THE BLACK DEVILS' MARCH

THE
BLACK DEVILS' MARCH

A DOOMED ODYSSEY
The 1st Polish Armoured Division 1939–45

Evan McGilvray

HELION & COMPANY

In Memory of Antoni Położyński
born 10 February 1914, Poland: died 30 June 2003, Pudsey, West Yorkshire
Sometime Soldier; Sometime Historian; Always a Patriot
For Your Freedom and Ours

Helion & Company Limited
26 Willow Road
Solihull
West Midlands
B91 1UE
England
Tel. 0121 705 3393
Fax 0121 711 4075
Email: publishing@helion.co.uk
Website: http://www.helion.co.uk

Published by Helion & Company Limited 2005
Designed and typeset by Carnegie Publishing Ltd, Lancaster, Lancashire
Printed by The Cromwell Press, Trowbridge, Wiltshire

The maps are drawn from *10 Pułk Strzelcow Konnych w Kampanii 1944–45* (no imprint, published 1947)

ISBN 1 874622 42 6

British Library Cataloguing-in-Publication Data.
A catalogue record for this book is available from the British Library.

For details of other military history titles published by Helion & Company Limited contact the above address, or visit our website: http://www.helion.co.uk.

We always welcome receiving book proposals from prospective authors.

Contents

Preface

This work covers the history of the 1st Polish Armoured Division from 1939 until the occupation of Wilhelmshaven in 1945. I have used Polish sources in order to try to use the authentic voice of the Polish troops as they attempted to liberate Europe and eventually their homeland. Western sources have been used to confirm certain aspects of the Division's history. The campaign diary of the 10th Mounted Rifles (10 PSK) has been extensively used as 10 PSK was a reconnaissance regiment and therefore the 'eyes' of the Division and generally met the enemy first.

I have several debts to honour, especially to my late neighbour, Mr Antoni Położyński, who first told me of the Division, of which I had never heard of before. We spoke many times about the Division and Mr Położyński lent me a great deal of material. I am also indebted to the following: Dr Andrew Maczek, who gave me valuable insights into his father's early career, Mr Bernard Astachnowicz of Bradford for his donation of material, to Mr Chaim Goldberg and his wife, Ruth, who had taken the time to answer my questions all the way from Canada. Likewise, Mr Tadeusz Walewicz has sent me material from Canada as well as answering my questions in full. I would also like to thank Mr Bolesław Mazur, formerly of the University of London, for teaching me how to translate Polish.

The biggest debt is owed by all of us to the members of the 1st Armoured Division who gave their lives during the Second World War.

Why the name 'Black Devils'? The Germans are supposed to have nicknamed the Division thus after the famous black leather coat of General Maczek.

Evan McGilvray
Pudsey, West Yorkshire
20 June 2004

CHAPTER I

Origins

The 1st Polish Armoured Division, formed during the Second World War, was comprised of soldiers who had fled their native Poland after the disastrous campaign following the German invasion of Poland on 1 September 1939, swiftly followed by the Soviet invasion of Poland on 17 September. The twin invasions and the subsequent fall of Poland led to another partition of the Polish state and the Polish people subject to every form of barbarity. Once again the only visible sight of Polish nationhood was to be found with its fighting men and women.

Poland has long been proud of its military tradition and its enduring legacy, which recently saw Poland become a member of NATO (1999). However Poland has not always enjoyed statehood. Between 1795 and 1918, Poland as a state did not exist, a processes that began with the First Partition of 1770 and ended with the Third and final partition in 1795. Until 1918, Poland was left partitioned between Austria, Russia and Prussia (after 1870, Germany). After 1795, many Poles went into exile or entered into conspiracies against the three partitioning imperial powers. The conspiracies manifested themselves in periodic insurrections and uprisings. A famous example of the Polish fighting spirit was found amongst the Poles who fought for the French under Napoleon Bonaparte.

The first Polish Legions were created in 1797 under the command of General Henryk Dabrowski. At first the legions were made up of Polish prisoners and deserters from the Austrian Army. This method of recruitment was to continue into the Twentieth Century as the Polish 1st Armoured Division took advantage of Poles who had been conscripted into the German Army. After the Normandy landings in 1944, Poles serving in the German armed forces were able to reach Polish lines and join the Polish Forces fighting in the West.

Three Polish legions were raised during the Napoleonic Wars. They may have marched under the French tricolour but they wore Polish uniforms. Their shoulder flashes bore the slogan, *Gli uomini sono fretelli* ('Free men are brothers') a forerunner of the later Polish slogan, *Za Wasze Wolnosci i Nasza* ('For Your Freedom and Ours').[1]

The Polish legionnaires, as today's Polish national anthem suggests, dreamt of marching under Dabrowski's command, from Italy, back to Poland. Sadly, as Norman Davies comments in his book *Heart of Europe*, their hopes were misguided, as the legionnaires never returned to Poland. Instead they were left on garrison duty in Italy before going to their deaths in Napoleon's wars, which included the ill-fated 1801 Haiti expedition which saw Polish troops put down a Negro slave revolt. This fulfilled the prophecy of the Polish patriot, Tadeusz Kosciuszko, who stated that the Poles should rely upon their own abilities and should not become involved with Napoleon, whom he described as a tyrant.[2]

After the defeat of Napoleon in 1815, the matter of Polish statehood was often raised in the form of insurrections, with revolts in 1830, 1846, 1863 and 1905. The Russians so utterly crushed the 1863 rebellion that Poland was silent for two generations.[3] Insurrection and revolt against the Imperial powers were not the only expressions of 'Polishness'. Literature played its part, even if it frequently related to struggle and to past military glories. Meanwhile, many Poles served as officers in the Imperial armies, which should have provided a sound base for a future Polish Army.

Many officers of the inter-war Polish Army (1918–1939) had previously served in the Imperial Austrian Army and this was to prove to be a problem. Once Poland regained it independence in 1918, the question of the loyalty of the officers who had served in foreign armies became a contentious issue. This problem was not resolved between the wars, which meant that the talents of some very experienced officers were ignored and squandered owing to the political ambition and intolerance of the Twentieth Century Polish hero, Marshal Jozef Pilsudski and his paramilitary followers, the Legionnaires. The friction between professional officers from the former Imperial and the Legionnaires was to weaken the potential of Polish defensive capability – especially after Pilsudski's coup during May 1926 – and this eventually allowed Poland to be easily overwhelmed in September 1939. Bluntly, the conflict should be seen in the terms of professionalism versus amateurism. Pilsudski and many of his Legionnaires had never attended a military academy, but had instead graduated from the military equivalent of the 'university of life'.

Much of Pilsudski's legend is derived from his determination to see an independent Poland. By 1918, he was Head of State (in Polish, *Naczelnik*). However much of this was due to good fortune and luck rather than the result of planning and military triumph.

Prior to the First World War, Pilsudski realised that the Balkan Wars (1912 & 1913) were a precursor to something much larger, which he was certain would bring the down the three empires ruling Poland and therefore allow nations such as Poland to emerge as independent states. To this end, Pilsudski formed, in the Austrian sector of Poland, a paramilitary organisation, known as *Strzelcy* or riflemen. Upon the outbreak of war in August 1914, the *Strzelcy*, later known as 'Legionnaires' fought alongside the Austrian Army until 1917 when Pilsudski and many of his followers were imprisoned in Germany after refusing to swear an oath of allegiance to the Central Powers. They remained in prison until the end of the war when suddenly the Germans released Pilsudski and gave him passage to Warsaw, where he assumed power. The recovery of Polish independence had very little to do with Pilsudski but was largely the result of the collapse of the three partitioning powers and the determination of the American President, Woodrow Wilson, to see an independent Poland as part of the Versailles Treaty.

Pilsudski was a visionary and wanted a federal structure in east-central Europe, in addition to the recovery of 'Polish lands' in the east.[4] He took advantage of the Russian Civil War and launched an invasion of Ukraine in 1919, hoping to recover territory, including the Polish city of Lwow (today in Ukraine and known as L'viv). This invasion took the Poles to the very gates of Kiev, the Ukrainian capital, from where the Bolsheviks counterattacked and forced the Poles into a full retreat, until Warsaw itself was imperilled in August 1920.

The Battle of Warsaw was a Polish victory and prevented the spread of Communism throughout east-central Europe for a generation, but it should have been a Bolshevik victory. Militarily the Bolsheviks had the upper hand and the fledgling Polish state appeared to be doomed. The battle was fought between 12 and 18 August 1920 and is sometimes referred to in Poland as *'cud na Wisla'* or the 'Miracle on the Vistula' – a reference to the zenith of the battle being reached on 15 August 1920 (the Catholic feast day of the Assumption of the Virgin Mary). Yet another legend was created as Mary was considered by many Poles to have saved 'Catholic Poland' from the 'Heathen Bolshevik' and thus prevented the creation of a 'Godless Europe'.

Some credit the victory to Pilsudski's tactical expertise, while others more realistically give the credit to the French general, Maxim Weygard and his 40-strong military mission which was present in Warsaw and may have exercised some influence upon the Polish victory.[5] Of equal importance was the fact that the Bolsheviks blundered, getting their lines of communications confused over the large and empty Polish terrain, which left troops bereft of both ammunition and orders.[6] No matter, who or what was responsible for the Polish victory, in Poland, Pilsudski is credited with the victory, even if he described the Battle of Warsaw as a 'brawl'.[7]

From this point, even allowing for the lack of direction from civilian politicians, Pilsudski (who left politics in 1923) using his Legionnaires, especially the 1st Brigade, remained the most important political figure in Poland.[8] In 1926, exasperated with civilian democracy, he launched a coup, supported by his Legionnaires, and was in effect, dictator until his death in 1935.

The Pilsudski legacy lay heavily on inter-war Polish military doctrine as the Polish-Soviet War had been largely cavalry orientated. The victory at Warsaw stifled any real improvement after 1920 in Poland in spite of re-armament in Europe during the 1930s, following the rise of Adolf Hitler and the Nazi Party in Germany after 1933. Not only were improvements in military technology ignored but capable officers, who were not *Pilsudski–ites*, were also overlooked for promotion.[9] Many of the non-Pilsudski officers came from the former Austrian Army and included such figures as the future wartime Polish Prime Minister and Commander-in-Chief (in the West), General Wladyslaw Sikorski (who had served in both the Austrian Army and the Legions) and the future commanding officer of the 1st Polish Armoured Division, General Stanislaw Maczek.

General Stanislaw Maczek was one of the many unknowns of the Second World War. Many are unknown owing to humble circumstances but Maczek's story is that of an intelligent, heroic and determined man, known simply to his men as *'Baca'* or 'Head Shepard'.[10] He was the only Polish wartime general to live to see a genuinely free and democratic Poland, even if it took over forty years following the end of the Second World War. However to fully appreciate Maczek's contribution to the Second World War would require a further book, therefore I shall confine my comments regarding Maczek to the salient points which will serve in the understanding of the story of the 1st Polish Armoured Division.

Stanislaw Maczek was born in Szczerzer, Eastern Poland, part of the Austrian Empire. In 1918, it became part of Poland, after 1945, it was incorporated into the Soviet Union and since 1991 has been part of the reborn Ukraine. Deimel observes that the military had not been Maczek's first choice of career, as he wanted to study either philosophy or psychology at university.[11] The outbreak of war in 1914 all but destroyed Maczek's hopes as he was conscripted into the Austro-Hungarian Army. He spent most of his war on the Italian Front following the opening of this campaign in 1915. He remained there until being wounded during the winter of 1917–18. Upon the re-independence of Poland in 1918, Maczek returned home. By 1919, he had formed a rapid mobile unit, which first saw action during the September of that year, following the outbreak of the Polish-Soviet War. This unit swelled rapidly under Maczek, who by now was a major in the Polish Army and the units became an assault battalion.[12]

The Polish title of Maczek's autobiography, *Od Podwody do Czolga* ('From Carts to Tanks') reflects his philosophy. The carts, farm carts, un-sprung, high-sided, wooded-wheeled and horse-drawn, were requisitioned from farmers, hence the word *Podwody* rather than the usual word in Polish for a cart, *furmanka*. By loading infantry and machine guns into the carts, Maczek was able to bring a greater mobility to the East European battlefields, which were dominated with the use of cavalry as a result of the underdeveloped terrain of Eastern Poland and Russia.[13] Maczek did not believe in trench warfare but saw war in terms of attack and withdrawal. He had no time for static warfare, as had been his experience during the First World War.[14]

Maczek's concept of rapid and mobile warfare with its application to Eastern Europe was groundbreaking. Armour, beyond the use of armoured trains, had played their role during the Polish-Soviet War and the Russian Civil War but their scope was limited. Armoured warfare using tanks had only arrived during the middle of the First World War; during the inter-war period, only about 10 officers from a handful of countries, including Charles de Gaulle of France, Guderian in Germany and Fuller and Liddell-Hart in Britain had taken tank warfare seriously. Therefore Maczek's interest indicates that he was a man of great military intellect and foresight.

Maczek's defence of Lwow during the Polish-Soviet War quickly brought him to the attention of senior officers, who persuaded him to remain in the armed services. After graduating from Staff College, Maczek returned to Lwow as second-in-command of an infantry regiment.[15] Keegan points to the fact that the Legionnaires were almost without exception to make up the inter-war command structure in Poland.[16] Such was Maczek's distinction during manoeuvres that Pilsudski himself made Maczek Deputy Divisional Commander of Czestochowa (Southern Poland) where he was to remain until the autumn of 1938. In 1938, Maczek was promoted to command of the 10th Mechanized Cavalry Brigade, the sole Polish cavalry brigade not mounted on horseback.[17] Keegan records Maczek's dismay at the lack of mobility of his brigade: his ideas had been ignored.[18] Pilsudski and his Legionnaires had been rather good at neglecting non-cavalry tactics and like Sikorski, Maczek's previous promotion had been a method of keeping a non-Legionnaire, yet capable officer, out of the way, allowing Pilsudski and his followers to continue to pursue their path of military ignorance.

By the autumn of 1938 Poland, along with Germany and Hungary, had taken part in an invasion of Czechoslovakia, but by March 1939 it was beginning to rue its close involvement with Germany, as after swallowing Czechoslovakia, Hitler turned his attention to Poland. Suddenly it became expedient for the Polish Government to at last make proper use of its more capable but not politically involved officers to defend Poland against the German threat. Stanislaw Maczek was to be counted amongst these men, and prepared to defend Poland.

Upon the outbreak of hostilities on 1 September 1939, 10th Motorized Brigade, under Maczek's command was entrusted with delaying XII *Panzerkorps* as it advanced into southern Poland. Despite heavy losses, the Brigade carried out every single order issued to it. Outside of Lwow, the Brigade even counterattacked a Mountain Division and regained territory from it.

The September 1939 Campaign as fought by the Brigade is well worth recording. Tadeusz Walewicz, a veteran of the campaign and now living in Canada recalls it well. During the middle of August 1939, Walewicz joined the Brigade in Rzeszow and was assigned to a reconnaissance unit under the command of Major Swiecicki. Later Walewicz was sent to a location near Bronowice Male. On September 1 1939, the Brigade was rushed southwest towards the direct of Spytkowice, where they encountered Germans for the first time. Later, the Poles learnt that before them had been the entire German XXII *Korps* under the command of General von Kleist.

Everywhere the Germans met with stiff Polish resistance but the Germans had superiority in numbers and equipment. Constantly, the Germans tried to outflank Polish positions. At night the Poles tried to retreat to new defensive lines, in order to resume fighting the next morning. Walewicz recalls seeing soldiers walking and sleeping. In this situation, he remembers that the only possible thing that the Brigade could do was to slow the German advance while the Polish line of retreat passed through Myslenice, Wisnicz, Rzeszow, Lancut and Jaroslaw, towards Lwow.

Outside of Lwow, at the Zboiska Heights, with the aid of other units in the area, the Brigade took part in heavy fighting between 14 and 17 September 1939, against the German 4th Infantry Division and actually retook the Heights from the Germans. But their actions were in vain, as on 17 September, the Soviet Union attacked Poland. At this time, Maczek, now a Colonel, was attending a meeting in Lwow. He returned to his Brigade, in order to give the order to cease fighting owing to the Soviet invasion. The Brigade was given orders to move south and reach the Polish-Hungarian border via Stanislaw.[19]

Deimel writes that the Brigade crossed the Hungarian border, complete with arms and colours flying.[20] Walewicz recalls that on 19 September 1939, the Brigade crossed the frontier into Hungary at Przelecza Tatarska, with less than half of its original strength. The Poles had to leave their half of its Beregiszosh and Walewicz's units were sent by trains to Komarno where they were housed in a very old fort. The living conditions in the fort were appalling, with the Poles being kept in large rooms which emitted very little light, and were only given straw to sleep upon.

Immediately the Poles began to hatch escape plans. They quickly found a tunnel, which led to the River Danube, but stones and rocks blocked the outlet of the tunnel. The fort was heavily guarded and it took some time to unblock the tunnel but on 15 January 1940, Walewicz and a group of 20 soldiers managed to escape and walked a short distance to a truck provided by the Polish Consul in Budapest who had already been alerted to the escape attempt. The plan was to drive to the Yugoslav border, but after an hour of driving in icy conditions, the driver lost control of the vehicle and crashed into a ditch. After this the group divided itself into smaller groups, each heading for Budapest. On the outskirts of a village Walewicz's group noticed a light coming from a small coffee shop. Despite being worried that the shop owner might call the police the Poles stepped into the shop.

Luckily, the shop owner proved to be friendly and arranged for a taxi to take the Poles to Budapest. The only problem was that the taxi driver, despite the fact that he did not mind taking them to the Polish Consulate in Budapest, insisted that the Poles leap out of the taxi once they got to the Consulate's gates, as the location was under constant police surveillance. This was done and the Poles were duly able to report to the Consulate.

After a week, once again the group was taken by truck to the small village of Barch, from where, at night, they were able to cross the River Drava, into Yugoslavia. Immediately, Yugoslav soldiers captured them and took them to their guard post. Once again the Poles' luck held, as the soldiers proved to be friendly and gave them warm food and the next day notified the Polish Consul in Zagreb of the presence of Walewicz's group. Shortly after, in yet another truck, they were taken to Zagreb and were provided with a place to stay by the Polish authorities. From there, travelling on student documentation, Walewicz, left for France, via Italy. Once in France, Walewicz was able to rejoin the Polish Army.[21]

Maczek had also escaped to Hungary but the possibility of internment in Hungary was not an option for him. His escape was somewhat swifter that that of Walewicz's and by October 1939, he had reported in Paris to General Wladyslaw Sikorski, Commander-in-Chief of Polish Armed Forces. Sikorski promoted Maczek to the rank of Major-General and awarded him the Gold Cross of the highest military decoration, the *Virtuti Militari*.[22] In France, Maczek, once again began to train a Polish light armoured division. However the German invasion of the Low Countries and France during the spring of 1940 meant that Maczek, with only part of the 10th Mechanized Cavalry Brigade, was able to take the field and meet the Germans once more.[23]

Walewicz is quite critical of the French and their attitudes towards the Poles after the fall of Poland. He had reached France from Yugoslavia. At first he was sent to a camp for Poles at Coetquidan before being sent to St Cecile, near Avignion, in order to rejoin the 10th Armoured Brigade. The French provided the Poles with a few, very old tanks, for training. When Germany attacked Holland and Belgium on 10 May 1940, this situation changed dramatically. Suddenly, the French wanted the 10th Armoured Brigade to join the French forces that were already fighting. As already discussed, the Brigade was not up to strength but still it was moved to a huge military depot near Paris.

The depot contained tanks, guns and ammunition. In short, all of the material necessary to fight a campaign. The Poles were given a brief time to study the equipment and despite not being familiar with the French weaponry, they were entrained for the front. The Polish assignment was to cover the French withdrawal, which was fighting along the way from Avise to Moloy, near Divon. At Montbard, the final battle took place. On 17 June 1940, the Brigade, lacking fuel and surrounded by Germans, was ordered to destroy the remainder of their equipment and try to escape in small groups to the unoccupied section of France (Vichy). Walewicz and his group reached Port Vandre in Southern France and very close to the Spanish border. The group had the idea of crossing with some French troops in the area, to Algeria. Sadly, the Poles were captured and placed in a French internment camp. Walewicz, with support from the Polish Red Cross, was able to get a studentship. This enabled him to study for the French matriculation examination before enrolling at the University of Grenoble.

At the same time, Walewicz's group, under the command of Colonel Jaklicz, became active in the under-ground movement. The group's task was to assist shot-down allied pilots, help them evade capture and escape back to Britain. After receiving a warning that he should leave France, Walewicz, in January 1943, once again found himself on the run. Using false papers, Walewicz, began his flight by train, heading once more for the Spanish frontier. On the train he was discovered. A German officer, fluent in French, was checking papers and noticed that Walewicz's travel documents indicated that he was a worker whilst his identification card stated that he was a student. The German said that Walewicz was to be taken off the train at the next station for interrogation. Shortly afterwards, the French policeman who had accompanied the German officer, returned to Walewicz and asked what his nationality was. When Walewicz replied 'Polish'; the police officer said 'You're lost'. He then told Walewicz that his only chance was to jump off the train before the next station, when the train had to slow down.

Walewicz took the Frenchman's advice and with the aid of a local French farmer was able to cross into Spain a day later. Walewicz tried to reach Barcelona but was arrested by the Spanish police, the first time he tried to travel by train, after trying to travel by walking at night and sleeping during the day. He was held for 3 months before Polish Consular officials in Barcelona managed to get him released. After his release he travelled by train to Madrid, where he stayed for a few weeks, reporting daily to the Polish Consulate for instructions. Eventually, via the Consulate, he was smuggled over the frontier into neutral Portugal. Once in Portugal, Walewicz and his travelling companions were given tickets to travel by rail to the small fishing village of Faro, on the Bay of Biscay.

From Faro, Walewicz and his comrades could see British ships heading for Gibraltar. In time, they were supplied with a small fishing boat and they left Faro to intercept a British freighter. The ship stopped and dropped a rope ladder. One by one the Poles boarded the ship. Eventually they reached Gibraltar and once again were able to put on uniforms. After waiting a while in Gibraltar, he was able to join a convoy sailing for Britain. On 28 August 1943, he landed in Liverpool. From there he was sent to a location near London for interrogation by the British security services. Once released, Walewicz was sent to Scotland to join 2nd Tank Regiment, under the command of Lieutenant-Colonel Stanislaw Koszutski.[24]

General Maczek was more fortunate. After the fall of France, he was forced to flee. Maczek reached Britain in a similar manner as that of Walewicz, travelling in *mufti* via southern France, Algeria, Morocco and Portugal. Upon reaching Britain, he was determined to rebuild his brigade as the foundation of a future armoured division. Early in 1942, his dream was realised when General Sikorski appointed him Commander of the 1st Polish Armoured Division.[25] As with all of the Polish troops in exile, Maczek must have begun to consider a triumphant return to the Continent and to Poland.

CHAPTER II

From Scotland to Normandy

After the fall of France and the retreat from Dunkirk by the British and French during May 1940, Polish troops continued to make their way back to Britain in order to continue fighting the war. The period between 1940 and 1944 was to be a period of frustration for the Poles and the 1st Polish Armoured Division was not to be spared.

The summer of 1940 saw the Battle of Britain, during which Allied pilots, including Poles, distinguished themselves and thwarted the planned German invasion of Britain. Other battles were fought at sea, especially upon the Atlantic Ocean, as German submarines played a deadly cat and mouse game with Allied and neutral shipping: a situation which was to last for nearly three years. As for the Polish troops who found themselves in Britain until 1944, there was little or no chance of getting to grips once more with the Germans.

General Maczek, as we have already seen, arrived in Britain during September 1940 and immediately sought to rebuild his armoured brigade. Szudek goes as far as to claim that Maczek in 1940 was the most experienced commander of armour located in Britain.[26]

Maczek's commanding officer, General Wladyslaw Sikorski, agreed with Maczek's desire to rebuild the brigade, but in 1940, the British had other priorities. Even if the Germans had been defeated in the air, the threat of invasion had not receded. A need for coastal defence arose while the country had to remain vigilant until such a time that the invasion threat could be lifted and Britain go onto the offensive. The Polish units stationed in Britain (I Polish Corps) were entrusted with the defence of the Scottish east coast, from Montrose to Dundee with its headquarters in Forfar.[27] Even if this did prove frustrating for the Polish troops, Maczek wasted no time in recriminations or protest; instead he began to train his troops to work and fight as an armoured unit.[28]

Szudek had detailed how the 1st Armoured Division was conceived and brought to life. As already discussed, Sikorski was in agreement with Maczek about the establishment of a Polish Armoured Division, using 10th Brigade as its basis. From this, it was hoped that a full armoured division would evolve. However a shortage of men posed a major problem. This situation changed dramatically once Germany invaded the Soviet Union in June 1941. As a result of the Sikorski-Maisky Pact,[29] a number of Polish prisoners of war (POW) and deportees were released by the Soviet Government, in order to join the Polish armed forces. This led to the decision of 14 February 1942, to form an armoured unit, with Sikorski formally appointing Maczek as its commander one week later.[30]

On 26 February 1942 a formal order confirming, the establishment of the division and its organisation was issued. The division was to consist of two armoured brigades, one anti-tank regiment, one anti-aircraft regiment, one infantry battalion, one engineering regiment and four signal squadrons. This type of establishment was considered by the British to be of the 'old establishment' with its large and powerful armoured section. But this had proved unsuitable for the British in combat situations in North Africa.

From the Polish point of view, it was highly desirable because the two armoured brigades allowed for the possibility of a rapid expansion of the two brigades into two armoured divisions, something which the Polish authorities had already planned.[31] At first the War Office in London agreed to the design of the Polish Division but in time, became steadily disenchanted with it[32] especially once pre-war Polish politics began to creep back into the Polish Army and threaten its fighting capability. Meanwhile the Division began to train hard in order to reach the high standards set by Maczek.[33]

The Division's final test came during the summer of 1943 when the Division took part in a major exercise in Cambridge, code-named STIRRUP. The Division acquitted itself well in this exercise but following several other major exercises, serious defects began to show in the old type of organisation. It was now obvious to both Polish and British officers that an all-armoured division could not manage without adequate infantry support if it was to hold ground when attacked. The British experience of North Africa had proved that the Division (or indeed any armoured formation) needed infantry to fulfil its role.[34]

The Polish High Command had recognised the need for re-organisation in early 1943; despite this early recognition and putting theoretical requirements of the Polish Armed Services aside, the ability to re-organise was compromised by a manpower shortage. Part of the problem was that the numbers of POWs returning from the Soviet Union had been overestimated. The numbers were far less than expected. Furthermore, Polish units serving in the Middle East received priority over other units. The Polish 1st Armoured Division received what was left.[35]

However there is another element to this story. The Poles who left the Soviet Union for the Middle East did so, often via a lengthy route, which took them through Iran and eventually to the Middle East. There was still a need in the area to forestall any German expansion into the Middle East. Furthermore, the idea of transporting large numbers of troops by sea to Britain, quite frankly would have been irresponsible. In addition, many Poles who had suffered hardship in the Soviet camps were not interested in Sikorski's idea of co-operation with the Soviet Union. The massacre of 16,000 Polish officers by the Soviet secret police at Katyn was proof of Soviet brutality against Poles, alongside the deportations and ill-treatment by the Soviets of Polish citizens from Eastern Poland between 1939 and 1941, following the Soviet invasion of Poland. These men did not want to aid the Soviets in any way and in fact many saw the Soviets as well as the Germans as the enemy.

To illustrate Maczek's manpower problem it is useful to consider one intake for his command, consisting of 1,238 other ranks (ORs). 30% were up to 30 years of age, 45% were up to 40 years of age and even more disconcerting, 25% were up to 50 years of age. Despite this apparent problem concerning the age of some of the Division's personnel it continued on its path towards combat readiness and received much praise from many directors of exercises in which it participated. However the problem of reaching full combat strength remained.[36]

The problem of recruiting Polish troops, putting politics and military necessity aside, also concerned the vast distances that Poles had to cross, often over inhospitable terrain, made all the more difficult owing to the conditions of wartime, when frontiers were all too frequently closed or tightly controlled. Britain being an island obviously served to increase the problem. Two examples are those of Antoni Polozynski and Chaim Goldberg. Both men left Poland illegally. Polozynski travelled eastward at first and then westward while Goldberg moved via the Soviet Union to Japan and then on to Canada.[37]

Polozynski, aged 25 when Germany attacked Poland, was working close to the Okecie Airport in Warsaw. He was a reserve infantry officer, working with the *Jumacki Hufce Pracy* (JHP), a voluntary youth movement, in which boys who had finished primary education (in Poland at the age of 15) were then trained for careers and professions. The JHP was organised along military lines, with Polozynski being in command of a platoon of 30 boys. At the airport, Polozynski saw the German bombers at work. After the Soviet attack upon Poland, he left Warsaw and returned to his family home, east of Warsaw, but owing to loyalty to friends in Warsaw, he quickly returned to the capital.

Polozynski returned once more to his family home for the Christmas and New Year of 1939–1940. During this festive period he realised that he was faced with two options: either to go underground or join the Polish Army in the West. On 5 January 1940, Polozynski set out illegally from Warsaw in an attempt to join the Polish Army. He chose to leave via the Soviet sector of Poland as he had realised that the Germans did not guard their side of the demarcation line between German and Soviet occupied Poland. From the Soviet sector, Polozynski planned to press on through the then unoccupied Baltic states and from there to Scandinavia.

The first attempt failed but upon the second attempt, conducted almost immediately, Polozynski's group crossed into the Soviet sector of Poland, via the loosely guarded demarcation line. Once inside the Soviet sector they travelled through Grodno (now in Belarus) and on to Vilnius (now the capital of Lithuania). In Vilnius, a Polish academic and his wife helped Polozynski travel to Riga, the Latvian capital. Once in Riga, Polozynski presented himself to the Polish Consulate and made his intention to rejoin the Polish Army quite clear.

The attitude of the Consulate was less than helpful and after only a few weeks Polozynski was sent to a camp for Poles at the winter resort of Siguld. There he learnt Russian and from Soviet newspapers discovered that the war had moved on and that Germany had invaded Norway and the Low Countries. He also learnt that Polish troops (the Podhalen Brigade) were fighting in Norway. The Polish troops in Siguld immediately went to the Consulate, demanding passage to Norway, via Sweden, in order to fight. But once again the Consulate refused to co-operate.

Polozynski, increasingly frustrated, decided to leave Latvia in secret. To this end, he packed what he needed for the journey and left the camp. Taking advantage of the good weather, he set out on foot for Estonia, which he reached within two days. In Estonia, he was given a lift to the capital, Tallinn. Once again, he made himself known at the Polish Consulate. The Consulate swiftly arranged for an Estonian fisherman to take Polozynski across the Gulf of Finland to Helsinki.

In Finland, Polozynski was sent to another camp for Poles in Ruukki. There he realised that the senior Polish officer at the camp, Colonel Los, had no intention of allowing Poles to escape to the West. Again, Polozynski set out illegally, heading for the port of Petsamo (now in Russia) where after one failed attempt, he managed to stow away on the ship, *American Legion*, bound for New York.

Once on board, a Polish woman travelling with her young daughter took him under her wing and made sure that he was able to disembark in New York without any difficulties, despite that fact that Polozynski lacked any form of travel document. The New York Polish community took care of Polozynski upon his arrival in the USA and he was able to stay there for several months. Eventually a passage to Britain was arranged for him. On 15 January 1941 Polozynski signed on as a 'deck boy' on the Polish ship, *Morska Wola*. On 1 March 1941, he arrived in Britain. Ten days later, he travelled from Kings Cross Station, London to Edinburgh, in order to rejoin the ranks of the Polish Army. Polozynski was never to see his parents again and he did not visit Poland again until 1965. A full quarter of a century had passed from the time of his escape.[38]

Chaim Goldberg, a 19 year old worker in the fur industry was living in Warsaw when Germany invaded Poland. The German invasion held serious consequences for Goldberg as he was not only a young Pole but also a Jew. Sadly, Goldberg was to lose most of his family in the Treblinka death camp.[39] Like Polozynski, Goldberg left Warsaw for Vilnius. Upon the entry of the Red Army into Poland, which included Vilnius, Goldberg, using false papers entered the Soviet Union and whilst there obtained a false Japanese visa. This allowed him to travel across Siberia, by train, to Vladivostok, where he waited for a ship to take him to Japan.

At the end of February 1941, Goldberg left the Soviet Union and arrived in Japan at the beginning of March 1941, where he stayed for around three months. During this time he obtained papers which allowed him to travel to Canada. He arrived in Vancouver and later travelled to Windsor, Ontario, where the Polish Army in Canada was located. There Goldberg was able to join the Polish Army in June 1941, and by October he was in Britain. At first he was sent to Liverpool and then onto Scotland, to receive training in the 9th Infantry Battalion of the 1st Polish Armoured Division.[40]

From our examples of Poles escaping from occupied Europe in order to join the Polish Army, the problems of recruitment are obvious. By 1 July 1943, the Division had 10,214 officers and men but the need was for 15,356.[41] The manpower problem seemed to defy all possible solutions, especially with the need for the substitution of one armoured brigade for an infantry brigade, in accordance with the new type of armoured division.

In May 1943, Sikorski proposed the transferral of an armoured brigade (personnel only) to 3rd Carpathian Infantry brigade, who were in the Middle East. According to Sikorski, this meant that the Poles would have acquired two armoured divisions of the new type: one in Britain and the other, temporarily, in the Middle East. The Poles thought that at a stroke, they had solved all of their manpower problems. General Nye, acting for the Chief of the Imperial General Staff (CIGS), General Brooke, refused the plan, claiming that transporting the troops would be difficult. Nye suggested that 16th Armoured Brigade should be disbanded and its personnel turned into an infantry brigade. The Poles were unimpressed and decided to leave matters as they were. Szudek observes that at this point, the 1st Polish Armoured Division continued to train as units which was already tactically obsolete.[42]

Following the death of Sikorski in July 1943, his successor, General Kazimierz Sosnkowski, brought the question of reorganising to the attention of CIGS. Even following a severe trimming of all Polish units in Scotland, the Division was still short of 3,150 men.[43] Once again the Sikorski plan was put forward and refused. The Poles, meanwhile, refused the British plan, which led to an impasse. However at this time the British were not content to let matters lay, as had been the case previously. This time the British were far more aggressive in their arguments and during the summer of 1943 pushed for the Polish acceptance of the new model of armoured brigade.

As the plans for the invasion of France were advanced the British put their case bluntly: either the Poles provide an armoured division of the new model or the Poles would not be allowed to take part in the invasion of Europe. With such a threat hanging over him, Sosnkowski ordered the final stripping of all the regiments in Scotland, leaving the most essential cadre with the exception of the Parachute Brigade.[44]

By 1 October 1943, the Division reached full strength minus 120 men, which seemed to satisfy the British. This final organisation was as follows:

10th Mounted Rifles	1st Field Artillery Regiment
1st Tank Regiment	2nd Field Artillery Regiment
2nd Tank Regiment	1st Anti-Tank Regiment
10th Lancers	1st Anti-Aircraft Regiment
10th Dragoons	Engineer Battalion
3rd Rifle Brigade (Podhalen Rifle Battalion;	Signal Battalion
8th Rifle Battalion; 9th Rifle Battalion)	Military Police Squadron[45]
Machine Gun Squadron	

After the summer of 1943 and the exercises of that season, the Division strove to reach optimal strength and performance. However owing to the loss of personnel following casualties during exercises, the deficiency in manpower continued. To add to the problem, there was also a need to replace 400 men of 'D' category (unfit for service) and who had probably been recruited originally to make up the numbers.

On 10 February 1944, Sosnkowski, in a meeting with the 21st Army's Commander-in-Chief (C-in-C), General Montgomery, said that the Division was still 510 men short but the deficiency would be made up in the near future. Sosnkowski asserted that the 1,280 men needed for the second replacement would not be made up until certain areas of Northern France, with large numbers of Poles living in the areas, were liberated. Sosnkowski also described the state of the Division's equipment as follows: 70% of establishment armoured fighting vehicles; 60% of the signal equipment; 40% of the engineer's equipment and 80% transport equipment. Montgomery expressed satisfaction with this, commenting that this was the situation generally with British units. He then promised to visit the Division on 13 March 1944.[46]

Montgomery's visit according to Szudek was tinged with spite, claiming that Montgomery was xenophobic in his treatment of the Poles (if not all foreign troops).

It was widely reported that in a conversation with Maczek, Montgomery, after meeting Poles who had served with the *Afrika Korps*, asked which language did the Division use when speaking amongst themselves, German or Russian?[47] It is difficult to decide whether Montgomery was indulging in some ill-advised humour, was being genuinely xenophobic, or whether the whole episode was simply just a sore point for the Poles. Furthermore, the Poles professed to dislike Montgomery's trademark eccentric mode of dress, which flouted, if not ignored all military discipline. It all cut no ice with the Poles, who took Montgomery to be patronising. In time, Sosnkowski requested that Polish forces be withdrawn from the first wave of the invasion. This was agreed to.[48]

However it must be observed that by September 1944, the Polish Government in London dismissed Sosnkowski, owing to his unwillingness to support any reconciliation with the Soviet Union. *The Economist* at the time commented that the ability of Polish military commanders to oppose Polish foreign policy was a 'regrettable legacy' of the 'Pilsudski-Beck' era.[49] Montgomery and other British commanders found the Polish commanders difficult to manage owing to the inter-war politics of the Polish Officer Corps. It is worth noting

Montgomery visiting General Maczek.
Imperial War Museum B11550

Six views of Montgomery's visit to the 1st Polish Armoured Division's HQ. Two of the photos show Montgomery posing with Maczek. **Imperial War Museum B12101, B12102, B12103, B12104, B12105, B12108 respectively**

General Anders's (Polish II Corps) reprimand from his British commander, General Leese, commander of the Eighth Army, following a complaint from Anders concerning the field newspaper, *Eighth Army News*, which contained anti-Polish information and pro-Soviet news. Leese reminded Anders that it was not desirable that he (Anders) as a corps commander should comment so publicly about political events that were taking place.[50]

This reflects the fact that there was actually very little understanding between the British and the Poles. The British ignored the fate of Poland under the Soviets but Polish officers should have realised that their task was to help in the defeat of Germany and not try to interfere in politics as they had done so frequently in Poland during the inter-war years.

In contrast with Montgomery's visit, General Eisenhower, the Supreme Commander of the Allied Expeditionary Forces Europe, made quite an impact on the Division when he visited it a month after Montgomery's visit. The Poles liked his sincerity and he immediately won them over. In May 1944, the Division moved to Yorkshire, where they exercised with General Leclerc's 2nd French Armoured Division. This was followed by an exercise which was inspected by General Sosnkowski. The Division then moved to Aldershot in July 1944, where they waited their turn to land in France.[51]

Men of the Division are shown being inspected by Eisenhower during his visit to the unit.
Imperial War Museum B12270, B12272

CHAPTER III

The Lessons of War (8–13 August 1944)

The Allied invasion of France began during the early hours of 6 June 1944. However the 1st Polish Armoured Division continued to wait in Southern England until 1 August 1944 before it returned to the European mainland. The Division by now numbered 13,000 officers and men and was equipped with 381 tanks, 473 artillery pieces and 4,050 vehicles.[52] The men of the 1st Polish Armoured Division had waited for a long time for their return to the Continent and for a chance to take the fight to the Germans. General Maczek, their proud and patient commander, was beginning to realise his dream of returning to Poland.

Ever aware of the need to boost moral, Maczek gave a short, warrior-like speech. He caused his men to remember why they were in France once more and he recalled the disasters of 1939 and 1940, which had left them weak and uncertain about their futures. He reiterated that after four years of hard work and training in Britain, they were now returning to battle in order to return to Poland, with the first steps being taken in France. Maczek said that after five years of conflict, they were still proud of themselves and now armed, they were to make the Germans pay for the war. At first Maczek stated that 'for every Polish life; a German life must be taken'. However, probably aware of the atrocities that had taken place in Europe since 1939, he quickly added that Poles must not become barbarians but fight as all Polish soldiers had fought in history, 'hard and chivalrously'. He concluded by expressing his and his troops 'belief in each other'.[53]

Maczek need not have worried about encouraging his soldiers with a sense of occasion in order to raise their fighting spirit, as they already believed in themselves and counted the days, weeks, months and years since the invasion of their homeland. Indeed, Lieutenant Jacek Stwora, of 24th Ulans, after his first engagement with the Germans in Normandy, was able to clearly recall, that it had been four years, eleven months and nine days since the Germans had attacked Poland.[54]

Lieutenant-General Guy Simonds, commander of Canadian II Corps with Montgomery. **Imperial War Museum B11552**

Despite the success of the Normandy landings, by August 1944, owing to a determined German counter-attack, the Allies had been unable to penetrate far inland, to such an extent that Maule is able to claim that there was a real risk of the Allies being forced back to the coast and experiencing another Dunkirk.[55] The arrival of the 4th Canadian Armoured Division and the 1st Polish Armoured Division was timely and they were assigned the task of executing the final breakout from the British sector, which would either trap or destroy the German armies in Normandy or drive them to the River Seine.

General Maczek wrote that the situation in Normandy was shaped thus: from the invasion beaches, along the eastern flank, throughout June and July, they had only reached the Caen area and had found themselves up against the largest German formation, *Panzergruppe West*, which consisted of five *Panzer* divisions. On the western flank, the Americans were denied

This series of eight photos show elements of the Division's 1st Tank Regiment going ashore at Mulberry 'B' harbour, Normandy 1944.
Imperial War Museum B8466, B8467, B8468, B8469, B8470, B8471, B8472, B8473

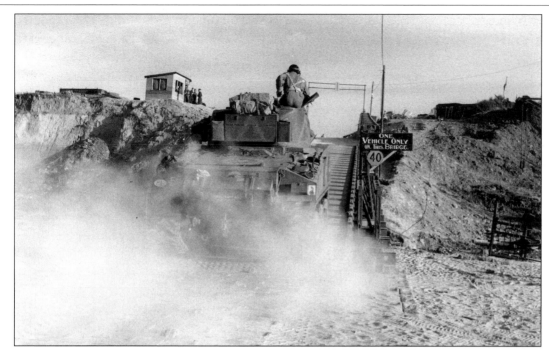

further gains as they sought to move on from the St. Lô region.[56] The near halt of the Allied advance was the reason for the offensive, Operation TOTALIZE, the first operation involving the 1st Polish Armoured Division.

As already discussed, the Poles were buoyant about fighting the Germans once more but at the same time, certain sections of the Allies saw the Poles as naïve and inexperienced.[57] However it would seem that the Poles considered some of the Allied commanders to be somewhat inexperienced in the nature of armoured warfare on the European mainland. Maczek acknowledged that Montgomery was the undoubted master of the North African desert but he doubted his experience in the high hedges and sunken lanes found in the Normandy *bocage* countryside.

The 1st Polish Armoured Division formed part of the 1st Canadian Army and very quickly the Canadians were told that the Division was to be used in TOTALIZE, set for 8 August 1944. As the Poles had only just arrived in Normandy, they had had very little time to become acquainted with other commanders. The Canadian commander, Lieutenant-General Guy Simonds, met Maczek and his staff for the first time on 4 August 1944n. Simonds only had time for a brief discussion with them before TOTALIZE began. British liaison officers were used by Poles for swift and effective communications but Simonds noticed that the Poles were different to the Canadian and British soldiers under his command and realised that they could not be controlled in the same way as he controlled British and Canadian troops.[58] Furthermore, the Canadian historian, Roman Jaramowcyz, asserts that not only was the language barrier a problem but Maczek as a 'modern tank officer' found Simonds's armoured tactics too restrictive.[59]

Senior officers of the Division with Montgomery at Sommerieu, Normandy.
Imperial War Museum B8761, B8762, B8763, B8764

On the eve of TOTALIZE, Maczek protested that the operational frontage of less than 1,000 yards allowed tanks no room for manoeuvre while allowing the Germans concentrated fields of fire.[60] Maczek was not alone in his reservations as Lieutenant-Colonel Franciszek Skibinski, Second-in-Command (2 IC) 10th Cavalry Brigade, was extremely worried with the planning, especially with Montgomery's briefing of 5 August 1944 to all squadron commanders. Montgomery's bypassing of Army and Corps commanders was typical of the Montgomery ideal as he wished that all commanders should understand his intentions, but the plan dismayed Skibinski.

Montgomery saw the Caen region as a 'hinge' or a 'pivot' from which the Allies could wheel southeast and strike at the flank of the German 7th Army. To achieve this, two divisions, the 2nd Canadian and 51st Highland, were to open the way through the German forward defences, ready for the 4th Canadian and 1st Polish Armoured Division to move through. The two armoured divisions were to charge the main line of German defence, which straddled the Caen-Falaise road. The Poles were to attack to the left and the Canadians to the right. Montgomery's briefing may have made an 'excellent' impression upon some officers but certain details caused dismay amongst the Poles. The Polish division was ordered to attack the German line frontally, with the Polish left flank dangerously exposed. Szudek compares this with the charge of the Light Brigade at Balaclava who during the Crimean War galloped ahead while passing waiting guns.[61]

Skibinski, a veteran of campaigns in Poland and France and a graduate of the Warsaw Military Academy, thought that the tactics suggested by Montgomery were contrary to everything that he had learnt in the classroom and on the battlefield. He reported his misgivings to Maczek, who was equally concerned with the plan. Maczek, ever the professional soldier, asserted that Montgomery, no doubt had made some provision for the unprotected flank: perhaps an aerial bombardment or artillery barrage, if not both. Szudek considers that in the circumstances this would have been a reasonable conclusion to have reached.[62]

The offensive began well, with an impressive infantry night attack on 7–8 August 1944. Skibinski recalled that the attack was a shock to the enemy, as the infantry managed to penetrate the forward German positions to a depth of four kilometres, which was to the German secondary line, leading from Fontenay-le-Marmion to Sequeville.[63] Maczek gives a detailed description of the night offensive. The attack began with a large aerial bombardment by the Royal Air Force consisting of 1,000 bombers and an artillery barrage. The first groups of infantry which had moved into the offensive were transported in improvised vehicles: dismantled artillery units. To obtain the maximum element of surprise, a system known as 'Monty's Moonlight' was deployed. This consisted of beams from searchlights being reflected down from clouds, while Bofor guns fired tracer shells

A fine photo showing tanks of 1st Polish Armoured Division moving up to support 51st Highland Division in an attack south of Caen, Normandy. (Imperial War Museum B8820

Men from the Division (probably tank crews as they are wearing British-pattern helmets designed for armoured troops) pose south of Caen. Note the Polish winged hussar insignia on the lorry's tailgate.
Imperial War Museum B8821

which indicated the flanks and objectives with the use of green shell bursts. The infantry moved rapidly, without loss, in the first phase of the offensive, to the first line of enemy reinforced defensive positions in the localities of May-sur-Orne; Roquancourt and Tilly-la-Campagne. The advance covered four kilometres, leaving behind isolated pockets of German resistance, who continued to fight on. From here the Canadian and Polish armoured divisions were to take advantage of this advance as already discussed.[64]

Maule describes how TOTALIZE was to have been performed in three stages. The first phase was to capture Fontenay-le-Marmion and la Hogue; the second was to capture Hautmesnil and St Sylvain with the third stage consisting of the Canadians, using their armour to exploit the situation as ordered. The first phase was carried out by the Canadian 2nd Armoured Brigade and the 2nd Infantry Division to the right and the British 33rd Armoured Brigade and the 51st Highland Division on the left. In the second phase, the Canadian 2nd Armoured Brigade was to move through the 2nd Infantry Brigade as the Canadian 4th Armoured Brigade captured highpoints at Hills 180, 195 and 206, about three miles further on.[65]

Maczek described his own formation as the Division moved into battle. The 1st Polish Armoured Division moved in two groups, past the 51st Highland Division. The 10th Armoured Brigade moved as the advance guard, reinforced by the 8th Infantry Brigade and 22nd Dragoons (British), equipped with half-tracked vehicles and support from the 1st Motorised Artillery Regiment. The second group was organised thus: 3rd Infantry Brigade accepted the task of clearing the area and consolidating important positions. They were supported by the 2nd Motorised Artillery Regiment and the 10th Mounted Rifles (in Polish, *10 Pulk Strzelcow Konnych*, 10 PSK). 10 PSK was the reconnaissance arm of the Division and was equipped with the faster Cromwell tank, while other armoured regiments in the Division were armed with either Sherman or Stuart tanks. 10 PSK was dispatched to reconnoitre the area in order to protect the Division's western flank.[66]

As we have seen, the night offensive had apparently gone well but daylight began to bring its own problems as the offensive began to run down, with the main armoured offensive being delayed until 13:45 hours, 8 August 1944. The wartime record of 10 PSK reveals some of the problems being faced by the Allies. Communication Nr. 3, dated 4 August 1944, which came from the Canadian sector revealed that 1st SS Panzer Division had widened its sector and had improved upon its positions, having moved from the left bank of the River Orne and was operating in an area between Bourgebus and the railway line which ran northeast to Caen. The report also revealed the disturbing news that a *Panther* battalion from 24th *Panzer* Division had moved from the Eastern Front into the area. A further piece of information that must have been of great interest to the Poles was that amongst 1st and 2nd SS Panzer Divisions were a 'certain amount' of Ukrainians, Czechs and Poles. This created a possible chance of ethnic divisions being exploited by the Poles within these formations owing to their very presence in the region. The report also confirmed that on the enemy's side of the Mezidon railway line there had been a lot of activity as supplies were being brought into the area. This did not reflect a beaten enemy but one which was confident; receiving supplies and reinforcements of battle-hardened troops coming from the fighting in Russia and Eastern Europe. The Poles were becoming more aware of the numbers and the type of soldier opposing them. Furthermore, the report gave information concerning the stalling of the Normandy offensive, due to the halting of the British offensive to the north-west of Caen.[67]

10 PSK moved to their position during the night of 7–8 August 1944 without incident. By 0800 hours, 8 August 1944, the Poles held the countryside north-west of Caen, but as already discussed, daylight began to bring problems. For example, the US Eighth Air Force, using 638 Flying Fortresses, accidentally bombed the Allied starting line. 60 men were killed, 300 were wounded, while guns and a large amount of ammunition was destroyed. This led to a German jibe, 'When the *Luftwaffe* comes over, the Allies duck; when the RAF comes over, the Germans duck; but when the Americans come over – everybody ducks!'[68] The enemy was also beginning to counter-attack. The 4th Canadian and the 1st Polish Armoured Divisions, who had been set the task of breaching the enemy's second line of defence between St Sylvian and Bretteville, were fighting the 12th SS *Panzer* Division, commanded by the 33 year old, General Kurt *'Panzerfaust'* Meyer. 12th SS Division had not been panicked by the Allied armour as expected, which had got to their rear and was now fighting off daylight attacks.[69] Maule claims that the Poles, owing to their lack of experience did not attack as aggressively as expected.[70] Even the Germans described the opening of the Polish attack as being hesitant.[71]

Antoni Polozynski, who fought from a Cromwell tank in Normandy points out that the Germans had far superior tanks and that the only way he could 'kill' an enemy tank was to hope that the German tank commander presented his tank sideways so that the Allied tank would get a chance to disable to enemy tank by hitting the bogies, along which the tank's caterpillar tracks ran, and then close in for the kill. Polozynski claimed that life and death on the battlefield is very much a matter of good and bad luck. One just hoped that the good luck was with you.[72]

An examination of the diary of 10 PSK illustrates the problems of the offensive in the Falaise area. 8 August 1944 saw 10 PSK positioned between 10th Armoured Cavalry Brigade (10 BK *panc*) and 2nd Tank Regiment (Polish). 2nd Tank Regiment was already fighting the enemy to the left and had the task of ensuring the safety of the offensive's left flank. 10 BK *panc* with 10 PSK to the rear, advanced further into the opening between Soliers and the Hubert-Folie railway crossing in the Bourgebus area. Here it was considered possible that the 51st Highland Division could have forced a breach in the enemy's line. But as soon as the offensive began, it became bogged down.

As it advanced between Sequr Le Campagne and Garceville Secqueville 10 BK *panc* met with strong enemy resistance, including armour and artillery, from the direction of St Aigan De Cramesnil. 2nd Squadron, 10 PSK,

A military policeman from the Division directs traffic moving up to support 51st Highland Division south of Caen, Normandy.
Imperial War Museum B8822

Polish Shermans lined up and ready to move forwards in Normandy. Their formation and lack of efforts at camouflage indicate the huge Allied air superiority enjoyed by this stage of the war. **Imperial War Museum B8823, B8826, B8830, B8835**

which had been assigned to protect the left flank, engaged the enemy and immediately lost a tank. Later, during the afternoon, 2nd Squadron moved again to hold Souling and also to reconnoitre the woods around Secqueville de Campagne. Despite encountering terrible terrain, 2nd Squadron was able to carry out its assignments but not without loss.

Encountering German *Panther* tanks, 2nd Squadron, 10 PSK, lost two tanks and suffered their first casualties: three dead, Lance Corporal Panko; Private Przybyszepski and Private Makarewicz, in addition to four wounded. During this time, 1st Squadron, 10 PSK, with the Armoured Car section, advanced to the north of Cramesnil (map ref: 083576) where the 24th Uhlans were already engaged in fighting to the north-east of the area. 3rd Squadron, 10 PSK, also engaged the enemy for the first time, when they held the area around Sequeville Le Campagne, supported by 2nd Tank Regiment and the Dragoons. All the units received casualties but took around 30 prisoners.

In the face of strong enemy resistance, the offensive became bogged down. The result was that 10 BK *panc* and other armoured units leading the offensive could not reach the Bretville Le Rabet – St Sylvian road. It became apparent that the objective of the offensive was unrealistic. At dusk, however, encouraging news began to filter through to the Polish lines; intelligence reports suggested that even though the Poles had failed to reach their objectives, the enemy was beginning to withdraw and that 10 PSK was to reconnoitre the Couvicourt area.[73]

If one looks at the larger picture of 8 August 1944, the Polish casualty rate is magnified. Maczek's fears about tactics were realised as within minutes, 2nd Tank Regiment lost 26 out of 36 Sherman tanks. Tadeusz Walewicz, a veteran of 2nd Tank regiment, recalled the events of 8 August 1944. Walewicz is anxious to assert just how slow and outgunned the Sherman was when compared with German armour. The only advantage of the Sherman was that owing to American mass production techniques, there were plenty of them available.

At zero hour, the order to attack came and the Poles did so, without any support, whilst the German positions remained intact. The Poles attacked along a narrow path, which contained well placed and well camouflaged enemy 88mm guns. As Walewicz writes, the result was not a surprise: 2nd Tank lost 26 tanks within a few minutes. They were all left burning on the battlefield. Walewicz remarks that everybody was shaken by this terrible experience and after the initial shock, the tactics of the Polish 1st Armoured Division changed.[74]

Wysocki gives a wider picture of the fighting of 8 August 1944. He records that at 14:00 hours, a platoon from 24th Uhlans and 2nd Tank Regiment moved onto the offensive straight into the murderous fire described by Walewicz. Nearby were twenty German heavy tanks, *Tigers* and *Panthers*, commanded by the veteran commander, Michael Wittman. On the Russian Front, Wittman was accredited with destroying 119 tanks and he had been in action in Normandy since 12 June 1944. His famous defence of Hill 213, to the north of Caen against the British 7th Armoured Division, when his *Tigers* destroyed 25 Cromwell tanks, was already legendary. Wittman was killed on 8 August 1944 in the Cramesnil region, which fell into 24th Uhlans' sector.[75]

German reports confirm what Walewicz and Wysocki have written concerning the attack by 2nd Tank Regiment but the Germans also made the observation that after the mauling of this unit, 24th Uhlans began to advance with caution and stopped inside a wide hollow to await the results of reconnaissance patrols. Owing to German artillery and tank fire, the Uhlans did not attack but still lost fourteen tanks before they returned to safety behind Canadian positions.[76]

The German observation was astute and it was the observation of experienced soldiers, as after 8 August 1944, the Poles paid closer attention to initial reconnaissance and closer co-operation between tanks, infantry and artillery. After 8 August 1944, the Poles began to enjoy more success. Maczek and Skibinski's fears had been justified and the Poles began to attack on broader fronts. Reconnaissance became more important, with 10 PSK and 1st Anti-Tank Regiment being deployed to reconnoitre the regions of Hills 140 and 132, which lay in the direction of Couvicourt, two kilometres northwest from Estree La Campagne.

The two hills were the objectives of 10 BK *panc's* next offensive. This was to prove risky as from Couvicourt, 10 PSK had to cross two kilometres of open country, and once again the left flank was exposed due to the lack of units available to cover it. In addition, the enemy had been alerted to the possibility of an offensive as the 4th Canadian Armoured Division was already fighting in the area. 10 PSK's operation plan was that after an artillery barrage, 1st Squadron was to reconnoitre the hills to the north of Couvicourt in order to investigate reports of *Tiger* tanks operating in the area. 2nd Squadron as a prerequisite to entering St Sylvian, had to secure the eastern approaches of the town. In turn, 3rd Squadron, with the anti-tank regiment, was to 'leapfrog' 1st Squadron, which was to provide covering fire for 3rd Squadron's operation. The whole area meanwhile remained under direct observation of enemy artillery that did everything to stall 10 PSK's offensive.

1st Squadron was ordered to pass Couvicourt from the east and Renesnil from the west, while 3rd Squadron successfully took the area of Couvicourt without meeting any enemy resistance, before moving north in order to hold the edges of both flanks. In contrast, 1st Squadron encountered very strong resistance from German anti-tank units and infantry, some of whom were equipped with a hand held anti-tank weapon, the *Panzerfaust*, positioned on the ridges of Hill 84. 3rd Squadron under the command of 10 PSK's commanding officer, Major Jan Maciejowski, went to the aid of 1st Squadron, giving support fire, but still 1st Squadron lost a tank to *Panzerfaust* fire, which left three men dead and one wounded. Eventually, 3rd Squadron was able to advance to the east of Renesnil. From there it moved to Hill 84 and then into enemy held woodland (map ref: 130520) where enemy infantry, about a company in strength, was overrun and taken prisoner. Furthermore the Poles destroyed two guns (88mm and 75mm). Allied tank crews especially feared the 88mm guns. 10 PSK's losses were slight, one tank, which had broken down, and one man wounded.[77] For the Poles it was a great victory and a morale booster. However the overall picture was not so good.

12th SS had been quick to counterattack and had destroyed many Sherman tanks. Cop is correct in his assertion concerning the weaknesses of the Sherman tank; Polozynski makes the same claim about the Cromwell tank being underpowered, under-armed and under-armoured when compared with the German tanks.[78] Frankly, the Germans had faster, better armoured and better armed tanks, often manned by veteran crews. The Allied advantage was that they had plenty of tanks compared with the Germans. To add to the misery being endured by the Allies, not only were the Germans better equipped and in prepared positions; the 12th SS Division was the *Hitlerjugend*, comprised on the whole of young fanatical Nazis, who would rather die than surrender, or so it seemed at the time. By the end of the Falaise operation, 12th SS Division had lost 80% of its combat troops. Its support personnel also suffered high losses owing to Allied air raids. The Division also lost 80% of its tanks; 70% of its armoured vehicles; 60% of its artillery and 50% of its motor vehicles. By September 1944, 12th SS Division amounted to only 600 men and no tanks.[79]

During August 1944 the Poles were beginning to get some idea of the nature of their enemy as seen from Communication Nr. 10, dated 13 August 1944. The report concerned the evidence of deserters from III Company /53rd Panzer Grenadiers from the Soignoilles area. The report revealed that casualties from Polish fire, especially heavy mortar fire, had been severe, with the firing being both very accurate and deadly. The differences between German officers and other ranks (ORs) are also very revealing. The officers were convinced of victory but the ORs were already certain that the war was lost. At this time, it should be noted that French civilians living in the area

Officers consult their maps during the offensives around Caen, Normandy. **Imperial War Museum B8825**

Polish Shermans in Normandy, August 1944. **Imperial War Museum B8836**

were still not certain if the Allies would succeed in their invasion. The report also revealed an irregular supply of food to German lines. Sometimes two or three days passed without any supplies reaching German positions. It was also discovered that three *Tiger* tanks had been hidden in a deep and camouflaged area with the crews having received orders to fight to the last without any thought for their own personal safety.[80]

Between 11 August and 14 August 1944, 10 PSK along with the rest of the 1st Polish Armoured Division, were involved in minor offensives designed to provide the breakout from Normandy while also trying to prevent the Germans escaping back beyond the River Seine. Part of the problem was that the Germans were fighting more stubbornly than had been expected, using their superior armour and anti-tank weapons.

10 PSK was ordered to advance along the road which ran from St Sylvain to la Bu sur Rouvres. By 10:00 hours, on 12 August 1944, 10 PSK had reached infantry lines and ran straight into enemy shelling, which caused 1st and 2nd Squadrons to move and seek a more suitable position that would allow them to avoid anti-tank fire. The terrain in Normandy, with its sunken lanes and thick dense hedges, meant that at any time the enemy might only be a few feet away and one would still be unaware of this.

1st Squadron, 10 PSK, advanced in two platoons to the fore, seeking to ensure a safety belt of 300–400 metres as they advanced. The Squadron Commander, with his 2ic, moved into the centre as two further platoons followed, giving good firing cover. In addition, two howitzers, from well-covered positions, were also able to give 1st Squadron excellent covering fire as it advanced towards the enemy lines. At 100 metres, in front of Scots infantry positions, the Squadron met with well-entrenched infantry and 400 metres further, they saw what appeared to be a German anti-tank gun traversing towards them.

Swiftly, the squadron advanced and opened fire. Artillery and machine gun fire was not enough to deter the Germans and the Polish tank crews were forced to defend themselves out in the open with sub-machine guns, revolvers and hand grenades against infantry, which was closing fast with *Panzerfausts*.[81] Those who may have observed the battle would not have distinguished who was firing at whom, owing to the ferocity of the artillery fire. This meant that it was impossible for the Poles to direct their own artillery. 1st Squadron was able to advance against continued waves of enemy infantry, who showed little sign of wanting to surrender.

After one hour of fighting, the Squadron was able to get clear of the wooded area and saw the first buildings of la Bu sur Rouvres, at last being able to see the enemy. But this was also short lived. Almost immediately it became apparent that the enemy was already in well-prepared defensive positions. This meant that in the thick of the battle, on the squadron's left flank, seven tanks could not advance, but merely provided artillery support. The German infantry began to attack the static Polish tanks with grenades and *Panzerfausts*. Once again the tank crews had to leave their tanks and engage the Germans in hand-to-hand fighting. Eventually the Germans were pushed back but the Poles discovered that the Germans had booby-trapped their trenches with grenades, which caused the Poles to advance with caution. As the Squadron advanced, the platoon on the left-hand side noticed a German anti-tank gun at 600 metres range and promptly destroyed it. On the right-hand side, a tank was not so fortunate, as it came into the view of German anti-tank gunners; it received several hits and caught fire. Three of the crew were wounded but were able to withdraw to safety.

2nd Squadron's offensive took place one kilometre to the right of 1st Squadron, to the north of la Bu sur Rouvres, and out of contact with, as a consequence of which it was unable to come to its assistance. 2nd Squadron was operating in extremely open terrain and met with anti-tank fire from the right. At 1600 metres north, *Panther* tanks were unleashed and attacked the squadron's right flank. Three of 2nd Squadron's tanks were knocked out, two men were killed and seven others wounded.

3rd Squadron, meanwhile, had been sent to reconnoitre the region and escaped without incident, except for a minor scrape with a mine. It became obvious that German resistance was stronger than expected and the Corps Commander demanded the withdrawal of 10 PSK. This proved to be difficult because of continued attacks by *Panthers*. Eventually under the cover of smoke, 10 PSK was able to withdraw, towing any tanks that could be salvaged from the battlefield. At a stop in the Renesnil area, 10 PSK once again came under artillery fire, which left one man dead, three wounded and damaged a tank. Once the Regiment was able to assemble properly, later that day, the casualty tally was 3 dead (one died from wounds), 14 wounded, 2 damaged tanks which could be repaired and 4 tanks destroyed.[82]

Wysocki makes the point that without a major offensive against the Quesnay Woods and the defensive area around it, which included heavy armour and anti-tank positions, the route to Falaise, which ensured the success of the Normandy Campaign, would remain closed to the Allies.[83] The account is interesting as it noted that on 9 August 1944, the Quesnay Woods had proved to have been a major obstacle, with *Panzers* dominating the open terrain to the east, north and west. The Allied attack upon the woods is recorded by the Germans as having started at 20:00 hours. According to the Germans, there were only about 23 *Panzers* in the area and a limited amount of infantry in the woods. The German trick was to wait until the combined Polish and Canadian forces were very close before they opened fire.

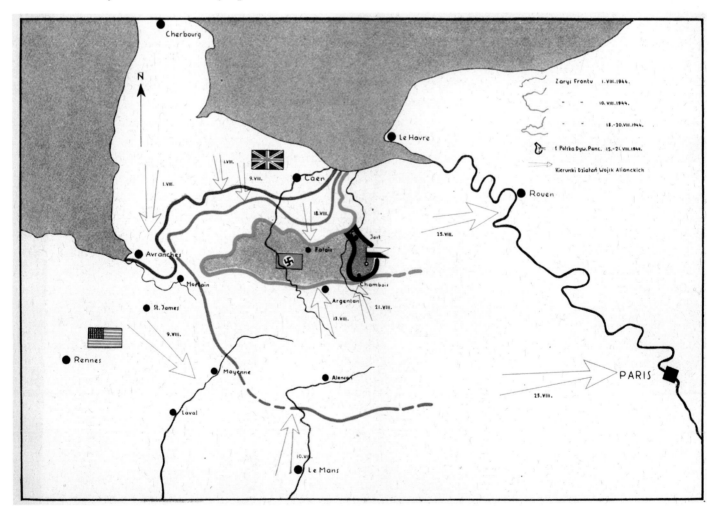

Battle for Normandy 1–21 August 1944. The lines indicate the frontline as it advanced – 1 August, 10 August and then 18–20 August respectively. The thick black line indicates the position of the Division 15–21 August. The thin arrows indicate the direction of Allied advances.

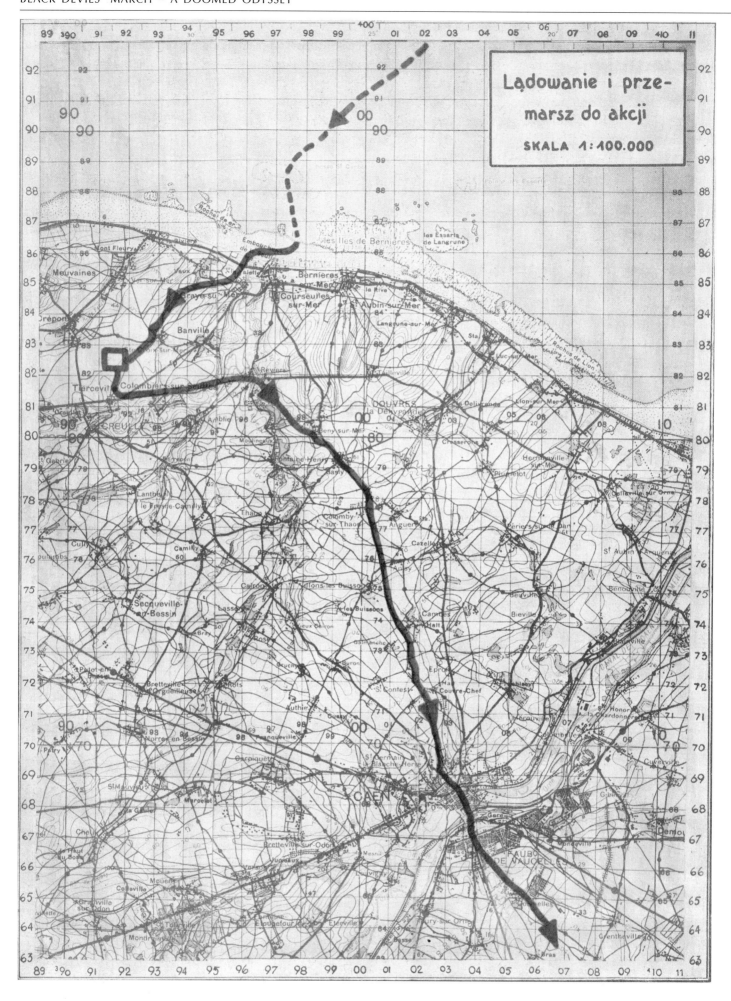

Landing and the march into action. On this and all subsequent maps, the bold line is always the operational route followed by 1st Polish Armoured Division.

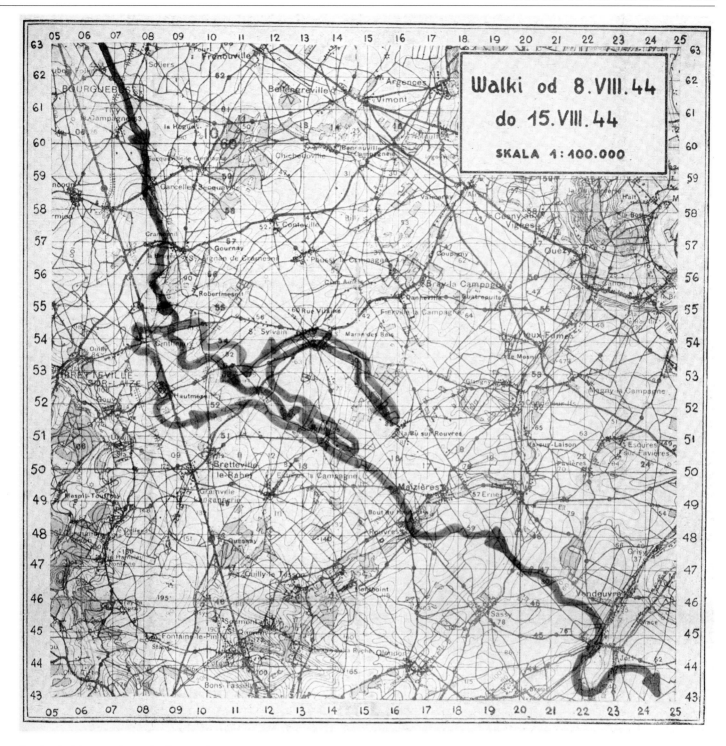

Battles in Normandy, 8–15 August 1944.

The 1st Polish Armoured Division had been ordered to follow the 3rd Canadian Infantry Division in order to capture Hill 140, cross the River Laison and then onto Sassy. The 3rd Rifle Brigade had been assembled in the area and in Estrees. The Germans comment that the official history of the 1st Polish Armoured Division indicated that any attack had been put off owing to heavy German artillery fire but the Germans claim that the offensive was more likely postponed because of the original attack upon the Quesnay Woods. However, 9th Battalion (3rd Rifle Brigade) did not receive a counter-command and started an attack upon Hill 111 (located 1.5 kilometres northwest of Hill 140) during the evening. Attacking with it were 10th Rifle Regiment and an armoured reconnaissance unit (10 PSK), which consisted of three Cromwell tank companies. The tanks came under artillery fire but one company managed to reach Hill 111. According to Polish reports, there was hand-to-hand fighting during which the Poles received significant casualties. A second assault upon Hill 111 was then attempted by the Poles and once again the Germans were able to repel this attempt and it was only once the Poles received reinforcements that as night fell, the Poles were able to capture the hill.[84]

CHAPTER IV

On to Falaise

Max Hastings notes that despite the setbacks during TOTALIZE, Montgomery was not downhearted as he continued to see scope for capturing and destroying the German forces in Normandy, thus denying them the opportunity of escaping eastward over the River Seine, in order to fight once more.[85] TOTALIZE had exposed the weaknesses of the Sherman tank; principally its armour, which was easily penetrated by German anti-tank guns, while its main 75mm gun was ineffective beyond ranges of 500 yards.

After TOTALIZE, the Poles learnt from other regiments the value of welding additional tank tracks to the hulls of their tanks in the hope of deflecting direct hits and therefore avoiding destruction.[86] The Poles lost 66 tanks during TOTALIZE but their Corps Commander, the Canadian, Lieutenant-General Guy Simonds, was critical of both the Canadian 4th Armoured Division and the 1st Polish Armoured Division. It is not certain if Simonds knew of the problems which the armoured divisions had faced during TOTALIZE or whether he merely chose to ignore them. He was especially disappointed with the Poles and for the next operation, code-named TRACTABLE, a massive daytime attack, on 14 August 1944, Simonds deployed the veteran 2nd Canadian Armoured Brigade alongside the newly blooded 4th Canadian Armoured Division, leaving the Poles in reserve. This was to prove to be fortunate as events turned out, as the Polish division was able to recover from its first battle and avoid another friendly 'bombing', this time by the Royal Canadian Air Force (RCAF).[87]

An examination of the regimental diary of the 10th Mounted Rifles (10 *Pulk Strzelcow* – 10 PSK) gives a clear account of events concerning the 1st Polish Armoured Division leading to the capture of an all-important crossing on the River Dives. The capture of this crossing by the Poles was to change events in the Falaise region, at the same time causing both the Allies and the enemy to come to respect the Polish fighting spirit.

On 13 August 1944, 10 PSK were bivouacked between Renesnil and Soignolles (118580) when an order came to move with the anti-tank regiment and units of 10th Motorized Cavalry (10 BK *panc*) to the Cintheaux region, to the north of their present position. The complete formation for the operation was that 1st Polish Armoured Division operated along the margins of the operation whilst 3rd Canadian Infantry Division prepared for action towards the south. During the afternoon of 13 August 1944 10 PSK moved to a position close to the main Caen-Falaise road, and once again bivouacked in wheat fields in which artillery positions were dotted around. Despite continued artillery fire from both sides, the Poles used the break to receive new personnel, equipment and carried out repairs.

On 14 August 1944, the Division began its operation at 16:00 hours and had two options to consider. The first (a) was to move via Falaise and southeast Falaise, the second (b) was to move via Brettville La Rabet in the direction of Sassy and then further onto the Rive Dives. Option (b) seemed the most likely to succeed as reconnaissance suggested that option (a) was impossible. Option (a) seemed almost suicidal because the Podhalian Battalion had to seize Villers Canivet, five kilometres northeast of Falaise, while 10 PSK, supported by anti-tank units and a squadron of Dragoons, were to be flung upon Falaise. This plan seemed to be lacklustre, ill thought out and lacking any real planning.

In contrast, option (b) seemed to be a more cautious plan. The plan called for 10 PSK, the Dragoon squadron and anti-tank units, to move via Rouvres and Sassy, to seek out a crossing at Jort, while 10 PSK and 24th Uhlans followed up behind. The operation was to be preceded by a two hour bombardment by RAF heavy bombers. At 14:25, a quarter of the bombs fell on 1st Squadron 10 PSK's position. The RAF continued to bomb the Polish positions until 15:40. Naturally, this was a disaster. 10 PSK alone suffered eight dead, eight wounded and two tanks destroyed.[88] Wysocki gives further figures, asserting that in total the Division suffered about fifty casualties, both dead and wounded. The 24th Uhlans are recorded as being bombed by 77 heavy bombers, which dropped 3,723 tons of bombs.[89]

The Poles were not alone in this disaster; the Canadians also suffered casualties from this 'friendly bombing'. The Germans were witnesses that day. They claim that two allied aircraft were shot down, one possibly by Allied anti-aircraft fire. The bombing according to the Germans caused confusion and resentment amongst the Allies, as the bombing had been worse than the previous bombing by Allied aircraft on August 8.[90] Not surprisingly, the offensive was called off but the need to cross the River Dives remained.

The following day, 15 August 1944, the results of the Division's actions of 14 August using option (b) were examined and looked promising. Also of great importance was information that elements of the Canadian infantry division had broken enemy defensive positions and reached the Sassy region. Major Jan Maciejowski, commanding officer of 10 PSK, decided that there was a need to enter the hilly region to the north of Sassy, where a squadron could reconnoitre the woods at reference 216 475. After securing this position, the squadron could then seize Hills 74 and 76, to the northwest of the town of Jort. From the two hills, sections of 10 PSK could reconnoitre the railway line and seize it. Following this, 10 PSK was to seek a crossing on the River Dives and force a crossing.

10 PSK set out, moving along two axes in the region of northern Sassy to complete their task. 3rd Squadron moved along the northern axis: Hautmensnil-Renemsnil-Soignoles-Rouvers-Sassy. 1st and 2nd Squadrons moved along the southern axis: Hautmensnil-Brettville la Rabet – northern axis: Estree la Campagne – Rouvers – Sassy. Before leaving to complete the assignments, 2nd Anti-Tank was ordered to remain at base while 1st Squadron was to reach the heights directly beyond this position.

3rd Squadron began their reconnaissance mission in the wooded area at 216 476, 1½ kilometres northwest of Vendeure. 3rd Squadron's mission was to protect and support 2nd Squadron and the anti-tank group assigned to it. 3rd Squadron engaged enemy infantry in the woods and in hidden positions northeast of Sassy. 3rd Squadron immediately opened fire very heavily at the enemy positions and destroyed them, thus allowing the advance to continue while heavy casualties were inflicted upon the enemy and scores of prisoners were taken. This action allowed the squadrons to move into the woods at 216 475, where once again, heavy fire was used to crush German infantry there.

Once clear of the woods, the Poles moved onto the slopes of Hill 74. Here they received a continuous flow of reports concerning the presence of the enemy along the railway line and in the wooded area in front of the tracks. As a result of these reports, Maciejowski, ordered reconnaissance and the protection of the left flank. He also gave orders for the reshuffling of 2nd Squadron and later for the anti-tank squad. Both were to move to the next set of slopes in the direction of the crossing at Jort.

Maciejowski realised that entry into the area of the crossing at Jort from the Polish right flank was impossible. Therefore he decided that the greatest profit could be gained by not only reconnoitring the railway line but also the locality and the crossing itself, while using 2nd Squadron and sections from the anti-tank group to tie up enemy armour to the north. The rest of the anti-tank group was deployed in a deeper formation in preparation for an enemy armoured counter-attack.

1st Squadron's offensive against the railway line at 225 451 and then to seize the line in order to enter the area to reconnoitre the possibility of crossing the River Dives, was supported by fire from 3rd Squadron and 2nd Artillery Regiment (Canadian). The artillery regiment was at the disposal of Maciejowski owing to the intervention of Bronisław Sachse, who had been sent by 10 PSK to communicate with Canadian units. Sachse had proposed the idea of an artillery observer from 2nd Artillery Regiment being sent to aid other divisions when artillery support was needed. This concept was agreed, to the benefit of 10 PSK in this case.

To execute its orders, 1st Squadron pushed through the enemy, crossed the railway track and moved into the suburbs of Jort. A 'snatch team' from a Cromwell tank under the command of 2nd Lieutenant Zbigniew Maksymowicz, reconnoitred the locality and took prisoners, which included two Russians.[91] The Poles assessed the strength of the enemy position in the town and on the river, while considering the approximate number of infantry battalions available to the enemy. From the prisoners, it was learnt that the best method of crossing was via the river, while mention was made of a bridge that was down over the river. At that time 1st Squadron still had not received support from the Dragoons, who could not reach them; therefore 1st Squadron requested that support be sent to them in order to enter Jort.

Maciejowski decided to move 3rd Squadron into Jort, in support of 1st Squadron, who were already fighting enemy infantry in the streets and buildings of Jort. Eventually the destroyed bridges, mentioned by the prisoners, were reached with the loss of one tank, set ablaze by fire from 12th SS *Panzer* Division. This left one man dead: Corporal Kazimierz Ambroz; and four wounded: 2nd Lieutenant Jan Sowa, 2nd Lieutenant Adam Bilski, Lance Corporal Bogusław Pontiatowski and Private Jan Kolat. The Canadian artillery fire was rapid and very accurate. Once 3rd Squadron had entered Jort, the artillery fire shifted to the region of Hill 62 (244 442), one kilometre from Jort. 1st Squadron using 10 PSK's radio network, completed observation and the direction of artillery fire.

1st Squadron could not enter the town because it was already full of tanks, but having enough information from prisoners about the crossing, the Squadron decided to bypass Jort form the south and cross the river using a ford. At the time, 1st Squadron, only had seven tanks fit for action. Three Cromwells had been damaged by

88mm anti-tank fire and a further two had fallen victim to the furrowed terrain and the railway line. 1st Squadron reported the marshiness of the riverbed and the steepness of the river banks, yet also the narrowness of the River Dives, with its firm edges, suggested the possibility of 'Sappers' Bridges' (Bailey Bridges).

3rd Squadron's battle in the town increased in intensity. 10 BK *panc* moved to support 10 PSK. For some unknown reason, 10 BK *panc's* tanks began to fire on the two 10 PSK squadrons in the region of the crossing. All attempts to get the Shermans of 10 BK *panc* to cease firing failed. Maciejowski, with elements of the anti-tank group pressed onto the area around the woods at 220 045, close to 2nd Squadron and the remainder of the anti-tank group. 1st Squadron, despite difficulties was able to find the ford situated in the region 228 439 and reported that four of its tanks had successfully crossed to the other side of the ford. At the same time, 3rd Squadron and the Dragoon Squadron were still fighting in the locality of 228 447 and in northern parts of Vendeure. The fighting left 2nd Lieutenant Jozef Eisler wounded. Maciejewski requested large amounts of infantry to be sent to support 3rd Squadron and the Dragoons. After a while, reinforcements from the Dragoons were sent into battle.

Antoni Położyński, Lieutenant 10 PSK, in 1947, gave the following description of the battle for the crossing at Jort. After the capture of prisoners as already described, 10 PSK already knew the best way to proceed in order to cross the River Dives at Jort. The commander of 1st Squadron, codenamed '*Wasil*' decided upon a new operational plan. Położyński's platoon, (Stefan Four) was to move to the left, along the railway line. Beyond the town, they were told to turn slightly to the left towards the direction of the river. At this time 3rd Squadron had received orders to enter the town and test the possibility of crossing the river. All the time, seeking a firing path, the squadron moved towards the railway viaduct, which Położyński passed under with a 'beating heart'. This admission reflected the fact that although German engineers had destroyed the viaduct, the Poles still pressed it into use, which left Położyński fearful that the entire structure may collapse onto the passing tanks. Happily, each tank passed through the viaduct without loss and entered enemy held territory.

The Squadron took to a wayside orchard, which prevented the Germans from mortaring them. The Squadron did not remain in the orchard long and moved off in two different directions, to reconnoitre for a crossing. Położyński's platoon took the route running parallel with the railway line. On its left, there was a high embankment and running along the right was the orchard. The platoon drove towards a building with a road on the left. It was possible that this route might lead to the river. Once inside the town, through open windows, it was possible to see traces of the German occupation. All the signs pointed to a panicky and rapid withdrawal by the Germans, as tables were laid out for meals and caps still hung on hooks along with parts of their equipment.

As per normal, the Squadron advanced firing at every window and chimney, thus denying snipers any cover. Every twist and turn of the road was advanced into slowly and with caution. An ambush could happen anywhere. Finally the lead tank stopped. At a distance of 100 metres, the Poles could see their objective: the bridge. Sadly, an inspection of it, through binoculars, revealed that the bridge had been partly destroyed.

The Poles decided to try and find a crossing point close to the bridge. To the right of the crossing, it may have been possible, but not at the point where the Squadron stood, as on the bank and in the water, mines were visible. To the left of the bridge there were no mines but the bank was under water. Even so the Poles decided to go to the left. The Germans on the opposite bank began to fire around the bridge. The Poles, buttoned up in their tank turrets, returned fire with their main guns, firing towards the wooded heights beyond the river. After several minutes, the German fire weakened. Immediately, one of the Polish tanks tried to cross the river. It moved slowly to the flat, boggy bank, its tracks indenting the mud. To its rear, another tank entered the water and got stuck. Several yards to the rear, stood another tank from the platoon, which immediately went to the aid of the stricken tank. A line was attached to the tank and in a few minutes it was pulled from the water. At this the Poles lost their last hope of crossing the river.

Meanwhile, the Dragoon Squadron had moved from Jort and was beginning to clear it of the enemy. The Germans put up an obstinate defence and under such resistance, the Dragoons were obliged to withdraw. The debris from the house that had either been blown up or set alight in the fighting began to block the route and stall any further movement. Running parallel to 3rd Squadron's abortive attempt to ford the River Dives was 1st Squadron, who were moving rapidly to the south of Jort and onto the ford. Not meeting any serious opposition, they moved through the orchard and scrubland until they reached the river. Sergeant Major (*Wachmistrz*) Łaskowski, was the first to drive his tank, like a powerful battleship, into the water. The conditions on the river were favourable that day and the tank reached the far bank. The next tank followed but this time not all went well as each following Cromwell got stuck in the middle of the river. This meant that each tank had to be hauled across along a line by the preceding tank. Położyński remarks that only by a miracle and perhaps with a faster

Three views of one of the Division's
Cromwell ARVs towing away a
disabled German *Panzer* IV tank,
Normandy 1944.
**Imperial War Museum
B6518, B6519, B6520**

approach did the tanks 'Wasila' cross the river unaided. The Squadron, once across the river, moved to a firing position, which the Germans had abandoned on the hills. From there the Poles fired upon the enemy.

2nd Squadron had been protecting 10 PSK's right flank against continuously circling by German *Tiger* tanks while 3rd Squadron continued to fight in Jort, helping the Dragoons clear buildings and give then firing support from the river crossing. The object of the Dragoon's task was crucial to the offensive with 4th Platoon, having to move along the main street in Jort to the ruined bridge. At the moment of moving forward to complete this task, the platoon commander's tank was hit several times by anti-tank fire and set ablaze. Four of the crew were able to bail out; three were badly wounded, including the platoon commander. The Polish tanks continued to return fire, refusing to yield any ground until eventually the German anti-tank guns fell silent, but by the same token, most of the Polish tanks were on fire as a result of this duel.

At dusk 1st Tank Regiment arrived in Jort. Elements of 1st Tank had already crossed the River Dives and had linked up with 1st Squadron 10 PSK. Around this time 1st Squadron suffered its greatest loss so far when their second-in-command (2ic) Lieutenant Jerzy Wasowski was killed when his tank received a direct hit from an anti-tank gun. 1st Squadron remained on the far side of the river until the following morning.

The Shermans of 1st Tank relieved the rest of the 10 PSK units, which had been involved in that day's fighting. Under the cover of smoke, 10 PSK withdrew to its night positions. While moving to its position for the night, 3rd Squadron came under heavy mortar fire, which wounded several people, including a platoon commander. This was the third platoon commander to have been wounded that day. Położyński remarks that the battle for the Jort crossing cost 10 PSK dearly as they received heavy losses in both personnel and equipment.

The following day, General Maczek, the commanding officer of the 1st Polish Armoured Division, sent word concerning the battle of Jort:

'You have had a splendid battle. But you don't realise yet what you have done.'

Położyński admits that at the time, he and his comrades did not understand the importance of the victory at Jort and the forcing of the River Dives but later it became clear that it prepared the way for the 1st Polish Armoured Division's victory at Chambois.[92]

A return to the narrative of 10 PSK's diary gives a wider view of the events of 15 August 1944. After Maciejowski had requested infantry support, not only did he receive Dragoon but also elements of the advance of 10 BK *panc* arrived at his position, in addition to reports of a platoon of sappers arriving to clear and prepare for the fording of the River Dives. This was then followed by a further report that 1st Squadron had reconnoitred, forced, taken and held the railway line in the locality of the river crossing at Jort. 1st Squadron had taken the eastern side of the Dives, 500 metres of Jort itself and was continuing to pour fire upon German infantry who were withdrawing from Jort and had formed a defensive 'nest'. It was here that Jerzy Wasowski, 1st Squadron's Commander, had been killed.

2nd Squadron reported enemy tank movements along the route in the region 243 435, which suggested that the Germans were withdrawing from the area. This meant that the town of Trun was now wide open to the 1st Polish Armoured Division. The victory had been costly for 10 PSK, which had not only encountered infantry armed with hand held anti-tank weapons but had also been arrayed against two companies of armour, consisting of Panzer Mk IVs to the east of Jort, and *Tigers* and *Panthers* on the west bank of the Dives, as well as armour in the stone quarries at la Breuil.

10 PSK's casualties were five dead and fourteen wounded. In material terms, two Cromwell tanks had been destroyed and four damaged. The estimated enemy losses were calculated as being: 103 prisoners; one *Tiger* tank destroyed; two 88mm anti-tank guns destroyed; thirteen guns of less than 75mm calibre destroyed. An ammunition dump was captured as well as seventeen lorries and trailers.[93] Wysocki notes that amongst the prisoners were members of 12th SS Division. This must have been quite a coup for the Poles as the 'Aryan Supermen' were now surrendering to the 'Sub-human Slavs', while the opening of the way to Trun allowed Montgomery to realise his plan to strike at Trun along the Dives river.[94]

On 16 August 1944, 24th Uhlans began to cross the River Dives using the ford which sappers had strengthened using metal netting and were shortly preparing to build a bridge over. The remainder of the Polish armoured division crossed to the east bank and surprised the enemy who had to bring reinforcements from the south and engage 2nd Tank Regiment (Polish) in a defensive action in the village of Homme Coulibeuf. In order to widen the advance guard it was decided that the Division should regroup for operations to the south.

This demanded some investigation, as during 14 and 15 August 1944 there had been a lot of activity between the *Luftwaffe* and Polish anti-aircraft units during which the Germans lost four aircraft. At night 10 BK *panc* was bombed causing several deaths. The following night, the Divisional Headquarters was bombed, killing four officers (unit masters) who had been holding a briefing in an armoured car used for command activities. After this incident, General Maczek ordered a reduction of such vehicles in case of future attacks. The vehicles were reduced to two or three armoured cars and tanks necessary to guard the immediate staff while the remainder of the Headquarters was positioned one or two kilometres to the rear.

For the next offensive, Maczek, created two formations. Lieutenant-Colonel Koszutski's group, which consisted of: 2nd Tank Regiment; 8th Rifle Battalion; an anti-tank group and a medical team. It was to operate along the Louvagny-Barou axis. The formation under the command of Major Kanski was made up of: 24th Uhlans, 10th Dragoons, an incomplete group of self-propelled anti-tank artillery and a medical team. It was to operate along the Viquette- Viques axis and along the River Dives.

24th Uhlans moved with the reserves from the Division across the new crossing on the Dives and straight into trouble. The Uhlan's commanding officer, Major Kanski, was badly wounded and his adjutant, *Rotmistrz* (Captain) Kozlowski was killed. The formation then came under the command of 10th Dragoons commanding officer, Major Zgorzelski. Kanski died from his wounds a few days later. The enemy was able to pour continuous fire down onto the endangered Polish position and Zgorzelski's group became involved in heavy fighting around Homme Coulibeuf. The armoured squadrons continued to press home their attacks and at around 18:40 hours encountered a weak armoured and infantry counterattack in the Coulibeuf-Barou region. The Germans were also aided by fighter planes, which strafed the Polish units. All of this activity by the enemy was in vain as by dusk the Poles had broken the counter-offensive and were preparing night positions.[95]

On 16 August 1944, 10 PSK, minus 1st Squadron, left its post to the east of Jort and spent the night in the area 216 456. The night was less than peaceful owing to enemy air attacks using rockets and bombs. During the morning of 16 August, Maciejowski had been to Division Headquarters to give a progress report to Maczek and to ask for further orders. The importance of Jort had not been immediately obvious but as the days passed it was realised that the Poles who had taken Jort, had not followed a plan from Corps but had instead, thought on their feet and had taken matters into their own hands and emerged victorious. The speed of the Polish action at Jort had made it impossible for the Germans to establish strongpoints of resistance while enabling tanks to link up with American units at Chambois, which closed the so-called 'bag' at Falaise and crushed the 7th German Army.

During this time, 10 PSK received orders to prepare for the next offensive. Their task was to reconnoitre in the direction of Trun. Preparations were moved from 14:00 hours and then to 16:00 hours and then put back until the evening. Finally 10 PSK was informed that Maczek had moved the offensive to dawn. 10 PSK had halted in the middle of the previous day's battle and at such close quarters was able to estimate the enemy's casualties for that day. The tank crews were interested to note the effect of the fire of their 75mm shells and rockets, as well as the effect of the fire of their 95mm howitzer, whose shot spread in a wide pattern. In the wooden areas, it was noted that shells fired into tree stumps at the height of one or two metres had burst horizontally below these heights and had caused great destruction within the enemy trenches. Throughout 16 August 1944 the Division was using units from 10 BK *panc* and 3rd Rifle Brigade, who after overrunning the Jort crossing, continued to fight the enemy to the south and southeast of Jort. Meanwhile, some units from 10 PSK occupied and cleared the localities of Courcy Lauvagny and Barou, as well as entering the outskirts of Morteaux-Couliboeut.[96]

By 17 August 1944 most of the units of the Division had been in continuous action for three days and in the case of 3rd Rifle Brigade and 24th Uhlans, four days. This meant that tired men were in fast moving action, continually exposed to danger and in constant contact with the enemy. The operation for that day was to take Hills 159 and 259.

The Germans were aware of Polish moves and Meyer reports that during the evening of 16 August owing to the threatening situation from the east of the Dives, the Germans moved two *Kampfgruppen* into the area in order to try to stop 1st Polish Armoured Division's attack from the Dives bridgehead towards Trun. The Poles had already reached Norrey-en-Auge (one of the destinations of *Kampfgruppe* von Luck) the previous evening. 10 PSK attacked the German formation from les Moutiers, in the direction of Trun. *Kampfgruppe* von Luck replied very effectively, knocking out four of the Polish Cromwells, while two more were damaged, but were able to retreat under the cover of a smoke screen. Two units from 10 BK *panc* were also able to reach Hill 259 by evening after what the Germans described as 'heavy fighting'.[97]

The Poles remark that the junction on the route to Trun was already under fire from Canadian artillery and tanks from 10 PSK. It was hoped that this would have the effect of denying the Germans a route out of Trun.[98] 10 PSK was given orders 'especially for 10 PSK' by Division, which explained the overall situation. 1st Polish Armoured Division continued in its task of pushing onto the hills, five kilometres northeast from Trun. From the west, 4th Canadian Armoured Division had moved during the night from the Perrieres area to take part in

Three photographs showing a German multiple-barrelled rocket launcher, or *Nebelwerfer*, captured by the Division in Normandy 1944.
Imperial War Museum
B7783, B7784, B7785

an operation, northeast of Trun. From the northeast of Jort, the 51st Highland Division was crossing the St. Pierre sur Dives while the Americans were four miles south of Trun. The task of 10 PSK was to be huge.

At 06:30 hours, 10 PSK was to overrun the high road for 500 metres below the co-ordinates at Level 41 in the Baron regions. 1st Squadron was to reconnoitre in the direction of Trun with the purpose of linking up with the Americans. The rest of the regiment had to reconnoitre in a broad fan from the direction of the Division which was on the Baron – Hill 159 axis (2836) in the region of Les Moutiers En Auge/ Hill 259 (3334). To the east of 1st Squadron, a reconnaissance patrol from 10 BK *panc* was to reconnoitre along the river. The estimated time of this patrol setting out was 10:00 hours.

1st Squadron, while moving towards the church in Trun, destroyed several 20mm guns, four 75mm self-propelled guns and an 88mm anti-tank gun, in addition to several enemy tanks. All this for the loss of one tank to an anti-tank gun. To the east, the situation remained unclear. 'A' platoon had been sent out to reconnoitre but had come under fire from two anti-tank guns. Both of these were destroyed but not without loss as Second Lieutenant Bolesław Rouppert was killed and Private Jan Ciechanowski was wounded, with one Stuart tank destroyed and another damaged. Meanwhile, 3rd Squadron signalled that they had captured Hill 159, where they had found an abandoned fuel dump and field guns.

Successive waves of squadrons from 10 PSK reached the area around Hill 102 and next to Hill 104. The enemy infantry had already withdrawn in confusion and as a consequence were captured by the Poles. There was a massive movement of mixed enemy vehicles fleeing the Allied advance along the route from the west and north-west from Moutiers En Auge. Despite the distance of the fleeing enemy column 10 PSK opened fire upon it. The Polish tank and artillery fire destroyed a large number of vehicles as well as causing disruption and panic amongst the enemy. Maciejowski reported that the River Dives valley looked like a 'giant cauldron' from which vehicles and entire German columns were to trying to flee to the east and the southeast. On the whole, the German position was hopeless and was in effect, trapped. This trap was reinforced by 4th Canadian Armoured Division's push from the west. Maciejowski requested artillery observers and further artillery fire in order to destroy the enemy and its route. 10 PSK was able to take prisoners from 21st *Panzer* Division, *Luftwaffe* units as well as individual Germans separated from their units.

The main Crocy-Fontaine les Bassets – Trun road was a scene of mass enemy movement while the strong fire upon it from the Poles increased. To the south of the road, enemy artillery and armour posts had been observed. At the same time reports were being received that suggested that the likelihood of linking up with the Americans during the day was small as the Americans had been unable to move directly to Trun. 3rd Squadron, however, had been able to move to Hill 259, its objective for the day. This was taken with little difficulty, with only Lance Corporal Jakubiec being wounded.

During the evening Maciejowski gave new orders: to move closer to Hill 259. After evacuating their wounded, 10 PSK moved via Louvieres En Auge (303 336) where they camped overnight with 3rd Squadron who had been fighting on Hill 259 and had decided to remain on the hill overnight. 10 PSK carried out its reconnaissance missions in the direction of Trun; moving around and enduring heavy fighting whilst reconnoitring the hills and looking for a base for the Division's operations for the following day which were designed to ensure panic and the disorientation of the enemy.

The casualty list for 10 PSK for 17 August 1944 was high: seven dead, ten wounded, four Cromwell tanks destroyed, three Cromwell tanks damaged, two Stuart tanks destroyed and one damaged. For the enemy it was far higher and could only be estimated as being 80 prisoners, one 88mm anti-tank gun, four 75mm self-propelled guns, three 20mm guns, one caterpillar tracked tractor, one fuel dump, seven lorries and a car. Despite the enemy losses it was noted that with the exception of 10 PSK and 9th Rifle Battalion, the 1st Polish Armoured Division did not reach any of its objectives set for 17 August 1944. However from captured German documents, the Division must have been aware of the fact that the Germans were in a tight situation. Most important for the Germans was the recovery of the area around Morteaux-Coulisboeuf from where they hoped to begin a new front. The German intelligence also revealed that the Allies had been worried about the presence of SS units and that the Poles actually had very little information about German positions and their strengths.[99]

Wysocki records that the general situation at the time was that there was a need for further effort. During the evening of 17 August 1944, General Simonds, command of 2nd Canadian Corps, came to the Division, from a meeting with Field Marshal Montgomery. Simonds expressed the highest recognition hitherto concerning the Division's operations, making reference to the crossing of the River Dives and both operations towards Trun. He played tribute to the tired units of the Division and noted that there was still need for a superhuman effort in the future.[100] It seemed that Simonds was beginning to respect the Poles.

The Division still had one further task to perform and that was that during the night, it was to take the intersection on the Chambois route, which was the remaining route eastward for the Germans and link up with the Americans, who were coming from Argentan. Maczek understood that the units were tired but they had to prevent the escape of German armed forces in the area. Therefore, he gave orders for the movement which if all went well meant the capture of the greater part of German Army Group 'B' which consisted of the Seventh and Fifteenth Armies in addition to *Panzergruppe West*.

The first order went to a group consisting of 2nd Tank Regiment, 8th Rifle Battalion (known to the Germans as the 'Bloody Shirts')[101] and an anti-tank group. Its commander was Lieutenant-Colonel Koszutski and its task was to move to Chambois and establish contact with 10 PSK who had been operating in the area, capture the town and at dawn, link up with the Americans, moving from the south. They were to move without delay.

After a day of fighting, this meant that they would have to replenish their fuel, ammunition, receive reinforcements and prepare marching orders – everything a soldier who has been fighting all day does not want to do. The column was formed up with armoured pickets leading the way, followed by tank units, commanders of the formation, a company of infantry and dragoons, infantry command, further armoured units and then the rest of the infantry – in total hundreds of vehicles. They moved into the night, into the Normandy dust, without lights, complete with overtired drivers. The column moved off at 02:00 hours; the nearest time possible following the issuing of orders at 19:00 hours.[102]

On 18 August 1944, 10 PSK was ordered to Chambois with 8th Rifle Battalion. Their task was to support 2nd Anti-Tank group, who had been trying to take Hill 259 since 17 August. General Maczek had given orders for a squadron of tank and an anti-tank group to be moved to the area around the hill, waiting for a move to Chambois, as well as the hoped for link with the Americans. 10 PSK pushed somewhat closer to Hill 259 (315 350). 3rd Squadron received orders to reconnoitre towards Chambois and moved out to execute this task at 11:00 hours, 18 August 1944, pushing towards Bourdon and Hill 124, about two kilometres north of Chambois. En route, 3rd Squadron evaded enemy columns but upon reaching Hill 124, they opened fire upon the Germans. The Polish shelling caused great destruction amongst the Germans and the Poles continued to fire, allowing German vehicles to pile up and block the route of the enemy withdrawal.

Destroyed German artillery equipment, Normandy. **Imperial War Museum B8832**

Units of 10 BK *panc*, who had no knowledge of the area, were sent to reconnoitre around the Chambois area. This turned out to be heavily defended by anti-tank units, *Panther* tanks and infantry. The fact that the Americans had still not reached Chambois also remained a problem for any offensive towards Chambois. 3rd Squadron, from a static position, continued to pour fire onto withdrawing German groups. This led to the enemy becoming boxed in and unable to withdraw from their positions. The amount of prisoners (40) taken by 3rd Squadron had also become a problem for the squadron as it compromised the squadron's safety.

Before dusk, Maciejowski ordered 3rd Squadron t return to 10 PSK's lines. 3rd Squadron's mission on 18 August 1944 had taken them twelve kilometres further than in any other region reached by Allied armoured units. On its way back, 3rd Squadron had to break through enemy columns. By the time it reached 10 PSK's position (around Hill 259), 24th Uhlans, coming from the direction of Chambois, had arrived to reinforce 10 PSK. 3rd Squadron had been the only squadron from 10 PSK in action that day and had not receive any casualties but had inflicted the following estimated casualties upon the enemy: one *Panzer* Mk IV destroyed, three 75mm self-propelled guns destroyed, four half-tracked ammunition tractors destroyed, four lorries destroyed, five cars destroyed, one 75mm anti-tank gun destroyed and 40 prisoners taken.[103]

Tadeusz Walewicz, who in August 1944 was serving with 2nd Tank Regiment, recalls the night moved to Chambois. 2nd Tank moved towards Chambois in the darkness, towards the German positions. On one of the tanks, sat a French guide, who Walewicz describes as 'disappearing at the first opportunity'.[104] At the intersection along the route, the Poles took a wrong turning and instead of going to Chambois, the Polish column headed eastwards towards Champeaux. On the way they passed German columns moving westward. In the darkness nothing was seen by either side as being amiss but upon reaching Champeaux at dawn it quickly became apparent that everything was wrong.

At the crossroad outside of Champeaux, a German 88mm anti-tank gun opened fire and disabled the lead Polish tank, killing one of the crew. At the same time, German infantry began to stream out of surrounding houses and began to attack the column. Walewicz remembers that the attack was easily repulsed using the Shermans' machine guns. From prisoners its was learnt that Champeaux housed the headquarters of 2nd SS Division.[105] A contemporary newspaper report provides further evidence of the significance of the 'Polish lucky mistake' as it revealed that not only did Champeaux contain 2nd SS HQ but also orders were captured which showed that I SS *Korps* should capture certain positions and hold them until II SS *Korps* broke through to Trun and Chambois. Champeaux lay between the two towns.[106]

Stanisław Koszutski, commanding officer, 2nd Tank Regiment, in his memoirs gave a vivid account of the action at Champeaux. 2nd Tank, as Walewicz described, took a wrong turn and passed German armour moving west. 2nd Tank Regiment was caught out on a narrow road with orchards and buildings to either side. There was no room for manoeuvre for the Sherman tanks. German infantry close to the Polish tanks began to flee from nearby houses whilst Polish infantry moved in to capture them; 80 prisoners were taken. From the right and slightly to the rear, 2nd Tank heard tank engines. There was a general assumption that they were Cromwells from 10 PSK. 2nd Squadron, 2nd Tank was dispatched to discover who the tanks belonged to but returned with information from local residents to the effect that the Germans had scores of tanks close to the Polish position.

The Poles advanced towards Champeaux and were met with barricades. Immediately 8th Rifle Battalion went into action, entering houses and gardens and once again took many prisoners. It was becoming obvious that the area was to the enemy's rear and was some kind of command post. The Poles even found two generals' uniforms. All around were documents concerning the staff of 2nd SS *Panzer* Division, including the documents already discussed. Furthermore there was evidence of looting as every car or horse drawn cart was loaded with silverware, clothing, furs, ladies lingerie, wine and food. Finally 2nd Tank found a guide who informed them that they were in Champeaux, which was about ten kilometres northeast from Chambois – their objective. Furthermore, they were deep in the German rear. From every side firing could be observed. The overall situation for the Poles looked bleak. Their biggest problem was how to get out!

Already 1st Squadron was under anti-tank fire. 1st Squadron made the following report: "There is a barricade along the road protected by two 88mm anti-tank guns, ringed by machine guns. To the left are steep slopes while on the right there is a precipice. To come off the road is impossible and the guide is wounded".

Virtually the entire column was under mechanized fire. The Polish infantry already had its hands full and were taking heavy casualties. They were climbing slopes so that they could take on Germans throwing grenades down upon them. The Polish tanks fired to the right, upon Germans. The Poles continued to receive casualties who were carried to the tanks. Once again the Poles were taking many prisoners. This mean that the Poles had nowhere to put the wounded and prisoners, therefore Polish wounded lay by the tanks alongside the German prisoners, literally in one another's arms and so died together under murderous fire.

A column of Polish Cromwells moves past an abandoned German gun, Normandy, August 1944.
Imperial War Museum B8833, B8834

Suddenly there was another wave of German attacks, from the right, aimed mainly at 2nd Squadron. The Squadron was able to deploy two platoons and doing so moved close to the nearest German group and was suddenly confronted with a full German company. The Poles let fly with a 'hurricane of fire' while on the move. The fire gave the desired effect: panic and the enemy fled unnerved and crazed by the ferocious Polish attack. The Germans tried to climb walls, they threw their weapons away and some merely wept. Most of the enemy was killed, either by Polish fire or were crushed under the tracks of the Polish tanks. At once 1st Squadron silenced the 88mm anti-tank guns and was able to sweep most the barricade while platoons from 2nd Squadron were able to join the column. From the tail of the column, (3rd Squadron) came reports of enemy infantry using grenades and *panzerfausts*. Koszutski was shocked at the futility of the German attacks: infantry against tanks. Once again the column was halted. Koszutski writes of being thirsty and his legs hurting. Heavy anti-tank fire and machine fire raked the column from the right. The tanks were quite secure but the infantry once again was suffering huge losses. Suddenly aircraft were spotted.

At first some of the tank crews thought that the aircraft were German *Messerschmitts* (such was Polish luck that day) but they were wrong. The aircraft were Allied, Thunderbolts (ground attack aircraft) about twenty in number. The Poles put up recognition smoke but this had no effect. The first plane came down and began to shoot up the column, followed by the other planes. The tanks could not make contact with Brigade as their communications had been damaged by the aerial attack. Bombs fell either side of the column and in the road between the tanks. The Poles suffered several wounded and it was only by a miracle that they did not lose any tanks. Both the Polish infantry and the German prisoners surveyed the scene in disbelief. It had only taken a few minutes to cause such destruction. Suddenly there was a second wave of aircraft.

The Poles watched the incoming aircraft with a sense of helplessness. They needed a miracle to escape total destruction at the hands of 'friendly' aircraft. But there was no miracle. 1st Squadron managed to clear away a damaged tank and began to attack a German anti-tank position. The position was destroyed along with an ammunition trailer which had been set ablaze.

A third wave of aircraft began its bombing attack but in time recognised the Polish tanks for what they were. The Poles were able to move from the area and got onto the road to Trun and were able to pick up with the rear of the column. After travelling several kilometres, 2nd Tank Regiment once again took post and prepared for further combat, as along the Trun – Vimoutiers road, which ran laterally to the Poles, was a formation of SS armour attacking from the east. However, the attack was of very little consequence as the Germans were already in a state of confusion and lacked co-ordination. German units withdrawing from Trun quickly fell into Polish hands. By the evening of 18 August 1944, 2nd Tank Regiment had reached the village of Bession-Rousseau, from where communication with Brigade was re-established.[107]

Before the Battle of Maczuga the Division was to be involved in further fighting before the climax of the Normandy Campaign. 10 PSK on 19 August 1944 was sent out with anti-tank units to reconnoitre the region towards Chambois. 10 PSK was to move along the axis: Church (323 340) area of Hill 147 (333 314) – Bourdon – Hill 124 (407 535) and Hill 113 (410 524). This route in fact retraced the route taken by 3rd Squadron the day before. However this time, 3rd Squadron advanced with anti-tank units as well as with 1st and 2nd Squadrons along with Maciejowski's squadron. One kilometre south of Bourdon, contact was made with weakened enemy units. The Poles immediately attacked them, causing the enemy to lose a large number of vehicles, two 105mm guns and a 75mm self-propelled gun, in addition to a large quantity of machine guns. An advance party belonging to 3rd Squadron, operating one kilometre north of Hill 124, met a reconnaissance patrol of 4th Canadian Armoured Division. The Canadians opened fire upon the Poles in the belief that they were a German patrol. During the afternoon 10 PSK reached Hill 124 where 1st, 2nd, 3rd Squadrons, 2nd Anti-Tank Battalion and the Regimental Command Post were established in deep firing groups.

On 19 August 1944 10 PSK led the fighting as they destroyed strong enemy positions as they worked their way from St Lambert sur Dives, moving in a south-east direction. The enemy resisted strongly, doing its best to thrust its way forward using an armoured attack. 10 PSK with its anti-tank units destroyed many medium vehicles, took prisoners as well as destroying an 88mm anti-tank gun, complete with towing trailer. The effect of the Polish destruction was to jam the enemy route between Hill 124 and Chambois owing to the resulting wreckage. Maciejowski moved 1st Squadron, followed by 2nd Squadron to the area of Hill 113. 1st Squadron was deployed to the west and 2nd Squadron to the east. The area around the position was covered by thick hedgerows which had its advantages as it was difficult for the Germans to fire from a distance with their 75mm and 88mm guns, equipped with extended barrels, thus reducing the efficiency of the German armour. This meant that German tanks were forced to come closer and therefore gave the Poles a better chance of defending themselves with their 75mm guns.

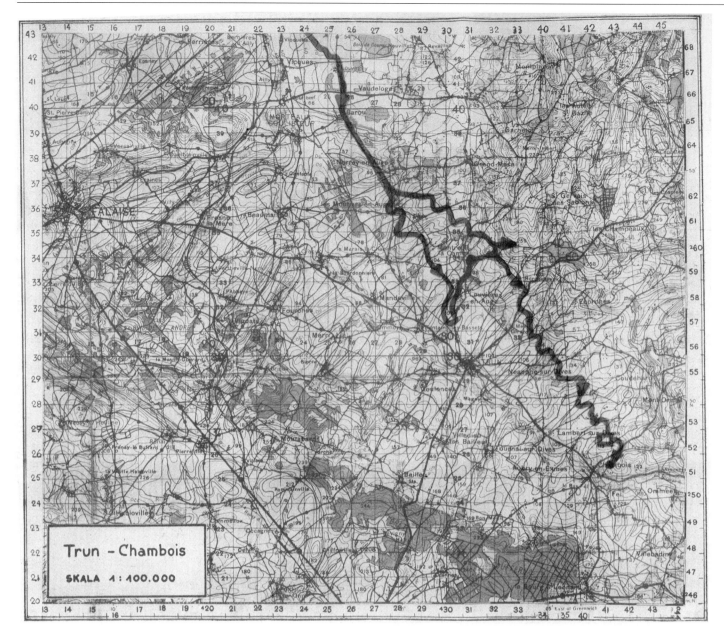

Trun-Chambois route.

At around 17:00 hours 10 PSK received orders to support an offensive of 10th Dragoons at Chambois. A great number of prisoners were taken. The Dragoons moved to the fore of 10 PSK while Maciejowski 1st, 2nd and 3rd Squadrons with 2nd Anti-Tank Battalion up closer to the front. 1st Squadron advanced to the cemetery (405 519) where they destroyed an 88mm anti-tank gun and fought off a second, while losing a tank. While 1st Squadron was engaged in the cemetery; 10th Dragoons occupied the countryside north of Chambois where many prisoners were taken. All operations ceased at dusk.

CHAPTER V

Maczuga – Hill 262

After the fighting at Champeaux, Koszutski and his tanks moved southwest towards Chambois, a mere six miles away. 10th Mounted Rifles (10 PSK) was moving to the right of Koszutski while 24th Uhlans headed down the Dives valley to Trun which was actually within the 4th Canadian Armoured Division's zone of operations, but still German hands. However this was more of an illusion as the Germans were already in flight, harried by Allied aircraft and artillery, as they trickled their way towards Mount Ormel, soon to be known as Hill 262 and nicknamed the *Maczuga* by General Maczek, commanding officer of the 1st Polish Armoured Division. *Maczuga* is the Polish word for 'mace' and from a relief map, Hill 262 resembles a mace.

By the night of 18 August 1944, twenty German divisions were trapped in the Falaise region. During the night there had been a let up in the Allied bombing of the Germans, which had allowed for the movement to the east by twelve of the twenty units, still operating as complete units: 3rd Parachute, 84th, 276th, 277th, 326th, 353rd, and 363rd Infantry Divisions, as well as, 1st, 10th, and 12th SS Divisions and 2nd and 116th *Panzer* Divisions.[108] However in the morning, the Allies resumed their aerial offensive against the retreating Germans.

The commanding officer of 10 PSK, Major Jan Maciejowski, foresaw that any activity scheduled for 20 August 1944 would take place in the east as the enemy fled from the allied advance. On 19 August 1944,

A Polish war correspondent covering the Division whilst in Normandy. **Imperial War Museum B8827**

Polish Shermans await orders to move forward in Normandy, 1944. **Imperial War Museum B8828**

10 PSK was gathered on Hill 113 and passed the night in a defensive square. 2nd Anti-Tank Self-Propelled Artillery Battalion was bivouacked with 3rd Anti-Tank Battalion, who had been seconded to the Dragoons. All the time, this position was being reinforced by crews who had been involved in the long battles of the previous days. As a result they were tired: very tired. Once within the safety of 10 PSK's position, they felt more secure and after camouflaging, they ate and then went to sleep.

During the evening, the Poles received an interesting communication (nr. 13: 19 August 1944, 21:00 hours). From interrogations of enemy prisoners, it had been disclosed that only the operations of the 1st Armoured Division, who had passed Jort on the River Dives, had caused any great alarm amongst the Germans. The lie of the land was discussed; the sunken lanes, woodlands and thick hedgerows, which made defence very easy and caused the Allies to take more time than they had anticipated. Furthermore, Allied casualties had been higher than the enemy had expected. A further revelation concerned the SS, in so much that despite the assumption that the SS were the cream of Hitler's fighting forces; the communication suggested that the SS were to be the first in line for withdrawal, while others came forward to surrender.

At this point, it is worth considering, were the Germans trying to preserve their 'elite' troops for the defence of Germany, the Fatherland? Furthermore, were those SS personnel who were surrendering, actually German and not committed to the Nazi ideal?[109] The communication does not reveal this but it does continue by saying that the morale of the SS units was far from enthusiastic.[110] It was obvious that the units, which had remained intact, continued to fight well.

During the night of 20 August 1944 at 02:45 hours, 10 PSK was attacked by a strong enemy reconnaissance offensive. The Germans lost their element of surprise owing to the vigilance of 3rd Squadron, under the command of 2nd Lieutenant Antoni Położyński. 3rd Squadron swiftly counter-attacked and ferociously beat off the German incursion. The noise of the fighting alerted the rest of the regiment who entered the fray firing from all directions. The fiery onslaught from 10 PSK, forced the Germans to withdraw. After this incident Polish pickets were doubled, while throughout the night the Germans continued to probe the Polish defences. On each occasion the enemy was beaten back. All around 10 PSK's position were more dead and wounded Germans, while prisoners tried to get to the safety of 10 PSK's defensive harbour.

At dawn, the enemy, after a mortar and artillery barrage, once again tried to storm the Polish position. In this attack, the Germans deployed 15 *Panther* tanks and 4 *Panzer* Mk IV tanks as well as several armoured cars. The

The crew of one of the Division's Shermans in Normandy. **Imperial War Museum B8829**

attack was fought at close range and was extremely bloody. Położyński's platoon destroyed four of the *Panthers*. Overall the Germans lost four *Panthers*, four Mk IVs and two armoured cars. Lieutenant-General Otto Elfeldt, commander LXXXIV Corps from 28 July 1944) headed the whole offensive.

The Germans risked huge amounts of infantry and equipment by pushing so close to the Polish tank positions. The heavy fire, by both the Polish artillery and tanks, totally destroyed the German attack. As the German armour was destroyed, their infantry became exposed to Polish machine gun fire, which denied them the chance to withdraw. Therefore entire companies began to surrender. In turn many senior German officers began to surrender until eventually, Elfeldt himself surrendered his pistol to Położyński, a mere 2nd Lieutenant.[111] In addition, Lieutenant-Colonel Gustav Fenstal (commanding officer *Panzer Grenadiers*, 2nd *Panzer* Division) along with two of his staff officers, followed by 22 officers, rising to the rank of Major, came forward to surrender. To complete the misery, 800 NCOs and other ranks also surrendered.

In the middle of 10 PSK's position, at the dressing station, which was treating about 300 men, the prisoners were collected. German medical orderlies helped the Polish medical staff and their work was model. In front of 10 PSK's lines were around 1,000 dead and wounded. This carnage reflected the desperation of the enemy as they tried to escape the Allied encirclement of their positions. As a result the Germans merely tried to overrun the Polish position without trying to make sure of the Polish numbers and strengths as they tried to escape the encirclement or as the Poles called it 'Kocioł' (cauldron). Frankly, the Germans could not see any exit from their position and to use the Polish metaphor, 'cauldron', a heady witches brew was being prepared for the Germans in Normandy.

At 08:30 hours, 10 PSK's Commanding Officer, Major Jan Maciejowski, was killed by sniper fire. Major Otton Ejsymont, assumed command. Owing to the continued fighting, 10 PSK was coming perilously close to running out of ammunition. 3rd Squadron, who had borne the brunt of the battle, had already used up its machine gun ammunition and shells for the main guns. Probably every unit was in a similar situation as basically, supplies had become cut off. Division could only contact 10 PSK by radio and therefore did not realise the position of the regiment.

General Maczek, meanwhile, demanded that General Elfeldt, with his staff, be sent to him at once. The regimental adjutant made the following reply: "Yes Sir (*Tak Jest*) but the regiment cannot guarantee the safety of transporting these prisoners to your (Maczek's) position." In the face of this testimony, Maczek withdrew his order.

In the afternoon, 10 PSK was able to establish contact with the American Army in the Chambois area. A forward Cromwell platoon, under the command of 2nd Lieutenant Kluz, managed to link up with the 385th Infantry Battalion. The Americans gave all possible assistance with the evacuation of the wounded and agreed to take responsibility for the removal of the prisoners from the battlefield, including Elfeldt.

Owing to the lack of supplies, 10 PSK's commanding officer, Major Ejsymont, in a radio communication, decided to move the regiment during the night to the America lines. At 19:00 hours, the Germans launched another armoured and infantry attack. This attack was broken with the fighting ending at around 20:30 hours. 10 PSK lost a tank but also destroyed a German tank. At dusk, 10 PSK in squadron formation, moved to the right flank of the American formation (416 515). The Polish casualties for 20 August 1944 were four dead: Major Maciejowski, Sergeant Wajnkopf, Corporal Horowski and Private Sirota. Four men were wounded and two Cromwell tanks were destroyed. The estimated German casualties were: 1,200 prisoners, including General Elfeldt, four *Panther* tanks destroyed, two armoured cars destroyed, one half-track and trailer, complete with ammuition captured as well as two motorcycle combinations.

Arrayed against 10 PSK had been units of 116th *Panzer* Division, 3rd and 5th Parachute Divisions, 12th SS Division *Hitlerjugend*, 1st SS Division *Leibstandarte Adolf Hitler*, 10th SS Division, 84th Infantry Division, 277th Infantry Division, 363rd Infantry Division and 27th Heavy Artillery Regiment. An extract from Information Communication Nr. 14 (20 August 1944, 18:00 hours) revealed that the enemy was desperate and was seeking to break out of Normandy, in the region around Hill 262 or the *Maczuga*.

During 21 August 1944, 10 PSK remained at the American infantry line. The Americans supplied them with ammunition, fuel and food, some of which was dropped by air. There was also a modest funeral for Major Maciejowski, killed the previous day. During the afternoon, 10 PSK was ordered to send a squadron to reconnoitre along the Chambois – Mount Ormel axis.

1st Squadron was assigned the task and set out with nine tanks. The Squadron could not use the roads owing to the large number of tank traps, which were destroying an increasing number of tanks. The terrain being crossed was difficult with the horizon being reduced to that of about ten to twenty metres. This restricted view allowed the enemy to slip away from Normandy in large groups. The possibility of enemy tanks escaping and then reappearing from an unseen direction posed a great threat to the Allies. Despite this 1st Squadron, during its patrol, took about eighty prisoners.

Cromwell tanks from the Division pictured in Normandy. **Imperial War Museum B8831**

The Mount Ormel area remained under fire from Sherman tanks operating around the church at Coudehard. Despite stubborn attempts to link up with the Shermans, their fire did not cease and further advance by 1st Squadron was impossible. At 20:00 Maczek decided to withdraw 1st Squadron, who promptly left the area, leaving two damaged tanks which they recovered later. 10 PSK grouped as the night before; on the right flank of the American infantry battalion. An information communication issued on 21 August 1944 (Information Communication nr. 15) stated what was largely already known. The fighting at Chambois had lasted all day and German pressure from the southeast had not been lifted, as a result a number of enemy tanks had slipped by. The enemy had been bombarded by an entire artillery division, which had set fire to a large amount of the enemy's equipment. There had also been reports of *Panzer* Mk IV, V and VI tanks being found amongst the enemy in the 'pocket' (the so-called Falaise pocket from which the Germans were desperate to escape). By the end of 21 August 1944, the 'pocket' containing the enemy was reduced to an area of five kilometres by ten kilometre, which was thought to contain 2nd *Panzer*, armed with a large number of tanks.

A further report received on 29 August 1944 but concerning the previous week, discussed the matter of gossip amongst the Germans. This gossip was of concern to General Schimpf, commanding officer of 3rd Parachute Division. This division had fought in the Falaise pocket and had taken 1,070 prisoners but Schimpf still felt the need to address the question of defeatism within the German ranks. He plainly railed against the idea of the German division being surrounded, which he claimed was merely enemy propaganda. Schimpf considered that gossip spread from units to the rear and that paratroopers, being front line soldiers, should ignore such gossip. He urged paratroopers not to lose spirit and fight as paratroopers always do. He added that the war would without doubt end in victory (for Germany) and that paratroopers would fulfil their duty to the end of the war. This was an interesting snapshot of the unrealistic views of the German high Command.

On 22 August 1944, Colonel Franciszek Skibinski arrived and, upon the orders of General Maczek, took command of 10 PSK. While the Poles continued to receive supplies, the British and American armies, pushing from the south and southwest, had the effect of reducing the Falaise pocket, which saw the surrender of many Germans in the area. Information Communication nr. 16 (22 August 1944, 18:00) revealed that the Falaise pocket or 'sack' was being closed with the enemy being harried from the air and by two British divisions moving from the west, with many prisoners being taken. It was alleged at the time that many Germans were afraid to surrender to the Poles.[112]

A German 88mm gun captured by the Division in Normandy. **Imperial War Museum B8847**

It was now obvious that the German High Command considered that the war in Normandy was over and that their duty was to get as many troops, with equipment, away in preparation for a later counteroffensive. One immediately thinks of the Arndennes Offensive during the winter of 1944–45. The views of the German military were also revealed from captured documents. Letters to German soldiers from home (Germany) that had been published in the German military press referred to 'secret weapons'. The weapons mentioned were the V1, V2, V3, V4 and the V5. The V1 and V2 rockets were to become familiar over southern England from autumn 1944. The sources of these letters were from those who had supposed to have visited the so-called 'secret factories'.

On 24 August 1944 Colonel Skibinski, received orders to take over command of 3rd Rifle Brigade, from Colonel Wieronski. Meanwhile, preparations were being made to make up the shortages of both personnel and equipment. It had been noted that after two weeks of heavy fighting, 10 PSK still functioned as a complete and efficeint fighting unit.[113]

After 10 PSK's victory at Chambois, the Germans began to move to the *Maczuga* or Mount Ormel. Mount Ormel is in fact an elongated ridge with two hills: one to the south and the other to the north. Maczek quickly realised the strategic importance of this geographic feature and ordered its seizure and holding.[114] 10 PSK's actions have already been described but the overall battle by the division deserves describing, if only to record in the English language this gallant, yet desperate action by the Poles.

1st Tank Regiment and two companies from the Podhalian Infantry Battalion seized the northern side of Hill 262 on 19 August 1944. Tanks could only enter the hill along a winding, rambling moutain road and about their deployment it was not possible to speak of. The Podhalians who reconnoitred the area saw action first and captured many prisoners (about a company). The enemy seemed thoroughly demoralised. 1st Tank was able to move squadrons in a column to the summit of the hill without meeting any difficulties. From the summit lay the Chambois – Vimoutiers route. 1st Tank was to protect the direction north and northeast. At 12:40 hours, it began to shell the pass between the hills, which made up the *Maczuga*. This came as a shock for the German armoured columns when it was realised that the Poles had taken the northern hill. The column nearest the Polish position (about forty metres distant) consisted of armoured cars, which were set ablaze and destroyed by the Polish fire. The Poles continued to fire upon the Germans for thirty minutes, setting further vehicles alight and caused mayhem amongst the Germans.

The German formation was extremely mixed and contained equipment such as *Tiger* tanks, 88mm and 105mm guns, armoured command vehicles, multi-barrelled mortars (*Nebelwerfers*) as well as trailers pulled

American troops examine a knocked-out German *Panther* tank whilst a Sherman from the Division drives past, Falaise Gap, August 1944. **Imperial War Museum B9589**

Polish troops examine a knocked-out German SdKfz 233 armoured car mounting a 75mm gun, Falaise Gap, August 1944. The German unit to which it belonged was 116th Panzer Division; its greyhound device can be seen on the front glacis of the vehicle.
Imperial War Museum B9591

either by vehicles or horses. The German reaction was swift and they returned fire using *Neberwerfers*, which wounded several members of 1st Tank. In addition, waves of anti-tank shells passed over the Polish tanks. Immediately, 1st Tank replied with far more accuracy than before, firing with impunity. The fire and the explosions along the pass was so intense tha for a while the horizon was completely hidden by smoke. 3rd Squadron (1st Tank) could not continue firing as it had exhausted its ammunition. The Poles only stopped firing when a group of Germans, moving under the cover of smoke, came forward with a white flag, bring their wounded comrades. It was difficult to move them over such unyielding terrain but eventually two ambulances, full of wounded men, were moved to the so-called *zameczek* (shooting lodge), a position on the northern slope of the *Maczuga*. Later Polish and German wounded were to lay together for two days and nights, without any possibility for evacuation.

Further action by 1st Tank Regiment, to the south, was not possible owing to the fires and smoke, which covered that direction; the result of their first attack upon the German convoy earlier that day. Furthermore, during the afternoon, 1st Tank received orders to leave the area, for the southern hill of the *Maczuga*, while two companies of Podhalian infantry were left on the northern hill. On the southern hill, 1st Tank was to join up with 9th Rifle Battalion (9BS) which was postioned around Hill 258. At 17:00 hours, Lieutenant-Colonel Koszutski's formation arrived on the northern hill. This formation was made up of 2nd Tank and 8th Rifle Battalion (8BS). The Podhalian Rifle Brigade came at 19:30 hours, followed immediately by a gross of men from 9BS. At this time Lieutenant-Colonel Aleksander Stefanowicz, commanding officer 1st Tank, delivered to Lieutenant-Colonel Zdzisław Szydlowski, commanding officer 9BS, orders concerning reaching the southern hill of the *Maczuga*. However it was considerd that owing to nightfall and the thick smoke from the burning enemy column, it would have been impossible to carry out the assignment on that day.

During the night of 19–20 August 1944, the Polish formation on the *Maczuga* began to realise that supplies were not going to get through as the enemy had managed to get behind the Polish rear lines. Keegan points out that the Polish position was desperate as from their vantage point on top of Mount Ormel, the Poles could see the road from Chambois to Vimoutiers fill up with German troops and equipment, moving along the Dives valley and head for safety. The two Polish armoured comanders on the *Maczuga*, Koszutski and Stefanowicz, conferred and realised that they had 15,000 infantry men and 80 tanks, cut off, surrounded and behind German lines. They lacked the fuel to break out. The only reasonable way out of their predicament was to hold fast and with their own weapons and by calling upon Polish and Canadian artillery, hinder German movements in the valley below. The Poles were described as being the 'cork' in the bottle, which held the Germans in until the Poles were relieved by the Canadians.[115]

Throughout the night, from the area around the German column along the Chambois – Vimoutiers route, noise relating to movement could be heard. Szydlowski asserted that his patrols had established that loose German groups were moving from the east and were digging in along the neighbouring roads. During the night 8BS were mortared several times while communications between the *Maczuga* and Brigade halted. Furthermore, the tank crews and infantry were extremely tired after two weeks of fighting and marching over the difficult Norman terrain. But overall the night passed quietly.

The Poles realised that if they were to turn events to their advantage they needed to look over the terrain once more. The 'handle' of the *Maczuga* which curved to the northwest sat in wooded hills and lacked any road or track. From each of these hills it was possible to establish redoubts and the Poles moved to this position. It was considered that from this direction it would be possible to receive supplies and evacuate the wounded. The establishment of redoubts also held the possibility of cutting the enemy withdrawal route as well as linking up with the Canadians, who were supposed to be moving towards the Polish position. The western opening of the Falaise pocket was cut by hedges and roads. All of this could be clearly seen from the *Maczuga*. The western slopes were unsatisfactory for armoured defence. To the northeast and east field-glasses revealed far horizons, in which lay thickly covered woods. To the south, in the direction of Hill 262, the horizon was rather shorter.

During the night of 19 –20 August 1944, the Poles had taken up defensive postions but with the morning they had to go on the offensive and follow the previous day's orders. On the morning of 20 August 1944, 1st Tank and 9Bs, in deep formation, attacked along the *Maczuga* axis, the fore being the pass between the twin hills of the *Maczuga*. The tail being at the *Zamecka* but fundamentally amongst the Podhalian Battalion and 2nd Tank lines. Lieutenant-Colonel Szydlowski's formation began the task of taking the southern hill. A reconnaissance platoon of Bren Gun Carriers followed 1st Squadron (1st Tank) and 4th Company 9BS. The formation could only move slowly along the pass because of destroyed enemy equipment from the previous day's fighting, in addition to the efficiency of the German defences. From the south, 2nd Squadron (1st Tank) moved with 2nd Company 9BS while 3rd Squadron moved with 1st Company. At 10:00 hours they all went on the offensive against the southern hill. 3rd Squadron (1st Tank), who had run out of ammunition on the previous day, being replaced by 3rd Squadron (2nd Tank), mius one platoon who had been sent to provide portection from the east.

1st Company 9BS could not move from the *Zameczka* where it was involved in fighting. 3rd Squadron (1st Tank) reached the wooded hills and from there the terrain to the west could be seen. Enemy columns could

A German *Panther* tank destroyed by the Division during the Falaise Gap fighting. **Imperial War Museum B9595**

German prisoners captured by the Division in the Falaise Gap.
Imperial War Museum B9621, B9624, B9626, B9656, B9662, B9670

Dead German on top of a destroyed *Panzer*, Falaise Gap 1944. **Imperial War Museum B9657**

be seen coming mainly from the northeast. Amongst these columns, the Poles could see several *Tiger* and *Panther* tanks. 3rd Squadron opened fire and fired for a full hour. This halted the German column and scattered the fleeing infantry. The Germans also suffered the loss of four self-propelled artillery guns.

At 09:00 hours, the Germans launched an attack from the north and northeast against northern parts of 8BS. The fighting was heavy but eventually the German attack was broken and at 10:30 hours, the Germans withdrew. At 10:00, a convey of supplies from 1st Tank arrived. This was made possible by the presence of Sherman tanks in the area. However once the convoy tried to get closer to the frontline on the *Maczuga*, at the *Zameczka*, the Germans opened fire, killing and wounding many men and destroying many lorries. 2nd Squadron (2nd Tank) received orders to support 3rd Squadron (1st Tank) and moved to the immediate area of 3rd Squadron. Once 2nd Squadron reached the area, it was able to relieve two platoon from 1st Squadron (2nd Tank). While this withdrawal was taking place, 2nd Squadron was attacked by Pz Mark IV tanks, firing from the east. Luckily the Poles did not suffer any losses. At the same time, 8BS with 3rd Squadron (2nd Tank) were under fire from the north and the northeast. At 11:00 hours, 3rd Squadron lost two tanks to Mk IV fire. Further away, two further platoons from 8BS were lying in deep formation, rather than under the direction of 2nd Tank which was in the woods to the south away from the fields, which contained the group from 8BS. As a result of communications between the two commanders of 1st and 2nd Tank Regiments, 2nd Squadron (2nd Tank) was sent at 10:00 hours to Hill 239 with the task of protecting this group and direction.

Observers on the 'Bare Ridge' (*łysego wzgorza*) had seen German tank movements towards Hill 239. Hill 239 was considered to be an important tactical position and if the enemy was successful in capturing the hill, the Polish units on Hill 262 would have been in considerable danger. However, 2nd Squadron (2nd Tank) could not move towards Hill 239 as it was still entangled in a battle with anti-tank guns in the *Zameczka* area. At around 11:00 hours, the commanding officer (CO) 9BS called 1st Tank's CO, to inform him of the increasing danger

A German casualty in the Falaise Gap. **Imperial War Museum B9659**

coming from the direction of Hill 239. At this time 3rd Squadron (1st Tank) came under fire from either a 75mm or an 88mm anti-tank gun, from the direction of Hill 239. Within a short while five tanks were wrecked with their crews being either killed or wounded. This forced 1st Tank and 9BS to make a decision about fighting either on the spot or move on towards the south of Hill 262. 3rd Squadron (1st Tank) after further losses regrouped on a formation with 3rd Squadron (2nd Tank). During the evening, 3rd Squadron (1st Tank) lost yet another tank to enemy fire from the north. At midday, the Germans laid down a large artillery and mortar barrage (mainly mortar fire) which caused casualties, mainly amongst the infantry. The barrage was maintained without a break throughout the afternoon.

During the afternoon it was decided that there was a need to co-ordinate the units found on the *Maczuga* and unite them under a single commander. It was decided that the CO of 9BS, Lieutenant-Colonel Szydlowski, should assume command. The *Maczuga* had become a fortress with surrender not being an option.[116] 4th Battalion Anti-Tank and an anti-tank platoon from 9BS, began to shell at midday, with great effect, German columns and formations whowere trying to turn in the valley to the west. The result of the Polish shelling was the dispersal and stalling of the German formations with the destruction of several tanks and armoured cars.

Captain (*Rotmistrz*) Zawisza, commander of the 4th Battalion Anti-Tank, assumed the co-ordination of the anti-tank defence. At 14:00 hours, the Germans, once again attacked the formation of 8BS, situated to the north. The German attack consisted of about a battalion of infantry, supported by several Mk IV *Panzer* tanks. 2nd Tank assisting 8BS, suffered a destroyed Sherman tank and another damaged. Eventually the German offensive was broken and the Poles were able to take a large number of prisoners. To the west of 8BS's position, further prisoners were taken and when they were counted, it was discovered that there was a total of 800. Later these prisoners were to suffer casualties from German mortar fire as the Poles were unable to remove them in time to a place of safety.

Two German *Panthers*
destroyed in the Falaise Gap.
**Imperial War Museum
B9664, B9665**

Throughout the afternoon there were various attacks aganst 1st Company 9BS in the *Zameczka* region as well as assaults upon 4th Company 9BS in the area of the Chambois – Vimoutiers route. Tanks in the area were attacked by German anti-tank guns firing from the north and southwest. Late in the afternoon, the Poles launched another offensive against Hill 239, using a formation consisting of 3rd Company 9BS and a squadron from 2nd Tank. At 16:00 hours, 3rd Company, moved into action but their attack was broken by German artillery and mortar, which caused heavy losses amongst the Polish infantry. At 15:00 hours, the Germans launched another attack. Once again they attacked in strength, using infantry supported by armour, coming from the east. By 17:00 hours, the attack was at its height when it reached the defences of 8th BS who lacked armoured support. Three German tanks came across crowds of German prisoners. In an exchange of anti-tank fire, the German tanks were destroyed and their crews killed. The prisoners panicked and fled into the woods but did not escape. A further German tank was destroyed by a Sherman tank from the range of several metres. At the moment of the anti-tank shell hitting the tank and exploding, the tank ran onto the legs of a Polish soldier, trapping him. He died on the spot from the fire in the tank and the resulting explosion of the German tank.

The German offensive continued to push forward but eventually the attack was broken. One of the principal reasons for the failure of the German assault was the stout defence by 8BS of their position, while making sure that their fire was extremely effective. The second reason was the counterattack by two sections of the reconnaissance platoon from 1st Tank and a mortar platoon from 9BS, which acted as infantry once its mortar bombs ran out. Simultaneously, to the north of the German offensive, which was on the right flank of 8BS as well as the gap between this flank and the left flank of 9BS and 1st Tank formation, the enemy was able to get to the rear of 8BS and was threatening the entire Polish position on the *Maczuga*. 3rd Company (Podhalian) managed to launch a determined counterattack from the southwest, while from the west, 2nd Company 9BS, launched a similar counter-offensive. The final assault by the Germans was broken at around 19:00.

Every German attack from the east on 20 August 1944 was organised by the German 21st *Panzer* Division, which had received the task of forcing open the routes necessary for the escape of German units fleeing the Falaise pocket. All other attackes appeared to have the characterisitics of chance and lacked any real determination.

After the German attacks, the formations on Hill 262 were as follows:

8BS without change, was charged with the defence of the general northeast direction.

1st Tank, also without change, was to provide support of rthe above sector.

2nd Tank, minus 1st Squadron, moved one kilometre in the direction of the Chambois – Vimoutiers main road, where 1st Squadron (2nd Tank) stood directly to the east and to the north of 2nd Tank. They were to be part of a formation with 8BS, with the task of providing support to the northern sector.

9BS, complete with the command battalion, remained without change and had orders to defend the general direction from the south.

The Podhalian Battalion was charged with the defence of the northwest.

The regrouping was done with very little difficulty even if the Germans periodically mortared the Polish positions. From 18:00 hours, it was hoped that units from 4th Canadian Armoured Division would arrive, which in turn would have meant that the route to the Polish positions would have been opened and allow for the supply of ammunition and fuel, as the Poles were becoming desperately short of supplies. Furthermore, the Division had to relieve the embattled units on the *Maczuga* very soon, if only to evacuate the wounded, of which 300 were in a very bad state and were also under German fire. The wounded could not be moved owing to the Poles being surrounded and therefore could only receive the most basic of medical care, owing to the siege-like conditions of the *Maczuga*. It soon became obvious that the Canadians would not be able to reach the *Maczuga* on 20 August 1944. The fighting continnued into the evening, with German raids on 2nd and 4th Companies 9BS. The raids were repulsed with infantry fire and artillery laidon by Division. The night was spent quetly with no further raids or ambushes.

At 07:00 hours, 21 August 1944, a platoon from 3rd Squadron (1st Tank) moved down from its postion, to the road heading for the direction of the *Zamaczek*, ready for linking up with the Canadians, who were already heading for Hill 239. The commander of the platoon paid particular attention to the area around the *Zamaczek* and attacked and destroyed a *Panther*, while taking note of the anti-tank and machine guns in the area before he withdrew with his platoon. At 08:00 hours, 1st Squadron (2nd Tank) relieved 3rd Squadron (1st Tank) which returned to its regiment. Before midday, once again, the Polish defences were tested, as the Germans once again launched a further attack along the Chambois – Vimoutiers road. Immediately on the road, the Germans began an artillery offensive and further, from the east, an infantry attack from the direction of Vimoutiers. The attack was strong, with mortars being deployed, which caused Polish casualties. At 11:00 hours, the Germans launched a suicidal infantry attack to the rear of 1st Tank, which served as a dressing station. The Germans had come in from the west, from the steep hills in the region of the chapel at Coudehard. The German assault was beaten back by 1st Tank, which used its machine guns, which were normally used against aircraft, to ward off this infantry attack.

There was plenty of fighting in the Coudehard direction. The German raids were partly successful as groups of Germans were able to penetrate Polish positions and take prisoners, including men from 9BS. Members of 4th Company 9BS were able to destroy a self-propelled artillery piece before being captured. Finally at 12:00, 21 August 1944, a platoon from 2nd Tank was able to link up with the Canadians. They met the Canadian vanguard between Hills 239 and 240, which was about three kilometres to the northwest of the northern hill of the *Maczuga*. By 14:00 hours, the Poles received their first supplies from the Canadians. The fight for the *Maczuga* was over.

Once the Poles were relieved by the Canadians, all of the fight went out of the Germans. The enemy casualties were high: around 500 dead, over 1,000 prisoners taken, most of the prisoners came from 12th SS *Panzer* Division with a certain amount from 1st SS *Panzer* and 116th *Panzer* Divisions as well as other units. Scores of German tanks had been destroyed, mainly *Tigers*, *Panthers* and Mk IVs. The Germans also lost similar quantities of artillery pieces, consisting of 75mm, 88mm and 105mm calibres. The Polish losses were rather less: sixteen officers were listed as killed, wounded or missing as well as 335 other ranks being listed as the same. The Poles only lost eleven tanks.[117]

After the battle for the *Maczuga* was over; the carnage was assessed. The commander of the Canadian Corps, General Guy Simonds, after visiting the battlefield said that he had never seen such wholesale havoc in his life.[118] Keegan makes the final tribute when he records that the sappers of the Royal Canadian Engineers, on the summits of the *Maczuga*, erected a temporary signpost, which read simply 'A Polish Battlefield'.[119]

CHAPTER VI

After Normandy

The Falaise Gap could only be considered closed once the Canadian 4th Armoured Division was able to link up with the Polish 1st Armoured Division at Coudehard and the Canadian 3rd and 4th Divisions were able to secure St Lambert and the northern route to Chambois. This was accomplished on 21 August 1944.

The German losses had been huge. In the northern sector alone, 344 tanks and self-propelled guns, 2,447 non-armoured vehicles and 255 artillery pieces had been abandoned or destroyed. The fighting for Normandy had cost the German Army: 1,500 tanks; 3,500 guns; and 20,000 vehicles The Germans also lost 450,000 men of which 240,000 had been killed or wounded. Whole divisions had been destroyed and those, which had been left, included armoured divisions, were in pitiful state regarding equipment and personnel. The Allies suffered 209,672 casualties of which 36,976 had been killed.[120] Having briefly examined the overall situation in Normandy we shall return to the 1st Polish Armoured Division and how the ending of the Normandy campaign affected it.

By the time the Falaise Gap was closed on August 21 1944, the 1st Polish Armoured Division had, for six days, defied ferocious and sustained attacks by two SS corps, often accompanied by *Wehrmacht* troops. The Poles replied by holding their positions and taking 5,000 prisoners, including General Eldfeldt and 140 other officers.[121] By holding their captured territory against determined German attacks the Poles had been crucial in the closing of the Falaise Gap.

Wysocki writes that 18 August 1944, when the Poles, through continued struggle, began to break the German strength, was a critical moment in the fight for Normandy. By being able to hold all of their captured territory and fight off waves of German attacks the Poles were able to deny the enemy a route to the west and out of Normandy. Basically by taking the high ground in the Chambois area, they were able to control the route out of the Falaise area. It is worth considering that in the final phase of the fighting, the Poles were only five miles from the Americans and Canadians but still had to endure waves of enemy attacks until the Americans were able to reach them, as we saw in the previous chapter.[122] Once the fighting in Normandy was over, the 1st Polish Armoured Division was able to calculate its casualties and then regroup.

Wysocki is able to give a detailed account of the 1st Polish Armoured Division's casualties between 8 and 22 August 1944. He calculated that the Division suffered 325 killed, including 21 officers. 1,002 wounded, of which 35 were officers, and 114 men were listed as missing. The overall casualty figure was 1,441. Generally speaking, the Polish units suffered casualty rates of 10%, which rose to 20% amongst the frontline units, with some receiving a 30% casualty rate.

Wysocki claims that such was the chaos and destruction visited upon the Germans that it was impossible to calculate the extent of their dead and wounded. Using Canadian records, Wysocki writes that German equipment losses in the Trun – Argentan – Chambois region amounted to 187 tanks, 157 armoured vehicles, 1,778 lorries, 669 cars and 252 guns. In total the Germans lost 3,043 guns, tanks and vehicles but did manage to move 1,270 guns, tanks and vehicles to the west. Wysocki agrees with Max Hastings in his assessment of the German strength (or lack of) after the German withdrawal from Normandy. Wysocki makes the point that after the battle for Normandy, the German 5th *Panzer* Army did not manage to recover its strength before the war's end.[123] Montgomery was moved to say that at Falaise, the enemy had been contained as if they had been in a bottle and the 1st Polish Armoured Division had acted as a cork and held the Germans in.

By referring to the diary of 10th Mounted Rifles (10 PSK) the situation after the fighting in Normandy becomes clearer, if somewhat mundane. Throughout the night of 23/24 August 1944, orders were received concerning the movements of the Division, for the next two to five days, to the Corps position in the region of Barou – Norrey en Auge – Les Moutries en Auge – Grand Mesnil. 10 PSK was ordered to move to a position on Hill 123 at co-ordinates 266 388. 10 PSK was to move from its present position at 06:00 hours and was to reach the area by 09:00 hours and establish a bivouacked location. During this time 10 PSK received information concerning the situation in France, following the German withdrawal from Normandy. (Information Communication Nr. 16 [23 August 1944] 18:00 hours). The communication revealed that in Paris, the French had risen against the Germans, while the Americans had crossed into the Paris sector in places to the north of Paris.

On the previous day an American division had already crossed to the eastern bank of the River Seine. From a variety of sources it was established that the Germans were trying to halt the 1st Canadian Army and the 2nd British Army, who were pushing from the River Touque at Lisieux and the River Risle at Bernam. The River Touque had already been reached while the Americans had to perform a flanking movement from the south to reach the Risle. The German Seventh Army and *Panzergruppe West* broke this ambition. Nothing went to plan during the American attack. Previously aerial reconnaissance had suggested that there had been no preparations for defence in the river's sector, however from the first line of defence it was obvious that the Germans were determined to defend the area, which also contained the rivers Somme and Marne. From this moment, the Pas de Calais region from where V1 'flying bombs' were launched against London and southern England, and to where the Allies wished to advance, became well defended.[124]

On 24 August 1944, the commanding officer (CO) of 10 PSK, Colonel Skibinski, received orders to take command of 3rd Rifle Brigade. During this time preparations were made to make up the shortages of equipment and personnel. On 25 August 1944, General Maczek, commander of the 1st Polish Armoured Division, made public his decisions concerning promotions within the Division. Major Otton Ejsymont was promoted CO of 1st Anti-Tank Regiment while 1st Anti-Tank Regiment's CO, Major Roman Dowbora, was moved to 24th Uhlans as CO. Dowbora replaced Major Kanski, the previous CO, who was seriously wounded at the Battle of Jort and died soon after from his wounds. Maczek also promoted *Rotmistrz* (Captain) Jerzy Wasilewski as CO of 10 PSK with *Rotmistrz* Michał Gutowski as his Second-in-Command (2ic).

At 19:00 hours, Wasilewski, in the presence of the entire regiment formally entered the ranks of 10 PSK, when he received and kissed the regimental standard. He gave notice of the following commands: Lieutenant Zygmunt Klodzinski was to succeed as commander of 1st Squadron with 2nd Lieutenant Kazimierz Szkuta as 2ic. 2nd Squadron was to be commanded by Lieutenant Jan Salwa with Lieutenant Nikodem Kluz as 2ic. 1st Squadron was to continue its task as reconnaissance platoon. Throughout the day, 10 PSK continued with repair and weapon checks. As a result of the latest battles, the Cromwell crews had learnt a valuable lesson about the protection of their tanks. The crews had learnt from the Germans the need to weld tank track links around the exterior of the drivers' hatch and to the sides of the turrets, thus helping to reinforce the tanks' armour against anti-tank fire.

A pause for rations somewhere in Normandy, 1944. **Imperial War Museum B8824**

During the morning of the following (26 August 1944) the Regimental Chaplain, Father Andrzej Glazewski, said Mass for those killed in the recent fighting, including Major Jan Maciejowski. General Maczek, Colonels Dworek and Skibinski, Major Stankiewicz, *Rotmistrz* Wysocki and other Divisional Staff officers also attended. Throughout the morning new supplies and personnel arrived, including Poles captured from the Germans and now wishing to fight in the Polish Army. 10 PSK also received two Challenger tanks armed with 17 pound guns. In the evening 10 PSK was entertained by ENSA (Entertainers to the Allied Forces).

The next morning saw further changes to 10 PSK. The most immediate was the posthumous award of the Gold Cross of the *Virtuti Militari* (the highest Polish awards for valour) to Major Jan Maciejowski, who had been killed at Chambois. There were also promotions for NCOs. Three Sergeant Majors (*Wachmistrz*) to the rank of Warrant Officer Class 1 (WO1 or in Polish *Starzy Wachmistrz*); three Sergeants to the rank of Sergeant Major and ten Corporals were promoted to Sergeant. 71 Lance Corporals were promoted to Corporal and 90 privates advanced to the rank of Lance Corporal. Further awards for valour were made by General Maczek, which included thirteen awards of the *Virtuti Militari* Class V, sixty Gallantry Crosses and two Silver Service Medals with Crossed Swords. Most of these decorations were made in reference to the Battle of Jort.[125]

Casualty Rate of 10 PSK during the Normandy Campaign from 8 August until 27 August 1944

Personnel	Officers	Ranks	Total
Killed	5	40	45
Wounded	16	75	91
Total	21	115	136

Equipment	Cromwells	Stuarts	Other	Total
Destroyed	16	4	1	21
Damaged	12	2	2	16
Total	28	6	3	37

10 PSK estimated that German losses against 10 PSK between 8 and 27 August 1944 amounted to around 1,600 prisoners, including General Eldfeldt, thirteen tanks, ten self-propelled guns, twenty six anti-tank guns and artillery pieces of over 75mm calibre, seven half-tracked tractors, thirty eight trailers for towing artillery and tanks, an ammunition dump and a fuel dump.[126]

After Normandy there was little will any longer to criticise the Division. Maczek was concerned about the high casualties that the Poles had suffered but he told General Sosnkowski, Comander-in-Chief of Polish Armed Forces, that the Division was anxious to contine fighting. Sosnkowski agree with him and by now, even Guy Simonds, the Canadian Army Commander, was happy to accept under his command a division that was at least 3,000 men short. In fact the Canadians also suffered high casualties but were equally ready for combat.[127]

The Poles had been truly blooded in Normandy and proved themselves to be worthy allies with their gallant defences of Chambois and of the *Maczuga*, which denied the Germans an escape route out of Normandy. After all of the difficulties between 1939 and mid 1944, the Poles really felt that they were on their way home and ready to chase the Germans back to Germany.

CHAPTER VII

The Chase – Northern France

Tadeusz Wysocki writes that after the difficult battles in Normandy, the 1st Polish Armoured Division was ready for further action. A decision was made which called for rapid movement on the part of the armoured and motorized units in the pursuit of the enemy across France. The Division prepared for this eventuality and waited impatiently to take part in further operations.

The Allies pursued the Germans in a wide formation, running from the left flank were the Canadian Army, 2nd British Army, 1st American Army and 2nd American Army. The line had been demarked so that the 2nd British Army would take the towns of Vernon, Beauvais, Amiens, Tournai, Brussels and Louvain.

Generally speaking the area in which the Allies moved across allowed for swift action on the part of the armoured and motorized units but in the Canadian sector, from where the 1st Polish Armoured Division was operating, the terrain was more difficult compared with that in the south where other Allied armies were operating.

In the Canadian sector, every river and canal flowed into the sea, which meant that the German method of defence was to oppose every river and canal crossing, which the allies were forced to attempt to cross. The Canadian Army had been given the task of destroying the enemy defences along the coast of Northern France. The Polish 1st Armoured Division was assigned the task of breaking enemy defences at Le Harvey, Dieppe and other centres of defence, especially any connected with the V1 ('Flying Bomb') sites. The assignment was to be difficult as it concluded in the terms of the chase but in the areas by the sea, which meant that the rivers, which flowed into the sea, were deep and proved difficult to force.

The Division moved the best over hard, flat, territory as its tanks were designed to cross water using bridges that the enemy had wrecked as they withdrew, before digging themselves into defensive positions on the far bank of a river or canal. It was as if the tanks were expected to leap across the water!

During the last days of August, the Division moved from the Falaise area towards a new area of operations, moving in pouring rain, along third-rate roads. After two days march, the Division reached its new sector along the meandering River Seine in the area of Elbeuf, a town to the south of Rouen. After crossing the Seine, via the 'Warsaw Bridge', constructed by sappers from the Division under the command of Major Dorantta, the Division decided to go on the offensive. That is to pursue the Germans but before any movement was made, 10th Mounted Rifle (10 PSK) had to reconnoitre the area. As the Poles were planning their next moves they became aware of the date, 1 September 1944. Five years to the day when Germany invaded Poland. The soldiers of the Division could not help but reflect upon the changes which they had seen during those five long, hard, and difficult years.

The enemy, with justification, was seen to be in a hopeless situation. They were trying to rescue units by literally travelling around, trying to locate units and then deploying hull-down tanks, often in open fields, defending stubbornly, if not fanatically until dusk. After dark the Polish tanks could not move forward while the enemy under the cover of night withdrew from their positions, destroying any crossings behind them, thus denying the Polish units their use the following day. This was a tactic that the Division was to experience until the end of the war. Every time the Germans withdrew, they left an open field for the Poles but destroyed any crossing places over rivers and canals in the area. However forward units from the Division would frequently ambush withdrawing Germans and take them prisoner. From information gleaned from prisoners, the Poles would generally be able to find a route that would allow them to bypass any major defensive positions in the area, therefore giving them a second chance. Thanks to the use of this tactic, the enemy was frequently surprised by the tempo of the Polish advance as well as those of individual British units.

There was little creation of defensive lines by the Germans in the area of operations, even along major rivers, for example along the River Somme, which flowed via Amiens and Abbeville. Thanks to this many towns avoided destruction. The area of such actions stretched for 400 kilometres. For reasons, as Wysocki comments, best left to those at a higher command, the flank of the Canadian Army divisions was positioned somewhere to the rear which created a situation in which the 1st Polish Armoured Division, in certain phases, acted as a wedge beaten into the enemy formations. The area to be covered in northern France, Belgium and later Holland was to provide a great test for the Division, which was to give tanks and sappers, especially the sappers, a greater role. Sappers, often under fire, were to build bridges swiftly, clear mines from crossing places and prepare tanks for further operations.

Before the Poles returned to action, further good news came. On 30 August 1944, Field Marshal Montgomery moved 11th Armoured Division to the Somme area. The next day in the vicinity of Amiens, General Eberbach, the new Commanding Officer of the German Seventh Army, surrendered with his staff. Amongst the documents captured at Eberbach's headquarters were the latest orders concerning the defence of the River Somme. This revealed a system of defences reaching from Switzerland to the North Sea. It would seem that the Germans were planning some form of defence system based upon the model seen in the First World War. Shortly afterwards the Guards Armoured Division crossed the Somme to the east of Amiens while a brigade of the 50th Infantry Division was able to establish a vanguard in the area.[128]

The Poles as we have seen, returned to the fight on 1 September 1944 and began with a reconnaissance mission and pursuit of the enemy towards Abbeville. As already discussed, the Front was moving swiftly but the sector towards the coast was cut through by at least seven major rivers and numerous smaller rivers and canals, over which tanks had to be forced and Germans ejected from. This had all the potential of reducing the Polish advance to a crawl.

The Germans had organised a defensive position on the River Sodde. The Division was given the task of reaching the area and breaking the enemy's defence. The Germans held their defence lines with anti-tank guns but the terrain was also a huge problem for the advancing Poles. The area to be crossed was mainly towns and woods, which gave the Polish armour no opportunity to advance rapidly. As the Polish tanks moved towards the area of operations, they were further hampered by a series of valleys, rivers and brooks. After crossing the sector, the Poles had to fight small groups of enemy determined to disrupt the Polish advance.

The task of 10 PSK was to move with 2nd Anti-Tank and 2nd Squadron from the Dragoon Regiment and reach advance elements of the Canadian 3rd Infantry Division, and then to reconnoitre and seize the crossing at Fourcarmount on the River L'Yeres and at Blangy on the River Bresle, where it was hoped that a bridgehead could be established and held while waiting for the arrival of Allied units. The operational plan was surprisingly simple. *Rotmistrz* Jerzy Wasilewski, commanding officer 10 PSK, ordered his armour to move swiftly and to take the enemy by surprise. In the case of the enemy making an organised defence of the crossing, the opposition was to be broken but the terrain was not to be cleared. Instead the tanks were to proceed forward. 10 PSK planned to advance along a single axis until the enemy was reached. Along one flank, a short-range search party was sent out looking for the enemy. The Axis was as follows: Blainville-Creven-Buchy-Somery-Neufchatel-Fourcarmount-Blangy.

At 07:00 hours on 1 September 1944, the formation moved from its position, heading for action once more. At the beginning of the march there were some problems as Poles tried to cross through Canadian columns but eventually the march got under way properly. The Poles entered Neufchatel using a weak bridge and met Canadian advance units. Local civilians reported that the Germans had withdrawn from the town during the morning. Some of the Germans had moved to the east whilst other had withdrawn to the north. It was considered that the Germans were going to concentrate in the regions of Gamanches and Abbeville. In Neufchatel itself no Germans were met but once the Poles began to move along the main road towards Fourcarmount, they encountered German 'marauders'. Whilst travelling along the Fourcarmount road, the Poles saw plenty of evidence of Allied aerial bombing, with burning vehicles, dead horses and destroyed buildings being very much part of the landscape. The Polish tanks also passed by launchers for the German V1 rockets.

At 13:00 hours the vanguard from 10 PSK seized Fourcarmount without any struggle and took many prisoners. The prisoners confirmed the reports from French civilians concerning an organised German defence at Blangy. At Fourcarmount, the Poles took a twenty-five minute break for checking equipment and ate. From there 2nd Squadron took over as advance guard. 2nd Squadron sent out a platoon, acting as a picket in addition to the search party. Before moving onto the woods at Foret D'Eu, the squadron captured the town of Fallencourt. At Foret D'Eu, the squadron took prisoners (mainly Russians) without any struggle before moving onto Blangy, which was defended as expected. With firing support from all of 3rd Squadron, 2nd Squadron entered the outskirts of Blangy, swiftly capturing the railway line and a bridge over the River Bresle. As the Poles attacked, groups of Germans with horse-drawn equipment were seen withdrawing towards the woods situated to the north of Blangy. Nevertheless, Germans from well concealed positions continued to harry the Polish tanks using machine guns, mortars and even hand grenades.

The Dragoons were ordered to clear Blangy while 2nd Squadron (10 PSK) was given the task of seizing the enemy complex in the woods north of Blangy. The Dragoons with the aid of a platoon of armour from 10 PSK cleared Blangy and took about 200 prisoners from 59th, 226th and 712th Infantry Divisions, as well as prisoners from the *Luftwaffe*. The prisoners posed a problem as to how to transfer them to the rear of the Polish lines. Eventually they were handed over to members of the French Resistance.

After leaving a platoon of armour from 3rd Squadron on the bridge in Blangy, Wasilewski decided that there was need for further action towards Abbeville. The commanding officer of 2nd Squadron (10 PSK) was given orders to proceed along the axis towards Abbeville. Meanwhile, via the radio network, came information that the Canadians had already occupied Abbeville. However the message came from such a great distance, that the signal was extremely weak. The Polish units upon hearing the news did not agree and taking into account enemy movements; reached the conclusion that the Germans were still in Abbeville and rather than having evacuated the town were actually prepared to defend it against any Allied attack.

2nd Squadron sent a platoon to reconnoitre Boullancourt-en-Sery and protect the passage from the direction of Gamaches. Two further platoons operated towards Translay and Framicourt. At Translay, the Poles came across the tail end of a withdrawing German horse-drawn column and promptly fired upon it. Twenty vehicles were destroyed with much of the German weaponry and ammunition. In addition, many prisoners were taken and handed over to the French.

About three kilometres northeast of Translay, 2nd Squadron encountered further enemy resistance at a railway station in the area. Wasilewski ordered 3rd Squadron to reconnoitre towards the town of Cerisy-Buleux and 2nd Squadron was to attack along the operation axis. 3rd Squadron moved to Cerisy-Buleux and opened fire upon covered field gun positions, anti-aircraft guns and their towing tractors. The Polish fire destroyed the

17pdr ammunition being taken aboard a Polish Sherman tank. **Imperial War Museum B8793**

guns and their crews fled thus allowing the squadron to return to the main operational axis via St Maxent en Vimeu while also taking fourteen prisoners.

2nd Squadron after breaking the enemy defences along the railway line and capturing St Maxent en Vimeu attacked the Huppy region which was followed by an attack on the Sevenways area (*Siedmiodrogu*) two kilometres northwest from Huppy. Sevenways was captured with many prisoners once again being taken. However there was an element of resistance as 10 PSK was attacked by artillery and mortar fire from the directions of Huchenville, Moreuil-Caubert and Bienfay, as well as machine gun fire from the immediate areas in front of the Polish armour. At dusk a Canadian communications officer arrived by motorcycle and asserted that the Staff of the Canadian 4th Armoured Division was indeed in Abbeville and that the Poles were to move their as well. Wasilewski totally disagreed with this report, pointing out that the enemy had prepared defences at Abbeville and at crossing places along the River Somme. It was decided that 10 PSK squadrons with the Dragoons should move out, attack the enemy and overcome their defences.

When the picket platoon from 2nd Squadron left Sevenways, it immediately came under fire from an anti-tank gun and from *Panzerfausts*. One tank was lost to the anti-tank gun while *Panzerfaust* fire set another tank ablaze. This left three men wounded: Sergeant Chojnacki, Corporal Baranowski and Private Zuba. The Dragoons also suffered casualties, both dead and wounded. Wasilewski ordered 1st Squadron to support 2nd Squadron's offensive, ordering to enter the battle from the right hand side of the main road. Once dusk fell it became impossible to continue further operations for the day and the units were ordered to cease operations and to take up a position of safety about one kilometre west of Huppy. During 1 September 1944, 10 PSK travelled 92 kilometres, of which for 42 they were in contact with the enemy, and were fighting for over 20 kilometres. The casualties for the day for 10 PSK were three wounded, one Cromwell tank destroyed and another damaged. The German casualties were estimated to have been: 250 prisoners (passed over to the French) thirty horse-drawn vehicles and two lorries, all destroyed.

The next day, 10 PSK was to begin to reconnoitre Abbeville. During the night information came via the radio network that the reports of Canadian units being in Abbeville had proved to be incorrect. It was probable that units of the Canadian 4th Armoured Division had forced a crossing over the River Somme, to the south of Abbeville and was barely operating towards Abbeville from the southeast. A formation under the command of Major Zgorzelski was to operate towards the woods, six kilometres to the west of Abbeville, in the direction of a bridge which stood one kilometres north of the wood. Then they were to move to a forest four kilometres to the northwest from Abbeville as an essential part of the Division's assault on Abbeville from the northwest. Throughout the day 10 PSK received waves of information concerning the enemy, which had been lacking the day before.

10 PSK with the 2nd Squadron (Dragoons) and 2nd Anti-Tank Battalion set out to reconnoitre in the direction of Abbeville in a belt from which its right border ran along the axis of the previous day's march while its left hand border ran along the main Moyenneville-Abbeville road. Wasilewski ordered that the hills overlooking the Somme valley were to be captured and from there the operation was to be switched directly towards a river crossing and then on to Abbeville. 1st Squadron was to operate along the Huppy-Caubert-Abbeville main road and 3rd Squadron was sent along the Moyenneville-Rouvroy-Abbeville main road. Wasilewski, with 2nd Squadron, a squadron of Dragoons and an anti-tank platoon, advanced between 1st and 3rd Squadrons in order to be ready to work with one of the other flanks. On 2 September 1944 at 08:30 hours, in pouring rain 10 PSK set out. Under the cover of darkness the enemy had withdrawn to the far side of the river and canal, leaving behind small groups, which acted as a rear guard. The rearguard was reinforced by minefields.

1st Squadron promptly suffered a damaged tank in the minefields with one man, Corporal Gorzko being wounded. By 10:30, 1st Squadron, without any resistance reached the hills in the St. Marferite area and 3rd Squadron reached the area of Hill 79. From these areas, the Poles had a splendid view of the Somme valley and of Abbeville, as well as allowing for the establishment of a splendid firing position. The Germans tried to halt the Polish advance with the use of artillery and anti-tank fire against 3rd Squadron. 10 PSK returned fire by shelling the distant road and any enemy vehicle movements that they could see. This caused great destruction amongst the enemy.

In further action towards the same crossing and town, 3rd Squadron without any fighting managed to move to the town of Rouvroy. The columns entering the town found that the bridge over the canal had been destroyed and that the enemy was defending the canal from the far side using small arms fire. 1st Squadron sent a platoon to a position about 500 metres from the tumbled down railway bridge (777 826). Wasilewski ordered the squadron to hold a firing position.

The regimental reconnaissance officer, Lieutenant Sachse with Corporal Kwiecinski and Sergeant-Major Mincer from 1st Squadron, with two Canadians from Corps, set out in an armoured car with the intention of reconnoitring the region southwest of Rouvroy. After fighting their way through enemy patrols, Sachse's groups finally made its way through to the area of the bridge over the canal. There the enemy sat 100 metres in front of them. Meanwhile Wasilewski ordered the Commanding Officer of the Dragoon Squadron as well as two platoons of tanks from 1st Squadron to seize the area around the railway station in addition to the canal bridges in Rouvroy. The tanks moved over sections of the ruined railway bridge and guided the Dragoons over as well. The area was seized but the bridges over the canals had been destroyed which prevented any further armoured advances. A foot patrol established that the bridge over the main channel of the Somme had already been destroyed while the enemy continued to resist using automatic fire as well as continuing to shell and mortar 10 PSK's tanks on the nearby hills.

3rd Squadron occupied the northwest fringes of Rouvroy's suburbs and was able to link up with 10 PSK's second-in-command in the area around the railway station. This action was furthered by the occupation of the region of this area and the suburbs to the west of the canal. At 14:00 hours, the Commanding Officer of the Podhalian Rifle Brigade (BSP) made personal contact with Wasilewski and informed him of orders which called for the forcing of the canal and river as well as the capture of Abbeville.

Wasilewski put BSP's CO in the picture. 3rd Squadron had been relieved by the Canadians and now under Wasilewski's orders had gone to the region of Hill 79 where it had been shelled. One man, Corporal Juszczyk, was wounded. 1st and 3rd Squadrons had also been shelling targets in the distance. At 16:30 hours, 10 PSK, under the orders of the 1st Polish Armoured Division's Commanding Officer, General Maczek, moved to a position at Huchenneville. The Polish causalities for the day amounted to two wounded men and one damaged Cromwell tank. The German casualty rate was estimated to have been one 75mm gun (confirmed as destroyed) one six-barrelled mortar (*Nebelwerfer*), one half-tracked vehicle and two trailers.

By 3 September 1944 the situation was that the British 1st Army had crossed the Somme and its advance guard (7th Armoured Division) had reached St. Pol as they continued their pursuit of the Germans. In the Canadian Army sector, the Canadian 4th Armoured Division had reached the Somme while the 1st Polish Division continued in the 'great pursuit' in the direction of Hesdin, Fruges, and St. Omer and further on towards Ypres. After the capture and clearing of Abbeville, divisional sappers built bridges, which were finished during the afternoon of 3 September 1944. 10 PSK took the opportunity to repair equipment, carry out maintenance checks of their equipment and wait for further orders.

There was little information about the enemy except that in front of the 1st Polish Armoured Division stood the 245th Infantry Division against whom they had fought at Abbeville. The terrain to be overcome once again consisted of a series of rivers, valleys and streams, thus making for difficult terrain to cross and the heavy rain made the ground very soft. Basically the whole area was not suited to armoured warfare. During the afternoon of 3 September 1944, Wasilewski received orders for 10 PSK who were to move in formation with 2nd Anti-Tank Battalion to the bridges belonging to the Canadian 4th Armoured Division (five kilometres to the southeast from Abbeville) because the bridges being built by the Polish sappers were yet to be completed. The formation moved to the St. Require region from where it was to begin a reconnaissance mission in the Foret de Cerci woods (ten kilometres north from Abbeville) as well as reconnoitring for a crossing on the River Lathy between Ponches-Estruy and Willencourt. 10 PSK was to cross the bridges late in the evening and during the night of 3–4 September 1944. Wasilewski decided that this operation was to be conducted swiftly as time was of the essence. The reconnaissance mission was successful and provided information about the crossing and how to contact the Canadian 4th Armoured Division, which was by the River Somme.

After 10 PSK had crossed the River Somme in the region of Pont Remy, 2nd Squadron with an assault platoon from the Buigny L'abbe area, reconnoitred in the direction of Neuf Moulin, Canchy and the northern outskirts of Foret de Crecy. Meanwhile the rest of the Regiment, in a single column, with 1st Squadron acting as vanguard, reconnoitred towards the town of Domvast from where 1st Squadron began its operations along the main road while 3rd Squadron moved along the right hand side of the main road towards the crossing in Le Boisle. At a briefing, held at around 14:00 hours, Wasilewski, whilst giving out orders to the squadron commanders, introduced for the first time a system of codes and ciphers which was to aid the regiment in the field. This practise, introduced at the briefing, proved to be so practical that it remained in place until the end of the European campaign. Wasilewski also insisted that the tanks should be supplied at all times with enough fuel and ammunition. This led to the introduction of half-tracked vehicles following the tanks, bringing them supplies of ammunition and fuel. Without doubt the lessons of Chambois and the *Maczuga* had been learnt.

At 16:00 hours 10 PSK crossed the Somme. In the St. Riquier area, the Poles met Canadian units. As information from the local population was proving to be contradictory and imprecise, 2nd Squadron sent out reconnaissance platoons. These operated via the town of Millencourt en Ponthieu-Neuilly L'Hopital-Canchy,

The crew of a Sherman clean its 75mm gun, France 1944. **Imperial War Museum B8795**

the woods to the northeast and via Marchville from the northeast. No resistance was met except for a small group of marauders who wounded Lance Corporal Bednarski. After the reconnaissance patrols had made their reports the entire regiment was ready to move.

1st Squadron acting as advance guard was able to defeat a weak German defensive position in the Domvast area. While moving only four kilometres from the crossing in Le Boisle, the Poles witnessed two huge explosions as the Germans destroyed bridges as they retreated. 1st Squadron linked up with 3rd Squadron in the hills that dominated the River L'Authie valley while seeing little evidence of the Germans. Therefore 3rd Squadron sent pickets down the valley to Le Boisle where they did meet the enemy. 3rd Squadron from its post began to shell the town, to which the Germans replied with mortar fire. The platoon from 3rd Squadron acting as picket in the outskirts of the town came under heavy German mortar fire and could not advance as the bridge needed for crossing the river had been destroyed.

German tanks began to attack from the hills to the southwest of Le Boisle but 2nd Anti-Tank Battalion beat them off and destroyed a *Panzer* Mk IV in the process. The reconnaissance mission for a crossing place in the immediate vicinity of Le Boisle was proving to be fruitless and by nightfall it was seen to be an impossible task owing to dogged German defence. 10 PSK withdrew for the night to a position in the area of the main road, one kilometre southwest from Le Boisle. Pickets from both 1st and 3rd Squadrons (about a platoon in strength) who were in contact with the enemy, who mortared them throughout the night, protected this position. During the afternoon and evening of 3 September 1944, 10 PSK moved about forty kilometres and suffered only one wounded man. The Germans were less lucky, losing fifteen prisoners to 10 PSK as well as one *Panzer* Mk IV tank, two 75mm anti-tank guns, two lorries and five trailers.

By the next day, 4 September 1944, the situation in the Polish sector was developing rapidly. The tasks of the 1st Polish Armoured Division remained unchanged. They were still pursuing the Germans, following tow axes, now in the direction of St. Omer but the speed of the chase was somewhat different to the pace that had been set in Normandy. Also German tactics were changing. Now their favoured method of defence was to destroy all bridges as they withdrew and then make stubborn defences from the far side of any obstacle (normally a river or canal) that the Allies wished to traverse. Therefore it was recognised by the Allies that they would have to fight for every inch of every crossing.

During the night of 3–4 September 1944, 10 PSK with 2nd Anti-Tank Battalion and a squadron of Dragoons, after finding a crossing on the River L'Authie, was to reconnoitre and seize the crossing on the river Ganche, to the east of the town of Hesdin. After this there was another reconnaissance mission to the north and northeast towards the crossing on the River Terenoizen. Maczek was determined that the Division should be responsible for its reconnaissance so that it could determine its own course of action concerning the seizure of crossings and the ability to advance.

Wasilewski had taken notice of the number of enemy defensive positions along the main communication line to the crossings over the River L'Authie and he decided that there was a lack of any serious amount of enemy armour in the area. This led him to conclude that a concentrated attack upon one of the crossings would give him the greatest chance of forcing a crossing over the L'Authie. 2nd Squadron had reported that there were three crossings in the sector west of Le Boisle while 3rd Squadron reported that there were four crossings to the northwest. Wasilewski's plan was that once a crossing place for the entire regiment had been identified and taken 10 PSK was to move on and seek a further crossing on the River Canche in a sector to the southeast of the town of Hesdin.

Between Hesdin and Wail every squadron was to move onto the offensive. After crossing the River Canche, it was probable that the next operation would be towards the crossing on the River Terenoizen, about fifteen kilometres from Hesdin towards the northeast. Throughout this offensive all squadrons were deployed simultaneously, with several reconnaissance platoons whose purpose was to seek out crossing places. The anti-tank battalion and the Dragoon squadron were kept as a reserve to be deployed as and when necessary.

At 07:30 hours 4 September 1944, 2nd and 3rd Squadrons set about their assignments. 2nd Squadron found that the bridges in its sector had been either totally destroyed or partially destroyed. 3rd Squadron reached the hill half a mile west from Willencourt, from where the crossing could be seen. Then news came that the Canadians had seized the bridge in the area of Auxi le Chateau. At once, 2nd and 3rd Squadrons seized bridges over the river and canal in Willencourt and La Neuville. The bridges had been damaged but the squadrons still managed to cross over, leaving a single platoon to guard the bridges.

After the crossing of the River L'Authie by the entire regiment, the commander of 3rd Squadron received orders to reconnoitre for a crossing on the River Canche in Hesdin while 1st Squadron was sent along the same river but in the Vieil Hesdin area and then further to the River Ternoize in the region of Auchy les Hesdin. 2nd Squadron after re-establishing contact with the regiment set out again looking for crossing on the River Canche, to the southeast of the region.

3rd Squadron, which was moving along the Le Boisle-Hesdin road, saw explosions in the valley below. This was evidence of the Germans blowing up more bridges as they withdrew from the area. The squadron continued travelling until it reached an intersection, two kilometres to the south of Hesdin. 1st Squadron had more luck in its mission, moving swiftly, with the efficient use of pickets and an advance party; it reached the crossing in Fontaine le Etalon and without encountering the enemy, captured the bridge in Vieil Hesdin at 10:30 hours. From there, 1st Squadron moved to its next operational task at Auchy les Hesdin on the River Terenoizen. 2nd Squadron operating in the far east of the sector reached a crossing already held by the Canadians and found a second bridge which had been blown up by the enemy.

Wasilewski directed 2nd and 3rd Squadrons to the crossing in Vieil Hesdin and with advance guards from other units crossed the bridge and reached Le Parcy. As 1st Squadron had already met enemy opposition in Auchy les Hesdin, 2nd Squadron was ordered to seek a crossing place further to the northeast while 3rd Squadron was to contact the remainder of the regiment in Le Parcy. By 11:30 1st Squadron had moved up to the area close to the bridge (already destroyed by the Germans) in Auchy les Hesdin. Immediately the squadron came under heavy anti-tank and machine gun fire. One tank was wrecked and four men wounded: Sergeant Dyszynski, Corporals Zdun and Skiba and Lance Corporal Kondol. The wounded were evacuated with a help from local French civilians.

The Squadron could not push on because of the heavy fire; therefore the Poles continued to shell the town. Meanwhile a platoon was dispatched to the northeast in order to reconnoitre a ford on the Terenoizen; near a mill in the town of Rollencourt. On the northern side of the river were German infantry but the platoon risked a crossing but the tracks of the lead tank became stuck on the marshy riverbank. Private Musinski was then wounded by German fire.

2nd Squadron, moving with its platoons spread out, was able to move without making any contact with the enemy as it moved through Fresnoy, Incourt and Eclimeux, from where two platoons searched in Blangy for a crossing on the Ternoize as the squadron's CO with two other platoons looked for a crossing in the Erin region. The CO's platoons were advancing at such a rate that they overtook a column of advancing Sherman tanks of

24th Uhlans and moved on swiftly towards a German infantry position which put up very little resistance. By 15:30 hours the little formation had captured a narrow stone bridge in the town of Tilly-Capelle. There the rest of the squadron caught up. Searches by 2nd Squadron for other crossings were fruitless as the remaining bridges had been blown up by retreating Germans and could not be used by tanks.

Wasilewski with 3rd Squadron and 2nd Battalion Anti-Tank, as well as a squadron of Dragoons had already moved to the Humerceuille area, where he received information concerning the capture of the crossing in Tilly-Capelle. He immediately left with 3rd Squadron and the Dragoons for Tilly-Capelle while 1st Squadron was sent orders to link up with the rest of the regiment. Acting simultaneously with 2nd Squadron, Sherman and Stuart tanks from 24th Uhlans entered 1st Squadron's area of operations. Despite the heavy enemy fire, one of the Shermans moved to a 1st Squadron tank, which had been destroyed by anti-tank fire. This enabled 1st Squadron to rescue the crew of the stricken tank from drowning in the ford there. Then the platoon from 1st Squadron was able to move to Humerceuille region.

2nd Squadron by attacking the Germans managed to break the strong German defensive stand in Teneur and took 25 prisoners, all the time shelling heavily the area. After this the squadron moved onto the main Fruges-Anvin road and captured the town of Crepy before Verchin where a bridge was captured (067 253). Throughout the entire operation the squadron was under heavy German mortar fire. During the time of 2nd Squadron's operation in Teneur and Crepy, parts of the Dragoon squadron cleared the woods in the Tilly-Capelle area while 3rd Squadron, moving along the western side of the same wood, reached Ambricourt and Crepieul, where they came under heavy artillery fire and mortar fire.

At 17:30 hours 10 PSK established a position for the night in a region to the north of Ambricourt. Throughout the day 10 PSK had moved about sixty kilometres with the armoured squadrons and platoons covering most of this distance. Their action was described at the time as being swift and forceful while for the first time the regiment deployed squadrons and platoons in wide formations which allowed them to cross three rivers in a single day. The casualty rate was also acceptable with only five men wounded, one Cromwell tank destroyed and another damaged. On the same day the enemy lost thirty prisoners, two 75mm gun, three jeeps and ten trailers. The overall situation on 4 September 1944 was that of success for the Division. 3rd Rifle Brigade captured Hesdin while elements of 10th Motorised Brigade's (10 BK *panc*) vanguard moved to Le Pit Senlins. During the night of 4–5 September 1944, 10 BK *panc's* formation moved to the southwest of 10 PSK's position. The task of the 1st Polish Armoured Division remained unchanged: the pursuit of the Germans in the direction of St Omer and further towards Ypres.

10 BK *panc* was to operate as the divisional vanguard along two axes with the purpose of capturing crossings between St Omer and Aire. Information concerning the enemy was also received; this revealed that generally the Division was fighting the 245th Infantry Division, which had been involved in most of the fighting during the river offensives. The German defences were considered to have been organised and that the next line of defence would probably be along the rivers and canals in the St Omer region.

During the night of 4–5 September 1944 new orders came for 10 PSK. With 2nd Anti-Tank Battalion and the Dragoon Squadron, 10 PSK was to reconnoitre for a crossing along the Neuf Fosse Canal between St Omer and Aire. Wasilewski decided to deploy his squadrons in a wide fan formation, operating simultaneously while searching for suitable crossings. 10 PSK in a single column moved to the main roads in the region of 141 420 where 3rd Squadron reconnoitred the crossing between St Omer and a crossing seven kilometres to the southeast. 2nd Squadron was to operate to the right of Aire while remaining in contact with 1st Squadron. The anti-tank battalion and Dragoons were to be deployed as necessary according to any situation that arose.

10 PSK began its operation at 08:00 hours on 5 September 1944. The enemy opposition was just about finished and was withdrawing, taking only essentials such as equipment, ammunition and plenty of fuel. The enemy had tried withdrawing entirely during the night but owing to tiredness and the Polish attacks of the previous days, the Germans had failed to decamp by daybreak. 10 PSK began to move along the Coupelle-Neuve-Fruges axes and along the main road towards St Omer. It was a difficult march because units from 10 BK *panc* were also moving along 10 PSK's route, therefore Wasilewski ordered 10 PSK to leave this route and travel across country via Wandonne and Andincthum to the crossing at 037 372 where 2nd Squadron was to begin operations along the Avroul-Clarque-Rocquetoire axes. 3rd Squadron was to conduct its operations from Herbelle towards Heuringhen and further on, continuously looking for crossings.

The effect of this was that units from 10 BK *panc* were already deployed along the main axis in the direction of St Omer and 2nd Squadron was having difficulty advancing in the direction of the crossing at Guarlinghem. Wasilewski altered part of the operational plan and decided that the main effort of the offensive was to be a reconnaissance of the northern parts of the canal. This led to the following orders being issued: 3rd Squadron

Troops from the Division examine a German V1 flying bomb site.
Imperial War Museum BU404, BU405, BU406

from Heuringhen was to reconnoitre for crossings at 153 495, 198 496 and 211 480. 1st Squadron from the Rocquetoire area was to reconnoitre for the crossings in the Blaringhem and Guarlinghem while 2nd Squadron was to look for a crossing in the Aire area. The remainder of 10 PSK was to follow 1st Squadron and move to the Rocquetoire area and later onto Wittes.

Between 11:00 and 12:00 hours all three squadrons came under enemy fire. The squadron's returned fire, moving along roads running parallel to the canal, firing heavily upon the enemy whilst leaving behind forward elements of 10 BK *panc*. A crossing was spotted while at the same time a series of explosions were observed in the canal valley and what appeared to be a bridge was seen. The enemy attacked the Polish tanks with mortars and artillery from the canal while a small group of Germans, armed with machine guns, fighting stubbornly, held the west bank of the canal. 3rd Squadron, which had been sent to reconnoitre the bridge, reported that it was unusual. After making this report it took up a firing position in the hills and shelled a column of Germans withdrawing to the far side of the canal. 3rd Squadron was able to take about twenty prisoners. 2nd Squadron moved to the north towards the outskirts of Aire where it met strong enemy resistance from anti-tank guns and mortars as well as anti-tank barricades. A platoon, which had set out on foot to reconnoitre a crossing in Guarlinghem, was attacked and suffered three wounded: Second Lieutenant Rozek, Corporal Garczewski and Private Apczynski. In Aire itself, 2nd Squadron broke the enemy resistance, destroyed the barricades designed to impede the progress of the Polish armour and then moved to the bridge which had been destroyed. Meanwhile, 1st Squadron, firing heavily whilst moving to the canal in the Guarlinghem region reported that the bridge over the canal was down while one platoon, fighting on the crossing in Blaringhem, met enemy resistance at Wittes, which it overcame and was able to advance further.

During this time information from Division reported a bridge on the canal (co-ordinate level 457) in Blaringhem which had been seized by one of the armoured regiments. Wasilewski knew nothing of this (from 1st Squadron) and so he sent out the Dragoons to clear Wittes while he went to Blaringhem in a scout car to check the information concerning the capture of the bridge for himself. At the crossing at Blaringhem, Wasilewski met members of a platoon from 1st Squadron but he could see for himself that the bridge had been destroyed. There was no further armour in the area and later Division denied the report concerning the bridge.

The clearing of Wittes by the Dragoons proved to be heavy work. The Dragoons suffered losses, both dead and wounded. The 2ic 10 PSK, sent in a platoon of armour from 2nd Squadron as support for the Dragoons' offensive. Eventually during the afternoon Wittes was cleared but not before 2nd Squadron suffered casualties: two dead, Corporal Mastuszak and Private Korta while Cadet Officer Klobukowski was badly wounded.

Once all of the daily reports had been collated it was established that every bridge over the canal had been destroyed and could not be used to cross armour over. 10 PSK was still fighting and had been reinforced by 8th Rifle Battalion (8BS) who were already firing upon the eastern side of the canal. At 18:00 hours 8BS seized a bridgehead in the area of the Blaringhem crossing. This meant that divisional sappers could now prepare to build a bridge over the canal ready for an armoured crossing. 10 PSK placed pickets (platoon from 1st Squadron) in the Guarlinghem area and in Aire (platoon from 2nd Squadron with a platoon of Dragoons). The remainder of the regiment was to secure a position in the Wittes area. There were still ambushes by the enemy during the evening, which saw the death of Sergeant-Major Karol Walczak (1st Squadron) and the wounding of Sergeant Terczynski (1st Squadron) on picket duty in Guarlinghem. However the pickets in Aire took about 60 prisoners. Throughout the day the regiment moved about 45 kilometres, most of it involved heavy fighting. 10 PSK's casualties were: three dead, five wounded and one tank destroyed by a mine. The enemy losses were 82 prisoners, one 105mm gun, two smaller calibre artillery pieces, one scout car and ten trailers.

Throughout the night of 5–6 September 1944, sappers of the 1st Polish Armoured Division rebuilt the bridge over the Neuf Fosse Canal, protected by units of 3rd Rifle Brigade while 10th Dragoons was to occupy St Omer. Despite this, the task of the Division was to continue in its pursuit of the Germans in the direction of Ypres and Roulers with 10 BK *panc* working along the two flanks as vanguard. There was also information concerning the enemy. The Division since morning had once more been fighting 245th Infantry Division and from observations made upon the fighting along the Somme and from information gleaned from prisoners, it seemed that all the opposition in the area was directed with great efficiency. 10 PSK received orders during the night to the effect that it was to reconnoitre with 2nd Anti-Tank Brigade and a Dragoon squadron on the 'blue flank' (the main flank), probe the 'red flank' (north flank) and seize the crossing on the Ypres Canal which was south of Ypres itself.

The method of operation was not to break any resistance found in the main flank (blue) but to move in wide lateral paths, heading to every consecutive crossing. In the opening phase of the operation the formation moved along a single axis to Staple. From Staple, the operation moved on two fronts. 1st Squadron moved along the axis: St Sylvestre Cappel-Mont des Cats-Westoutre, while 3rd Squadron moved very much towards the north of the sector but parallel to 1st Squadron via Caestre and Fletre. The remainder advanced behind 1st Squadron. In the Westoutre area the operation split into three: 2nd Squadron moved towards the crossing at Ypres, 1st Squadron to the east and northeast of Voormeszeelle and 3rd Squadron to the very south, towards the crossings in the regions of Hollebeke and Houthem. 2nd Anti-Tank's duty was to reinforce the armoured squadrons and was deployed in a ratio of a platoon of anti-tank to a squadron of armour. The Dragoons were deployed in a similar way but were more flexible and was able to adapt to any developing situation.

1st Squadron moved to the Erzenwalle region where it constantly fought the enemy while looking for a crossing place. The advance guard platoon went to crossing one kilometre to the south of Ypres. There the bridge was heavily defended with barbed wire entanglements as well as violent mortar fire, not to mention long-range anti-tank fire. Despite this, the platoon fought its way across to the other side of the canal while Wasilewski sent the Dragoons and Second Squadron (10 PSK) under the command of 10 PSK's Second-in-Command with the purpose of creating a bridgehead and securing the crossing.

At the same time, 1st Squadron was ordered to reconnoitre for additional routes and bridges, to and over the canal (596 577). In this region, the squadron seized a bridge and established a bridgehead there. 3rd Squadron, which was in the north-eastern suburbs of Wytschaete where they met enemy opposition. Two men were wounded: Second Lieutenant Antoni Położyński (the officer who captured General Eldfeldt in Normandy) and Corporal Golej. A tank was also damaged. An enemy column, which tried to move westward, past the squadron's rear, was immediately fired upon. This spelt the end of German resistance in Wytschaete.

Every element of 10 PSK was in action on that day. The regiment's command post met a column of enemy vehicles and infantry in the Elzewalle region. The CO's platoon with 2nd Assault Squad, the remainder of the Anti-Tank Battalion and the Reconnaissance Platoon, destroyed the enemy and took 34 prisoners, including officers, in addition to capturing the orders for the commanding officer of XXVI Corps.

2nd Squadron with the Dragoon squadron and a platoon from 1st Squadron held the crossing at 584 596, secured from the direction of Ypres. From this crossing the Poles were able to fire, with great accuracy, upon enemy units withdrawing from Ypres. Later twenty prisoners were taken. At 17:00, 1st Tank Regiment (Polish) arrived at the crossing. During this time further orders were received in preparation for further operations. It was decided that the entire regiment (10 PSK) was to cross at 596 577 and begin to reconnoitre in the general direction of Roulers. 3rd Squadron was to act as advance guard followed by 2nd Squadron and the Dragoon squadron. 1st Tank, after crossing at 584 596 was to link up with 10 PSK while 1st Squadron took up the rear of the regimental column.

At 17:30 hours the reconnaissance operation began. 3rd Squadron made an inspection of Ypres from the southeast, crossing the Ypres-Menin, upon which there was much abandoned and destroyed enemy equipment. 3rd Squadron moved in the direction of Zonnebeke, firing upon withdrawing enemy vehicles and groups of soldiers. In the hamlet of Frezenberg, two kilometres northeast of Zonnebeke, enemy resistance was met. Wasilewski ordered 1st Squadron to the left of 3rd Squadron and attacked on two fronts: 3rd Squadron to the south and 1st Squadron on the northern side of the railway line. The squadrons then moved to a region, one kilometre from Zonnebeke. As dusk fell Wasilewski broke off operations and by dark 10 PSK had formed a harbour, one kilometre south of Zonnebeke.

During this day 10 PSK had moved about sixty kilometres and had taken the fight to the enemy. The actions of 2nd Assault Squad and 2nd Anti-Tank Battalion was considered by 10 PSK to have been invaluable; the lessons concerning their deployment with armoured units had been learnt. The casualties for the day were five Poles wounded with the loss of a single Cromwell tank and two others damaged. The enemy suffered 55 prisoners, the loss of two 75mm anti-tank guns, ten 37mm guns, two ammunition trucks, four lorries and seventeen trailers.

A communication which was made known to 10 PSK revealed the results of the Allied pursuit of the Germans into Belgium and serves to help in the understanding of the situation concerning the fighting. The communication opened by stressing that the 'bag' (the German position) was closing and was closing rapidly since the Allied occupation of the Belgian port of Antwerp. Until this time the Germans had considered withdrawing from France by sea and in the best case scenario fall back five kilometres to the River Sklady. However it should be noted that both examples called for a maritime evacuation. By a curious quirk of fate it seemed that the Germans were heading for the beaches at Dunkirk, as the British and the French had done during May 1940. From the captured German orders, destined for XXVI Corps, it could be seen that the general direction of the withdrawal changed from the east to the north on 5 September 1944 as a result of intelligence concerning the allied entry into Antwerp. The Germans had also considered the possibility of reinforcing Dunkirk and treating it as a fortress. From various sources it was also revealed that the German garrison in Boulogne remained until it was finally overwhelmed by the allies. The 3rd Infantry Division fought all day against the German 64th and 245th Infantry Divisions, which did not immediately surrender until the fall of Boulogne. From the changing of the above German orders it was apparent that the occupation of Ypres by the 1st Polish Armoured Division was a shock to the Germans. Sappers from the German 17th Engineer Battalion had been preparing to destroy the bridge over the River Lys in sector H 8055-J 0573 during the night of 5–6 September 1944.

For the Germans the greatest pressure from the Allies had come from the south but the Poles had come from the west, which was to the rear of the German position. In the allied opinion it had become obvious that the Germans were planning to withdraw to the coast while leaving units behind to fight a rearguard action, using the same methods since they had been forced from Normandy. This meant the destruction of every bridge and crossing, forcing the allies to fight their way over every river and canal.

The 1st Polish Armoured Division after clearing Ypres continued in the pursuit of the Germans along two flanks in the directions of Roulers and Thielt and then further north-west to the Canal d'Gand. 10 PSK's task was that with 2nd Anti-Tank and the Dragoon squadron, to reconnoitre in the direction of the Division's operational area, first in Roulers and later in Thielt. Wasilewski decided that the best operational plan for 10 PSK was that it should clear the Division's route. To this end he moved his armoured squadrons forward with the purpose of smashing any opposition that they may encounter. There was an expectation of strong opposition being moved from the north. At the beginning of the offensive the squadrons moved along a single axis with 3rd Squadron acting as an advance guard until the intersection at Passchendale was reached. From there the squadrons advanced on two fronts. 2nd Squadron was sent on a reconnaissance mission along the Westroosebeke-Sleijhagen-Hooglede axis and then further in the direction of Thielt. 3rd Squadron moving via Roodkruis was deployed in a reconnaissance of the western suburbs of Roulers. 1st Squadron with the Dragoons followed 3rd Squadron to the Roulers area. Their part of the operation depended upon how the entire operation developed. 2nd Anti-Tank Battalion was split into platoons and assigned to squadrons on the same basis as that of the previous day.

At 08:00 hours, 7 September 1944, 10 PSK began its operations. 3rd Squadron moved to the western suburbs of Roulers and was met with barricades and anti-tank fire. The Poles returned fire and destroyed an anti-tank gun, a staff car and two lorries. It was asserted that the enemy anti-tank defences were to be found towards the south-western and western outskirts of Roulers. Therefore orders were given to encircle the town from the northwest and to cut the road which ran north from Roulers.

At Sleijhagen, 2nd Squadron came under artillery, mortar and anti-tank fire. Courageous action on the part of 2nd Squadron broke the enemy resistance and several dozens of prisoners were taken before the squadron was able to return to its offensive and move on towards Hooglede. After 2nd Squadron's battle in Sleijhagen, Wasilewski sent the Dragoons into the town in order to clear it as well as deciding to greatly expand the operation to the north. 1st Squadron received orders to follow 2nd Squadron and advance further to the west. In Lindeken, the squadron was to move north and move to the region of St Joseph. From there 1st Squadron was to begin its operation properly by moving two kilometres west of Lichterville and begin a reconnaissance mission and generally spy upon the enemy and its movements. After 1st Squadron had finished its immediate tasks it moved to engage enemy infantry in the St Joseph's area. Statements from prisoners taken in the St Joseph's suggested that there was only a single infantry battalion which lacked any anti-tank guns in the area. The German's only anti-tank defence in that area was hand-held *Panzerfaust* and the arrival of armour had been a shock for the Germans. During the fighting for the St Joseph's area, the squadron did not move into the built-up area of St Joseph but moved directly upon the enemy infantry and from their tanks, the Poles caused mayhem amongst the Germans, inflicting huge casualties and taking many prisoners. The Squadron did not have time to escort the prisoners to the rear but instead allowed the Germans to move alone to the rear of the Polish lines.

From the Drijevegen area, Wasilewski, by radio, ordered 1st Squadron to move towards Gits with the purpose of entering the flanks and rear of the enemy's defence in Hooglede. Hooglede was very heavily defended. Wasilewski advanced to the Rigerije region. In the Hooglede offensive, 2nd Squadron sent a platoon as an armoured advance guard along the right hand side of the road which led to the church. The rest of the Squadron moved to the same place and met organised infantry and anti-tank fire. Two men, Sergeant Wojcik and Corporal Dąbrowski, both from 1st Platoon 2nd Anti-Tank battalion were killed. Corporal Grabowski and Lance Corporal Szczepański, from the same platoon were wounded. In further fighting, the squadron suffered more losses. Corporal Zylber was killed and Corporal Doruch was wounded. The Squadron still managed to destroy two anti-tank guns. In view of the strong enemy resistance and upon learning that 2nd Tank Regiment (Polish) and the Dragoon Regiment had been ordered to attack and capture Hooglede, Wasilewski ordered 2nd Squadron to break off their attack and withdraw which they did and retired several hundred metres to the rear.

3rd Squadron while moving to Roulers encountered very difficult terrain due to ditches and water channels cutting through the area which it was trying to cross. Throughout its journey to Roulers the squadron fired upon withdrawing enemy units and actually destroyed two Pz Mk III tanks but not before suffering two dead when Private Jan Wibart and Sergeant Strozik were killed by mortar fire. The tank of the commanding officer of 1st Squadron was hit five times by anti-tank fire, as was the tank of his 2ic. The advance platoon also suffered losses, losing one tank but the platoon commander, Sergeant Major Mincer, managed to lead a platoon through enemy lines and via a round about route was able to return the platoon to 10 PSK. By now the Squadron had lost one man and had had three others wounded. It also lost three tanks to anti-tank fire and yet another damaged. The wounded were evacuated under the cover of a smoke screen while heavy fire from the Assault Squad totally dislodged the enemy. Following this, the enemy withdrew from Roulers, leaving much of its equipment behind, including five 75mm guns.

After 10 PSK's battle in Roulers, 10 BK *panc*, who were next in line, positioned northeast of Roulers, took Hooglede. Wasilewski told 1st Squadron to wait for further orders while 3rd Squadron was considered to have been the 'star' of the day, having been in action from morning until 17:00 hours. 10 PSK, as a whole, had inflicted heavy casualties upon the enemy, had broken every point of enemy resistance and had provided every possible assistance needed to aid the Division's commanding officer, General Maczek, in reaching operational decisions. By 18:30 hours, the regiment had taken a night position ½ kilometre south of Hooglede. 1st Squadron finally reached this position at 20:00 hours. During this day 10 PSK advanced twenty five miles. The Polish casualty rate (10 PSK): three dead, five wounded. Five Cromwell tanks destroyed and two damaged. (2nd Anti-Tank Battalion): two dead, one wounded and a gun damaged. The German casualty rate was determined as being: forty seven prisoners, two Pz Mk III tanks, one 155mm gun, eight 75mm guns, five lesser calibre guns, ten lorries, two half-tracked tractors, two jeeps, one motorcycle and a field kitchen.

A German prisoner is brought in. **Imperial War Museum BU407**

The following day, the 1st Polish Armoured Division was reorganised in order to continue with its offensive. 10 BK *panc* and 3rd Rifle Brigade were to be used for the occupation of Roulers. 10 BK *panc* was supposed to continue towards Thielt and further on towards the northeast. 10 PSK was to move in the Divisional column ready for several days rest in the southern outskirts of Thielt. The Regiment was to march with 2nd Anti-Tank Battalion, taking every tank, including those damaged or unsuitable for combat. The column moved at 09:00 hours on 8 September 1944. Wasilewski had expected 10 PSK to be sent to Thielt and receive living quarters somewhere along the Roulers-Ardoye axis. At Ardoye, the column received news that 10 BK *panc* was having great difficulty taking Thielt. 10 PSK received the following orders: first to seize the area in which they were to operate in the southern outskirts of Thielt and then to reconnoitre the area around southern Thielt and from there give support to the 24th Uhlans offensive in Thielt.

Wasilewski decided to take every combat worthy tank from the convoy and sent them straight into action. The tanks were grouped into two squadrons and moved forward into action along the right hand side of the road of Thielt. 1st Squadron was sent in the direction of Marialoopkauter while 3rd Squadron moved hard to the north. The Marialoopkauter region was seized and from there on further action depended upon how the overall situation developed. 2nd Squadron and 2nd Anti-Tank Battalion were then deployed behind 1st Squadron. From the Ardoye region the squadrons moved across a variety of surfaces ranging from main roads as well as heavy and difficult terrain. By 11:00 hours they had crossed the main road from south to the north in region 847 730 and during the afternoon had reached the railway line two kilometres to the southwest of Thielt.

1st Squadron after crossing the railway track was met with heavy mortar and anti-tank fire. The squadron from a partly covered position returned fire and reported the presence of a column of twelve Pz Mk III or IV tanks in the Krommendijk region, moving to the east. After hours of fighting the enemy appeared to run out of steam and ceased firing. The squadrons advanced a little and fired upon a second enemy rearguard. After a while, orders were received to reconnoitre Marialoop and the 'hills with windmills', 2 ½ kilometres to the southeast of Thielt. 2nd Squadron received orders to scout around the outskirts of Thielt, on the eastern side of the railway track. 2nd Anti-Tank Battalion was to accompany 2nd Squadron. 3rd Squadron was to reconnoitre Meulebeke. The squadrons were told that after completing their assignments, they were to fire upon any withdrawing enemy columns that they could see and not to allow the enemy to organise any resistance.

2nd Squadron having learnt that Thielt had already been captured changed their direction of operations and headed directly for the hilly area of Poelbergmolen. Meulebeke was already free of the enemy. This left the Marialoop and the 'windmill hills', which were captured by the squadrons with no struggle and prisoners were taken. By dusk Thielt was clear of the enemy. 10 PSK made its night position in the southern suburbs of Thielt. 10 PSK had moved 28 kilometres without any casualties. The enemy casualties were: 24 prisoners, one artillery tractor, seven lorries, six trailers and a scout car.

Polish Casualties (10 PSK) During the 'Chase', 25 August 1944 – 22 September 1944

Personnel	Officers	Ranks	Total
Killed	—	12	12
Wounded	8	21	29
Total	8	33	41

10 PSK Equipment Losses During the Same Period

Equipment	Cromwells	Stuarts	Other	Total
Destroyed	12	—	—	12
Damaged	8	—	—	8
Total	20	—	—	20

Enemy Losses to 10 PSK, same period:

535 prisoners
3 tanks
13 75mm anti-tank guns
6 anti-tank guns and anti-aircraft guns greater than 50mm calibre

1 *Nebelwerfer*
17 artillery pieces of 50mm or less in calibre
42 military vehicles
81 trailers
1 motorcycle.[129]

CHAPTER VIII

On to Belgium

During the previous chapter we saw how the 1st Polish Armoured Division with the Allies pursued the Germans across northern France and denied the enemy any chance of putting up a sustained resistance. During the course of that chapter reference was made of the Division fighting – principally 10th Mounted Rifles (10 PSK) in their reconnaissance role – using the faster Cromwell tank. In this chapter the role of the 1st Polish Armoured Division in Belgium as a whole will be discussed further.

Wysocki recorded that the Division crossed the Belgian frontier on 6 September 1944 when it moved into Ypres with no opposition from the enemy as the Polish armour swept through enemy defences and 9th Rifle Brigade (9BS) took prisoners.[130] Captain Stefan Drozak (9BS) put the Polish date of entry as 5 September 1944. He also recalls seeing the tragic results of the First World War when he saw the huge cemeteries with their long rows of white crosses dating from the epic battles for Ypres during the 1914–1918 War. In 1944 the town was captured in one day with few casualties. In 1947 Drozak recalled that information about the enemy's position was sketchy but it seemed that most of the opposition was coming from the western side of the town around the area of the railway station. Apart from that, the armour (2nd Tank Regiment [Polish]) had captured all the entrances into Ypres.

The commanding officer of 9BS, Lieutenant Colonel Szydlowski, decided that 3rd and 4th Companies 9BS were to close down the German defences from the rear while 4th Company was to capture the railway station. 4th Company hurried in two columns from the northwest to the centre of Ypres. Without any opposition they moved to the market place where they took prisoners including staff officers. The Polish action finished any idea of resistance as they had no idea that the Poles would move upon them from such a direction. It was a total shock for the Germans. Very quickly the market square filled with local Belgians, all very happy to see Allied troops. The people sang. They shouted and danced. They drank and waved banners, which read *Vive la Pologne*. Young girls kissed the Polish troops, not caring that the soldiers were dirty, unshaven and had red sunburnt faces. Drozak remembered Belgians throwing flowers as if it was a *Corpus Christi* procession until finally his Bren Gun carrier was transformed from being a vehicle of war to a mobile flower shop! It became impossible for the Poles to move forward as the locals pressed against their vehicles and then suddenly there were a series of shots from a church tower.

The crowds melted away and once again the streets were empty. The enemy fire appeared to be strong and accurate; Polish casualties began to mount up. Reports suggested that there were two bases for the enemy defences. One was in front of the railway station and the second by the canal in the area of the cemetery. Drozak not wishing to test the entire enemy system decided to attack the area around the cemetery and that of the school in the area and then afterwards attack the railway station.

The Poles launched a fierce attack against the school, including the use of PIATs, a handheld anti-tank weapon. The fire from the PIATs caused the enemy to believe that the Poles were reinforced with armour. The Germans wanted to parley with the Poles and so the commander of the German company facing 9BS came out waving a white handkerchief. The German commander was willing to surrender but wanted a guarantee that he and his men would not be handed over to the Belgian Underground. This was agreed and the Poles took 72 prisoners. After the capitulation of the force in the cemetery the opposition at the railway station needed to be dealt with. The commander of this garrison was a major who had been wounded and lay in a nearby house. After he heard the report of the German officer who had surrendered his company; the wounded major surrendered his pistol without a word.

This was by no means the end of German resistance around Ypres as small pockets of Germans decided to hold out. Drozak completes his memories of Ypres by relating the story of a Private Smolinski, who during a mortar attack took refuge in a nearby house. Upon seeing Smolinski the Germans defending the house surrendered, and he then had the pleasure of taking five officers and 45 other ranks to the rear as prisoners. Eventually the skirmishes in Ypres died down as the Poles completely took over the town and a further eleven officers and 159 other ranks were added to the tally of prisoners in the market square.[131]

Second Lieutenant Stanisław Trembacz of the 2nd Tank Regiment claimed that 2nd Tank entered the pursuit of the rapidly withdrawing Germans on 8 September 1944 at around 12:00 hours when it received orders to capture the northern escape routes in Ruysselede. The distance between Ruysselede and 2nd Tank's position was only five kilometres therefore the regiment had to move swiftly in order to cut the enemy's sole escape route. 1st Squadron acting as an advance guard was given orders to move to an area two kilometres to the north of Ruysselede with the purpose of closing both main roads which ran north and northeast. The Regiment moved immediately; not even having time for a briefing.

The squadron commanders moved as directed along the march and via radio learnt their objectives and the manner that they were to be executed. Luckily, for once, the terrain was hard and without any obstacles, perfect for rapid movement of armour, ranging from the heavier Sherman tank to the lighter swift Cromwells, all of which were travelling as fast as possible. Eventually the tanks reached more undulating territory and in the distance along a single route out of the area, the road was black with mechanised and horse-drawn vehicles and constantly swarming with infantry along the edges of the road.

A short order was given, 'On them!' and the Polish tanks fell upon the enemy. Surprise was total. Before the Germans knew what was happening, the first Polish tanks were already on the road. Within a few moments the first two platoons were busy firing upon the enemy and moving through their ranks, crushing their foe with their terrible tank tracks and then sped off towards Ruysselede. One of the platoons returned from Ruysselede without any misfortune. The rest of the squadron moved like an avalanche through the overcrowded road and headed towards the next route. The Germans were totally demoralised by the speed and ferocity of the Polish attack and did not even attempt to fight back. Not one shot was fired in response to the Polish offensive; such was the surprise that the Poles had on their side. The Germans merely took shelter in nearby houses or in ditches, anywhere to escape the tanks.

In the meantime the rest of the Regiment rushed to the scene and took a position parallel to the road and began their offensive to complete the German misery. For about two kilometres the road was crowded with all manner of equipment and remains of soldiers, blown to pieces by Polish anti-tank shells and churned into a

Belgians greet the first tank to cross the border. Note the extra track links and stowage added to the front of the tank to increase armour protection. **Imperial War Museum BU372**

gory mess owing to the use of hand grenades. The picture of slaughter was completed by Polish artillery shelling Ruysselede.

With the Germans held, the Polish operation, having outflanked them on the last withdrawal route while tanks from 10th Motorised (10 BK *panc*) had moved up from the south, meant that the Germans were bunched up in Ruysselede, caught like fish in a net. In spite of their casualty rate, the Germans still managed to mount a counterattack in a vain attempt to punch their way out of the Polish lines. The counterattack was finally beaten back by 1st Squadron (2nd Tank). After this fight, 2nd Tank received orders to reach the Altre region on the Ghent Canal. 1st Squadron was left in the Ruysselede area in order to guard the road while the reminder of 2nd Tank advanced towards Altre.

After the first counterattack, the Germans mounted yet another, this time supported by *Panzer* Mk IVs which endangered the Polish position but with artillery support the German counter-offensive was destroyed. The fighting in Ruysselede cost the Germans dearly: 250 dead and over 300 prisoners taken. The loss of equipment was uncountable save for twenty artillery pieces captured. General Maczek commented the following day, upon seeing the carnage in the Ruysselede area, 'it was a small Chambois'.[132]

The increasing desperation of the Germans was reflected in an information communication (nr. 27) seen by the Poles in early September 1944. It opens by claiming that the enemy's intention was to defend the Channel ports of Boulogne, Calais, Gravelines and Dunkirk. The enemy considered that these positions would be defended to the end. Allied intelligence suggested that about 30,000 troops were trapped in these areas and were a mixed bunch of units including anti-aircraft and artillery units minus their guns and fighting as infantry. The Allies also seriously considered that the Germans were thinking of flooding the area as a defensive measure. The area to be flooded generally corresponded to towns on the map, which related to a network of small canals.

During the night of 7–8 September 1944, 712th Infantry Division (German) withdrew towards the north from the south via Thielt. Units around 712th Infantry Division were designated as a battle group, or *Kampfgruppe*, under the command of Major Frazkowski. The strength of these units was estimated to have been around two battalions with 20–25 light and heavy anti-tank guns. It was also revealed that 712th Division also had a nearby mobile anti-aircraft unit at its disposal. This meant that the Poles might have to deal with the dreaded 88mm gun, which functioned either as an anti-aircraft or an anti-tank gun. In either role it was deadly.

There was also an indication that the Germans were running low on fuel and ammunition. In the Allied opinion it seemed that the enemy would try to leave the area via a bridge over the Ghent Canal, getting as many units over before the arrival of 2nd Tank with the Dragoons at the bridgehead. It was also considered that the enemy would be restricted in its activities owing to a shortage of material and the fact that the German troops were no doubt exhausted.[133]

The fighting for Thielt began at dawn 7 September 1944 with 24th Uhlans under the command of Lieutenant-Colonel Dowbora moving towards the town while 10 PSK on the right moved to the very north of region, outflanking Thielt. During this time great events were taking place in Belgium as the Guard's Division had liberated Brussels, 11th Armoured Division had taken half of Antwerp complete with the dockyard and 7th Armoured Division had captured half of Ghent as far as the canal network and were making a stand there. Dowbora's group moved towards Thielt, a distance of about ten kilometres to the northeast of Roulers where 2nd Tank and a Dragoon squadron were waiting to be moved if required in any operation against Thielt. Dowbora's group consisted of a reconnaissance platoon (24th Uhlans), mortar platoon, tank squadron, reconnaissance platoon (8th Rifle Battalion, 8BS), Commander of 24th Uhlans (four tanks), a squadron of tanks carrying infantry men from 8BS, a further squadron of tanks, a squad of anti-tank guns and motorised artillery. The formation took shape during the night of 7–8 September 1944 before moving out at dawn. The reminder of 8BS under the command of Colonel Nowaczynski was to link up with the formation during the fighting in Thielt.

In Thielt, the Germans were unaware of the capture of Roulers and did not realise the danger that their position was in. When Lieutenant Dzierzka's reconnaissance platoon entered Thielt, passing in their tanks between the first houses, they saw nobody and continued driving through the empty streets of the suburbs until they finally reached the market square by the town hall. There they came across three German officers sitting in a car. A burst of machine gun from the Polish Stuart tank ended the Polish element of surprise. The enemy was alerted and fighting broke out in the streets. The Germans defended with machine-guns and *Panzerfausts*. The platoon withdrew from the area after coming under mortar fire and requested support from 8BS. The fighting continued for a couple of hours before the enemy realised that the Polish offensive was too strong and gave up fighting. After leaving a strong rearguard the enemy withdrew their main strength to neighbouring parts of the town.

As this was happening, Colonel Majewski at Brigade decided to send 2nd Tank under the command of Lieutenant-Colonel Koszutski with the Dragoon Squadron on an outflanking movement from the left side of the

Crossing the Alhelt Canal at Bermuge.
**Imperial War Museum BU716, BU717,
BU719, BU721**

offensive. A German column was seen by Koszutski's formation leaving Thielt moving northeast towards Altre. Koszutski moved his group across country and deployed his armour from the east where it attacked the German column between Ruiselede and Thielt. Shortly after Brigade sent 1st Tank onto the offensive and in the long-term bypass Koszutski's position, it came under fire from anti-tank guns already fighting Koszutski's group.

However the deployment of 1st Tank meant that sections of the German column were destroyed. The attack by the two Polish formations upon the withdrawing German convoy became known as the 'mini Chambois'. The result of the joint action of 24th Uhlans and 8BS with 1st and 2nd Tank Regiments operating to the left and 10 PSK being deployed on the right hand side of the town was that 12,000 prisoners were taken, several divisional orders from *Kampfgruppe* Frantzkowski, six anti-tank guns and a great number of mechanical and horse drawn vehicles were also captured. The commander of the *Kampfgruppe*, Major Frantzkowski, was killed fighting in the streets of Thielt.[134]

The operations of the 1st Polish Armoured Division towards the north and northeast were hampered because of the destruction by the enemy towards the Ghent Canal. From dawn, 9 September 1944, 10 PSK and 2nd Anti-Tank Battalion stood ready for action. At noon the operation was cancelled. 10 PSK was quartered in abandoned factories in the southern outskirts of Theist for several days rest. For the first time since leaving the Britain in August the soldiers were living in quarters. This rest period was spent in equipment and weapon maintenance. The next day, once again, 10 PSK prepared for action before being stood down again in the afternoon. Finally orders came from Division.

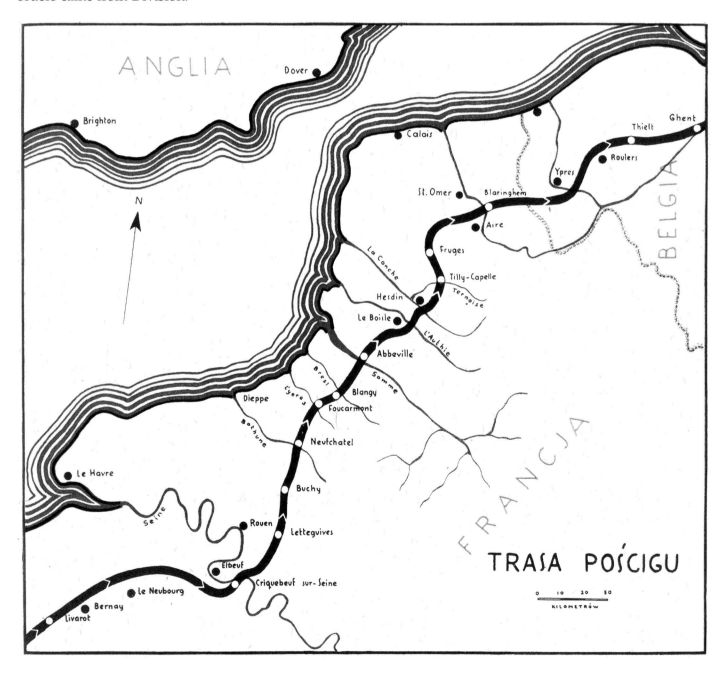

The main route of the 1st Polish Armoured Division into Belgium.

Davison briefly outlined the situation that was to face 10 PSK. The main problem was that the enemy was re-organised and giving rigid resistance to any allied advance. The German 59th and 712th Infantry Divisions were stubbornly defending the Ghent Canal in the sector from Bruges to Hansbeke. Information about the defences further to the east was totally lacking. The enemy had taken advantage of width of the canal using it as an obstacle and were able to defend their positions in excess of their ability, given the limited arms and ammunition available to the German armed forces by this stage of the war. There were successive waves of opposition as in the previous areas; once again the Germans had as far as possible destroyed all bridges and then opposed all attempts to cross by giving the most stubborn of resistance.

The Poles dominated the southern banks of the canal and unleashed continuous barrages of fire. However the enemy was growing in confidence since its withdrawal from France and was even beginning to send out reconnaissance patrols, for example along the northern canal bank. The 1st Polish Armoured Division received orders to move to the Ghent region and to clear an area which bordered from the south and east of the River Schelde from the northern mouth of the Schelde and from the west of the Terneuzen Canal, incorporating the Ghent area. The 4th Canadian Armoured Division had to continue in its operation concerning crossing along the Ghent Canal in addition to clearing the region to the west of the 1st Polish Armoured Division's sector.

10 PSK was assigned to reconnoitre the crossings on the Lys Canal, to the east of Thielt, in the Vive Saint Bavon Beynze sector. Wasilewski sent a reconnaissance platoon to conduct this task. The platoon reported that every bridge in this area had been blown up by the enemy and was unsuited for any attempted crossings. After this they linked up with 15th Scottish Division which held the eastern side of the canal. The following day the 1st Polish Armoured Division entered Ghent. 3rd Rifle Brigade (3BS) who entered first was greeted by the citizens of Ghent with wild acclaim but it was obvious that there was still a long way to go before the Germans could be finally ejected from the area. Even so the enemy was slowly being forced from Ghent but once again the enemy was using the canal as a method of defence and as obstacle to the Poles. The enemy firing was as usual resolute but rather weak as ammunition was beginning to become scarce but a battery of 105mm guns reinforced the German position. 10 PSK was ordered during the afternoon of 11 September 1944 to move to the Ghent area while during the day the main road to the northeast of Ghent had been cleared and the presence of British armour was reported in the nearby regions of Lokeren and St Nicolas.

3BS took over Ghent from 131st British Infantry Division while the enemy still held the northern parts of the town. The eastern frontline in Ghent was determined as running from the canal to point 2588 and then from there to the northeast along the river to Wachtebeke and then to the east to Boschdorp and again northeast to Callo. Throughout the night of 11–12 September 1944 with 3BS already in Ghent, the remainder of the 1st Polish Armoured Division moved into the Ghent area while 10 BK *panc* moved to the Lokeren region. On 12 September 1944 10 PSK moved behind 10 BK *panc* along the Thielt-Deynze axis and then to the centre of Ghent before moving to a position to the east of Ghent, towards the suburbs of Ablbroekstraat. During the evening 10 PSK received their orders for the following day.

The situation in Ghent on 12 September 1944 was that units from 10 BK *panc* were in Lokeren and St Nicolas area while a formation from 3BS were still clearing the enemy from the northern areas of Ghent. The enemy was about a battalion in strength and was making quite a stand. Information concerning the enemy at the time was somewhat patchy and contradictory but it seemed that the German strength was based upon a mixed group of sappers who had become separated from their home units and stragglers from the 59th Infantry Division. There was also a dearth of information concerning enemy movements to the northeast of Ghent. 10 PSK's orders for 13 September 1944 was to reconnoitre sections of the canals and bays along the Zuidleedle and the d'Hoerwart Canal from 223 883 towards the railway line which ran from Lokeren to Moerbeke.

The commanding officer of 10 PSK, Captain Wasilewski, decided that the best way to execute his orders was to send out armoured patrols from a single squadron to patrol designated areas. The patrols were to move along the route from the south towards the north of the canal with the purpose of reconnoitring bridges and crossings as well as eventually being deployed beyond the canal. The patrolling was only to be done during daylight hours. A night harbour was established with pickets from the reconnaissance platoon acting with the anti-aircraft platoon. The following day the entire regiment remained at its night position save for 3rd Squadron, which undertook the reconnaissance patrolling. 3rd Squadron reconnoitred every crossing within its designated area along the River Zuidleedle. Every bridge over the river was either blown or had been rendered unsuitable for further use. During the day the Squadron met with small enemy patrols moving towards the d'Moerwaart Canal. At dusk the squadron returned to 10 PSK's position. On 14 September 1944, 2nd Squadron took over 3rd Squadron's patrolling duties and as a result of enemy fire was able to identify enemy firing positions, which appeared to be well hidden.

Once 2nd Squadron reached the destroyed crossings on the d'Moerwaart Canal it began to shell the town on the opposite side. The Germans replied with mortar fire from the area of Winkel Sainte Croix. There was also some wildly inaccurate long-range anti-tank fire falling around the Polish position. Local civilians from the town of Steenburg told the Polish tank crews that the Germans had been patrolling the day before. Civilians who had been evacuated from Mendoch also spoke of German patrols.

Attempts by the Polish tank crews to cross the canal by foot came to nothing owing to the intensity of the German fire from the opposite bank. Members of *Brigade Blanc* (Belgian Resistance) informed the 2nd Squadron that at about 07:00 hours, a company of German infantry had moved to nearby Desteldonck. A platoon was dispatched to investigate this report but owing to becoming involved in fierce fighting around the railway line beyond the Ternouzen Canal, it was unable to assert if the Belgian report was accurate. Around the railway line the enemy was holding off the Polish tanks with mortar and machine gun fire. According to a port worker the Polish shelling achieved some results as he saw the destruction of several railway wagons and a large barge set alight as a result of the Polish tank fire. At dusk, 2nd Squadron returned to 10 PSK's position without any casualties.

On 15 September 1944, General Maczek gave orders for a re-grouping of formations within the Division and assigned units to the command of Lieutenant-Colonel Deka with the purpose of holding Ghent. 10 PSK minus 1st Squadron moved to regroup with 3BS and throughout the day moved to the region approximately four kilometres to the north of St Nicolas. 1st Squadron (10 PSK), which came under the direct command of Maczek, reconnoitred sections of the River Zuidleedle. The area to be reconnoitred was the area to the north of the Zuidleedle river in a sector, which ran from the Terneuzen Canal to the woods, two kilometres to the northeast of Exarde.

1st Squadron carried out this task by moving in a wide platoon formation. One platoon moved to the east with the purpose of reaching patrols from 10 BK *panc*. The rest of the squadron patrolled on foot along the Moerwaart Canal as well as shelling an area where the day before there had been reports of enemy patrols. The enemy replied with weak and occasional mortar fire. During the evening, on a section of the right flank, German officers with a flag of truce approached and asked for the terms of surrender. The commanding officer of the platoon, Second Lieutenant Sztumpf, dictated the terms: 'Come in close order with full arms and surrender unconditionally'. The Germans accepted these terms. 22 Germans, bearing full arms, used a footbridge to cross over to the Polish position. The platoon took the prisoners to the squadron from where they were transported back to Division.

At Divisional Headquarters the Germans claimed that they had surrendered because the German authorities had deceived them by telling them that the canal was the Albert Canal, from which the German Army had links and hoped to rescue the situation. But this group of Germans had already realised that they were surrounded. At 19:00 hours, the squadron returned to the region to the east of Ghent and received orders to carry on with the same duties the following day.

10 PSK's position on 16 September 1944 remained very much the same as that of the previous day, except that Maczek ordered 1st Squadron to find a crossing, where a bridge, which could carry tanks, could be easily built. At 08:00 hours, 1st Squadron set out to do this. During the afternoon, Maczek ordered 1st Squadron to return to 10 PSK. Moving swiftly the squadron moved along the route via: Saffelaere, Schebken, Exaerde, Sinay St Paul and Kemseke Stekene. The squadron caught up with the regiment in the region of Het Zand. The 1st Polish Armoured Division was once again advancing, this time towards the Axel-Hulst Canal.

The situation before the advance towards the Axel-Hulst Canal was that the Division was still in two formations. One formation, under the command of Lieutenant-Colonel Skibinski, was concentrated in the St Paul's region. To its right was 10 BK panc in the St Nicolas region while to the left of Skibinski's formation was Colonel Deca's group. The enemy to the north of Ghent was bottled up in an area which ran from the north (mouth of the River Schelde) while from the east, elements of the Second British Army in the Antwerp area were pushing forward, as in the west units of the 1st Canadian Army pressed forward and in the north, the Polish 1st Armoured Division added its pressure. The enemy endeavoured to keep back the pressure from the south in order to escape across the River Schelde and into Holland. The enemy took advantage of the terrain, which was intersected by canals, dykes, weirs, dams and ditches as well as being comparatively flooded in order to defend against the allied advance. In the 1st Polish Armoured Division's sector it was asserted that elements of the 59th and 712th Infantry Divisions were withdrawing to the north, leaving a rearguard at the Dutch frontier.

Lieutenant-Colonel Skibinski's group's task was to reconnoitre for a crossing on the Hulst Canal and at least conduct artillery observation in order to guide the shelling of the port of Terneuzen. Skibinski decided on the morning of 16 September 1944 that 3BS should seize the Drie Hoefijzers-Koewacht Line as a basis for further operations. Therefore there was a need for a reconnaissance mission in the direction of Hulst. During 15 September 1944 Wasilewski received orders for 10 PSK from General Maczek. Maczek ordered 10 PSK minus 1st Squadron but with a battalion of anti-tank to move to a position four kilometres north of St Nicolas, where they were to re-group with Skibinski's group. At 16:00 hours 10 PSK moved quickly to the area. Four hours later, at 20:00 hours, Skibinski sent a movement order to Wasilewski, which required 10 PSK to move to the Terlink area.

The following day, 16 September 1944, at 07:00 hours, 10 PSK minus 1st Squadron moved to Terlink via St Paul, Kemseke and Stekene to Terlink where the regiment was received as reinforcements. 10 PSK operated to the north while 9th Rifle Brigade (9BS) moved to the northwest and crossed the Dutch frontier at 09:30 hours and advanced further until they made contact with the enemy along the Axel-Hulst Canal line. At 11:00 hours, 10 PSK received orders to push further on in the direction of Axel and crossed the Dutch frontier at Koewacht at 12:15 hours. Eventually they reached the Het Zand region where as before they continued to act as reinforcements except for 3rd Squadron who operated to the northwest as support for 9BS.

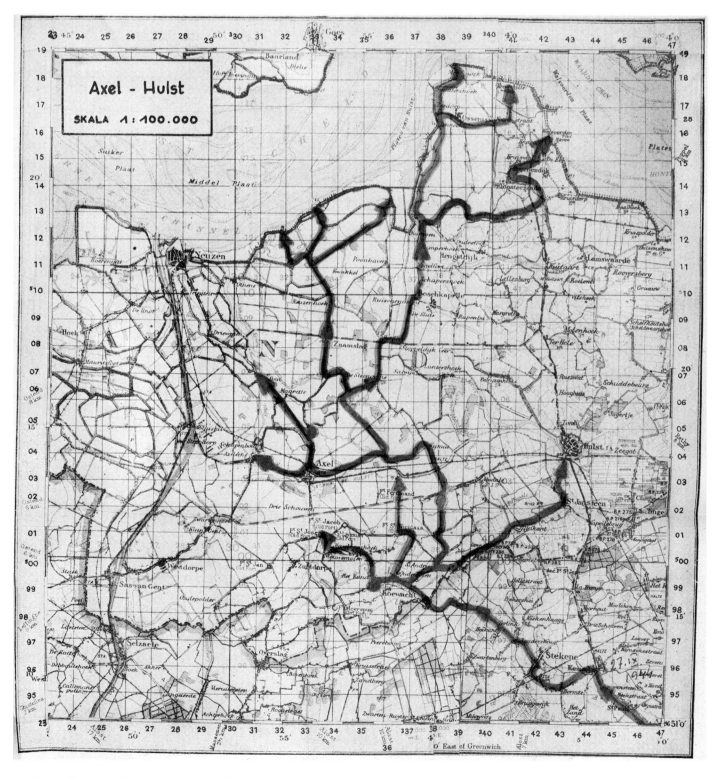

Axel to Hulst. Note the annotation dated 27.IX.1944, clearly written by a Polish hand.

3rd Squadron found itself operating over very difficult terrain while supporting 9BS's offensive in the direction of Axel. The enemy had prepared defences along the roads in the form of anti-tank ditches and barricades. Furthermore, the Germans had flooded the area. From a distance of one and a half kilometres to the south of Axel, 3rd Squadron came under anti-tank fire, losing one tank. 9BS also received heavy casualties. The armoured platoons rendered 9BS great assistance with their fire and by evacuating the large amount of wounded. 3rd Squadron continued fighting until dusk and remained in the area west of Nieuwemolen throughout the night with 9BS. The remainder of 10 PSK moved to a position for the night, on the outskirts of Het Zand, protected by artillery formations from the south and the west. At around 15:00 hours, 1st Squadron returned to the ranks of 10 PSK. Despite all of the activity during the night, 10 PSK lost only one Cromwell tank while the Germans lost a single tank and one anti-tank gun of either 75mm or 88mm calibre to 10 PSK.[135]

After the fighting in Belgium the Division was able to continue in its eastward advance towards Poland. However, first the Poles were to become involved in further battles for canal and river crossings as they advanced into Holland, which was stubbornly defended by the enemy as the Allies steadily moved towards Germany itself.

CHAPTER IX

The Dutch Campaign

The people of Holland have great respect for the Polish soldiers who helped to liberate the Netherlands during 1944 and 1945 and they continue to honour their memory.

Much of this is a result of the fighting in Arnhem during September 1944 during which the Polish Parachute Brigade played a significant part. Another side to this relationship concerns the Dutch and the 1st Polish Armoured Division. The citizens of Breda in particular are grateful to the men of the 1st Polish Armoured Division, as we shall see during this chapter.

In the previous chapter the 1st Polish Armoured Division had just crossed into Holland and its armoured units had reached the Axel-Hulst Canal. Wysocki notes that the terrain in Holland, as could be expected, was largely flat and below sea level and promised heavy going for the Division's armour. Once inside Dutch territory the Division changed the direction of its front, which had been to the east. Suddenly it turned 90°, moving directly to the north in the direction of the wide mouth of the River Schelde. By moving in this direction and along the river, the Division was assuming responsibility for an area of Dutch territory measuring 100 kilometres long and between 15–20 kilometres wide. Not only was this area flat and below sea level, it also contained many reinforced positions, forts and redoubts, scattered throughout the area.

Once again most bridges over the river and canals had been destroyed which meant that the Germans could defend their positions relatively easily against slow moving armour which could so easily become stuck in the waterlogged conditions found in Holland. The Polish 1st Armoured Division was once again working as two formations. On the left flank, a formation under the command of Colonel Deca from 8th Rifle Brigade (8BS) consisted of 3rd Rifle Brigade (3BS), 24th Uhlans as well as a battalion of artillery and anti-tank artillery which had been released from guarding Ghent once Canadian units relieved them there. On the right hand flank, an armoured brigade under the command of Colonel Majewski was operating. The armoured brigade consisted of most of the Division's armour less 24th Uhlans. Overall, the Division was operating in a wide formation towards the north.

1st Tank Regiment (Polish) first reconnoitred the area to the north and on 14 September 1944 conquered an area from the north of St Niklaas to the towns of Stekene, La Trompe (with Dragoons) and St Gilles. Immediately in front of the Division, parallel to the banks of the River Schelde ran the Axel-Hulst Canal. The canal needed crossing but the Germans had already destroyed the crossings over it. Therefore a crossing was required and the task fell to 3BS under Colonel Skibinski in co-operation with 10 PSK and the Dragoon. On 16 September 1944 9th Rifle Battalion (9BS) was operating from the south towards Axel but was hampered in its operation owing to defensive firing from the north. The terrain to the north, from the forts of St Niklaas and St Ferdinand and to the south from Kijkuit was firm and allowed for the passage of most of the Division's regiments to the canal. At the canal the regiments established a weak bridgehead, which lacked anti-tank defences.

Sappers from 10th Company, under fire, began to build a bridge over the canal but quickly it was asserted that the length of bridge sections being used to construct the bridge were insufficient. Upon receiving wide bridge spans, the sappers were able to construct a covered footbridge as well as building a link that would carry the Dragoon's heavy equipment to the other side of the canal.

Rotmistrz Giery's squadron from the Dragoons was the first to cross and they moved to the south, followed swiftly by two further squadrons. The enemy put up weak resistance while the squadron to the right managed to advance on Stenbosch and there for a while lost radio contact with the rest of the formation. Because of the lack of a bridge, the tanks could not cross the canal and Bren Gun carriers fell from the link into the water. This put the Dragoons in a very dangerous position. Therefore the Brigade Commander ordered the Dragoons' commanding officer, *Rotmistrz* Kownas, to prepare for the reception of a squadron from 10 PSK and sections of the Podhalian Infantry Brigade (PBS) at the bridgehead during the night.

At dawn on 17 September 1944, in thick fog, the Dragoons' position came under continuous artillery and mortar fire, which heralded an enemy armoured car attack. This pushed the Dragoons, who suffered heavy casualties, back onto the southern bank of the canal. The thick fog and high earth banks, which ran along the canal, meant that the bridgehead did not help the Dragoons. In this attack the Dragoons' casualty rate was two officers and 72 other ranks dead and wounded. *Rotmistrz* Kownas was transferred to the 2nd Tank Regiment and was killed in 2nd Tank's next battle. Later that day 3BS regrouped. The returning Dragoons and 8BS formed up with advance units of 1st Tank and 10 PSK. The following day the formation forced a crossing over the Axel-Hulst Canal.[136]

After the German counter-attack the Poles had to concede that the enemy's defence was well organised. This caused Majewski to look at the Polish gains. The object of Majewski's formation became that of holding the territory gained on the previous day. The infantry was to be protected along a line which ran along the main road from Fort Ferdinand to Drieschouwen, which would also provide safety on the canal line. This task was to be performed by reserve tanks held ready for the purpose of counter-attacking as well as reconnoitring the end of the safety flank. 10 PSK minus 1st Squadron was sent to the disposition of Majewski. At around 08:00 hours 17 September 1944, 1st Squadron moved to the Dubosch and Kijkuit area on the Hulst Canal and reported to the commanding officer of BSP, who held the Fort Ferdinand region, ready for an offensive on the canal and beyond it. One platoon was deployed at the Dubosch crossing to reinforce a BSP company already fighting on the crossing while another company was sent to the Kijkuit crossing. The Germans had blown up all of the bridges along the canal. Enemy infantry heavily defended the northern bank of the canal with artillery fire, while both sides deployed machine guns. At Kijkuit the Germans were also using anti-tank guns. As a result of the unsuccessful attack by 10th Dragoons in the suburbs of Dubosch, new orders came during the afternoon.

The remainder of 10 PSK was assigned new tasks. 3rd Squadron throughout the day provided protection from the direction of Zuiddorpe and Fort Moerspuij without engaging the enemy. 3rd Squadron was not able to advance far along this direction because of damaged roads and the general flooding of the area. At 12:00 hours, 2nd Squadron was sent to reconnoitre to the northeast of the region with the object of taking St Jansteen, then to reconnoitre towards Kappelenburg and La Trompe. 2nd Squadron reached the town of Chuekje without meeting the enemy. There a platoon seized a bridge on the Papale Canal. The entire squadron came under heavy mortar and artillery fire from the direction of Hulst. Some of the following platoons moved onto St Jansteen where there was further fighting towards Hulst and La Trompe. Owing to anti-tank fire 2nd Squadron asserted that it was not possible to advance any further north. However the Poles continued to shell Hulst and an enemy position in the countryside, north of Hulst. Enemy infantry then began to withdraw north from the direction of La Clinge while La Trompe was cleared of the enemy. 2nd Squadron also destroyed two 75mm anti-tank guns, in addition to overrunning a mortar position where two prisoners were taken. At 18:00 hours, 2nd Squadron was ordered to return to a position of safety in the St Andries area. At dusk, 1st Squadron regrouped in the BSP region acting as self-propelled artillery.

On 17 September 1944 10 PSK suffered no losses while the enemy lost five 75mm or 88mm anti-tank-guns, one mortar, three machine gun positions and two prisoners. Throughout the day two tanks from Wasilewski's (CO 10 PSK) platoon during the fighting on the canal in the Dubosch area came under heavy anti-tank fire and machine gun fire. This caused the Second-in-Command's tank to become stuck on the canal bank. After several hours of attempting to rescue the tank in the very teeth of enemy fire; tanks, one from 3rd Squadron and a platoon form 1st Squadron, finally managed to get the tank free.

On 18 September 1944 information from Skibinski's group revealed that, as a result of the previous day's operations (holding occupied lands against enemy attacks), the formation could not move beyond the Axel-Hulst Canal line. The inability to advance further was simply due to the pressure that the Allies put upon the enemy. The Germans responded by giving a more determined and stubborn defence than had been expected. The failure of the Dragoons' offensive merely encouraged the enemy in its determination to resist the Allied advance.

1st Squadron, which had been put at the disposition of the CO of BSP since early morning (18 September 1944) had been shelling the enemy from a position along the canal bank. The resulting fire from 1st Squadron was that infantry was able to force a crossing over the canal, which led to firing from both sides of the canal. Wasilewski, during a briefing with Skibinski, proposed a forced crossing of the canal in the Kijkuit area. Wasilewski's plan was that two squadrons of Cromwell tanks would be used to fire on the canal, giving cover for a company of infantry who could seize the far side of the canal. Once the crossings was completed the way for the sappers to build a bridge, which would bear the weight of tanks, would be open. Skibinski accepted the idea.

At 13:30 hours, 3rd Squadron took a position to begin the previously mentioned operation. However immediately a problem arose. The terrain did not allow for the squadron and its platoons to be deployed in its entirety and was forced to move along the canal road but came under anti-tank fire from the direction of Kijkuit. The platoons were hit several times causing the deaths of two soldiers and the loss of a Cromwell tank. Eventually 3rd Squadron was able to subdue the source of the enemy fire. 2nd Squadron (Wasilewski's squadron) with 1st Squadron moved to the right flank. Both squadrons then lay down heavy fire directly beyond the canal, which destroyed points of enemy resistance and caused enemy anti-tank fire to break off firing. However, heavy mortar and artillery fire continued to fall upon the crossing and onto 10 PSK's position. 1st Squadron meanwhile remained sandwiched between the Fort Ferdinand and the Dubosch crossing.

At 15:00 hours a general order from Skibinski was verbally dispatched to 10 PSK and other units operating along the canal. BSP, with a squadron from 10 PSK, were ordered to immediately force the Axel-Hulst Canal in the Kijkuit area. A bridgehead was to be seized and held in preparation of 10th Sapper Company building a bridge over the canal. Once the bridge was built, enemy resistance was to be rolled as far west as possible along the canal where it was hoped that a second bridge could be built in the Dubosch region. 10 PSK minus one squadron was required to support and cover the forcing of the canal and building of the bridge in the Kijkuit area.

During the afternoon infantry units from BSP moved to the canal. There under covering fire from Cromwell tanks and artillery, several BSP companies were able to cross the canal and take prisoners in the bridgehead area. The sappers immediately began to prepare to work on the bridge but mortar and artillery fire was so intense that it was impossible to continue the work. The sappers suffered heavy casualties while 3rd Squadron (10 PSK) lost a Cromwell tank. The fighting for the bridge continued into the evening as the enemy's fierce fire refused to die down and the bridge remained unfinished. At 20:00 hours special orders were received concerning the area in front of the bridge. BSP and 10 PSK squadrons were ordered to hold the area in front of the bridge throughout the night (18–19 September 1944). At dawn the Poles launched a further offensive with three companies of infantry in a western direction and reorganised in the outskirts of Dubosch. A squadron from 10 PSK, which had crossed the sappers' bridge at 06:00 hours, covered the eastern flank of this offensive.

When dusk fell on 18 September 1944, 2nd and 3rd Squadrons (10 PSK) remained at their posts before the canal. 90% of their ammunition had been used in the fighting of that day. The squadrons, platoon by platoon, went to the rear to replenish their supplies, including ammunition, and then swiftly returned to their previous positions along the road. The crews slept in their tanks that night. 1st Squadron passed the night in a region, one kilometre from the Kijkuit crossing. Throughout the night the sappers completed the building of the bridge which allowed squadrons from 10 PSK to cross to the northern bank of the canal at 06:00 hours and begin their operations. 10 PSK's casualties for 18 September 1944 were two dead and two destroyed Cromwell tanks destroyed. The German casualty rate in the fighting with 10 PSK was three 75mm anti-tank guns, four cars, an ammunition dump and a half-tracked vehicle.

That evening, orders for operations for the next day (19 September 1944) were issued. 1st Squadron was moved to the disposition of the commanding officer of BSP with the task of moving to the canal and supporting the Podhalian offensive to the west of the north side of the canal. After a bridgehead had been created by BSP in Dubosch, the squadron was to move to the disposition of 8BS, which was moving further to the northwest in an attempt to reach the Zeldenrust-Rondeputten-Pavliet-De-Steevons area, which was cut through with ditches and dykes.

2nd Squadron was to support 9BS's offensive on the far side of the canal to the west, heading towards Axel. 3rd Squadron was to cross the bridge first at 06:00 hours, occupy Kijkuit and ensure the safety of the whole area from the northeast. The reconnaissance platoon in the area of the Kijkuit crossing was to ensure the security of the entire operation from the east side of the canal. The offensive as already discussed began at 06:00 hours when 3rd Squadron crossed the bridge, built by Polish sappers, over the canal during the night of 18–19 September 1944 and captured Kijkuit. In the fighting for Kijkuit, 2nd Squadron destroyed four German anti-tank guns, took twenty prisoners and captured a 50mm gun.

From Kijkuit, 3rd Squadron moved on to reconnoitre to the north and northeast. 1st Squadron after crossing the canal began to work in co-operation with BSP towards the west. The nature of this joint operation was support which meant that a platoon of tanks was assigned to each infantry company. In very thick fog, 1st Squadron, moving with infantry, reached the Dubosch area and the riflemen began to organise a bridgehead.

Upon the arrival of 8BS in the Dubosch area, 1st Squadron and BSP came under the command of 8BS's commanding officer, who was conducting an offensive to the northwest. The enemy did not put up a very strong defence, being somewhat surprised by the arrival of the Polish formation. The infantry was able to take many prisoners whilst 1st Squadron destroyed a self-propelled gun, an ammunition towing truck and defeated a patrol of German officers armed with *Panzerfausts*. At midday 8BS moved to its designated area (1½ kilometres to the south of Zaamslag) and settled in it to defend the area. 1st Squadron provided cover from the east and southeast of the position.

2nd Squadron it its turn crossed the bridge at 10:00 hours, carrying infantry (9BS) on its tanks. The squadron reached the Axel area before any enemy opposition was met. At the moment of meeting the enemy, both infantry and armour sprang into action. Two armoured platoons with a company from 9BS moved to Axel while the remainder of the squadron with infantry support attacked from the east. This prevented the enemy from withdrawing to the north. During this operation about 40 prisoners were taken (including two officers) and an anti-tank gun was destroyed.

At 12:30 hours, 3rd Squadron was required to push on from the Kijkuit region towards the northwest into the Magrette region for the purpose of reconnoitring the main Axel-Terneuzen Road. 3rd Squadron, meeting little opposition, easily got to Magrette but, in the hamlet of Doornhof, the squadron encountered anti-tank and strong mortar fire. A platoon of armour was sent from Doornhof to reconnoitre a bridge further north in the Spui area. The bridge was found to have been destroyed by the enemy. Upon reaching the Spui region, the squadron shelled the enemy until dusk and was able to defeat an infantry motorcycle attack. 2nd Squadron after capturing Axel with 9BS reached the left flank of 3rd Squadron's operational area and began to fire upon the enemy in the town of Schapenhout. Meanwhile the regimental reconnaissance platoon, after advancing to 3rd Squadron's position in the northwest, was able to take over some of the squadron's sectors.

At 16:00 hours Sherman tanks from 1st Tank Regiment (Polish) were able to provide covering fire for Skibinski's operation from the east and northeast, thus relieving the reconnaissance platoon, which then linked up with Wasilewski's squadron in Axel. 1st Squadron once again came under the orders of 8BS and began to reconnoitre from Rondeputten, towards the north. The group met a platoon of Cromwells under the command of Second Lieutenant Sztumpf, a platoon of Bren Gun carriers, a platoon of infantry from 8BS and a squad of sappers, all moved towards Zaamslag. The reconnaissance platoon fired upon an enemy column of about ten vehicles, which were towing artillery pieces from the east and heading towards Othene; the enemy had already abandoned Zaamslag. Upon the fall of dusk this mixed group moved to 8BS's region.

1st Squadron passed the night within a formation of self-propelled artillery aligned with 8BS. 2nd Squadron took a night position, one kilometre north from Axel while 3rd Squadron formed a protective harbour in the Magrette region. During the evening 10 PSK received renewed supplies of ammunition, food and fuel. During the day's operations, the regiment had only suffered two wounded: Corporals Matuszak and Salo. The German losses to 10 PSK were quite incredible: five 75mm anti-tank guns, one self-propelled artillery piece, two field guns, one 50mm gun, two half-tracked tractors, one ammunition truck, five artillery towing tractors, three cars and eighty prisoners. Later during the day Majewski sent his thanks to all the squadron commanders of 10 PSK for their co-operation with 3BS.

Throughout the night of 19–20 September 1944 Allied artillery heavily shelled the area of the Terneuzen port. The enemy in turn shelled 10 PSK during the night. The enemy in the area of the 1st Polish Armoured Division, once its defences on the Axel-Hulst Canal was broken, ceased to operate as a single unit. Instead the Germans began to make their way towards the northern ports with the purpose of evacuating by sea. From early morning (20 September 1944) 10 PSK's armoured squadrons operating with infantry battalions received orders to reconnoitre as directed by the infantry commanders. 1st Squadron moving from Zaamslag went to Reuzenhoek while 3rd Squadron, via Spui, moved in the direction of Terneuzen. 2nd Squadron which had been under the orders of 9BS's commanding officer, received orders from Wasilewski instructing it to move to the northeast via Zontepand-Het Ver to the Vogelfort region where there was a chance of intercepting a German column withdrawing north to the ports.

1st and 3rd Squadrons both moved without incident to the areas which they had been ordered to. 2nd Squadron moved quickly to the Vogelfort region where it did indeed intercept withdrawing German units and promptly opened fire upon the column. 2nd Squadron's fire destroyed two military buses full of infantry as well as three anti-tank guns in addition to taking about 30 prisoners.

At 10:00 hours 10 PSK received orders to clear the region from the north to the main road, which ran through Zaamslag to the east. 1st and 3rd Squadrons left the Rifle Brigades and returned to their parent regiment in order to receive orders for the coming offensive. 1st Squadron was to clear an area, which ran from co-ordinate 365 on its eastern border to co-ordinate 300 on its western side, in reference to the above-mentioned routes to the north from the southern shores of the Schelde Gulf. 2nd Squadron was to move from the Vogelfort region to the north and northeast while 3rd Squadron was to move to the town of Kampen from where it was to operate northeast of Klootserzande and the port of Waalsoorden.

1st Squadron operating in a wide platoon formation over a network of sandy roads reached their operational area on the banks of the Schelde Gulf in the De Griete region by 13:30 hours without any problems. On its way the squadron even managed to destroy an 88mm anti-tank gun. From the banks of the gulf, 1st Squadron opened fire with great effect on the sandbanks of Middelplaat (2 ½ kilometres to the northeast of Terneuzen) where four huge sea-going barges, crammed with infantry, were stuck fast. The fire from the Polish tanks destroyed the barges and the enemy (about a battalion) had little chance of escaping as the sandbanks were totally isolated from the shore.

The commander of 1st Squadron also directed artillery fire upon the sandbanks. The tide, which came in at 16:30 hours, completed the work of the Cromwell tanks and the artillery. A few of the enemy were rescued later by motorboat and it is believed that about 600 German soldiers lost their lives on the sandbanks that day. By the end of the afternoon, 1st Squadron had exhausted its ammunition therefore Wasilewski sent more to its half-track. At 17:00 hours the squadron moved to Rapenburg (already captured by 10 PSK). 2nd Squadron reached the Kampers area and then moved further north in order to reach the shore of the Zeedorp Gulf, moving via Koningsdijk and Ossenisse. Along the route the squadron took ten prisoners and from Molenhoek and Krever Hill areas it fired upon a sea-going barge, which was in the middle of the gulf, and destroyed it.

At dusk Polish infantry patrols moved to the banks of the gulf which allowed 2nd Squadron to move to Rapenburg. 3rd Squadron during the day destroyed two anti-aircraft and took eighteen prisoners in the Kloosterzande region before moving onto their objective in Waalsoorden Port. After handing over the port to the infantry, the squadron moved to Rapenburg. The capture of the port in Terneuzen was a most extraordinary escapade. Lieutenant Bronisław Sachse (Intelligence Officer 10 PSK) with Corporal Kwiencinski swam out to a German vessel in the Kniatershoek area. The German boat turned out to be a fully equipped patrol boat which had been abandoned because its diesel engine was broken and on fire. Sachse and Kwiencinski with great presence of mind managed to float the boat over to the shore where mechanics from 10 PSK put out the fire and repaired the engine. Then Polish infantry was packed into the boat and set sail for Terneuzen. At Terneuzen, German artillery, fooled by the correct livery, actually guided the boat into port. At the last possible movement the Polish infantry rushed from the boat, stormed the German position and captured the port.

By evening all of 10 PSK was quartered in Rapenburg while the reconnaissance platoon made an inspection of the area to the east of the shores of the Graaw region. 10 PSK during the day did not receive any losses in either men or equipment but the German losses to the regiment were grievous, losing not only the port but many men and much equipment and is listed as follows: 60 prisoners (including three officers) five anti-tank guns, one anti-aircraft gun complete with trailer, two anti-tank guns complete with trailers, four sea-going barges destroyed, two sea-going barges damaged, one captured patrol boat, two lorries, one motorcycle and one infantry battalion (600 men approx) killed on the sandbanks at Middelplaat. To sum up the recent operations, Polish units had moved from the Gulf of Schelde to the sector from Waalsoorden and onto the port of Terneuzen, destroying any enemy activities on the way.

On 21 September 1944 Skibinski thanked 10 PSK for their co-operation in a difficult yet successful operation. At 12:30 10 PSK returned to their usual formation and moved in a normal formation. At 15:00 hours the regiment moved to Kemseke via Luntershoek, Kijkuit, Drije Hoefijzers, Heikant, Hellestraat and Stekene. In Kemseke, the squadrons received orders from Wasilewski concerning their next deployments, which established 1st Squadron in Drie Shouwen, 2nd Squadron in La Trompe and 3rd Squadron in Meuleken. 10 PSK established quarters in Meuleken and spent several days there, taking the opportunity to repair their equipment and weapons in addition to taking a well-deserved rest.

10 PSK Casualty Rate in the Fighting on the Axel-Hulst Canal: 15–22 September 1944

Personnel	Officers	Ranks	Total
Killed	—	2	2
Wounded	—	5	5
Total	—	7	7

Equipment State	Cromwells	Stuarts	Other	Total
Beyond Repair	3	—	—	3
Repairable	—	—	—	—
Total	3	—	—	3

After the fighting on the Axel-Hulst Canal, the Poles at rest took stock of the situation in Europe. During an unceasing pursuit of the enemy throughout the first twenty days of September the Allies had reached the Siegfried Line. Most of France and Belgium had been liberated while a deep wedge had been driven into the enemy defences in Holland as a result of the Arnhem offensive. Sadly the airborne operation in the Arnhem region was not to realise its objectives despite the bravery of the forces involved. The Allied communication lines were fully stretched by September 1944 as a result of not being able to take advantage of the French and Belgian ports along the northern coast which had either been destroyed or were still in the hands of the enemy.

By mid-September the Polish 1st Armoured Division was putting the final touches to capturing and clearing regions in the Axel-Hulst area. The command headquarters were in Lokeren, 10 BK *panc* was in the St Nicolas region and 3BS was in the Axel area. 3BS continued to receive orders, which required the patrolling, and maintaining of order in the captured regions. It was also a time for resting and re-organising after two weeks of hectic movement and fighting, before moving on once more.

Once again the Division was feeling the pinch concerning the lack of experienced soldiers. On 24 September 1944 10 PSK received back into their numbers three officers and ten other ranks who had been lightly wounded in previous fighting, in addition to eleven Polish volunteers from France who lacked military service. The following day, twenty-five Poles who had been conscripted into the German Army, captured by the Allies and now wished to fight for the Polish Army, were sent by base to 10 PSK. Not one of the twenty-five had any experience with tanks.

As a consequence of the shortage of experienced tank crews, General Maczek decided to re-organise the structure of 10 PSK's armoured squadrons (HQ Squadron, 1st, 2nd and 3rd Squadrons, which operated in platoons). The swiftest way to achieve this was to strip the anti-aircraft platoon of its personnel and then pass them onto the squadrons. By this stage of the war the Allies were virtually masters of the air and Maczek felt that air attacks posed little threat to the Polish armour. The re-organisation of 10 PSK had begun in Thielt but this had been limited to matters of supply but as in the European campaign the problem of supplying the front line squadrons with trained men continued to plague the Division.

On September 1944 preparations for operations in southern Holland began. For the 1st Polish Armoured Division this meant moving from the command of II Canadian Corps to the command of I British Corps of the 1st Canadian Army (28/9/44). During this time Wasilewski received orders from Maczek concerning operations for 29 September 1944. The situation was that Antwerp, minus the dock area and the west of the city and the River Schelde, was already in the hands of the Allies. On the right flank, the 2nd British Army had driven

The Watch on the Rhine – one of the Division's M4 Shermans along the banks of the River Waal (Rhine), Netherlands, 1945.
Imperial War Museum B10996

a wedge from beneath Nijmegen which linked them to Allied airborne troops who were fighting for a crossing over the River Rhine as far as Arnhem. The 1st Canadian Army's task was to conquer the rest of southern Holland to beyond the River Maas which would cover the left flank of the 2nd British Army's wedge and open the port at Antwerp. The opening of the port in Antwerp would be very important for the Allies as it would mean that the front close to the Rhine could be supplied far more directly than it had been previously.

The 1st Polish Armoured Division served under the command of I British Corps who were operating towards the towns of Tilberg and Breda. I Corps had to relieve XII British Corps, which had been deployed around the Eindhoven – S'Hertogenbosch region. I British Corps had been fighting in the north of Antwerp and to the east, along the Antwerp – Turnhout Canal. Meanwhile the 49th British Infantry Division had seized a bridgehead higher up on the Antwerp – Turnhout Canal in the Ryckervorsel region. It was asserted that there were three enemy divisions defending the northern outskirts of Antwerp and the Antwerp – Turnhout Canal. 711th Infantry Division with the 14th Machine-Gun Battalion with units of *Panzer* Mk IVs defended the sector to the west of Antwerp. 346th Infantry Division defended the position to the east of 711th Infantry Division to St Leonard while 719th Infantry Division defended the eastern sector.

From a wide cross-section of recently captured prisoners it was learnt that the above enemy divisions were, in reality, gravely weakened and contained elements of what were considered second-rate soldiers. The intention of the enemy was to oppose all Allied operations, using at every crossing point anti-tank weapons and other water obstacles by destroying bridges and leaving the Allies to struggle over or around canals and dykes in the area. The 1st Polish Armoured Division by now concentrated in a region east of Antwerp with its reconnaissance regiment, 10 PSK, in position in Borsbeek, ready and waiting for its next operational role. The 2nd Anti-Tank Battalion was also in position waiting with the regiment.

At 14:00 hours following a briefing, Maczek gave his operational orders: the Division was to capture Tilburg and the crossing in the same region. The operation was to be conducted in two phases. In the first phase 10 PSK in co-operation with 3BS was to capture Merxplas and then the Lipseinde region. In the second phase 10 BK *panc* was to capture Tilburg and the crossings in the area. 10 PSK with the Anti-tank battalion moved to 3Bs's position in preparation for their joint offensive. At 19:00 hours, following a briefing between Skibinski and Wasilewski, the following orders were given:

1. Reconnaissance missions to be carried out upon reaching forward units of the 49th British Infantry Division

2. Reconnoitre for an entry to Merxplas from the south

3. The operations to begin tomorrow (29 September 1944) crossing the bridgehead on the Antwerp – Turnhout Canal from both flanks at 08:30 hours.

At 07:00 hours on 29 September 1944 10 PSK moved out to begin their operation and reached the canal crossing at the revised time of 09:30 hours. After crossing the canal 10 PSK were ready for action. By 10:00 10 PSK had made contact with forward Allied elements in the area. The direction of the Polish armour was dictated by the situation found on the front line. British infantry was attacking Depot de Mendicite and was having difficulty in achieving their objective, therefore 2nd and 3rd Squadrons were sent to support the British offensive. Further action by the armoured squadrons continued to depend upon the nature of the enemy's defences, which appeared to be in the direction in which 3rd Squadron had moved to and the rest of the regiment headed in the same direction. 2nd Squadron at 09:30 hours had already established contact with the commander of the British Infantry Brigade, which was engaged in a mixed infantry and armoured attack on the industrial complex of Depot de Mendicite. The British commander did not want additional units moving with those already allocated to the task at a time when the battle was intensifying. This meant that 2nd Squadron could not advance any further than beyond the main road.

As a result, the commander of 2nd Squadron sent a platoon forward to seek forward infantry units. This probing action was made impossible by anti-tank fire coming simultaneously from several places. This left two men dead: Sergeant Kwiencien and Lance Corporal Trochimowicz and one man wounded: Private Rokicki. In addition, a Cromwell tank was damaged. Attempts to enter Depot de Mendicite, from both the north and the south were impossible because the terrain was soft and riven with dykes.

At 17:00 hours, after the Allied artillery barrage, the British infantry once again went on the offensive and this time 2nd Squadron went with them. The squadron moved forward as the infantry spread through the buildings, firing upon enemy infantry and artillery positions. The enemy counter firing was tremendous, consisting of mainly mortar and artillery, which caused serious losses amongst the British infantry. On the right flank, 9BS with a unit from 24th Uhlans launched an offensive, which had the effect of relieving most of 2nd Squadron's problems in its offensive. At dusk 2nd Squadron was ordered by Wasilewski to cease firing and return to 10 PSK's lines. Following a roundabout route, 2nd Squadron returned to 10 PSK at 22:00 hours.

3rd Squadron after crossing the bridge over the canal in the morning, moved to the east and reached British infantry in the region 965 076. The British were on the defensive with no intention of going over to the offensive. 500 metres further the squadron came under heavy mortar fire while the lead tank ran into a mine and then was hit by *Panzerfaust* fire. Shortly after 10:30 hours, Wasilewski with the rest of the regiment arrived in the area.

From reports and observations it was possible to establish the enemy's position. A line had been built from 972 076 to the canal to the south, as well as running beyond the canal in the region of 097 068, which was strongly held by infantry. From nearby woods in the Luystenborg area the Germans were using mortars and artillery fire against the Allies. During the early afternoon infantry units from BSP covered by an artillery barrage moved towards 3rd Squadron's position. 1st Squadron remained as an extension of 3rd Squadron, on the left and both squadrons gave support to BSP's offensive. In the next round of fighting BSP suffered heavy casualties from mortars, mines and snipers. The tanks were able to evacuate the wounded, which included BSP's Adjutant, Captain Jan Rozwadowski. The commander of the reconnaissance patrol from 3rd Squadron, Sergeant Jerczak, was killed by a sniper while trying to rescue a tank stricken by a mine. Just before evening the enemy opposition weakened and the Allied offensive was able to advance. 1st and 3rd Squadrons advanced according to the operational plan.

Wasilewski pushed on beyond 1st Squadron while the remainder of the regiment owing to difficult terrain moved along the shortest route beyond the forward units of 10 PSK. 3rd Squadron advanced parallel to the canal and reached the main road, which led to Merxplas. From there the squadron turned north and reached Wolfsputten. Along the way the squadron destroyed two anti-tank guns and took several prisoners. 1st Squadron moved parallel to 3rd Squadron on the left without any great opposition. To the west of 1st Squadron, the fire of advancing Allied units could be clearly seen. At dusk, 10 PSK received orders to make a position on the canal (2 ½ kilometres to the southwest of Merxplas). Before dark the squadrons were already in the area. At 22:00 hours, 2nd Squadron rejoined the regiment and shortly after fresh supplies arrived. During this time Private Guzowski was wounded when a group of enemy infantry was found in the Polish lines; about twenty prisoners were taken by the Poles.

10 PSK's casualties for the day were three dead, three wounded, one Cromwell tank destroyed and one damaged. The enemy casualties as a result of action by 10 PSK were thirty-five prisoners taken, one anti-tank gun destroyed, two 37mm guns destroyed and a car destroyed. During the night, orders for the next day's offensive came from Skibinski.

The plan for the following day was that the Wolfsputten-Merxplas axis was to be attacked and two crossings seized one kilometre to the north of Merxplas. The object of the offensive was to establish a base for further action towards the north. This was achieved with the deployment of BSP who were to capture Merxplas and the next crossing to the east and also protect the left flank of the offensive. 10 PSK was to provide protection for the 3BS offensive's eastern flank while closing the western exit of the woods that lay to the east of Merxplas. The rest of the regiment was to co-operate with BSP in an attack to the north leaving Merxplas from the northeast.

The offensive was set to begin from co-ordinate level 09 at 08:30 hours on 30 September 1944. At 06:30 hours Wasilewski received the following operational orders: 1st Squadron was to act as vanguard beyond the axis of the crossroads, three kilometres to the south of Merxplas – Obstal, the squadron was to seize a crossing one kilometre to the northeast of Merxplas. 3rd Squadron was to advance beyond 1st Squadron into the Wolfsputten region where they would be in position to cover the network of western exits from the woods in the region 013 110. The main task of the offensive was to reconnoitre the western exits from the woods. The regimental reconnaissance platoon was to move beyond 3rd Squadron and reach point 018 088 from where it could protect the northeast side of the offensive while a group to be known as 'Bober' (broad bean) a free ranging group under the direct command of Wasilewski was to reach point 015 100 where they were to protect the offensive from the east. Wasilewski with a platoon and 2nd Squadron was to advance beyond 1st Squadron's position.

At 08:00 hours 10 PSK moved to their starting place after experiencing difficulties owing to congestion along the route. On the Merxplas – Beersse road 10 PSK's column ran into enemy mortar fire which killed Lieutenant Nikodem Kluz, 2ic of 2nd Squadron and badly wounded Corporal Urbanowicz and Lance Corporals Imiolek and Klimkowski. In the Wolfsputten area and around the woods, 1st Squadron was attacked by enemy infantry armed with machine guns and *Panzerfausts*. 1st Squadron's task was made even more difficult because of the heavily wooden terrain that was also intersected with ditches and dykes. It was impossible to go around an enemy position or to bring up another squadron of armour. Therefore the squadron, firing heavily, stormed through the woods and any building that got into the way. A platoon of infantry moved with the armour and cleared the way, taking fifteen prisoners. After breaking the enemy resistance at a farm, east of Wolfsputten, 1st and 3rd Squadrons moved on, in order to begin their offensives.

1st Squadron whilst moving to Obstal fired constantly upon the enemy while hard by them; Wasilewski's Squadron and a platoon of riflemen were clearing the region. As 1st Squadron was moving onto Obstal it ran into anti-tank fire. Sergeant Laskowski's tank was hit but without casualties. The crew were able to leave the area under the cover of fire and smoke. However the BSP formation fighting in the northern outskirts of Merxplas had run into difficulties. 10 PSK's advance had been rapid and was already in front of the infantry which meant that Wasilewski was able to rush 1st Squadron to 004 117 and seize the crossing there.

2nd Squadron was sent to the northern outskirts of Merxplas. 3rd Squadron continued with its original task and was already firing on the northern side of the canal. The *Bober* group also made a courageous sally on Koekhoven in order to assert the presence of the enemy. 1st Squadron reached point 006 112 but was attacked from the left by anti-tank fire. Lieutenant Borzemski's tank was destroyed and Lance Corporal Gustaw Hodzidło was killed. 2nd Squadron once again gave covering fire while tanks from Wasilewski's squadron moved to 1st Squadron's position and rescued the situation. In addition to providing for 1st Squadron, 2nd Squadron also captured the northern outskirts of Merxplas and was able to move to the rear of the enemy, thus making the infantry's job of capturing Merxplas much easier.

1st Squadron after their rescue pressed forward and surprised a party of Germans preparing to destroy a crossing. The crossing was captured while two vehicles containing explosives were destroyed. 1st Squadron topped this by taking five prisoners including an officer who had important documents in his possession. 10 PSK after completing all of their tasks took up a position on the captured bridge over the canal, which guarded the right flank of 3BS and waited there for further orders.

At 15:00 hours further orders arrived. The 3rd Rifle Brigade formation was to continue towards Lipseinde. This meant that 10 PSK was to reconnoitre the woods to the north from the captured crossing in the Merxplas area. 10 PSK also had to reconnoitre for a crossing in the direction of Zondereigen. 1st, 2nd and 3rd Squadrons were mobilised to undertake this task. 1st Squadron was ordered to the main Lipseinde road with purpose of seizing the crossing in the Zondereigen. This was done but almost immediately from the nearby woods the squadron came under attack from infantry supported by strong anti-tank fire. 1st Squadron linked up with BSP and a squadron from 24th Uhlans. Together with further assistance from 10 PSK's reconnaissance squadron it led an offensive through the woods. 2nd Squadron then moved towards the fighting and came across a withdrawing enemy column. The squadron opened fire and destroyed vehicles and captured an officer and five other ranks. After this the squadron lost its sense of direction and 3rd Squadron's axis and so struck out as far as Strikken. The result of this move was the capture of two crossings at 022 152 and 018 152.

As a result of 2nd Squadron's mistake, 3rd Squadron was left heading directly into the woods where it had to fight hordes of enemy infantry. Upon gaining an exit from the woods, the squadron came up behind 2nd Squadron and together reached Strikken without any opposition. The rapid movement of the squadrons cut off the enemy's withdrawal route and further reached the German rear, which no doubt contributed to the enemy's defeat and the clearing of the T'rond Punt Wood.

1st Squadron's offensive moved at a much slower tempo but enjoyed as much success. To the north of the woods, the squadron with infantry, captured a gun battery of 155mm guns, which were used against enemy positions by Polish artillery the following night. As dusk fell it was decided that the infantry should stay put while 1st Squadron was ordered to move up to Lipseinde in order to link up with 2nd Squadron. Even though the move to Lipseinde was relatively short, the squadron was able to destroy several enemy vehicles and take fifty prisoners. Further action was impossible because of the dark and the roads were blocked with either destroyed or abandoned enemy equipment. It was noted by lights and firelight that the enemy was taking advantage of the dark to slip away and take up defensive positions elsewhere.

2nd Squadron was relieved during the evening by tanks from 24th Uhlans which allowed 1st and 2nd Squadrons to link up with 10 PSK in a region, two kilometres to the north of Merxplas. 10 PSK's losses for the day were three dead, three wounded and one tank destroyed. The German losses to 10 PSK were eighty prisoners, six 155mm guns, one 37mm gun, one mortar, eleven cars, three motorcycles and eight trailers.

The loss of the Merxplas region was a blow for the Germans but still they continued to defend their positions, bridge by bridge, which led to many individual operations and battle along the road to Tilburg. It was noted by the Poles that defensively, the enemy held all of the cards owing to the flat terrain which denied the Poles artillery observation points and gave their tanks short fields of fire, while the Germans lurked in dykes and canals and were able to defend every bridge head. The next line of opposition lay along the Dutch border and was defended by the 719th Infantry Division commanded by General-Major Sievers.

At 08:00 hours, 1 October 1944, 3BS went into action with the tasks of capturing 1) Zondereigen and 2) Baarle-Nassau. 10 PSK was to go into action operating along the east flank of 3BS. 3BS's offensive had failed. From Zondereigen, the enemy had throughout the night, led stubborn resistance in a line running from the main road to the church spire, while the west flank reached Height 017 160 where the enemy was ensconced in bunkers. Likewise there were reports of strong anti-tank fire along the Dutch coast to the east. This led to a mixed group of infantry and armour (10 BK *panc*) attacking the enemy while 10 PSK with a company of infantry was to attempt an outflanking movement in the Ginhoven area with the object of capturing northern parts of Zondereigen and reconnoitre the Dutch frontier to the north of Zondereigen. At 14:00 hours, 10 PSK left its position and very quickly reached Ginhoven, picking up infantry support en route. From Ginhoven, 10 PSK met with some rather futile anti-tank fire from the northwest. At 14:30 hours the offensive began properly.

2nd Squadron, firing heavily, moved against Height 017 160 and reached the first buildings in Zondereigen. The infantry support followed closely behind the tanks and by taking full advantage of the ceasing of enemy tank fire broke the resistance of the enemy, cleared the area and took prisoners. The enemy replied with continuous mortar fire and also began to shell the Polish position. During this time, 1st Squadron moved to the right towards the Dutch frontier (towards the east) without meeting any real enemy opposition. Unfortunately some of the tanks became stuck in the marshy terrain. The squadron left one platoon behind and began advancing to the northeast and was able to link up with 2nd Squadron.

The Polish fire from both 1st and 2nd Squadrons in Zondereigen was extremely effective and the Germans began to realise that they were endangered from the rear and began to withdraw selected units. Some of the German units tried to hide in buildings but this served no purpose as the Polish 2nd Assault Battalion blew up the buildings. The Germans opened fire with artillery which destroyed two Cromwell tanks and a German tank but despite this, the Poles only suffered one man wounded: Sergeant Tkaczyk, who was only slightly wounded. 2nd Squadron with infantry support managed to clear the suburbs and moved towards the church. Wasilewski's squadron took up a position by the chapel at 025 160 while 1st Squadron provided protection from the north at position 023 163.

3rd Squadron took advantage of the enemy retreat and began to reconnoitre along the Zondereigen road, towards the northeast. Near dusk the squadron had reached the Dutch frontier where they encountered enemy infantry supported by a field gun and anti-tank fire. 3rd Squadron found the fight difficult as they could not leave the road and were therefore exposed to *Panzerfaust* fire. The squadron's commander's tank was hit, leaving Captain Herman Cieslinski and Corporal Olszowy wounded. 3rd Squadron continued to return fire, firing so heavily that eventually the enemy was obliged to cease firing and withdraw. The tanks in a surprise attack, moved swiftly upon the Germans, destroyed two 155mm guns and killing their crews. After this the squadron remained in the area until infantry and tanks from 24th Uhlans relieved it after dark. During the night 10 PSK was shelled by enemy artillery, which hit a captured German tank.

The following day the Poles received an information communication concerning the state of the enemy's defences. The Germans fighting the Poles were asserted to be principally the 719th Infantry Division and was to continue to be so for the immediate future. In addition, German paratroopers (II/6 *Fallschirm*) had entered the area together with three companies of infantry and a mortar company during the early hours of the morning (02:00) 1 October 1944. Furthermore a battalion of infantry had been moved from Germany to Tilburg and had fought at Galen and later then at Reusell before moving into the Polish sector. A prisoner also revealed that to the right of his battalion was a battalion of the *Luftwaffe* Field Division Hoffman. The prisoner also underlined the fact that there were eighteen mortars in the area where he had been captured. It was generally considered that the enemy strength amounted to three average sized battalions and that as the fighting proceeded towards Germany itself, the battle for the enemy would become one of principal and that German resistance would become even more stubborn than it had been previously. A Divisional report was also received which stated that since the offensive in Antwerp, the Davison had captured twenty five officers and 609 other ranks. In the last two days of September, the Division had captured four officers and 218 other ranks on 30 September 1944 and seventeen officers and 227 other ranks on 29 September 1944.

It was decided that the 3rd Rifle Brigade formation was to move to the Dutch frontier on 1 October 1944 and at 10:00 hours, the following day begin further operations towards Baarle-Nassau. 10 BK *panc* on 1 October 1944 tried to capture the railway station, five kilometres south of Baarle-Nassau but failed despite fighting all night. At 09:00 hours, 2 October 1944, 10 BK *panc* renewed its attack against the railway station. The enemy, about a battalion in strength, was identified as being elements of the 719th Infantry Division, reinforced by the remaining units of 203rd *Ersatz* Battalion as well as elements of 331st Division. After receiving its operation orders 10 PSK moved out at 08:45 hours on 2 October 1944. While already on the march, information was received from the reconnaissance platoon to the effect that in the direction of 3rd Squadron's march, the enemy had throughout the night organised strong defences and that the Polish advance guard was already fighting along the Dutch frontier. 3rd Squadron reached the intersection of the route (one kilometre to the northeast of Zondereigen) that it was to follow. There the squadron found three wrecked tanks belonging to 24th Uhlans as well as dug in infantry.

As a result of the terrain being soaked and intersected with ditches in addition to being under artillery and anti-tank fire, 3rd Squadron established a firing position and began to shell the German positions. While the tanks were establishing their firing positions, Second Lieutenant Franciszek Rozwadowski's tank was hit by anti-tank fire and set alight. Nobody was hurt but any further advance was ruled out. The remainder of 10 PSK remained stuck in the Zondereigen region, under heavy artillery fire with 10 BK *panc* also finding itself in a similar uncomfortable position.

General Maczek ordered a cessation of any further action; the offensive was to continue only after aerial and artillery bombardments. The Division waited for its support which came in the form of an aerial bombardment, led by Spitfires and Typhoons. After the aerial bombardment came an artillery barrage. However as soon as 3rd Squadron tried to move again it came under heavy anti-tank fire. Once more a tank was lost but without any casualties. The assault platoon had lost a tank which caught fire, killing its commanding officer, Second Lieutenant Raczynski and his driver, in addition to three crewmen being wounded. The enemy fire intensified but the squadrons were able to beat them off. Only the anti-tank fire caused the Polish tank crews any real alarm. In the region where Wasilewski's squadron was fighting, a tank from the reconnaissance platoon was hit by anti-tank fire and Lance Corporal Zmyslany lost both of his legs.

The battle for the Dutch frontier continued into the afternoon of 2 October 1944 and from prisoner statements it was learnt that the enemy had partly withdrawn from the sector between co-ordinate levels 01 and 02. Even so the enemy's position had improved as during the night of 2–3 October 1944 it had received over ten anti-tank guns as well as several self-propelled guns, not previously seen in the area. During the morning of 3 October 1944, the 1st Polish Armoured Division tried to capture Baarle-Nassau and Baarle-Hertog. At 09:00 hours, 10 PSK moved out and reached Ginhoven. A small bridge over the canal at Heesbom-Heining (008 167) broke after the entry of 2nd Squadron and the squadron's reconnaissance platoon failed to locate an alternative crossing in the immediate area. This led to the canal being crossed using fencing and fascine to shore up the damaged bridge.

1st Squadron moving through the woods was able to bypass the enemy positions while 3rd Squadron with infantry support following immediately behind was able to clear the area and took about fifty prisoners. 10 PSK continued to move north as the enemy continued to withdraw but fighting all the way. However the Poles were still able to take prisoners as they went. At one point the tanks were outpacing the progress of 3BS's offensive, which greatly endangered the Cromwells of the forward armoured squadrons. Wasilewski suspended operations until 14:30 hours when the offensive moved on again. Eventually 2nd Squadron reached Reuth when it came under heavy artillery fire and further advance was impossible.

While 3rd Squadron with infantry support was clearing the woods in the Eikelen-Bosch area, 1st Squadron advanced with tanks from Wasilewski's squadron to the farm at 013 197 from where it could be seen that the infantry offensive had caused the enemy to flee from the woods and make for Baarle-Nassau from the northwest. It was also noticed that the Germans were withdrawing with assault guns. The squadron moved swiftly firing as it went. Its intention was to encircle Baarle-Nassau from the northwest. Once the squadron reached the suburbs of Baarle-Nassau it came under close range anti-tank fire, which damaged one tank.

1st Squadron responded with such violence that the enemy was swiftly silenced. In addition the squadron destroyed a self-propelled gun. After reaching the intersection of the main road in the northwest of Baarle-Nassau, the squadron set up a patrol, which passed through the burning buildings of the area. The fires were so fierce that the crews were scorched. At dusk the infantry moved into the area while 10 PSK held the Hoogeinde region.

Throughout the day's fighting 10 PSK suffered only three wounded and one Cromwell tank was damaged. The Germans facing 10 PSK suffered the loss of eighty prisoners, the destruction of a self-propelled gun and three motorcycles. More importantly 10 PSK captured a series of tactical orders and maps which gave the enemy's exact position. Much of this documentation should have never found its way onto the front line but the Poles made two points: the first was the main Polish tactic of surprise; Polish tanks appeared from directions that the Germans had supposed that the Poles would not be operating from and the second point was that

German officers, riding motorcycles, rode straight up to the Polish tanks in order to surrender. One can only surmise that the Germans had had enough of the war and wished to ingratiate themselves with the Allies.

On 4 October 1944 at 12:00 hours, General Maczek himself came to 10 PSK's position in the Hoogeinde farm area to personally give operational orders. Once again the 3BS formation including 10 PSK was to move towards the north and northwest, engaging and clearing the enemy as it moved. Once Wasilewski received his orders for 10 PSK, he gave operational orders to his squadrons. The squadrons were to outflank the withdrawing Germans and cut off their withdrawal routes. 10 PSK moved out on its mission at 14:00 hours. 2nd Squadron reached its position at an intersection at map reference 025 207 where a firing position was to be established. Immediately upon arriving at its position the squadron came under mortar and artillery fire. The infantry which had ridden upon the tanks dismounted and dug in. From its position 2nd Squadron's view towards Ulicotsche-Heide was perfect and it was able to report the presence of German tanks in the woods in the region (024 223). Wasilewski immediately changed 10 PSK's operational orders and sent 1st Squadron to act as a reserve to 2nd Squadron.

2nd Squadron and a platoon of armour from Wasilewski's squadron opened fire upon the woods. Only a single vehicle emerged from the woods. Wasilewski's tank crews destroyed a 105mm self-propelled gun while the rest of the enemy tanks and self-propelled guns were eventually forced to withdraw to the northwest as a result of the Polish shelling. By 17:40 the Goordonk wood was captured. 10 PSK was able to link up with 9BS and received orders to make a position for the night in a region two kilometres to the south of Baarle-Nassau. Units of the British 49th Infantry Division eventually captured the region around the Hoogeinde farm.

At 20:00 hours new orders came. As a result of every enemy offensive being supported by armour, 8BS, which was positioned in the woods one kilometre to the west of Baarle-Nassau, was forced to withdraw to Baarle-Nassau. Because of the possibility of further enemy attacks, 10 PSK moved to a region ½ kilometre to the southeast of Baarle-Nassau which then closed down the northeast to the enemy. At dawn, 5 October 1944, 10 PSK, under the orders of 3BS, advanced to a position which was to the fore of elements of 10th Dragoons, where they reached the Nijhoven road. There an infantry patrol reconnoitred the immediate area and was promptly fired upon by enemy infantry. As a result of this, the Poles were unable to establish if the German armoured units had withdrawn from the area or not. The 1st Polish Armoured Division prepared for an offensive along the Nijhoven Road in the direction of Alphen Boschoven. The 3BS formation was to move along the left hand side of the road.

After an artillery and aerial bombardment at 11:00 hours the offensive began. 10 PSK was to move to a region, one kilometre to the north of Baarle-Nassau and protect the offensives of 3BS at both Baarle-Boschoven and Alphen Boschoven before the enemy had time to counterattack. Despite the armoured support of the offensive; it came to a halt. The enemy stoutly defended Baarle-Boschoven and the Polish infantry could not advance while 2nd Squadron came under anti-tank fire. On 10 PSK's right flank, two Sherman tanks from 10 BK *panc* had been set on fire by German anti-tank fire. At 16:15 hours Skibinski ordered 10 PSK to break the enemy resistance in Baarle-Boschoven. This was done by striking at the left flank at Alphen Boschoven, moving through the woods across the railway line and attacking the west of the town.

At 16:30 hours 10 PSK went onto the offensive. 3rd Squadron quickly outpaced the Allied infantry and without any great opposition reached the railway line in the area and then the infantry moved to the fore of the armour. 1st and 2nd Squadrons crossed the railway line and surprised a group of retreating Germans. After an aerial bombardment; the enemy's resistance was entirely broken. The operation was completed within thirty minutes. The infantry cleared Alphen Boschoven while 10 PSK reconnoitred the eastern and western outskirts in order to ensure the safety of the new position. Once this was done the Baarle-Boschoven region was considered safe and the Poles made their position there.

The result of the fighting was that the 1st Polish Armoured Division broke the enemy's defence line of Esbeek- Poppel- Baarle-Nassau- Meerle and had captured the important Baarle-Nassau junction. The enemy withdrew to the woods of Alphen, to the region of Klein Hoef and into the woods to the east of the town. The enemy strength was estimated to have been two battalions of infantry supported by an artillery division as well as relatively large numbers of anti-tank guns. The entire German organisation was split into two battle groups (*Kampfgruppe*). The Polish 1st Armoured Division had driven a deep wedge into the enemy formation. As a result 10 PSK was sent to reconnoitre the area on 6 October 1944. In addition 1st Squadron was sent to a position where units of the British 49th Infantry Division felt threatened by the appearance of German *Tiger* and *Panther* tanks. 1st Squadron spent the day with the British units but the German tanks failed to reappear.

After several days of reconnaissance missions and minor skirmishes, the Division returned to the offensive on 27 October 1944. At 08:00 hours, in thick fog, 3BS went onto the offensive with the task of capturing the

Alphenschedijk region as well as the woods to the west of the town. 10 PSK provided the armoured support. 2nd Squadron in a single leap captured the woods, ½ kilometre to the north of Brakel. From the woods, the squadron shelled Brakel while two platoons of armour moved into the town, firing continuously at buildings. The enemy relied on a single machine gun and then without any further opposition the town was captured.

Wasilewski ordered 2nd Squadron to move on to Vijhuizen. 10 PSK began to suffer casualties when one of Wasilewski's tanks while crossing the Brakel railway line struck a mine. The tank was completely wrecked, killing Private Zbiegieł and wounding Sergeant Tomiak, Corporal Megiera and Privates Osipacz and Radola. Once again, 2nd Squadron firing as it went, reached Vijhuizen at 10:40 hours. There it took up a position guarding the west and southwest from enemy attacks. As the Poles advanced, the operation began to intensify and such was the success that by 11:00 hours it had moved towards Gilzen to prevent the enemy escaping from the area.

Upon reaching Gilzen, the Poles acted with caution. Before entering the town, they checked it from every side as it was known that a large group of infantry was withdrawing from the area. After checking the town 1st Squadron moved further on. The tanks reached the eastern side of Gilzen while the reconnaissance platoon and a platoon of infantry took Gilzen without any opposition. At around 13:40 hours, 2nd Squadron received orders to reconnoitre the southeast of Gilzen airfield and from the Verhoven region provide protection for further regimental operations from the west. 2nd Squadron captured Verhoven with no opposition. At the same time 1st and 3rd Squadrons were to cut the Tilburg-Breda road. 1st Squadron moved swiftly to the Gilzen airfield and onto Haanberg where a firing post was established. From its firing position 1st Squadron spotted a railway

Polish infantry wearing the British M44 pattern steel helmet emerge onto the banks of an unknown watercourse in the Netherlands, 1944. **Imperial War Museum B11442**

line and began to shell the area, destroying a Sherman tank previously captured by the enemy and pressed into use by the Germans. 3rd Squadron moved quickly from Vossenberg to Hultenseint where it took prisoners and captured a 155mm gun.

At 16:00 hours 1st Squadron received orders to reconnoitre a bridge over the Wilhelmina Canal in the Dongen area. It was not possible to move via the Rijen main road because the town was strongly defended. Instead the squadron moved directly across country, to the north, heading towards the canal but six tanks became stuck in the marshy ground. This meant that over half of the squadron's tanks were stuck and meant that the remainder of the squadron was forced to spend the night with the marooned armour. At dusk, 3rd Squadron received orders to reconnoitre Rijen but as the squadron approached the town it came under *Panzerfaust* fire. The squadron returned fire and was able to stifle enemy resistance before remaining in the area until late into the night when it was relieved by 24th Uhlans and Dragoons. 3rd Squadron then returned to 10 PSK's position in Gilzen. 10 PSK's casualties for the day were one dead, seven wounded and two Cromwell tanks destroyed. The German losses against 10 PSK were: eighty four prisoners, one 155mm gun and limber, one 75mm gun and limber, one mobile canteen complete with provisions, one lorry and one motorcycle combination.

Throughout the night of 27–28 October 1944 Wasilewski received orders for 10 PSK concerning the Division's offensive against the town of Breda. 10 PSK and 2nd Anti-Tank Battalion were to reconnoitre and seize crossings on the canal and on the River Mark, to the north of Breda. From there they were to move onto the next offensive in the direction of Moerdijk. Breda was to be passed from either the south or the east, depending upon the situation.

On 28 October 1944 at 09:30 hours, 10 PSK minus 1st Squadron moved on to the offensive and found that it was able to advance somewhat rapidly, overcoming any enemy resistance with infantry support. Whilst moving from Eikberg to Bavel, 2nd Squadron came under anti-tank fire and the tanks on the left flank reported the presence of Panzer MK IVs. By laying down a smoke screen the squadron sped past the enemy. 3rd Squadron which was moving north met dug in infantry in the Lage Aard region who promptly surrendered once the Polish tanks began to shell their positions. 2nd Squadron had moved on towards Bavel with the purpose of cutting the Bavel-Ginneken road and was continually fighting the enemy who used artillery and mortar fire. Eventually the Poles were able to take over a 100 prisoners; five guns of varying calibres were also captured. 2nd Squadron was able to enter Bavel and to the west of the town cut the road to Ginneken. The reconnaissance platoon and a platoon of infantry moved into Bavel and took several score of prisoners. In total in the day 10 PSK took 161 prisoners.

By 29 October 1944 the situation in Holland was as follows. A formation of the 4th British Armoured Brigade had captured Rijen and was fighting to the west and the north. Elements of the advance guard from the 2nd Canadian Armoured Brigade were patrolling the crossroads three kilometres to the north of Ginneken while 104th American Infantry Division had captured the Rijsbergen area. It seemed that the enemy was heading towards the River Maas in order to escape the Allied advance but the fight had not left the enemy.

At dawn in 29 October 1944 the Germans had counterattacked and taken some of the towns in the area. This led to the orders being given which demanded armoured protection from 10 PSK and 10 BK *panc* along the right flank of the Breda offensive. The German counter offensive had endangered the right flank and the rear of 10 BK *panc*. 10 PSK by moving to the nearby town of Dorst and breaking the enemy resistance in the area was able to secure the Polish position.

Second Lieutenant Tadeusz Krzytzaniak of 8th Rifle Battalion recalled the liberation of Breda by the 1st Polish Armoured Division on 29 October 1944. 8BS at 10:00 hours moved onto the offensive against Breda. At the entrance of the town, Krzytzaniak records that 1st and 3rd platoon from 4th Company 8BS were decimated by mortar and fire from 88mm guns but still 8BS pressed on towards the centre of Breda using Bren Gun carriers and machine guns as they fought house to house. A single group of Germans had also crossed over the canal into downtown Breda but were reached by a Bren Gun carrier patrol which also scattered a group of German troops on bicycles which was close to the hospital. A second infantry captured a German motor pool after a short exchange of fire and the capture of twelve prisoners.

Further into town the enemy was firing heavily from hidden positions in bunkers and had established a barricade on the bridge. Luckily Polish tanks were in the area and were able to break the enemy resistance, which left the area and had only slightly damaged the bridge over the canal. A second bridge was then reached but anti-tank guns had already fired upon the Poles when suddenly white flags were seen over the guns. The German position had surrendered as the overjoyed Dutch celebrated the surrender of the guns.

German resistance continued in the entrance to the Princeshagen district in the western outskirts of Breda. The Germans fought from concrete bunkers as well as deploying a battery of mortars and a group of machine

Three different views of
flooding in the Netherlands.
**Imperial War Museum
B11712, B11713 and
B11714 respectively**

Passing a knocked out Sherman during the advance to Eindhoven. **Imperial War Museum BU925, BU926**

guns. The Poles had to take each house, one after the other, which led to huge casualties. The first patrols were to move into the area and after very hard fighting were able to clear a factory and capture the main road from the Breda side. After the crossroads at Princeshagen were captured, the Polish offensive pushed on from the north towards the southern suburbs heading for the Ginneken Weg crossroads. The Germans continued to resist stubbornly, firing from windows and cellars. Time after time, sniper fire could be heard. The fighting was brutal as the Poles used hand grenades and hand-held PIAT anti-tank weapons against German machine gun positions in cellars. Even when some of the Germans had surrendered the difficulties continued as sometimes they concealed weapons and Polish troops had to be vigilant against this. Krzytzaniak records an incident where a Polish corporal shot dead a German soldier who had surrendered but then attacked a Polish soldier with a hidden knife.

Eventually the crossroad at Ginneken Weg was captured and the Polish troops upon capturing an enormous bloodied swastika flag vented their anger, ripping it into shreds. As Breda was liberated, the people danced in the streets with joy as their historic town had been spared the destruction of modern warfare owing to the rapid advance of the 1st Polish Armoured Division and its resolute action in attacking the Germans with such conviction that the enemy's will to resist swiftly evaporated.[137]

The following day it was decided to end resistance in Breda and clear the town. 10 PSK was sent to reconnoitre towards Beek with the task of seizing the bridge on the River Mark, four kilometres to the northwest of Beek. In the case of successfully crossing the river, 10 PSK was to move along the motorway towards the railway track, which ran toward Zevenbergsche – Hoek – Hoelske – Moerdijk to a region of large bridges in the Gulf of Holland Diep with the purpose of preventing the enemy from crossing. On 30 October 1944 at 07:00 hours, 10 PSK moved out according to plan. The motorway was reached but it was only partially built. The high embankments denied the tanks a place to enter along the west side. The reconnaissance platoon was then sent out to look for a point of entry onto the motorway.

At 10:20 hours 2nd Squadron took Beek without any opposition. Local civilians told the Poles that the enemy had already withdrawn over the River Mark at 07:00 hours. There was still no information concerning the state of the bridges over the rivers and canals. The stay in Beek was brief and at 11:00 hours the squadron was on the move again. Eventually from the heights at Klein Overfeld it could be seen that the bridges over the river had been destroyed. The enemy began to mortar and shell the Polish position and owing to the enemy's fine field of fire it was considered that to rebuild the bridge was impossible. It was finally decided to rebuild a crossing about 300 metres to the left of the broken bridges. To this end Wasilewski sent for sappers to build a bridge. At about 15:00 hours, under the cover of 2nd Squadron's fire which was positioned by the riverside, two platoons of infantry crossed the river and seized a small bridgehead, destroyed enemy resistance and took prisoners, in addition to holding the bridgehead for ninety minutes. During this 2nd Squadron fired non-stop upon columns of withdrawing enemy vehicles moving in the direction of Zevenbergsche Hoek. Later 1st Squadron replaced 2nd Squadron at the river's edge as 2nd Squadron had exhausted its ammunition.

The following day, 31 October 1944 at 08:30 hours, 2nd Squadron returned once again to the river and continued with its work of the previous day. At 10:00 hours with artillery and armoured support, units from 8BS crossed to the far side of the river. Enemy artillery, mortar and self-propelled guns turned the crossing into hell. The sappers could not build the bridge and the infantry could not advance. At 14:30 hours a squadron from 2nd Tank Regiment (Polish) replaced 2nd squadron but the bridgehead on the River Mark was abandoned at dusk as a result of heavy shelling and enemy counterattacks. Eventually on 3 November 1944 a formation from 10 BK *panc* forced a crossing on the Mark Canal and created an extensive bridgehead and eventually a bridge was built on co-ordinate level 988. The fighting in Holland for the 1st Polish Armoured Division finished on 8 November 1944.

10 PSK Casualty Rate in Fighting in Southern Holland: 22 September 1944 – 8 November 1944

Personnel	Officers	Ranks	Total
Killed	1	8	9
Wounded	12	66	78
Total	13	74	87

Equipment	Cromwells	Stuarts	Other	Total
Destroyed	—	—	—	—
Beyond Repair	11	2	8	21
Damaged	19	—	—	19
Total	30	2	8	40

Enemy Casualties Inflicted by 10 PSK During the Fighting in Southern Holland: 22 September 1944 – 8 November 1944:

528 prisoners, three tanks (1 *Panther*, 1 captured Sherman, 1 *Panzer* Mk IV) 8 self-propelled guns, one 150mm gun, 9 field guns over 75mm calibre, 12 guns of less than 50mm calibre, 2 *Nebelwerfers*, one motor barge, 18 lorries, 3 caterpillar tracked tractors, 1 staff car, 21 limbers,8 motorcycle combinations.[138]

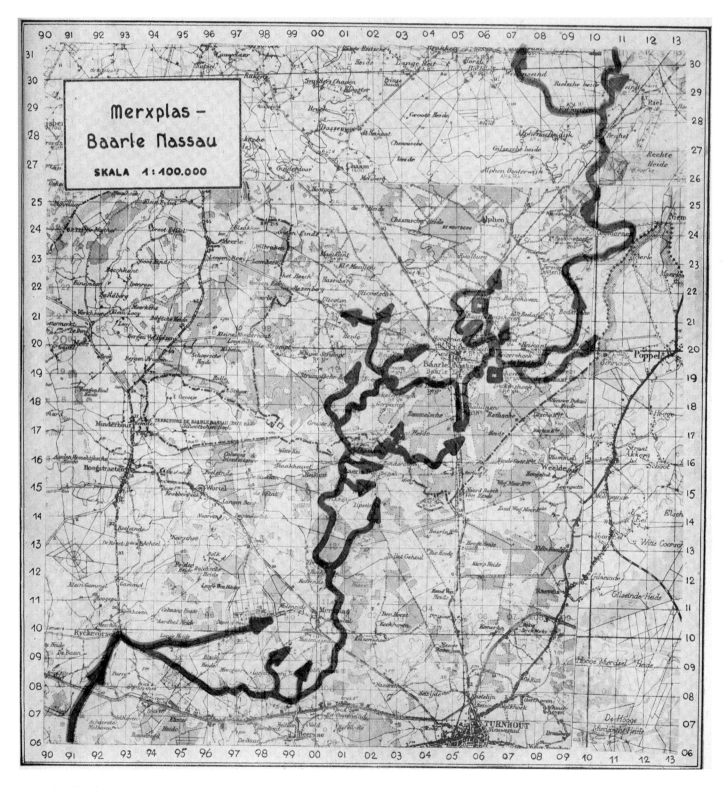

Merxplas-Baarle Nassau route.

The fighting in Holland, which culminated with the capture of Breda, was as hard as any of the fighting that the Division had experienced in France. Tadeusz Walewicz, a veteran of the 2nd Tank Regiment, now living in Canada, recently recalled the problems of fighting in the Low Countries. The Dutch Campaign, he writes, was totally unsuited for armour 'but the objective had to be accomplished'. Everywhere he recalls was water, dykes and bridges, which had to be secured. Walewicz expressed his high esteem for the valour of infantry and sappers who paid a heavy price for every crossing. Their losses are marked with white crosses.

As we have seen, and as Walewicz still remembers, day after day it was the same. Bridgeheads had to be secured. Each bridgehead was usually defended by mortar and artillery. As the German and Polish artillery and mortar fire slugged it out, the sappers and infantry tried to force crossings and construct bridges. In addition they also had to clear minefields, which the Germans used effectively and in great numbers. Not all approaches were the same. Some were steep sided, some swampy while many bridges were only suitable for local traffic and could not support the weight of tanks. Walewicz also points out that the weather was atrocious, raining most of the time, which served to make the ground very soft and marshy, hardly ideal for heavy armoured vehicles. Walewicz claims that many of the Poles – despite the slow and painful pace of the campaign – felt that the war was coming to an end but feared what was to become of the Poles.[139] No doubt the relentless westward march of the Red Army was beginning to concern the Polish troops in the west.

Wysocki records the overall casualties of the Dutch Campaign between 27 September 1944 and 9 November 1944. The German losses were huge and Wysocki claims that they can only be estimated, although he records that the Division captured 53 officers, 2,892 other ranks as well as large amounts of German equipment which included eight 155mm guns, six 88mm guns, fifteen 75mm guns, three 50mm guns, 4 tanks and 8 self-propelled guns. Polish casualties amounted to 69 officers and 876 other ranks, killed or wounded. Equipment losses are not recorded at divisional level.[140] Overall it was a brutal and bloody campaign.

CHAPTER X

The Final Round – Victory?

The fighting in Holland saw Queen Wilhelmina of the Netherlands and her Government award the 1st Polish Armoured Division the Order of the Orange Nassau with Swords. The Belgian Royal Family and the Mayor of Breda all sent proclamations expressing gratitude for the liberation of their people by the 1st Polish Armoured Division. To this day the Division is still deeply respected by both the Belgians and the Dutch. However to return to the situation after the liberation of Breda – the war still had to be won; Germany invaded and defeated.

After moving, fighting and suffering huge casualties, the Division captured Moordijk and its surrounding area. The Division as before operated between the Canadian 1st Army and I British Corps. The 1st Polish Armoured Division held an area about 25 kilometres in depth between the Holland Diep Gulf and the River Maas. To the left was the Canadian 10th Armoured Car Regiment and to the right, the 4th Canadian Armoured

Some indication of the difficult nature of the Dutch terrain is given by this photo of Royal Engineers making fascines near a small waterway, 1944. **Imperial War Museum B11711**

Division. During this time 21st Army Group was already planning for the next offensive: the destruction of the enemy between the sea and the River Rhine.[141]

The British Corps was the custodian of the River Maas and the Holland Diep Gulf while the 1st Polish Armoured Division held a sector of the Dutch frontier. This sector consisted from the right hand side, the route from Dongen (051 346) to the intersection (050 472) along the canal to the junction with the River Maas (042 500), which incorporated the route to Drie Sluizen. The left-hand frontier included Hoeven, the rail intersection and high road (819 401), canal junction and river (818 413), the canal to Zevenberg and the north along the canal to position 8348.

The task of the Division was to prevent the penetration of its sector by either enemy patrols or its agents. In addition Dutch civilians fleeing the area were to be stopped. The enemy, the Fifteenth Army, was pushing towards the northern bank of the River Maas. While they were waiting for further instructions the Germans began offensive patrolling as well as engaging in strong and aggressive forays. The immediate task of the Division was to make a check of its area. 10th Motorised Brigade (10 BK *panc*) without a single armoured squadron was sent to check out the sector at Made and Raamsdonkveer and received reserves in the frontier sector of Oosterhout which lay to the right of the Division.

The 3rd Rifle Brigade (3BS) was to be reinforced by an armoured regiment, either 10 BK *panc* or 10th Mounted Rifles (10 PSK) for the purpose of overseeing the Division's left sector. Eventually 3BS was reinforced by armoured regiments in turn by the following regiments: 1st Tank Regiment, 10 PSK, 2nd Tank Regiment and 24th Uhlans. The expected length was eight days and the armoured regiments were under the direct orders of the commanding officer (CO) 3BS. On 17th November 1944 at 10:00 hours, two groups 'W' and 'T' under the command of the Second-in-Command 10 PSK relieved 1st Tank and took over the River Maas sector. 1st Squadron (10 PSK) was sent to the northern outskirts of Zevenbergsche Hoek while 2nd Squadron was sent to Blauwe Sluis and 3rd Squadron to Wagenberg.

Each squadron had two pickets to each platoon of armour. 1st and 2nd Squadrons in turn operated in Moerdijk while 2nd Squadron operated in Lage Zwaluwe. The pickets in the Moerdijk area were to reconnoitre Strijenas and Wilhelmsdorp while the second group operating from the Lage Zwaluwe area were to observe Anna and Jakomina Plaat. The pickets operating in these areas, which had bridges, were expected to note and immediately report any activity on the enemy bank. Every piece of information went straight to the squadron commander. In the event of the enemy coming too close, the Polish pickets were to illuminate the immediate area with rockets, red and green, the signal fired at a time of alarm. Civilian movements also had to be controlled.

The responsibility for the sector fell to the CO of 9th Rifle Brigade (9BS) and throughout this period of observation by the Poles; the enemy merely replied with weak artillery and mortar fire. The period of operations concluded on 25 November 1944. On the same day in Breda, Field Marshal Montgomery decorated soldiers of the Division with British awards. The CO of 10 PSK, Jerzy Wasilewski, now a Major, was awarded the Military Cross while Second Lieutenant Józef Doruch was awarded the Military Medal.

From 25 November 1944 until 20 December 1944, 10 PSK with the rest of the Division, if not the entire front, fell into a period of virtual inactivity. A German counter offensive, which began in the Ardennes, afforested area between Belgium and Germany, rudely awakened the Allies. The offensive, led by Field Marshal von Rundstedt, a veteran of the 1939 Polish Campaign and both the 1940 and the 1944 French Campaigns, endangered Brussels and threatened to destroy most of the Allies' gains made since June 1944. Antoni Położyński makes the point that Montgomery was preparing to leave the Continent for London as Christmas approached.[142] It was certain that the Allies were confident of victory and had forgotten to continue in their pursuit of the Germans. The following eight days were to be a sharp reminder to the Allies that the war was not yet over and that it was not time to relax one's guard.

The first order relating to the Ardennes counter-offensive to concern the 1st Polish Armoured Division was issued at 09:30 on 20 December 1944 which put the Poles at the disposition of the 1st Canadian Army. A review of the situation relating to the Poles was that I British Corps was in defence of the River Maas and that in front of the 4th Canadian Armoured Division were the German 711th and 712th Infantry Divisions. General Maczek noted the aggressive nature of German patrolling and began to contemplate the possibility of enemy raids. The 1st Polish Armoured Division, minus 24th Uhlans, was to reinforce the RAF Regiment (British) and replace the Canadian 4th Armoured Division and take over its sector between Lihoijen and Raamsdonk. The Poles immediately handed over their sector to the 18th Reconnaissance Regiment (Canadian) who was to be the left hand neighbour while 7th Reconnaissance Regiment from Second Canadian Corps, which was defending the River Waal, was the right-hand neighbour. The Poles were to maintain the formation already established by the Canadian 4th Armoured Division.

Local inhabitants help to free a Sherman bogged down near the River Maas, Netherlands. **Imperial War Museum B11781**

Even though the Ardennes Offensive did not directly involve the Polish 1st Armoured Division, it still became part of the defensive measures put into place to guard against paratroop landings either in the immediate area of the Division's sector or elsewhere. 10 PSK minus its armoured squadrons and with a squadron from 10th Dragoons under the orders of 10 BK *panc's* CO established a formation with the task of operating to the advantage of 3BS and prepare for counterattacks, mainly from the direction of the Walwijk region and from Loon Op Zand. In the event of 3BS being able to force a crossing over the Afwatering Canal defence, tanks were to cover the operation. The precautions against German counterattacks led to a policy of 'joint management'. The main concern was the possibility of attacks by paratroops. The CO of the formation ordered the establishment of a series of lookout points in the Undenhout area. This was to ensure that reports concerning aerial landings would be with Division within five minutes of any such landings being observed.

Until the need for intensive vigilance was removed the commanders ensured strong patrolling as well as external guards and sentry posts at every strategic objective (bridges, equipment dumps as well as Command Head Quarters). Every armoured regiment was to have a squadron on stand by to move within thirty minutes of any alarm being raised. All equipment and all vehicles had to be camouflaged to evade detection by enemy aircraft. All radio communication was directed via 10 PK *panc* and 3BS.

On 26 December 1944 1st Squadron (10 PSK) went onto the offensive with a platoon being sent to Walwijk for the purpose of engaging enemy pickets. Upon reaching Walwijk the platoon opened fire. The destroyed terrain made any approach towards the enemy side of the River Maas impossible. However the efficiency of the tank's fire, corrected by Polish infantry pickets acting as artillery observers, made it possible to advance to the river level. From there on, the armoured units were able to move to the sea with the purpose of shelling further enemy pickets. The shelling was considered to be very tactical; very similar to that at 'Shooting School' for fresh tank crews.

At 02:45 hours on 31 December 1944, on the command of the CO 3BS, one platoon from 1st Squadron was sent to Capelle to support an infantry offensive. The objective of the offensive was the destruction of enemy infantry pickets who were operating on the Polish side of the Oude Maasje Canal and then to cross the canal and clear the 'islands' between the canal and the Maas River (Kapelsche Veer). The platoon supported the offensive throughout the night until 10:00 hours and received casualties: Corporal Majda was killed and four men wounded: Privates Mackowiak, Suchocki and Popiołkiewicz along with Corporal Rozdzynski, with one tank destroyed.

The Polish infantry achieved one objective of their offensive as the enemy pickets on the Oude Maasje Canal were destroyed but the offensive on the 'islands' failed. At 10:00 hours the armoured platoon was relieved by another from 1st Squadron. Later this platoon took eight prisoners and ceased operations at 13:00 hours.

Once again at 03:00 hours, 2 January 1945, a platoon from 1st Squadron moved to the Kapelsche Veer region for the purpose of supporting infantry pickets. The pickets felt threatened by the presence of tanks and self-propelled guns, which could be heard from the other side of the River Maas. The platoon took up a position on the Oude Maasje hoping to provoke a reaction from the Germans. There was no such reaction and it was considered that the threat from armour or artillery did not exist and so the platoon returned to the squadron.

From 3 January 1945, under Divisional orders, 10 PSK in its entirety fell under the command of 3BS and changed its position. 10 PSK's command post and special squadrons with 1st Squadron moved to Kaatsheuvel, 2nd Squadron went to Walwijk and 3rd Squadron moved to Henstraat. The squadrons' command headquarters was in Loop Op Zand. The perceived wisdom at Army and Corps level was that the enemy was liable to launch large scale attacks across the River Maas in the following directions: Geertruidenberg – Breda, between co-ordinate levels 17 and 10 and also between co-ordinate levels 15 and 19 at S'Hertogenbosch. The 1st Polish Armoured Division was to reinforce 47 Royal Marine Commando and a Canadian battalion. Its purpose was to prevent the Germans overrunning the River Maas. In the event of the river being overcome by a strong enemy force and the north being put under pressure by the Germans, the Division was to defend the Tilburg direction in support of the north-west outskirts of the Loonsche woods and Drunensche as a foundation for operations by 10 BK *panc*. If any defence was required it was to be conducted in three phases:

1. Battle of the river

2. Battle of the islands

3. Slowing from the south, defending towards the Loonsche and Drunensche areas thus giving time for the creation of a reserve force.

In the first phase a formation from 8BS supported by 2nd Squadron 10 PSK was expected to halt any crossing of the River Maas by the enemy in the area. In addition there was also further formation consisting of a machine gun squadron with 3rd Squadron 10 PSK and a squadron of Sherman tanks which had been assigned to 8BS and had been deployed in the area. 9BS minus one company and 10 PSK minus two companies acted as a reserve for the whole formation. In the second phase, the Polish formation was to attempt to deny the enemy access to the islands and strongly defend the towns of Waspik and Beerdwijs. It was to use the canals in order to impede the enemy's progress. The 8BS formation was to defend the approach from the north to the line of the Waspik – Deerwijk main road. In this event the machine gun company formation was to move to 8BS's position. The reserve force was to then move to the area in order to shore up the defences there. It was expected that 1st Squadron 10 PSK would be deployed to cover the Division's western flank. In the third phase, 10 PSK from the Loop Op Zand region was prepared for operations from the north and northwest.

By 5 January 1945 the Poles had returned to the offensive when 2nd Squadron (10 PSK) took part in Operation TROJAN. This offensive had been pencilled in for 2 January 1945 but the Ardennes Offensive and its repercussions throughout the front along the Belgian – Dutch – German frontiers had caused its postponement. The essence of TROJAN was to test the formation on the River Maas in the sector which ran from co-ordinate level 14 to the S'Hertogenbosch region with the purpose of reconnoitring the enemy, its artillery and reaction to aggressive Polish patrolling.

The entire operation was to be opened with an aerial bombardment and an artillery barrage by the entire artillery corps. 3BS carried out three raids on the northern bank of the Maas. In each case the Polish infantry was supported by armour. 10 PSK gave a squadron for the offensive in the region to the north of Doeveren. The purpose of this attack was to reconnoitre Gederen. TROJAN began at 13:45 hours with a ten-minute barrage followed by a period of silence for five minutes in order to allow the artillery to check its bearings. Then at 14:00 hours, a further barrage consisting of artillery, mortar and tank fire erupted while the infantry hidden behind a smoke screen crossed the River Maas. The operation finished at 15:00 hours with everything going to plan. The enemy responded with strong small arms fire but cold only manage weak mortar and no artillery fire at all.

At 03:30 hours on 7 January 1945, the CO 3BS requested that 1st Squadron (10 PSK) send a platoon of armour to a farm (097 403) in order to support an attack by a company from 9BS upon the enemy bridgehead at Kapelsche Veer. Despite having had artillery and armoured support, the Poles could not capture the enemy position that was being fought from a reinforced position and doggedly defended. Three members of the platoon from 10 PSK were wounded: Second Lieutenant Andrzej Mincer, Corporal Gize and Private Nadzieja. At 10:30 hours the platoon was relieved by a platoon from 3rd Squadron which remained at its post until dusk, giving the infantry supporting fire which made it possible for the infantry to withdraw. At dusk the platoon returned to its squadron's position. On 8 January 1945 10 PSK moved to Teteringen where it remained until 4 March 1945.

During the afternoon of 5 March 1945 10 PSK minus 2nd Squadron save for two platoons moved to a subsection in the Raamsdonkveer and Raamsdonk areas. The task of 10 PSK with a squadron of Dragoons and a unit of thirty eight Dutch soldiers was to defend the River Maas in the subsection 'Poznań' which ran from co-ordinate level 065 to the east and from the canal (010 500) in the west and to the Dongen canal to the south. 10 PSK organised the following defensive points: 1st Squadron with a platoon from 2nd Squadron with eight Dutch soldiers established a position in the northern outskirts of Raamsdonkveer and advanced armoured pickets entered the regions of 019 488 and 024 484 and relieved a picket in the area of the bridge at 033 503. 3rd Squadron and the Dragoon Squadron, two scout cars complete with a communication platoon and eleven Dutch soldiers organised a defensive picket at Raamsdonk and placed armoured pickets in regions 042 478 and 052 472. 2nd Squadron (Dragoons) put in two pickets: Nr. 12 in region 053 502 and Nr. 13 in region 054 495. The assault platoon organised a picket Nr. 15 in the industrial area at 039 501 while 1st Platoon from 2nd Squadron placed pickets on the bridges at 023 464. 10 PSK also established a regimental position in Raamsdonkveer.

Throughout its stay in the section 10 PSK received sporadic mortaring upon its pickets. On 7 March 1945 Lance Corporal Kucbajski was killed and Corporal Guzik was wounded (both were from 1st Squadron). On 9 March 1945 a platoon from 10th Dragoons launched a ten man raid upon the northern bank of the Maas with the purpose of seizing prisoners. The raid came under the command of 10 PSK but failed to achieve anything because as soon as the patrol landed it came under heavy machine gun fire and was forced to withdraw. On 13 March 1945 10 PSK handed their section over to 24th Uhlans and returned to Teteringen for further training. The training killed more men than the recent fighting as four men were killed and two wounded when their tank ran over a mine.

10 PSK Casualty Rate between 9 November 1944 and 6 April 1945

Personnel	Officers	Ranks	Total
Killed	—	5	5
Wounded	2	17	19
Total	2	22	24

Equipment	Cromwells	Stuarts	Other	Total
Destroyed	—	—	—	—
Beyond Repair	13*	—	—	13
Damaged	1	—	8	9
Total	14	—	8	22

*12 of these tanks had reached the end of their service lives.

Estimated German Losses against 10 PSK between 9 November 1944 and 6 April 1945:

Eight prisoners and four barges.

By the beginning of April 1945 the situation in Western Europe had changed so much that final victory by the Allies was beyond doubt. The general situation was that 6th Army Group via the 1st French Army had captured Sulzfeld and Klingenburg while 7th US Army had reached Kitingen, Wurzburg, Hammelburg and Bruckenau. The 3rd US Army from 12th Army Group had reached Frotha, Ohrodruf, Lanensalz and Mulhausen. 1st US Army had reached Kassel and Hofgeisman while the 9th US Army had crossed the River Weser and had reached Minden.

The 2nd British Army from 21st Army Group after crossing the Weser reached Wietersheim, Petershagen, Osnabruck, Salzbergen and the Lingen region. Finally the 1st Canadian Army had captured Neufhaus, Emlicheim, Wilsum and Achtervener and had reached the suburbs of Coevorden. The Canadians had also captured Almelo and had reached the suburbs of Zutphen. Plans for the conquest of Germany were already well under way.

At 22:00 hours on 6 April 1945 during a divisional briefing, the CO 10 PSK, Major Wasilewski, received orders for the forthcoming campaign. The 1st Polish Armoured Division was to become part of the Canadian II Corps.

It had been foreseen that Coevorden was to be the area for concentrating forces ready for an offensive towards the north and southeast. Maczek ordered the establishment of two formations which were charged with the tasks of seizing and making the area around Coevorden safe. 10 PSK was part of a formation under the command of Lieutenant-Colonel Zgorzelski, Commander of 10th Uhlans. 2nd Squadron (10 PSK) was assigned to the other formation commanded by Lieutenant-Colonel Complaka, CO of Podhalian Rifle Brigade (BSP). Zgorzelski's formation was to go to Coevorden and Complaka's to Neede. 10 PSK moved in two squads to Neede: 'A' and 'B'. 'A' Squad consisted of tracked vehicles which were carried upon transporters while 'B' Squad consisted of wheeled vehicles. 'A' moved out at 21:00 hours on 7 April 1945 and 'B' at 03:00 hours on 8 April 1945.

The route from Teteringen to Neede was via Tilburg, S'Hertogenbosch, Reek, Gennep, Henkens, Goch, Rees (crossing the River Rhine) and then further along the 'Diamond Route' axis until reaching the dispersal point. From there both squads moved to their designated operational areas. The column carrying the tanks repeatedly stopped throughout the march. Along both routes support was added in order to deceive the enemy of its intension. The transporters carrying the tanks were unloaded during the early hours of the morning en route between Goch and Clewe (Germany). Although the entire regiment was assembled there were long delays waiting for individual transporters to arrive. 1st Squadron even lost a tank before any action as it fell of its trailer en route.

At 14:00 hours the tanks crossed the Rhine using a platoon bridge in Rees. From there, moving rapidly, the armoured column covered 65 miles and reached Neede by 19:00 hours where a post for the night was established. Squad 'B' had to make a night post before crossing the Rhine as the bridge was closed for several hours so that it could be repaired. At dawn on 9 April 1945 2nd Squadron (10 PSK) moved to Complaka's formation. 10 PSK minus 2nd Squadron cleared the assembly point at Neede and at 14:00 hours after travelling sixty miles reached the Coevorden concentration area where it stopped in Agterhorn, five kilometres to the southwest of Coevorden (Germany).

In the first phase of the operation Zgorzelski's formation had to take over Coevorden from Belgian paratroopers and then organise defences in the town from the north and west. In the second phase, the formation was to reconnoitre towards Emmen along the Division operational axis as well as checking every road to the west and northwest. Complaka's formation had to clear the Division's left axis along which 3BS had to operate.

A fine image of one of the Division's Sherman Firefly tanks dug-in near the German town of Gangelt, very close to the Dutch border. **Imperial War Museum B13283**

There was very little information about the enemy. German defences were conducted in small groups ranging from a company to a regiment in strength. In the area were soldiers from the 6th, 7th and 8th Parachute Divisions as well as soldiers from the 245th, 331st, 346th and 361st Infantry Divisions. The terrain once again was difficult for tanks as it was flat with large numbers of canals, dykes and peat marshes. Furthermore the whole area was flooded.

At 15:00 hours Wasilewski received orders to rush a squadron of armour to the Dragoons and Belgians who had seized and were guarding a bridge to the north of Coevorden. The axis for this operation went from the main road between Coevorden to Dalen and further in a northwest direction to the crossing and to Oosterhesselen. 3rd Squadron received this task. The Dragoons and Belgians, without any real opposition, had captured the bridge, which was partly damaged. The enemy who had been using weak patrols had withdrawn to the north side of the canal. After a temporary repair on the bridge, 3rd Sqaudron moved to the other side of the canal where they established a post for the night and then settled down to guard the bridge. During the evening, Wasilewski received orders for the following day.

10 PSK and the Dragoon's squadron after crossing the bridge searched the area in the direction of Westerbork. In this area they were supposed to find a group of French paratroopers, dropped during the night of 8–9 April 1945 with the task of seizing a bridge over the Oranie Canal. On 10 April 1945 at 07:00 hours the operation began. By 13:00 hours, both groups had reached their destinations and had found 64 paratroopers. It seemed that some of the paratroopers had been dropped on the wrong side of the canal and were presumed to be dead. In the Westerbork region 1st Sqaudron liberated a Dutch concentration camp for political prisoners. The Dutch guards were retained to guard the camp but under the control of a Dutch officer from the Polish contingent.

After reaching the Oranie Canal, two kilometres north of Westerbork, 1st Squadron's commander sent a foot patrol over the canal. The patrol clashed with the enemy who used machine guns. Privates Turkowiak and Kosztubajda were killed. After completing its task, 10 PSK minus 2nd and 3rd Squadrons moved at 14:00 hours to a position at Dalen where Wasilewski received fresh orders. At 15:00 hours, further orders came. 3rd Squadron was to go into action along two axes: two platoons moved via Holsloot and Erm in a northeast direction to the crossing on the Oranie Canal in Noordbarge while a further two platoons went to the crossing to the north of Noordbarge. At 17:00 hours the Poles encountered the enemy and shelled and destroyed several enemy bunkers from which the Germans had been defending the bridge. Eighteen prisoners were taken. After driving the enemy away, 3rd Sqaudron was able to support the Dragoons in crossing the canal. Once the canal was crossed, the squadron established a bridgehead and guarded it throughout the night. At the same time sappers built a Class 40 bridge over the canal while the Dragoons cleared Noordbarge and Emmen of the enemy.

During the evening orders for the following day arrived. 10 PSK after leaving Emmen was to reconnoitre and clear an area of terrain from the Oranie Canal to the woods, one kilometre to the northwest of Odorn and from the main road from Emmen to Ter Apel. Wasilewski decided to manage the entire operational belt in two sub-sections. The right line of the offensive included the express railway line from Emmen to Buinen. In the left sub-section, 1st Sqaudron starting from Klijndijk was to reconnoitre and clear Odorn, Veerdinge, Valte and Exlo, while 3rd Sqaudron was to reconnoitre the main route from Emmen to Ter Apel as well as clearing the town.

On 11 April 1945 10 PSK moved out to begin its operation. Upon reaching Emmen, the squadrons separated to begin their individual tasks. Two kilometres away from Odoorn, 1st Squadron met with barricades and mines. This led to fighting with enemy infantry in both Odoorn and Exlo. After overcoming the barricades and mines, the Poles reached both towns by 14:00 hours. Sergeant Major Laskowski, commander of 3rd Sqaudron was killed in the fighting. The enemy suffered great loss in both towns and the Poles were able to take 100 prisoners. It was noted that much of this was achieved with co-operation between the Assault Squad and Cromwell squadrons. 3rd Squadron in the first phase of the operation did not meet the enemy but met with difficult territory as the bridges along the route had been destroyed. This meant that the Squadron had to move across country and use bridges which had been designed to bear only a few tons and certainly not heavy armour. In spite of this by 13:00 hours, the Squadron was in the Ter Apel region and had engaged the enemy. Entry into the town proved to be impossible owing to the lack of a suitable bridge therefore a large barrage against the town was organised. By dusk, both 1st and 3rd Squadrons had achieved their objectives and rejoined the remainder of 10 PSK in Weerdinge.

The following day, 12 April 1945, 10 PSK in a joint operation with 10th Dragoons cleared an area as a continuation of 1st Squadron's section by moving further to the north of the canal. It was decided that an armoured squadron was to act as a vanguard working along three axes. On each axis there was to be one platoon of armour and a platoon of Dragoons. The left axis was to run via Odoorn, to the north of the town towards Eesgroen and Westdorp. The central axis ran along the main Odoorn-Borger road and the right axis ran along the railway line from Exlo to Buinen. One armoured squadron from 10 PSK was to be retained in Odoorn as a reserve.

The tanks moved out at 10:00 hours with Wasilewski leading the vanguard. By 12:00 hours each formation had passed through Odom and Exlo and was preparing to carry out their allotted tasks. Every platoon of 3rd Squadron had encountered the enemy. As a result of Polish fire, the enemy had withdrawn beyond the canal and had blown up the bridges along the central axis in Borger and Westdorp. Using an armoured offensive the Dragoons attempted to force a crossing of the canal in the Borger region but owing to a huge loss of life and equipment, was obliged to withdraw from the bridgehead under a smoke screen provided by the tanks.

During the morning of 13 April 1945, a 10 PSK squadron operating with the Dragoons was to reconnoitre along an axis reaching from Buinen and Veendam and then further northeast towards Winschoten. At 08:00 hours 2nd Squadron set out to undertake this task. After encountering terrible terrain but not meeting the enemy, the Squadron reached Gieten where it linked up with elements of the 3rd Canadian Infantry Division. The Canadians told the Poles that the enemy was in the northern outskirts of Wildervang. This report proved to be true. En route to Wildervang, 2nd Sqaudron was forced to remove barricades and finally reached the canal close to the town. There the Squadron was forced to halt owing to the bridge over the canal being raised. Attempts to capture the town using dismounted tank crews proved to be futile owing to heavy machine gun fire. Eventually with the help of local civilians the bridge was lowered and repaired which allowed the tanks to enter the town itself. Wildervang was captured and significant casualties were inflicted upon the enemy. A large magazine was discovered also captured. The magazine had been housed partly in buildings and partly in barges (40 in total) on the canal. In the magazine were several hundreds of tons of military equipment and rations. After the capture of the magazine sections from the squadron were deployed to prevent theft from it.

On 14 April 1945 Maczek dissolved Zgorzelski's formation and placed 10 PSK under his direct command. At 17:00 hours Maczek ordered 3rd Squadron to be sent to Haren under the command of 10th Dragoons. The following day, 15 April 1945, 2nd Squadron attempted to move north but after a few kilometres were held in Munterdam. The reason for this was that in every direction the bridges had either been destroyed or were too weak to bear the weight of armour. This obliged 2nd Squadron to return to 10 PSK's position in Klijndijk.

The following days continued along these lines until the night of 17–18 April 1945 when an urgent request came from Division asking for an armoured platoon to be sent to a camp in Niederlangen which contained women prisoners from the Polish Underground. It was crucial that the Poles freed these women as it was feared that the Germans might try to use them in some form of diversionary tactic. A platoon from 3rd Squadron was sent to Niederlangen. No doubt the women were overjoyed to see Polish troops. A woman known simply as *Mieczysława* described her liberation from *Stalag VI C Oberlangen* by troops of the 1st Polish Armoured Division. At first the women thought that the soldiers, owing to their uniforms were British but upon hearing them speak realised that they were Polish troops. The most important thing for the women captives was that the troops spoke to them in Polish.[143] To the women being liberated by Polish troops was nothing short of a miracle. It is interesting to note that one of the women liberated in 1945 wrote to General Maczek on his 100th birthday in 1992, still expressing her gratitude for her liberation so many years before.[144]

During the morning of 18 April 1945 1st Sqaudron was sent to clear territory from the west of the River Ems, moving north form Walchum to Heede. The Dragoons had already been in the area for two days but it was felt that the presence of enemy troops could endanger supply lines. At 10:30 1st Squadron operating with an assault platoon set out. Local civilians claimed that SS patrols which had been withdrawing from the north were still prowling around the area. During the evening the squadron linked up with the Dragoons as well as establishing a 'harbour' in the Heede area. The platoon which was sent to the north of Rhede in order to establish contact with the Dragoons actually captured a four man enemy patrol.

The next major operation for the Division was on 20 April 1945 when territory to the southeast of Papenburg was to be cleared. Maczek placed 10 PSK into a formation commanded by Lieutenant-Colonel Nowaczynski. The formation was to operate from a region 3 ½ kilometres to the south of Aschendorf, clearing the area enclosed with a region which ran from Klusterkanal in the south, Borgerwald canal in the east, co-ordinate level 750 in the west and co-ordinate level 740 in the north. To complete the operation, Nowaczynski divided the formation into two groups. The first group commanded by Major Gryziecki consisted of 1st Squadron (10 PSK), a company from 8BS and a platoon of Bren Gun carriers from 8BS. The objective was to clear a belt of territory 2½ kilometres to the west of the Borgerwald Canal in the north and to the formation's southern frontier on the Kusten Canal.

Captain's Rozwadowski's formation, which contained 3rd Squadron (10 PSK), was to clear the remaining part of the designated area in a northern direction towards Neu Herbrum and Neulehe. 2nd Sqaudron (10 PSK) and a company of infantry from 8BS were retained as a reserve force. The formations moved onto the offensive at 10:00 hours with Rozwadowski's group moving swifly and with no trouble to their objectives. After reaching the Kusten Canal in Neulehe it even captured a 75mm gun. In the Herbrum area the Polish formation liberated a

Sherman Fireflies of the Division move through an unidentified village during the winter of 1944/45.
Imperial War Museum B13400, B13401

concentration camp which had been bombed by Allied aircraft during the crossing of the Kusten Canal. Most of the barracks had been burnt with the prisoners still inside. In the barracks area laid hundreds of unburied bodies. Forty prisoners proved to be Polish; the camp was taken care of by the Division's Medical Corps.

Major Gryzieck's group moved towards the east; Tanks from a platoon from 1st Sqaudron acted as vanguard. After moving only three kilometres it was realised that it was not possible for all of the tanks to travel. Therefore a platoon of armour with an infantry platoon moved to the southern suburbs of Papenburg and seized a bridge on the Borgerwald Canal at point 818 942. The remainder of the squadron with a company of infantry from 8BS walked along the route towards Gut Borgermoor and the junction of the Kusten Canal with the Borgerwald Canal. The infantry was carried upon tanks and without incident came upon the enemy at Gut Borgermoor. At the canal junction the vanguard encountered enemy opposition which was well dug in and armed with *Panzerfausts* and used with great effect. After nearly exhausting its ammunition the vanguard finally attacked the enemy with hand grenades, broke the enemy's opposition and overrun the canal. The armoured platoon only suffered two wounded but 8BS who were under heavy enemy fire suffered both dead and wounded.

Another armoured platoon with an infantry platoon moved to the left in a circular route and was able to come across to Borgermoor. While the entire armoured squadron fired upon the enemy, a company of infantry was able to capture Borgermoor and seized a bridge there. The bridge then needed guarding day and night against constant enemy raids.

During the night a platoon of Bren Gun carriers from 8BS reached the bridge. After taking the canal junction and seizing the bridge in Borgermoor, 1st Squadron remained at a night post close to the canal. 10 PSK could not receive supplies due to the state of the roads. At 09:00 hours on 22 April 1945 10 PSK continued its march into Germany. After crossing the Borgerwald the Poles met with terrible roads and so began to repair them using telegraph poles and wayside trees. While they were carrying out this work a group of Poles who had escaped from a concentration camp told Wasilewski that the Germans were holding prisoners from the camp in peat bogs about two kilometres distant. Crews from two tanks and scout cars with an infantry platoon from 8BS set out on foot to rescue the prisoners. This was done and the camp guards (fifty three in number) were taken prisoner. 2nd Sqaudron without meeting the enemy reached the intersection at 857 914 where yet another camp containing 300 prisoners was discovered.

Throughout most of the day many Polish tanks fell victim to the terrain rather than to the enemy as tanks became stuck fast in mud. However 3rd Squadron's vanguard was ambushed after entering the southern suburbs of Bockhorst. German infantry using *Panzerfausts* destroyed two tanks as they entered the area. The platoon fought back like devils and used every available weapon including hand grenades. Eventually it was able to break up the enemy attack and evacuate the crews from the disabled tanks. A platoon of armour was sent to reinforce the vanguard and took an enemy platoon, complete with officers, prisoner. 2nd Squadron, which was clearing a firing path, destroyed an enemy position and was able to take prisoners before reaching Neu. In Neu itself the squadron destroyed a 75mm gun and four 20mm co-axial guns and forced the enemy to withdraw to the north.

At dusk 2nd Squadron reached the bridge (883 949) where five aerial bombs (over 250 kgs each) were found. These were later exploded and buried by prisoners. The advance to the north continued on incredibly soft marshy terrain and into the next day 23 April 1945. Prisoners were made to repair roads in order to make the Polish advance possible. During the afternoon 3rd Squadron occupied Langholt and took sixty seven prisoners including the commander of a battalion of Marine Infantry. During the evening further repairs were carried out while during the night 3rd Squadron and infantrymen repaired and reinforced two bridges. The bridges were dubbed the *Maciej Bridge* and the *Krwawa Koszula Bridge* ('the Bloody Shirt Bridge') a reference to 8BS.[145]

In spite of the chronic roads Wasilewski decided that 10 PSK was to press further northeast. Operations began at 08:00 hours on 24 April 1945. 1st Squadron cleared a firing path and advanced three kilometres to the north and found a canal crossing but with its bridge destroyed. 1st Squadron took up a firing position and began to shell the enemy from the other side of the canal. A section of infantry attempted to cross the canal but heavy enemy fire made this impossible. From information obtained from prisoners it was asserted that the Marine Infantry Battalion which had been captured the day before had been replaced by a Parachute battalion.

2nd Squadron was given the task of supporting an infantry company which was to capture the enemy defensive position in the southern outskirts of Idafehn. After a strong barrage by artillery and tanks from 2nd Sqaudron, the infantry began its attack but the Germans defended stubbornly and the infantry was forced to retire. The marshy terrain did not allow the tanks to advance with the infantry. The following day, 25 April 1945, at 09:00 hours, a company from 8BS supported by 2nd Squadron again attacked Idafehn. This time owing to the enemy having withdrawn from the town it was captured with very little opposition. The infantry moved to the north with 2nd Sqaudron moving parallel from them, 500 metres to the east. In this manner they soon linked up with an infantry company, which had been operating with 1st Squadron. The squadron moved to point 934 052 where a destroyed bridge over a canal was found. From this point 1st Squadron began to shell the enemy on the other side of the canal.

During the afternoon 2nd Squadron received orders to seize Strucklingen (where all of 10 PSK was to pass through) and reconnoitre the crossings towards Bollingen and Ramsloh. 2nd Squadron, bypassing the bridge on the canal, moved across open country to Strucklingen. There the enemy opened fire with artillery and mortar fire but their opposition was swiftly broken. After the capture of Strucklingen, the squadron commenced its reconnaissance operation towards Bollingen where a destroyed bridge was found over the river in the area. As the squadron moved towards Ramsloh, three kilometres to the north of Strucklingen, it was discovered that the canals in the area had been damaged and the area flooded. Therefore it was impossible to move in this area and the squadron was forced to return to Strucklingen.

During the night 27–28 April 1945, Lieutenant-Colonel Nowaczynski's formation was ordered to clear the islands in the marshes in the towns of Ramsloh, Hollen and Scharrel. These ran along the length of the express route to the south from Bollingen to the Kusten Canal. Two groups were formed in order to carry out this task. Group 1 came under the command of Major Wasilewski and consisted of 10 PSK minus one squadron and a company of infantry from 8BS. Their task was to clear the operational area from Strucklingen to the south. Group 2 came under the command of Major Gryziecki and consisted of 1st Battalion Anti-Tank with 1st Squadron (10 PSK) and a company of infantry (8BS) and was to operate from the Kusten Canal in the north from Scharrel.

The operation began at 09:00 hours with Nowaczynski directing the action from 10 PSK's position in Group 1. The operation went smoothly as the tanks moved over ruined territory and by 15:00 hours, Group 1 had reached the outskirts of Scharrel. En route sappers were able to repair roads and bridges. It seemed that the enemy had fled the area. Any further movement beyond Scharrel was deemed impossible, as the bridge over the river had been destroyed. 1st Squadron which had been moving with Major Gryziecki's formation as with Wasilewski's group was able to move around unhindered by the enemy and was able to cross the east side of the Sagter Ems river and reached southern Scharrel. There, the squadron was able to link up with a platoon from 2nd Squadron. Once this link was established 8BS was able to clear the town. It had been estimated that the enemy would take two days to withdraw from the area; they withdrew within one day.

The following days 28–29 April 1945 were days of reflection for 10 PSK as it prepared for its Regimental Day on 29 April. On the day itself, a role call of the regiment's dead was called. This was followed by a short speech by Wasilewski, recalling the regiment's history and its link to the present war. Mass and the distribution of souvenir pamphlets to all soldiers followed. During the evening, General Maczek with his Chief of Staff, Lieutenant-Colonel Ludwik Stankiewicz, paid a visit to 10 PSK.

Owing to the very bad roads and the high number of destroyed bridges, the 1st Polish Armoured Division gave up trying to operate along its present axis and decided upon a second route. The new Divisional axis ran using a bridge on the River Leda, via Leer, which had been captured by the 3rd Canadian Infantry Division and then further to the northeast via Hessel and Remels towards Wilhelmshaven. On the march to Hessel, 10 PSK was allocated to the 10 BK *panc* formation. At 06:00 hours, 1 May 1945, 10 PSK began its march to Leer. At 08:00 hours it crossed the river by pontoon bridge. 10 PSK was to move upon Hessel while the way was being cleared by 2nd Tank Regiment (Polish) but after two hours of waiting Wasilewski realised that 2nd Tank was not going to make rapid penetration into Hessel, therefore he formulated his own plan. Wasilewski decided to bypass Hessel and the Friedeburg woods by taking his tanks along the southern side road via Nordmoor and enter the main route at a point four kilometres to the east of Hessel from where they could begin operations as according to plan. At 12:00 hours, Wasilewski attempted this manoeuvre using 2nd Squadron as vanguard. However a problem arose once 3rd Sqaudron reached the intersection (932 210) as the previous squadrons had ruined an already wrecked road. Wasilewski returned with 3rd Sqaudron along the route which they had just gone along and moved along the originally proposed route which 2nd Tank had finally opened and had linked up with 10 PSK along the main operational axis. After an hour, via a very marshy route, 10 PSK minus 3rd Sqaudron reached the main road leading from Hessel to Remels.

Upon engaging the enemy 1st Squadron captured an area towards Schwerinsdorf and later Grossoldendorf, where they captured quarters, taking prisoners as well as an artillery magazine and communications centre. In further action, the squadron, once more moving over difficult terrain, seized a bridge over a canal four kilometres to the north of Remels. The bridge was made of concrete and had been taken by surprise. The squadron also captured a pair of 20mm guns.

2nd Squadron, which operated along the main operational axis, came across a partly destroyed bridge over the River Ehe. The squadron moved swiftly to destroy enemy defences and captured the bridge. The bridge was left under the guard of two infantry platoons while the squadron began to reconnoitre further north towards Remels, moving in a circular route via Klein Oldendorf (already captured by 1st Sqaudron). After a bitter battle, the bridge over the River Ehe was seized and Remels captured. During the fighting an 88mm gun and six 20mm guns were destroyed. Sixty prisoners were also taken. After clearing Remels, 2nd Squadron moved towards the crossings to the east and to the south of Remels. Owing to the rapid and energetic action by 2nd Squadron both bridges in these directions were captured before the Germans could destroy them. The Germans had prepared many bridges for destruction but the speed of the Polish armour prevented them completing their plans and the bridges were saved.

The following morning, 2 May 1945 at 06:00 hours, the enemy laid down a heavy artillery barrage onto 10 PSK's lines, killing one man, Lance Corporal Jaroszewicz of 1st Squadron and wounding Private Kopowski. 1st Sqaudron counter-attacked, crossing the bridge and moving into the Grossander area. There the squadron was confronted by destroyed roads and enemy opposition (about a company of infantry). As a result of the strong assault by the squadron and its accurate firing, the enemy's resistance broke. A small bridge was captured and the wrecked routes were cleared in thirty minutes and the town fell to the Poles. When 1st Squadron wanted to push on it came across many obstacles, which included a cratered road, two anti-tank barricades and a mined bridge; all stoutly defended by the enemy. The squadron also came under a mixture of heavy artillery, mortar and machine gun fire. Furthermore, marshy terrain stopped the tanks from exiting the road and so bypassing obstacles.

A reconnaissance party from the squadron with a section from the assault squad set out to reconnoitre the infantry obstacles, firing at them in an attempt to destroy them. A squadron of Dragoons was also sent as support. At 11:25 hours the enemy opened fire with anti-tank weapons, including a mixed group of 75mm and 88m guns, in addition to heavy and accurate artillery fire. The assault by the enemy was furthered by lively attacks along the cratered route which caused considerable casualties to the squadron. 1st Squadron's Commander, Lieutenant Paweł Borzemski was killed along with Sergeant Jankowski, Corporal Zielinski and Private Jurkowski. Lance Corporal Łas and Private Piaskowski died later form their wounds. Three men Corporal Dragun, Lance Corporal

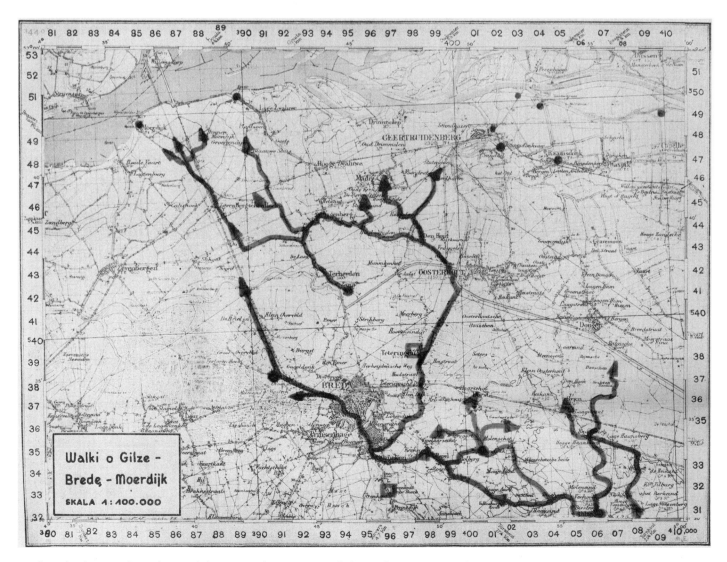

Battles of Gilze, Breda and Moerdijk. Dots indicate extent of planned operations at this time.

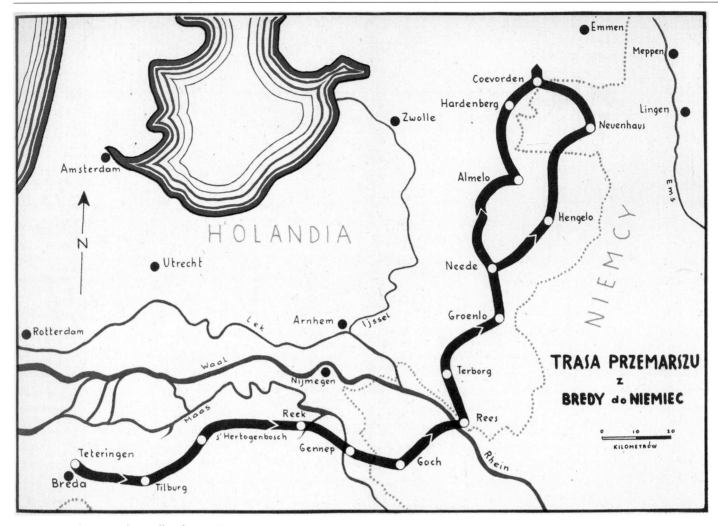

Main route from Breda, Holland into Germany.

Fron and Private Nadzieja were all wounded. One tank was destroyed and three damaged but 1st Squadron still held its position. As reinforcements arrived in the area the enemy was force to withdraw.

During the night of 2–3 May 1945 the enemy left Remels and withdrew towards the north and the east. 10 PSK with a company of infantry from 8BS entered Remels while 10 PSK throughout the day captured Moorburg, Hellweg, Westerstedde and Halsbeck. During the evening Wasilewski received orders for the following day: 10 PSK with a company from 8BS was to reconnoitre towards Neudenburg and further north towards Wittmund. The operational plan was that owing to the lack of suitable roads, 10 PSK was to move along a single axis with 3rd Squadron acting as vanguard. The regiment was to reconnoitre from Halsbeck, northwards towards Neuenburg and further to the northwest towards the Neuenburg woods and the towns of Marxs, Strudden, Friedeburg and Repsholt. There were reports from Allied aircraft concerning the presence of German tanks in front of the Division.

On 4 May 1945 at 07:15 hours, 3rd Squadron moved to the Halsbeck region where it met 1st Tank Regiment who during the night had lost contact with the enemy. 3rd Squadron upon reaching the intersection in the Asterfeld area met with the enemy and took four prisoners. About 200 metres from the intersection was a large crater in the road. As there were further craters in the road and obstacles en route, the squadron was forced to travel across country. The destruction of local routes was part of the enemy's defence and eventually the squadron was forced to halt its advance. Once halted the squadron poured fire upon the enemy until dusk. At dusk a company of infantry from 9BS came to 3rd Squadron's position with the purpose of attacking the enemy position. These preparations were not needed because of the surrender of the German Army in the 21st Army Group sector. 10 PSK ordered 3rd Squadron to withdraw one mile southwest of the main road and from there take up a guard position.

At 21:00 hours the official news of the capitulation of the German Army came and the cessation of further action at 08:00 hours, 5 May 1945. 10 PSK remained at this post until 8 May 1945 when the 1st Polish Armoured Division moved to the regions of Wilhelmshaven and Jever where it supervised the capitulation of the German Army in that region.

At last for the Poles the war was over.

10 PSK Casualty Rate between 7 April 1945 and 8 May 1945

Personnel	Officers	Ranks	Total
Killed	1	16	17
Wounded	1	26	27
Total	2	42	44

German Losses against 10 PSK between 7 April 1945 and 8 May 1945:

517 prisoners, one 88mm gun, two 75mm guns, 17 guns of 50mm or less calibre, two scout vars, one motorcycle, forty barges containing supplies for a Corps and one artillery dump.

Overall German Casualties against 10 PSK from 8 August 1944 and 8 May 1945:

3,328 prisoners (including a general), 19 tanks, 21 88mm and 75mm self-propelled guns, 135 anti-tank guns, four *Nebelwerfers*, three armoured cars, 24 half-tracked tractors, 11 motorcycles, one fuel dump, forty barges with material for a Corps, six sea-going barges and one fully armed patrol boat.

10 PSK Casualty Rates between 8 August 1944 and 8 May 1945:

Personnel	Officers	Ranks	Total
Killed	7	83*	90
Wounded	41	192	233
Total	48	275	323

* Three Sergeant Majors were promoted posthumously to officer rank.

Sequel

Tadeusz Wysocki records that when the 1st Polish Armoured Division took charge of Wilhelmshaven the amount of prisoners and equipment was incredible. The prisoners numbered 19,000 officers including two Admirals and a General. The haul of equipment was impressive: three cruisers, 18 submarines, 205 minor battleships and support vessels, 94 fortress guns, 159 field guns, 560 machine guns, 40,000 rifles, 280,000 artillery shells and 64 million rounds of small arms ammunition. In addition there were also stores of mines and torpedoes as well as supplies of food for 50,000 troops for a six month period.[146]

The Poles who had been driven from their homes nearly six years before should have felt that this was a moment of triumph but for one thing: they still had no country to return to. From my time as an undergraduate at the University of London, I recall the distinguished historian, Norman Davies, assert that often a war and its conclusion is seen in the simplistic terms of good defeating evil. Davies added that the conclusion of the Second World War did not bring such an ending. The Soviet Union was on the side of the victors but for the next forty-five years it tyrannised East-Central Europe. The Polish troops on the whole felt that they could not return to Poland as some had already felt the injustice of the Soviet system while others knew that by fighting for the west they would be labelled in Poland as fascists – quite ironic.

I will conclude by illustrating what happened after the war to some of the men who fought in the 1st Polish Armoured Division. General Maczek remained commander of the Division until only 20 May 1945. After that he took command of the Polish Resettlement Corps, based in Scotland. He lived until he was 102 years of age and died in December 1994. He was the only Polish wartime general to live to see a free Poland and is recognised today in Poland as a true Polish war hero; following years of being denied Polish citizenship. Sadly though, Maczek was too frail to travel to Poland after the collapse of Communism there in 1989. After leaving Poland in 1939 he was never to see his beloved homeland again. He is buried at Breda; the scene of his greatest triumph.[147]

Antoni Położyński was demobbed in 1947 and settled in West Yorkshire where he went into business, married and had children and grandchildren. He did not return to Poland until 1964. When he left Poland in 1940 he was never to see his parents again as they died in the intervening twenty-four years. He died aged 89 during 2003.

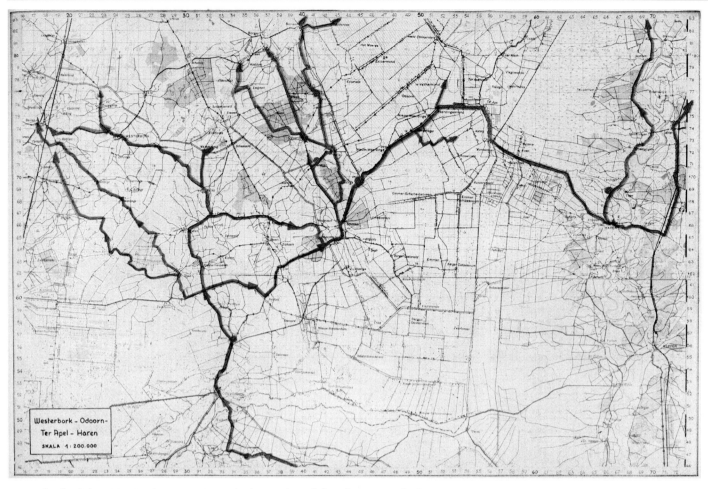

Westerbork, Odoor-Ter Apel-Haren. Towards the war's end, heading towards Germany.

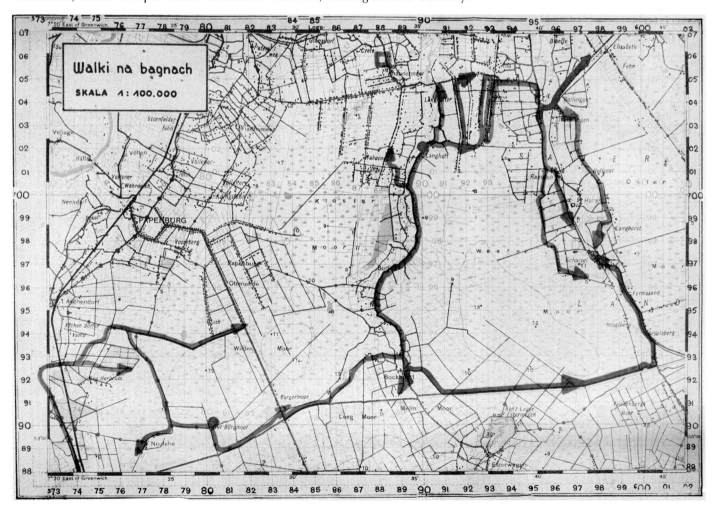

Battle of the Marshes.

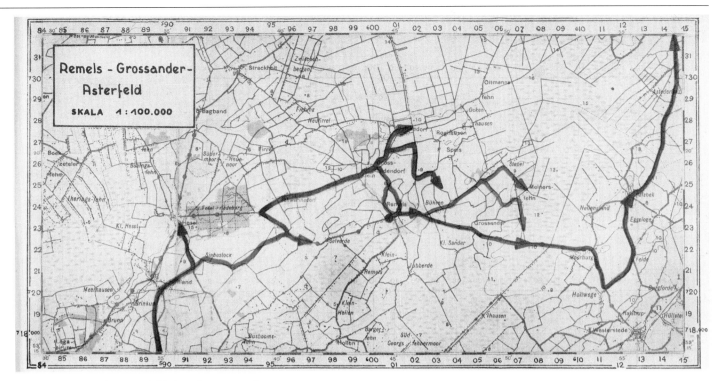

Remels-Grossander-Asterfeld, heading towards Germany.

Chaim Goldberg has never returned to Poland. As all of his family perished in the Treblinka death camp he feels that he has nothing to return to. Instead Goldberg made a new life in Canada where he married, opened a fishmonger's and raised a family.

Tadeusz Walewicz was warned by his mother in a letter not to return to Poland. He too made a new life in Canada. Franciszek Skibinski did return to Poland. He was tried by the Communist regime and sentenced to death but the sentence was never carried out. For five years he remained in a limbo between life and death. After the ending of Stalinism in Poland during 1956 he was quietly released and resumed his military career in the Polish Army under Communist control, known as the Polish Peoples' Army.[148] This same army was to be instrumental in putting down workers' protests in Poland during the Communist era.

In 1945 Europe was in chaos and as Położyński points out, no Pole knew what was really happening in Poland. It was difficult for Polish soldiers to decide whether to return to Poland or not. All that they knew was that Poland had suffered horribly and that the Soviet Army was occupying the country. It led many Poles who had fought across Europe to decide that at present there was no free Poland to return to; but that there would be one day. None of them suspected that it would take fifty years to see such a reality.

Order of Battle,
Polish 1st Armoured Division, August 1944

Headquarters & Divisional Support Units

Division HQ incl HQ Squadron
Quartermaster Section
Chaplain Service Section
Provost Squadron
1st Traffic Control Squadron
Field Security Section
8th Court Martial Section
Paymaster Section
Field Post Section
1st Forward Tank Delivery Squadron
10th Mounted Rifle Regiment

10th Armoured Brigade

Staff & HQ Squadron
10th Dragoons
24th Uhlans
1st Tank Regiment
2nd Tank Regiment

Each of the four armoured regiments consisted of a HQ Squadron, 1st-3rd Squadrons and a Support Squadron.

Each standard Squadron consisted of 1st-3rd Troops, Scout Troop, Service Troop, Mortar Section.

Each Support Squadron consisted of 1st Troop (Machine Gun), 2nd Troop (Machine Gun), 3rd Troop (Anti-Tank), 4th Troop (Anti-Tank), 5th Troop (Anti-Tank).

3rd Rifle Brigade

HQ Company
8th Rifle Battalion
9th Rifle Battalion
Podhalanski Rifle Battalion
1st Independent Machine Gun Squadron

Divisional Artillery

HQ
1st Artillery Regiment
2nd Artillery Regiment
1st Anti-Tank Regiment
1st Anti-Aircraft Regiment

Divisional Engineers

HQ
10th Engineer Company
11th Engineer Company
Field Park Company
Bridging Troop

Divisional Signals
(Designated Signal Battalion on 15 January 1945.)
HQ Signal Squadron
2nd, 10th & 11th Signal Squadrons

Divisional Transport Troops

HQ, Divisional Service Troops
Transport Company, Divisional
10th Transport Company, Armoured Brigade
3rd Transport Company, Rifle Brigade

Divisional Workshops & Ordnance Service

Workshop Company, Armoured Brigade
Workshop Company, Rifle Brigade
1st Field Park

Divisional Medical Services

10th Light Field Ambulance
11th Heavy Field Ambulance
1st Field Dressing Station
1st Field Hygiene Station

Medal Recipients

Medal Recipients of
10th Motorised Cavalry Brigade, Polish Campaign, September 1939

The Order of the Virtuti Militari Class IV – Gold Cross

Deskur, Jerzy, Major.
Dworak, Kazimierz, Colonel.

Maczek, Stanisław, Colonel.

The Order of the Virtuti Militari Class V – Silver Cross

Bielatowicz, Józef, Second Lieutenant (P) [Posthumously]
Bukraba, Zygmunt, Lieutenant. (P).
Duszynski, Stanisław, Corporal
Dziechciarz, Wincenty, Corporal. (P).
Dziuba, Franciszek, Corporal. (P).
Eustachiewicz, Kazimierz, Second Lieutenant. (P).
Franczak, Antoni, Cadet Officer.
Hempel Zdzisław, Captain. (P)
Hojnacki, Bronisław, Sergeant.
Howrysz, Kazimierz, Second Lieutenant.
Jozefowicz, Henryk, Lieutenant.
Kała, Stefan, Cadet Officer.

Kański, Jan, Corporal. (P)
Katz, Lejb, Gunner.
Kiersz, Wiesław, Lieutenant.
Kowerski, Andrzej, Second Lieutenant.
Krachelski, Stanisław, Captain.
Kubacki, Feliks, Sergeant.
Manka, Józef, Corporal.
Medwecki, Adam, Cadet Officer.
Moszczenski, Zygmunt, Lieutenant-Colonel.
Mroz, Józef F. Second Lieutenant.
Pawlowski, Wincenty, Captain.
Radiwiłłowicz, Romuald, Captain.
Rupniak, Marcin, Second Lieutenant.

Siemienski, Roman, Warrant Officer Class 2 (WO2).
Stanko, Aleksander, Captain. (P).
Sum, Józef, Cadet Officer.
Swiecicki, Ksawery, Major.
Uberman, Leon, Corporal. (P).
Urban, Walenty, Cadet Officer.
Waliłko, Antoni, Sergeant.
Zakrzewski, Jan, Cadet Officer.
Zawadzski, Alfred, Lieutenant.
Żarski, Jerzy, P. Lieutenant.
Żmudziński, Kazimierz, Major. (P).

Krzyż Walecznych (Cross for Valour).

Abramowicz, Józef, Lance Corporal.
Andryszczak, Jan, Corporal.
Arciszewski, Mikołaj, Trooper.
Augustyniak, Stanisław, Corporal.
Badowski, Henryk, Trooper.
Banach, Kazimierz, Sergeant.
Bara, Stanisław, WO2.
Bassa, Feliks, Lance Corporal.
Bator, Roman, Corporal.
Bauer, Kazimierz, Corporal.
Balka, Franciszek, Corporal.
Bernecki, Stefan, Corporal.
Bielczyk, Jerzy. M, Second Lieutenant.
Bieniasz, Konstanty, Sergeant Major.
Bieniek, Leopold, Sergeant.
Bieniek, Władysław, Corporal.
Bilski, Kazimierz, Lieutenant.
Biszewski, Edmund, Cadet Officer.
Błaszak, Feliks, Sergeant Major.
Bober, Antoni, Second Lieutenant.
Bogut, Aleksander, Trooper.

Borcholski, Mieczysław. T, Second Lieutenant.
Borych, Edmund, Corporal.
Boś, Jan, Trooper.
Bosztak, Kazimierz, Trooper.
Bosztak, Kazimierz, Trooper.
Breś, Jan, Trooper.
Broda, Adolf, Corporal.
Broś, Stanisław, Trooper. (P).
Brzeziński, Zbigniew. R, Second Lieutenant.
Buczkowski, Mateusz, Sergeant.
Burniewicz, Jan, Corporal. (Awarded Twice).
Bury, Stefan, Second Lieutenant.
Cegłowski, Antoni, Corporal.
Chałupa, Jan, Trooper. (P).
Chmaj, Franciszek, Corporal.
Chodor, Roman, Cadet Officer.
Chojnowski, Bolesław, Sergeant.
Cholewa, Piotr, Lance Corporal.
Chuchnowski, Rudolf, Corporal. (P).

Chwicewski, Bolesław, Sergeant.
Cieśliński, Herman, Lieutenant. (Awarded Twice).
Cobulski, Mikołaj, Private. (P).
Cup, Kazimierz, Corporal.
Cwikliński, Jerzy, Second Lieutenant. (P).
Czajkowski, Wiesław, Cadet Officer.
Czajkowski, Władysław, Corporal.
Czarnecki, Marian. N, Lieutenant. (Awarded Twice).
Czerkirda, Władysław, Corporal. (P).
Czerwiak, Józef, Lance Corporal. (Awarded Twice).
Dąbek, Władysław, Lieutenant.
Dejner, Franciszek, no rank given. (P).
Doleżek? Lance Corporal.
Domaradzki, Jan, Trooper.
Dręgiel, Tadeusz, Corporal.
Drwięga, Józef, Corporal.
Drygała, Jan, Corporal.
Duda, Feliks, Corporal. (P)
Duda, Józef, Sergeant.

Dudek, Stefan, Corporal.

Dymski, Krzyżostan, Warrant Officer Class One (WO1).

Fedasz, Taras, Lieutenant.

Ferenstein, Ludwik, Captain.

Fliski, Zbigniew, Corporal.

Florian, Józef, Second Lieutenant.

Franczak, Antoni, Corporal.

Gano, Władysław, Corporal. (P).

Garczyński, Marian, Second Lieutenant.

Gasiewicz, Kazimierz, Gunner.

Gełesz, Ludwik, Sergeant.

Głudko, Stefan, Private.

Gniady, Bronisław, Lance Corporal.

Goj, Franciszek, Corporal.

Golej, Aleksander, Corporal.

Goreczny, Roman, Lance Corporal. (P).

Grabowski, Stanisław, WO1.

Gradowski, Kazimierz, Corporal.

Grajkowski, Jan, Major.

Greiner, Henryk, Second Lieutenant.

Grudziński, Lieutenant. (Awarded Twice).

Gurbiel, Kazimierz, Cadet Officer.

Gurdak, Jan, Trooper.

Gwozdziewski, Aleksander, Trooper.

Haduch, Antoni, Cadet Officer.

Haluszkiewicz, Wladysław, Sergeant.

Hamera, Kazimierz, Trooper.

Hołub, Stanisław, Corporal. (Awarded Twice).

Horowski, Edward, Corporal.

Hunka, Stanisław, Sergeant Major.

Irzykowski, Józef, Lieutenant. (P).

Jagniński, Andrzej, Lieutenant.

Jancewicz, Włodzimierz, Sergeant. (Awarded Twice).

Jandula, Wilhelm, Bombardier.

Jarosz, Michał, Lance Corporal.

Jasiński, Stanisław, Corporal.

Jastrzębski, Adam, Trooper.

Kaczmarek, Teodor, Lieutenant.

Kański, Jan. W, Captain. (Awarded Twice).

Kardasiński, Michał, Trooper.

Karst, Henryk, Corporal.

Kida, Jan, Corporal. (Awarded Twice).

Kleszcz, Józef, Corporal.

Klin, Michał, Trooper.

Kloc, Stanisław, Corporal.

Kluska, Józef, Trooper.

Kłyś, Józef, Trooper.

Kociuba, Wacław, Lance Corporal.

Kociuk, Maksymilian, Lance Corporal.

Kocjan, Stanisław, Corporal.

Koliński, Piotr, Corporal.

Kominek, Stefan, Lieutenant (Doctor).

Konicki, Stefan, Captain.

Kopeć, Stanisław, Corporal.

Koprowski, Edward, Trooper.

Koronkiewicz, Zygmunt, Second Lieutenant.

Korytkowski, Włodzimierz, Captain.

Korzeniowski, Stanisław, Sergeant.

Kos, Stanisław, Corporal.

Kozak, Józef, Corporal.

Krawczyk, Eryk, Gunner. (P).

Krogulec, Zygmunt, Corporal.

Król, Stanisław, Trooper. (P).

Kubala, Józef, Trooper.

Kubiak, Leon, Corporal.

Kucharczyk, Stanisław, Sapper.

Kucza, Stanisław, Corporal.

Kudła, Jan, Lance Corporal.

Kuhlman, Tadeusz, Second Lieutenant.

Kuna, Aleksander, Gunner.

Kupiec, Tomasz, Corporal (P).

Kurzawa, Zygmunt, Corporal.

Kwiecień, Wladysław, Corporal.

Laszczewski, Stanisław, Trooper.

Laszczyk, Władysław, Corporal.

Lech, Jerzy, Officer Cadet.

Lencewicz, Władysław, Lance Corporal.

Leśkow, Jan, Corporal.

Leśniak, Stanisław, Bombardier.

Leśniak, Tadeusz, Corporal.

Lipiec, Stanislaw, Sergeant.

Łazowicki, Stanisław, Trooper. (Awarded Twice).

Łeczyński, Antoni, No rank given.

Łoboda, Zygmunt, Corporal. (P).

Łoś, Stanisław, Trooper.

Łukaszewicz, Edward, Second Lieutenant. (Awarded Twice).

Łukowski, Stefan, Captain. (Awarded Twice).

Macek, Władysław, Private.

Mackiw, Bazyli, Sapper.

Mackiewicz, Piotr, WO1.

Madej, Józef, Bombardier.

Maj, Bolesław, Lance Corporal.

Majer, Roman, Bombardier.

Makowski, Karol, Corporal.

Maksymowicz, Stanisław, Bombardier.

Maksymowicz, Zbigniew, Second Lieutenant.

Malawski, Henryk, Corporal.

Maleszewski, Tadeusz, Captain.

Malicki, Władysław, Corporal. (Awarded Twice).

Marczuk, Edward, Lance Corporal.

Marczak, Michał, Corporal.

Maszkiewicz, Jerzy, Corporal.

Matiuszyn, Marian, Corporal.

Mazurek, Tadeusz, Trooper. (P).

Menderek, Stefan, Trooper.

Michalski, Stanisław, Lieutenant.

Mikiewicz, Zdzislaw, Bombardier.

Miller, Henryk, Sergeant Major. (Awarded Twice).

Mincer, Bohdan. A, Captain.

Młodzinski, Jakub, Lance Corporal.

Mocha, Dominik, Private.

Mordal, Stanisław, Corporal.

Moskaluk, Jan, Private.

Mucha, Władysław, Sergeant.

Mucha, Krzysztof, Corporal.

Niecko, Władysław, Trooper. (P).

Niemira, Lucjan. Sergeant.

Niedzieliński, Alfons, Corporal.

Nitrus, Edmund, Lance Corporal. (P).

Niziołek, Józef, Corporal.

Nowak, Aleksy, Gunner.

Nowakowski, Janusz, Lieutenant.

Nowakowski, Jerzy, Lieutenant. (Awarded Twice).

Nowicki, Maciej, Lieutenant. (Awarded Twice).

Nyka, Franciszek, Lance Corporal.

Okapiec, Antoni, Corporal.

Olczak, Feliks, Trooper.

Olechowski, Stefan, Corporal.

Olewicz, Aleksy, Corporal.

Onak, Franciszek, Corporal.

Opitek, Henryk, Lance Corporal.

Osiecki, Wincenty, Lance Corporal.

Ostaszewski, Józef, Second Lieutenant. (Awarded Twice).

Ostrombski, Mieczysław, Second Lieutenant. (Awarded Twice).

Ostrowski, Stefan, Corporal.

Ostrzycki, Jerzy, Lieutenant.

Ożog, Józef, Trooper. (P).

Pałycha, Leon, Corporal.

Pasek, Wincenty, Corporal.

Pasternak, Michał, Corporal.

Patalas, Antoni, Corporal.

Paul, Konrad, Corporal.

Pawelczak, Józef, Corporal.

Pawłowicz, Władysław, Major (Doctor).

Pelc, Stanisław, Sergeant Major.

Pest, Jan, Sergeant.

Piechocki, Jan, Corporal.

Piechota, Józef, Corporal.

Pieregorodzki, Anatol, Captain.

Piklikiewicz, Stefan, Lieutenant. (Awarded Twice).

Piotrowski, Antoni, WO1.

Piotrowski, Jan, Corporal.

Piotrowski, Stanisław, Captain.

Piwoński, Marian, Lieutenant. (Awarded Twice).

Piwowar, Kazimierz, Corporal.

Pizoń, Stanisław, Trooper. (P).

Plichta, Marian, Second Lieutenant.

Płachciński, Adam, Trooper.

Podleśny, Jan, Corporal. (P).

Podolak, Władysław, Corporal.

Polit, Władysław, Captain.

Polończak, Józef, Corporal.

Porczyński, Leon, Corporal.

Porębski, Adolf, Sergeant Major.

Potapczyk, Wacław, Corporal.

Powroźnik, Zbigniew, Sergeant.

Pozdniak, Jan, Lance Corporal.

Proc, Michał, Trooper. (P).

Przanowski, Jan, Second Lieutenant.
(Awarded Twice).

Przezdziecki, Tadeusz, Lieutenant
(Doctor [Awarded Twice]).

Racki, Franciszek, Corporal.

Rakowski, Władysław, Lieutenant,
(Awarded Three Times).

Rapa, Stefan, Trooper. (P).

Raube, Ryszard, Corporal.

Romaniuk, Aleksander, Sergeant.

Roniker, Stefan, Second Lieutenant.

Runge, Brunon, Sergeant.

Runkowski, Mieczysław, WO1.
(Awarded Twice).

Rut, Stanisław, Corporal.

Ryś, Jan, Lance Corporal.

Ryszkowski, Czesław, Sergeant.

Ryzner, Jan, Lance Corporal.

Rzewuski, Stanisław, Corporal.

Sadowiec, Henryk, Trooper.

Sadownik, Jerzy, Second Lieutenant. (P).

Samujło, Antoni, Corporal.
(Awarded Twice).

Sasim, Tytus, Lieutenant.

Sawczuk, Emilian. G, Second Lieutenant.

Serwata, Józef, Lance Corporal.

Siczek, Franciszek, Corporal. (P).

Siedlecki, Eugeniusz, Second Lieutenant.

Sienko, Czesław, Corporal.
(Awarded Three Times).

Sikorski, Jan, Captain.

Skowronek, Ludwik, Lance Corporal.

Skrok, Stefan, Corporal.

Skrzypek, Franciszek, Trooper.

Slusarczyk, Aleksander, Private.

Słatyński, Emil, Major.
(Awarded Three Times).

Smagła, Stanisław, Lance Corporal.

Smiech, Stanisław, Corporal.

Smok, Bolesław, Corporal.

Smołucha, Stanisław, Trooper.

Smotryś, Karol, Lance Corporal.

Smutek, Andrzej, Lance Corporal.

Sokołowski, Stanisław, Trooper.

Solecki, Józef, Private.

Stachura, Jan, Lance Corporal.

Stala, Jan, Corporal.

Stankiewicz, Ludwik, Captain.

Starzomski, Bronisław, Corporal.

Starzyński, Zygmunt, Lieutenant.

Surdacki, Wacław, Trooper.

Suska, Kazimierz, Sergeant.

Swist, Dominik, Corporal.

Synowiecki, Józef, Gunner. (P).

Synówka, Antoni, Cadet Officer.

Syrokosz, Aleksander, Trooper.

Szabat, Jan, Corporal.

Szaleniec, Wilhelm, Sergeant Major.

Szałkowski, Zygmunt, Sergeant.
(Awarded Twice).

Szarko, Jan, Trooper. (Awarded Twice).

Szczeniowski, Wacław, WO1.

Szczepanik, Bronisław, Corporal.

Szczepański, Stanisław, WO2.

Szeszko, Jan, Sapper.

Szewczak, Paweł, Trooper.

Szewczyk, Franciszek, Sergeant.

Szewerniak, Leon, Sergeant. (P).

Szmigiel, Jan, Sergeant Major.
(Awarded Twice).

Szmuc, Julian, Cadet Officer.

Sznajder, Edward, WO1.

Szpejnowski, Aleksander, Sergeant Major.

Szpunar, Józef, Corporal.

Szpunar, Władysław, Corporal. (P).

Szumniak, Zygmunt, Lance Corporal.

Szydłowski, Emil, Corporal.
(Awarded Twice [P]).

Szylberg, Wacław, Corporal.

Szymik, Jan, Corporal.

Szyszko, Józef, Corporal.

Szyszko, Tadeusz, Corporal.
(Awarded Twice).

Taras, Stanisław, Second Lieutenant.

Taraszka, Jan, Lance Corporal.

Targoński, Leon, Trooper (P).

Tarkowski, Tadeusz, Lance Corporal.

Tomaszewski, Stanisław, Corporal.

Tomczyk, Julian, Corporal.

Tomczyk, Stanisław, Corporal.

Tomkowicz, Antoni, Captain.

Toruń, Bronisław, Trooper.

Trojan, Ludwik, WO1. (Awarded Twice)

Tymiec, Piotr, Lance Corporal.

Walarowski, Bolesław, Corporal.

Walas, Ignacy, Corporal.

Walter, Władysław, Sergeant.

Warzocha, Stanisław, Corporal.
(Awarded Twice).

Wasilewski, Jerzy, Lieutenant.

Wasilewski, Leon, Trooper. (P).

Warzocha, Karol, Corporal.

Weber, Józef. H, Second Lieutenant.

Weclewicz, Władysław, Gunner.

Widomdski, Edward, Sergeant Major.

Wiech, Michał, Lance Corporal.

Wielus, Józef, Trooper. (Awarded Twice).

Wijas, Albin, Lance Corporal.

Wilewski, Michał, Corporal.
(Awarded Twice).

Witkowski, Wacław, Corporal.

Wnuczek, Szczepan, Corporal.

Wojcik, Jan, Corporal.

Wojtowicz, Mieczysław, Corporal.

Wolańczyk, Piotr, Sergeant Major.

Wołkowicz, Wiktor, Sergeant. (P).

Wołódko, Franciszek, Trooper.

Wołos, Wawrzyniec, Trooper.

Wróbel, Józef, Corporal.

Wydmuch, Jan, Trooper.

Zając, Jozef, Corporal.

Zajączkowski, Franciszek, Corporal.
(Awarded Twice).

Zarembiński, Wiktor, Captain.
(Awarded Three Times)

Zaruba, Czesław, Second Lieutenant.

Zarzycki, Roman, Trooper.
(Awarded Twice [P]).

Zdun, Józef, Corporal.

Zdybel, Józef, Corporal.

Zgórka, Edward, Corporal.

Zięba, Edward, Second Lieutenant.

Zieliński, Czesław, Corporal.

Zieliński, Józef, Corporal.

Ziental, Bolesław, Sergeant.

Zioło, Stanisław, Corporal.

Zmroczek, Franciszek, Second Lieutenant.
(Awarded Twice).

Medal Recipients from the
10th Motorised Brigade for the French Campaign, 1940

Order of the Virtuti Militari Class V Silver Cross

Bućko, Michał, Corporal.

Czapliński, Władysław, Captain.

Czerniewicz, Witold, Captain.

Hornowski, Witold, Cadet Officer. (P).

Jabłoński, Stanisław, Cadet Officer. (P).

Jurecki, Marian, Lieutenant.

Łatka, Andrzej, Trooper.

Maciejewski, Zbigniew, Lance Corporal.

Martini, Sforza, Kazimierz, Captain.

Niepokojczycki, Włodzimierz, Lieutenant.

Slaski, Ludomil, Lieutenant.

Stankiewicz, Ludwik, Captain.

Trocki, Adolf, Cadet Officer.

Krzyż Walecznych

Andrzejewski, Henryk, Second Lieutenant.

Andrzejewski, Walerian, Sergeant.

Babańczyk, Stanisław, Second Lieutenant.

Banaś, Jan, Cadet Officer.

Bartnik, Jan, Sergeant.

Bilon, Edward, Cadet Officer.

Bojkowski, Felicjan, Corporal. (Awarded Twice).

Budkowski, Edward, Lance Corporal.

Bugajski, Tadeusz, Lance Corporal.

Brzeziński, Stanisław, Trooper. (P).

Chojnowski, Bolesław, Sergeant. (Awarded Twice).

Chomentowski, Eugeniusz, Second Lieutenant.

Chrost, Wacław, Trooper. (P).

Chylak, Jan, Trooper.

Czarnecki, Jerzy, Cadet Officer.

Czarnecki, Kamil. B, Lieutenant.

Dębowski, Jan, Corporal.

Domanski, Stanisław, Second Lieutenant.

Doskoczyński, Tadeusz, Cadet Officer.

Duchowny, Michał, Corporal.

Dziedzic, Jan, Corporal. (P).

Flis, Kazimierz, Lance Corporal.

Forster, Paweł, Second Lieutenant.

Fudakowski, Zygmunt, Second Lieutenant.

Gaj, Józef, Trooper.

Gajewski, Roman, Trooper.

Gargula, Kazimierz, Corporal.

Gąsiorowski, Jerzy, Cadet Officer.

Giertowski, Wojciech, Trooper.

Gniadek, Tadeusz, Corporal. (P).

Godorowski, Jerzy, Trooper.

Godunow, Borys, Captain.

Goj, Władysław, Corporal.

Góral, Józef, Lance Corporal. (P).

Grabowski, Stanisław, WO1. (Awarded Twice).

Grabski, Józef, Captain.

Grzebalski, Mieczysław, Cadet Officer.

Gumiński, Wacław, Sergeant.

Hajman, Roman, Second Lieutenant.

Huk, Andrzej, Trooper (Awarded Twice).

Iwanowski, Władysław, Second Lieutenant. (Awarded Twice).

Janas, Henryk, Corporal.

Jebwabny, Bolesław, Sergeant.

Juchab, Wojciech, Sergeant.

Kamala, Mirosław, Second Lieutenant.

Kaszubowski, Jan, Captain.

Kiercul, Edward, Sergeant. (P).

Kiersz, Wiesław, Captain.

Klej, Seweryn, Sergeant.

Kochański, Mikołaj, Sergeant.

Kociołek, Edmund, Corporal.

Koliński, Piotr, Corporal. (Awarded Twice)

Kołosowski, Stanisław, Corporal.

Konarski, Aleksander, Cadet Officer. (Awarded Twice).

Kopczyński, Zbigniew, Lieutenant.

Kostuch, Tomasz, Second Lieutenant.

Kowalski, Aleksander, Corporal.

Kozubowski, Tadeusz, Second Lieutenant. (P).

Krajewski, Edmund, Cadet Officer.

Krajewski, Franciszek, Sergeant.

Kramarczyk, Bolesław, Trooper.

Krasicki, Stanisław, Cadet Officer.

Krasiński, Stanisław, Second Lieutenant.

Kubasiński, Stanisław, Trooper.

Kukuła, Kazimierz, Corporal.

Kula, Eugeniusz, Corporal.

Kulesza, Tadeusz, Lance Corporal.

Kurnik, Leopold, Staff Sergeant.

Lebelt, Zenon, Second Lieutenant.

Lemański, Konstanty, Corporal.

Leśko, Stanisław, Corporal.

Lisowski, Franciszek, Bombardier.

Liwiński, Józef, Corporal. (P).

Łomacki, Hermenegild. Trooper.

Majchrzak, Piotr, Corporal.

Majewski, Leon, Corporal.

Majewski, Feliks, Trooper.

Majewski, Tadeusz, Lieutenant Colonel. (Awarded Twice).

Major, Józef, Corporal.

Malanowski, Władysław, Lieutenant. (Awarded Twice).

Marek, Stanisław, Second Lieutenant.

Marszałek, Jan, Corporal.

Matuszewski, Stefan, Staff Sergeant.

Miastkowski, Stanisław, Trooper. (P).

Michałowski, Jozef, Lieutenant.

Mielec, Andrzej, Sergeant.

Miller, Stanisław, Trooper. (P).

Mincer, Bohdan. A, Major. (Awarded Twice).

Nalepa, Eugeniusz, Trooper.

Neklaws, Wiktor, Captain.

Nowakowski, Kazimierz, Cadet Officer.

Ostromęcki, Adam, Cadet Officer.

Pasieka, Kazimierz, Corporal.

Pasionek, Tadeusz, Second Lieutenant.

Pelczarski, Eugeniusz. J, Cadet Officer.

Piątkowski, Jerzy, Lieutenant.

Pieregorodzki, Anatol, Captain. (Awarded Twice).

Pietrzak, Feliks, WO1.

Piłat, Czesław, Corporal. (P).

Piotrowski, Antoni, WO1. (Awarded Twice).

Piotrowski, Jan, Corporal. (Awarded Three Times).

Pokutyński, Feliks, Trooper. (P).

Polański, Henryk, Second Lieutenant.

Popiel, Janusz, Second Lieutenant. (Awarded Twice).

Proszek, Roman, Lieutenant.

Rogowski, Janusz, Corporal.

Sajnog, Ignacy, Trooper. (Awarded Twice).

Sakiewicz, Władysław, Second Lieutenant.

Saphieha, Leopold, Cadet Officer. (P).

Scipio del Campo, Andrzej, Trooper.

Serafin, Ludwik, Corporal.

Sikora, Roman, Second Lieutenant.

Skibinski, Franciszek, Lieutenant Colonel.

Skulski, Stanisław, Cadet Officer.

Smigiel, Jan, Cadet Officer.

Stala, Stanisław. K, Trooper.

Stefanowicz, Aleksander, Captain.

Stwora, Jacek, Cadet Officer.

Strzelecki, Wiktor. J, Corporal.

Superson, Jan, Corporal.

Szczepański, Stanislaw, Cadet Officer.

Szleifer, Brunon, Corporal.

Szwiec, Waldermar, Cadet Officer.

Thoma, Jerzy, Second Lieutenant.

Wentel, Antoni, Corporal.

Więcław, Florian, Sergeant.

Witek, Józef, Sergeant.

Witosławski, Jan, Trooper. (P).

Wolaniecki, Aleksander, Corporal.

Wójcik, S. Cadet Officer.

Wysocki, Eugeniusz, Corporal.

Zgorzelski, Antoni, Major. (Awarded Twice).

Zieliński, Antoni, Sergeant.

Zieliński, Ryszard, Corporal.

Zwierzanski, Michał, Corporal.

Zwil, Roman, Lieutenant.

Żuryn, Włodzimierz, Corporal.

French Awards

Croix de Guerre

Berbeć, Aleksander, Lance Corporal.

Blay, Czesław, Corporal.

Chyzyński, Stanisław, Corporal.

Czapliński, Władysław, Captain.

Czarnecki, Kamil. B, Lieutenant.

Gąsiorowski, Józef, Cadet Officer.

Irzykowski, Józef, Lieutenant.
Iwanowski, Władysław, Lieutenant.
Kacałaj, Władysław, Corporal.
Kiercul, Edward, Sergeant. (P).
Kiersz, Wiesław, Captain.
Klisowski, Kazimierz, Corporal.
Krasicki, Stanisław, Regimental
Sergeant Major.
Kwaśnik, Stanisław, Cadet Officer.
Łopata, Stanisław, Corporal. (P).
Maj, Mikołaj, Corporal.
Majewski, Tadeusz, Lieutenant Colonel.

Majewski, Leon, Corporal.
Makiełło, Ludwik, Lieutenant.
Maniak, Stanisław, Major.
Martine, Sforza, Kazimierz, Captain.
Mincer, Bohdan, Major.
Nowakowski, Kazimierz, Corporal.
Ostromęcki, Adam, Cadet Officer.
Pasieka, Kazimierz, Corporal.
Piłat, Czesław, Corporal. (P).
Popiel, Janusz, Second Lieutenant.
Sapieha, Leon, Sergeant Major. (P).

Siewertacki, Wacław, Captain.
Skibiński, Franciszek, Lieutenant Colonel.
Soja, Wacław, Corporal.
Stankiewicz, Ludwik, Captain.
Staziński, Private.
Swidziński, Kazimierz, Corporal.
Szklarz, Bronisław, Corporal.
Terlecki, Jerzy, Corporal.
Witek, Józef, Sergeant.
Wójcik, Bolesław, Cadet Officer.
Zgorzelski, Władysław, Major.

Medaille Commemorative Française De La Guerre 1939–1945 Avec Barratte 'France'

Every soldier from 10th Motorised Cavalry Brigade.

Medal Recipients of the 1st Polish Armoured Division for Campaigns in France, Belgium, Holland and Germany, 1944–1945.

Order of the Virtuti Militari Class III – Krzyż Kawalerski (Knight Companion)

Maczek, Stanisław, General of Division (Lieutenant General).

Order of the Virtuti Militari Class IV – Gold Cross

Maciejowski, Jan, Major. (P).
Majewski, Tadeusz, Colonel.

Noel, Bronisław, Colonel.
Skibinski, Franciszek, Colonel.

Wasilewski, Jerzy, Major.
Zgorzelski, Władysław,
Lieutenant Colonel.

Order of the Virtuti Militari Class V – Silver Cross

Akimow, Paweł, Corporal.
Andrzejewski, Edmund, Lieutenant.
Antonczyk, Alojzy, Corporal.
Antonowicz, Mikołaj, Lieutenant.
Bachurzewski, Zbigniew, Lieutenant.
Bagiński, Stanisław, Sergeant. (P).
Baraniak, Józef, Sergeant Major.
Bartosiński, Marian, Captain.
Baskowski, Wilhelm, Lance Corporal.
Bednarczyk, Bolesław, Private.
Biały, Zdzisław, Lieutenant.
Bielawski, Jacek, Captain.
Biliński, Józef, Sergeant. (P).
Blicharski, Antoni, Corporal.
Błaszkiewicz, Dariusz, Second Lieutenant.
Błaszczyk, Czesław, Second Lieutenant.
Bniński, Roman, Lieutenant.
Bochniewicz, Michał, Lieutenant. (P).
Bogdanowicz, Tadeusz, Staff Sergeant.
Bohdanowicz, Konrad, Lieutenant.
Bohm, Zbigniew, Cadet Officer.
Bojanowski, Zbigniew, Captain.
Borecki, Mikołaj, Lance Corporal.

Borkowski, Henryk, Lance Corporal.
Borowicz, Edward, Second Lieutenant.
Boryna, Józef, Sergeant Major. (P).
Borys, Franciszek, Lieutenant.
Borzemski, Paweł, Lieutenant. (P).
Borysławski, Marian, Lieutenant Colonel.
Bucholz, Bronisław, Sergeant.
Buryło, Piotr, Lieutenant.
Chmura, Władysław, Sergeant Major.
Chrostowski, Bronisław, Chaplain.
Chura, Piotr, Bombardier.
Cichocki, Władysław, Sergeant.
Cichocki, Józef, Corporal. (P).
Ciesielski, Jan, Lance Corporal.
Cieśliński, Herman, Captain.
Cybulski, Edwin, Lance Corporal.
Cymański, Piotr, Lance Corporal.
Czarnecki, Marian. N, Major.
Czerny, Stanisław, Cadet Officer.
Czyrko, Stanisław, Sergeant.
Derych, Jan, Bombardier.
Dębicki, Wacław, Second Lieutenant. (P).
Dembiński, Edward, Lance Corporal. (P).

Dorantt, Jan, Lieutenant Colonel.
Dowbór, Romuald, Lieutenant Colonel.
Drobot, Jan, Second Lieutenant.
Drozdowicz, Leopold, Lieutenant.
Dubicki, Zdzisław, Lieutenant.
Dudek, Wacław, Lieutenant.
Dulka, Bronisław, Sergeant.
Dzierżek, Adam, Second Lieutenant.
Ejsymont, Otton, Major.
Gabalewicz, Władysław, Lance Corporal.
Gadzikiewicz, Witold, Cadet Officer.
Gasior, Edward, Corporal.
Gardziel, Kazimierz, Dragoon.
Gardyasz, Stanisław, Second Lieutenant.
Gawski, Józef, Sergeant.
Goldin, Michał, Corporal. (P).
Golis, Leon, Sergeant Major.
Gozdziewicz, Marian, Corporal.
Góralik, Jan. E, Second Lieutenant.
Grabinia, Tadeusz, Second Lieutenant. (P).
Greiner, Henryk, Lieutenant.
Gros, Henryk, Sapper.
Gryziecki, Kazimierz, M. Captain.

Gruszka, Antoni, Sergeant.
Grzebalski, Mieczysław, Corporal.
Grzegorzewski, Franciszek, Lieutenant.
Grzywa, Jan, Corporal.
Gutowski, Michał, Captain.
Habant, Bronisław, Lance Corporal.
Handelsman, Józef, Lieutenant.
Hardulak, Władysław, Private.
Hasiuk, Stanisław, Corporal.
Herz, Leon, Lieutenant. (P).
Hołdys, Franciszek, Corporal.
Hupa, Piotr, Chaplain. (P).
Iskrzyński, Zbigniew, Cadet Officer. (P).
Jabłoński, Lucjan, Corporal.
Jakiemow, Tadeusz, Corporal.
Jakubczyk, Franciszek, Second Lieutenant.
Jamorozik, Józef, Gunner.
Jankowski, Józef, Sergeant. (P).
Janowiak, Roman, Cadet Officer.
Jaworski, Zbigniew, Captain.
Joworski-Zubowicz, Jan,
Second Lieutenant.
Jaźwinski, Kazimierz, Sergeant.
Jodko-Narkiewicz, Janusz,
Cadet Officer. (P).
Judkowiak, Edward, Captain.
Jurgielewicz, Stefan, Second Lieutenant.
Juśków, Roman, Lieutenant.
Kaleta, Mieczysław, Corporal.
Kalinowski, Władysław, Corporal.
Kałwa, Franciszek, Corporal.
Kański, Jan, Major. (P).
Kaper, Ludwik, Sergeant.
Kasprzak, Marian, Captain.
Kida, Jan, Sergeant Major.
Kieliszek, Modest, Corporal. (P).
Klajman, Chaskiel,
Second Lieutenant (Doctor).
Kluz, Nikodem, Second Lieutenant.
Kłodziński, Zygmunt, Lieutenant.
Kobielski, Wilhelm, Sergeant. (P).
Kobierski, Bolesław, Private.
Koblański, Józef, Sergeant.
Kochanowski, Marian, Captain.
Komosiński, Zbigniew, Cadet Officer. (P).
Konieczny, Władysław, Corporal.
Kononowicz, Edmund, Lieutenant.
Konstanty, Antoni, Cadet Officer. (P).
Kończak, Józef, Lance Corporal.
Kostecki, Adam, Cadet Officer.
Kostka-Juszczyk, Tadeusz, Cadet Officer.
Koszutski, Stanisław, Lieutenant Colonel.
Kościukiewicz, Michał, Sergeant.
Koślacz, Aleksander, Captain.
Kotłowsk, Jan, Lance Corporal.
Kowalczyk, Jan, Captain.
Kowalski, Eugeniusz, Sergeant Major.
Kownas, Wacław, Captain. (P).
Kozanecki, Witold, Lieutenant.
Kozień, Marian, Second Lieutenant.

Krawczyk, Anastazy, Lance Corporal.
Krayer, Erwin, Corporal.
Krupa, Gustaw, Sergeant.
Krupowicz, Władysław, Captain.
Krystyniak, Leopold, Corporal.
Krzyżaniak, Tadeusz, Second Lieutenant.
Kubatek, Stanisław, Lance Corporal.
Kuczowicz, Wilhelm, Lieutenant. (P).
Kudelski, Józef, Lance Corporal.
Kula, Kazimierz, Lieutenant. (P).
Kumela, Henryk, Lieutenant.
Kurek, Hieronim, Lieutenant.
Kurpiel, Stanisław, Captain.
Kuś, Władysław, Lance Corporal.
Kusmirek, Henryk, Lieutenant.
Kwidziński, Franciszek, Sergeant.
Lampa, Bernard, Lance Corporal.
Lancberg, Jan, Corporal.
Lange, Józef, Sapper.
Leszczyński, Tadeusz, Cadet Officer.
Lewandowski, Walerian, Cadet Officer.
Lewicki, Zdzisław, Cadet Officer.
Lewoniewski, Kazimierz, Lance Corporal.
Limberger, Władysław, Captain.
Lisowski, Franciszek, Corporal.
Lubański, Jan, Sergeant.
Łabno, Edward, Captain.
Łasłowski, Marian, Captain.
Łochocki, Konstanty, Sergeant.
Łucki, Jerzy, Major.
Łuczak, Wojciech, Sergeant.
Łukasik, Mieczysław, Lance Corporal.
Magoński, Władysław, Lieutenant.
Majerski, Edward, Sergeant.
Majranowski, August, Lance Corporal.
Makarus, Paweł, Lance Corporal.
Maksymowicz, Zbigniew, Second
Lieutenant. (P).
Malczewski, Kazimierz, Major.
Malkiewicz, Paweł, Lieutenant.
Małachowski, Józef, Corporal.
Małżyński, Aleksander, Corporal.
Marcinkowski, Bronisław, Second
Lieutenant.
Maresch, Karol, Colonel.
Marowski, Jan, Major.
Marszałek, Władysław, Private.
Martynoga, Stanisław, Lieutenant.
Matejak, Henryk, Sapper.
Matosz, Tadeusz, Corporal.
Mejsnerowicz, Jan, Lieutenant.
Michalak, Stefan, Lance Corporal.
Michałek, Albert, Dragoon.
Mincer, Bohdan, Major.
Mincer, Andrzej, Sergeant Major.
Miś, Sebastian, Cadet Officer.
Mitka, Bronisław, captain.
Mizerka, Henryk, Sergeant.
Młodzki, Lech, Cadet Officer.

Młynek, Stefan, Private.
Mnich, Bolesław, Corporal.
Mogilski, Władysław, Second Lieutenant.
Mortun, Józef, Corporal. (P).
Morawski, Czesław,
Second Lieutenant. (P).
Moszczyński, Eugeniusz, Sergeant Officer.
Neklaws, Wiktor, Major.
Niewiadomski, Jerzy, Cadet Officer.
Norski, Brunon, Sergeant.
Nowaczyński, Aleksander, Lieutenant
Colonel.
Nowak, Władysław,
Second Lieutenant. (P).
Nowak, Józef, Sergeant.
Nowakowski, Marian, Second Lieutenant.
Nowakowski, Roman, Corporal. (P).
Nytkowski, Edward, Private.
Ojrzanowski, Marian, Second Lieutenant.
Oksiak, Edmund, Sergeant.
Oleksy, Jan, Corporal.
Olendzki, Edward, Lance Corporal.
Olensiński, Józef, Lieutenant.
Oliwka, Edward, Private. (P).
Oses, Jan, Second Lieutenant.
Oslizło, Daniel, Lance Corporal.
Owczarek, Edmund, Cadet Officer. (P).
Padewski, Ignacy, Dragoon. (P).
Pater, Wawrzyniec, Corporal.
Patkowski, Piotr, Corporal.
Pawłowicz, Władysław,
Lieutenant Colonel (Doctor).
Pelc, Antoni, Sergeant.
Pilch, Władysław, Bombardier. (P).
Piotrowicz, Marian, Private.
Pirog, Jan, Corporal.
Plichta, Marian, Lieutenant.
Płaszczyca, Stefan, Bombardier.
Podleski, Czesław, Second Lieutenant.
Pogorzelski, Władysław, Major.
Pokorny, Stanisław, Captain.
Polak, Stefan, Second Lieutenant.
Położyński, Antoni, Second Lieutenant.
Poniatowski, Andrzej,
Second Lieutenant. (P).
Popek, Antoni, Lieutenant.
Popiak, Aleksander, Second Lieutenant.
Przystupa, Stanisław, Sergeant.
Przanowski, Jan, Captain.
Przyborowski, Zygmunt, Second
Lieutenant. (P).
Puszyński, Godfryd, Lance Corporal.
Purzycki, Stanisław, Second Lieutenant.
Pytlak, Edmund, Lieutenant.
Raczkowski, Wiesław, Dragoon. (P).
Raczyński, Konrad, Second Lieutenant. (P).
Radomski, Edmund, Lance Corporal.
Rakowski, Władysław, Major.
Ratuszyński, Jan, Dragoon.
Rembowski, Szczepan, Chaplain.

Rewer, Wojciech, Captain.
Romanek, Stanisław, Second Lieutenant.
Romaniak, Józef, Trooper.
Romer, Stefan, Second Lieutenant.
Rostkowski, Józef, Trooper.
Rozum, Jan, Corporal.
Rozwadowski, Jan, Lieutenant.
Ruca, Franciszek, Private.
Rugalski, Ryszard, Cadet Officer.
Rzeznikowski, Stefan, Lance Corporal.
Sachse, Bronisław, Lieutenant.
Sadłowski, Mieczysław, Cadet Officer. (P).
Salwa, Jan. S, Captain.
Samulski, Bohdan. P, Second Lieutenant.
Seid, Henryk, Second Lieutenant (Doctor).
Seroka, Henryk, Trooper.
Sichulski, Jerzy, Lieutenant.
Siemieniuch, Stanisław, Second Lieutenant.
Sikora, Roman, Second Lieutenant. (P).
Siudut, Franciszek, Lieutenant.
Skibinski, Piotr, Sergeant.
Skirmunt, Jan, Second Lieutenant. (P).
Slesorajtis, Mieczysław, Second Lieutenant.
Smoleński, Kazimierz, Sergeant.
Smolny, Kazimierz, Cadet Officer. (P).
Smyczek, Rejnhold, Second Lieutenant.
Sokól, Stanisław, Lance Corporal. (P).
Sołtys, Henryk, Staff Sergeant.
Sołtysiak, Jan, Second Lieutenant.
Sołtyski, Jan, Major.
Starzomski, Bogusław, Sergeant. (P).
Starzyński, Zygmunt, Captain.
Stasiłowicz, Stanisław, Dragoon.
Stawiński, Mieczysław, Second Lieutenant.
Stefanowicz, Aleksander, Major.
Stępień, Tadeusz, Lieutenant.

Stępień, Konrad, Captain.
Straszewski, Ryszard, Cadet Officer.
Suchecki, Jan, Second Lieutenant. (P).
Suchoń-Prella, Stefan, Corporal.
Sumiński, Kazimierz, Private. (P).
Sumiński, Albert. M, Captain.
Surma, Jan, Corporal.
Swierszcz, Czesław, Second Lieutenant.
Swiokło, Kazimierz, Lance Corporal.
Szczeniowski, Wacław, Lieutenant. (P).
Szeliga, Wojciech, Lieutenant.
Szewerniak, Leon, Sergeant. (P).
Szłamas, Leonard, Lieutenant.
Szperber, Adam. W,
Second Lieutenant. (P).
Szpunar, Józef, Sergeant.
Szydłowski, Zdzisław, Lieutenant Colonel.
Szydłowski, Kazimierz, Captain.
Szymański, Marian, Private.
Szymański, Jan, Lance Corporal.
Szynkaruk, Czesław, Second Lieutenant.
Szubarga, Andrzej, Lieutenant.
Tarnowski, Janusz, Second Lieutenant. (P).
Tkacz, Stanisław, Captain.
Tucewicz, Zygmunt, Captain.
Typer, Roman, Lieutenant.
Urbaniak, Józef, Captain.
Uściński, Edward, Captain.
Wajnkopf, Roman, Sergeant. (P).
Walicki, Tadeusz, Second Lieutenant.
Walkowski, Jan, Captain (Doctor).
Walter, Paweł, Sergeant.
Wanic, Wiesław, Cadet Officer.
Warchoł, Paweł, Cadet Officer.
Wartak, Stanisław, Captain.
Wasilewski, Jerzy, Captain.

Wasilewski, Roman, Lieutenant.
Wąsowski, Józef, Lieutenant. (P).
Wiatrkowski, Tadeusz, Second Lieutenant.
Wielogórski, Tadeusz, Lieutenant.
Wiercioch, Artur, Corporal.
Wieroński, Marian, Colonel.
Winczakiewicz, Jan, Second Lieutenant.
Wisz, Kazimierz, Cadet Officer.
Witek, Czesław, Lance Corporal.
Włosowicz, Edward, Corporal.
Wnęk, Zygmunt, Second Lieutenant. (P).
Wojciechowski, Marian. G,
Second Lieutenant.
Wojciechowski, Olgierd, Lieutenant.
Wojtowicz, Adam, Lance Corporal.
Wojtynowski, Leon, Sergeant.
Wolny, Józef, Corporal.
Woroniecki, Stanisław, Sergeant.
Wysocki, Tadeusz, Major.
Zagórski, Jerzy, Captain.
Zagórski, Jacek, Second Lieutenant.
Zając, Karol, Lance Corporal.
Zając, Franciszek, Sergeant.
Zaleski, Andrzej, Second Lieutenant.
Zamecznik, Władysław, Cadet Officer.
Zawadzki, Józef, Corporal.
Zawadzki, Adam, Lieutenant.
Zawalski, Zygryd, Lieutenant. (P).
Zawisza, Andrzej, Captain.
Zatorski, Ryszard. J, Second Lieutenant.
Zbroski, Jan, Major.
Zieliński, Czesław, Sergeant.
Zienkiewicz, Wincenty, Lieutenant.
Zipser, Gustaw, Second Lieutenant.
Zubrzycki, Tadeusz, Lance Corporal.
Żukowski, Adolf, Lieutenant.

Krzyż Walecznych

Abelski, Józef, Corporal.
Adamczak, Franciszek, Corporal.
Adamczak, Jerzy, Lance Corporal.
Adamczewski, Kazimierz, Lieutenant, (P).
Adamczyk, Teodor, Dragoon.
Adamczyk, Emil, Private.
Adamek, Władysław, Sergeant.
Adamek, Edward, Lance Corporal.
Adamiak, Jan, Sergeant. (Awarded Twice)
Adamik, Gerard, Lance Corporal.
(Awarded Twice)
Adamski, Jan, Private.
Adamski, Leon, Lance Corporal,
(Awarded Twice).
Adamowicz, Mikołaj, Sergeant.
Adamowski, Konrad, Lance Corporal.
Aliński, Feliks, Trooper.
Ambroż, Kazimierz, Corporal. (P).
Ananicz, Leon, Second Lieutenant.
Andrearczyk, Edwin, Dragoon.

Andrelczyk, Antoni, Corporal. (P).
Andrus, Zygmunt, Lance Corporal. (P).
Andruszkiewicz, Romuald, Lieutenant.
Andryszczak, Jan, Sergeant.
(Awarded Twice)
Andrejewski, Henryk, Corporal.
Andrejewski, Henryk, Sergeant. (Awarded
Twice)
Andrejewski, Tadeusz, Lieutenant.
Aniserewicz, Stanisław, Second Lieutenant.
(Awarded twice)
Ankierski, Stanisław, Corporal.
Antachow, Michał, Lance Corporal.
Antonowicz, Mikołaj, Lieutenant.
(Awarded Twice)
Antosiak, Józef, Sergeant.
Antoszewski, Eugeniusz, Gunner.
Apacz, Jan, Lance Corporal.
Apczyński, Stanisław, Lance Corporal.
Apfel-Czaszka, Tadeusz, Private.

Arciszewski, Adolf, Lance Corporal.
Augustyniak, Stanisław, Sergeant.
(Awarded Twice).
Avrel, Kazimierz, Bombardier.
Babiński, Jan, Private. (Awarded Twice).
Babiuk, Roman, Corporal.
(Awarded Twice)
Bachen, Gerard, Private.
Bączek, Józef, Corporal.
Bączkowski, Mieczysław, Sergeant.
Badowski, Henryk, Corporal.
(Awarded Twice).
Badura, Piotr, Lance Corporal.
Bagiński, Stefan, Corporal.
(Awarded Twice)
Bagniewski, Roman, Lance Corporal.
Bahrynowski, Leszek, Cadet Officer.
Bajek, Franciszek, Corporal.
Bajek, Henryk, Corporal.
Bajer, Antoni, Sergeant.

Bąk, Antoni, Sergeant.

Bąk, Ludwik, Corporal. (Awarded Twice)

Bąk, Stanisław, Lieutenant.

Bąkowski, Zygmunt, Corporal.

Bąkowski, Tadeusz, Corporal.

Balas, Roman, Bombardier.

Balcer, Franciszek, Lance Corporal.

Balcer, Tadeusz, Sergeant.

Bałtowski, Kazimierz, Lance Corporal.

Banaś, Tadeusz, Trooper.

Banek, Franciszek, Private. (P).

Bańkowski, Józef, Sergeant.

Banot, Paweł, Corporal.

Bara, Waldermar, Lance Corporal.

Baran, Franciszek, Sergeant. (P)

Baran. Jan, Lance Corporal.

Baraniecki, Józef, Second Lieutenant.

Baranowski, Franciszek, Lance Corporal.

Barbacki, Janusz, Lieutenant.

Barcikowski, Stanisław, Lance Corporal.

Barczak, Piotr, Dragoon.

Barczyk, Stefan, Lance Corporal.

Bardziński, Sylwester, Corporal. (Awarded Twice)

Bargier, Władysław, Lance Corporal.

Barski, Józef, Corporal.

Bartczak, Bronisław, Lieutenant.

Bartel, Jacek, Cadet Officer.

Bartnicki, Marian, Lance Corporal.

Bartosiewicz, Adam, Sergeant.

Bartosiński, Marian, Major. (Awarded Twice [P])

Bartoszewski, Paweł, Private.

Bartoszek, Franciszek, Bombardier. (P).

Bartosz, Stanisław, Second Lieutenant.

Barycz, Aleksander, Second Lieutenant.

Basamon, Tadeusz, Corporal.

Basara, Marian, Lance Corporal.

Basista, Józef, Corporal.

Baista, Tadeusz, Lieutenant.

Baska, Paweł, Sergeant.

Baszma, Bronisław, Private.

Bator, Jan, Sergeant Major. (Awarded Twice).

Baumgart, Franciszek, Second Lieutenant.

Bawicz, Czesław, Lance Corporal.

Bazgier, Władysław, Lance Corporal.

Bebnik, Aleksander, Dragoon.

Bech, Jerzy, Corporal.

Beck, Stanisław, Corporal.

Beckowicz, Wiesław, Lieutenant.

Bednarski, Edward, Captain, (P).

Bednarski, Stanisław, Corporal.

Bednarski, Stanisław, Cadet Officer.

Będziejewski, Józef, Gunner.

Beger, Leon, Lance Corporal.

Benc, Nikodem, Corporal.

Berlicki, Andrzej, Corporal.

Benek, Stanisław, Corporal.

Benita, Edward, Lance Corporal.

Bentkowski, Stanisław, Captain.

Berent, Jan, Lance Corporal. (P).

Bergander, Stefan, Corporal. (Awarded Twice).

Berger, Aleksy, Lieutenant.

Bereziński, Józef, Lance Corporal.

Bernard, Jan, Corporal.

Beszczyński, Władysław, Corporal.

Besztelechman, Kazimierz, Sapper.

Bekter, Adam, Second Lieutenant.

Biały, Józef, Lieutenant.

Biały, Robert, Lance Corporal.

Białkowski, Leon, Gunner.

Biedrzycki, Józef, Lance Corporal.

Bielaszewski, Alfons, Lance Corporal.

Bielawiec, Jacek, Lieutenant. (Awarded Three Times).

Bielecki, Roman, Lance Corporal.

Bielicz, Edward, Sapper.

Bielski, Adam, Second Lieutenant.

Bielski, Henryk, Private. (P).

Bieniecki, Augustyn, Corporal.

Bieniek, Zygmunt, Corporal.

Bieńko, Hieronim, Lance Corporal.

Bieńkowski, Stefan, Corporal.

Bieńkowski, Tadeusz, Second Lieutenant.

Biernacki, Wiktor, Lance Corporal.

Biliński, Kazimierz, Dragoon.

Binkowski, Stanisław, Lance Corporal.

Biskup, Adolf, Corporal.

Bissinger, Jan, Corporal.

Bizański, Andrzej, Lieutenant. (Awarded Twice).

Blank, Edward, Gunner.

Blanik, Walenty, Lance Corporal.

Blaszyk, Czesław, Cadet Officer (Awarded Twice).

Bletek, Tadeusz, Second Lieutenant (Awarded Three Times).

Blicharski, Antoni, Corporal.

Bloch, Janusz, Second Lieutenant.

Blot, Erwin, Lance Corporal.

Bluszcz, Józef, Lance Corporal.

Błajda, Edward, Lieutenant.

Błasiak, Władysław, Sergeant.

Błaszczyk, Jan, Lance Corporal.

Błaszkiewicz, Dariusz, Cadet Officer.

Błatowski, Kazimierz, Lance Corporal.

Błażejewski, Sylwester, Corporal.

Błażejewski, Tadeusz, Cadet Officer.

Błażejowski, Franciszek, Lance Corporal.

Błędowski, Władysław, Second Lieutenant.

Błoński, Bronisław, Sapper (Awarded Twice)

Bniński, Roman, Lieutenant.

Bober, Antoni, Lieutenant. (Awarded Twice)

Bober, Stanisław, Lance Corporal.

Bobkowski, Włodzimierz, Trooper.

Bobula, Adam, Second Lieutenant. (Awarded Four Times).

Bobula, Bolesław, Private.

Bocek, Jan, Lance Corporal.

Bobhuszewicz, Kazimierz, Lance Corporal.

Bocian, Zbigniew, Lance Corporal.

Bogacz, Jan, Sergeant.

Bogdanowicz, Henryk, Second Lieutenant (Awarded Twice)

Bogdanowicz, Tadeusz, Sergeant (Awarded Twice)

Bogucki, Kazimierz, Lance Corporal.

Bogun, Franciszek, Sergeant (Awarded Twice)

Bogusz, Stanisław, Corporal (Awarded Twice)

Boguszewski, Stanisław, Cadet Officer.

Bohdanowicz, Konrad, Lieutenant (Awarded Twice)

Bohun, Józef, Corporal.

Boiński, Józef, Corporal. (P)

Bojan, Bolesław, Corporal.

Bojanowski, Kazimierz, Private (Awarded Twice).

Bojanowski, Zbigniew, Lieutenant.

Bojarski, Zbigniew, Captain.

Bokatczuk, Michał, Corporal.

Bolechowski, Henryk, Lieutenant (Awarded Twice)

Bolesławski, Feliks, Private.

Bolek, Franciszek, Lance Corporal.

Bomba, Ignacy, Private.

Bończoszek, Bronisław, Trooper.

Boniecki, Stanisław, Sapper.

Bony, Franciszek, Lance Corporal.

Borcholski, Mieczysław, Second Lieutenant (Awarded Twice)

Borecki, Mikołaj, Private.

Borek, Kazimierz, Corporal.

Borkowski, Antoni, Bombardier.

Borkowski, Leon, Private.

Borkowski, Stanisław, Trooper

Boronkiewicz, Franciszek, Lance Corporal.

Borowiec, Adam, Captain.

Borowski, Bohdan, Captain.

Borowski, Jan, Lance Corporal.

Borowski, Jan, Bombardier.

Borowski, Michał, Sergeant.

Borowy, Stefan, Lance Corporal.

Borsuk, Aleksander, Staff Sergeant.

Borsukiewicz, Bronisław, Lance Corporal.

Borus, Alfons, Private.

Borut, Jerzy, Lance Corporal.

Borys, Franciszek, Lieutenant. (Awarded Twice)

Bosak, Antoni, Lance Corporal.

Boslak, Stanisław, Corporal.

Bors, Józef, Lance Corporal.

Borzemski, Paweł, Captain. (Awarded Twice [P])

Borzychowski, Jerzy, Trooper.

Borzycki, Adolf, Dragoon.

Borzysławski, Marian, Lieutenant Colonel.

Bozanowski, Aleksander, Corporal.

Bożniecki, Brunon, Lance Corporal.

Bożek, Stanisław, Corporal.

Brandys, Stanisław, Private.

Brandys, Rudolf, Lance Corporal.

Brankiewicz, Jan, Corporal.

Bramorski, Edward, Lance Corporal.

Bratek, Franciszek, Staff Sergeant.

Bratkowski, Bolesław, Second Lieutenant.

Brodowicz, Kazimierz, Sergeant Major.

Brodzisz, Stefan, Private.

Brud, Józef, Sergeant.

Brudnicki, Stanisław, Lieutenant.

Bruski, Bronisław, Lance Corporal.

Brych, Edward, Sergeant.

Brychcy, Jan, Trooper.

Bryczek, Stanisław, Corporal.

Bryl, Mieczysław, Mirosław, Corporal
(Awarded Twice)

Brzeski, Brunon, Bombardier
(Awarded Twice)

Brzeski, Jan, Lance Corporal
(Awarded Twice)

Brzeski, Stanisław, Lance Corporal.

Brzeski, Wincenty, Lance Corporal.

Brostek, Zygmunt, Corporal.

Brzezicki, Antoni, Lance Corporal.

Brzezinka, Jan, Lance Corporal.

Brzeziński, Bronisław, Lance Corporal.

Brzeziński, Jan, Lance Corporal.

Brzoza, Alojzy, Private.

Brzoza, Brunon, Lance Corporal.

Brzoza, Edward, Lance Corporal.

Brozozowiak, Bronisław, Private.

Brzozowski, Bohdan, Second Lieutenant.
(Awarded Twice).

Brzozowski, Henryk, Lance Corporal.

Brzozowski, Leon, Private.

Brzozowski, Stanisław, Bombardier.

Brzozy, Jerzy, Regimental Sergeant Major
(Awarded Three Times)

Brzyski, Stanisław, Corporal
(Awarded Twice)

Buchholz, Bronisław, Corporal. (P)

Buchta, Grzegorz, Lance Corporal.

Buczek, Jan, Lance Corporal.

Buda, Jan, Trooper.

Budziak, Alojzy, Sergeant.

Budzisz, Edward, Corporal.

Budzyński, Władysław, Corporal.

Bugla, Edward, Lance Corporal.

Bugła, Leon, Gunner.

Bujan, Bolesław, Corporal.

Bukowczyk, Eugeniusz, Captain.

Bukowski, Alfons, Sergeant.

Bukowski, Czesław, Lieutenant.

Bukowski, Feliks, Lance Corporal.

Bulik, Kazimierz, Corporal.

Buliński, Alojzy, Lance Corporal.

Buller, Tadeusz, Corporal (Unclear how
many times awarded)

Buła, Józef, Cadet Officer

(Awarded Three Times)

Buniak, Aleksander, Corporal.

Bunkowski, Jan, Private.

Buraczewski, Józef, Sergeant
(Awarded Twice)

Burdzy, Władysław, Corporal.

Burek, Oskar, Lance Corporal.

Burek, Wacław, Corporal (Awarded Twice)

Burszta, Zygmunt, Cadet Officer.

Bursztyn, Kazimierz, Second Lieutenant.

Bury, Leon, Private.

Buryło, Piotr, Lieutenant. (Awarded Twice)

Burza, Edmund, Sergeant

Byra, Stanisław, Lance Corporal.

Byrdy, Tadeusz, Lance Corporal.

Bystram, Antoni, Cadet Officer.

Bzdal, Stefan, Bombardier.

Bzikot, Konstanty, Corporal.

Bzowski, Tytus, Lieutenant.

Cabański, Ludwik, Second Lieutenant.

Całus, Wacław, Lieutenant.

Cebula, Jan, Corporal.

Cebulak, Jan, Corporal.

Cegielniewski, Marian, Lance Corporal.

Cegłowski, Bronisław, Bombardier.

Celebański, Jan, Corporal.

Cena, Piotr, Sergeant.

Centner, Antoni, Corporal.

Ceptowski, Alfons, Lieutenant.

Chabasiewicz, Zbigniew,
Second Lieutenant.

Chackiewicz, Marek, Gunner.

Chaj, Antoni, Trooper (Awarded Twice).

Charatak, Michał, Sapper.

Charżewski, Czesław, Captain.

Chatys, Czesław, Sergeant.

Chęciński, Witold, Corporal.

Chełchowski, Piotr, Captain.

Chetkowski, Zdzisław, Cadet Officer.

Chlebicz, Mieczysław, Corporal.

Chmal, Adam, Lieutenant.

Chmielewski, Józef, Corporal.

Chmielewski, Stanisław, Corporal.

Chmura, Józef, Lance Corporal.

Chozidło, Augustyn, Lance Corporal. (P)

Chojnacki, Franciszek, Lance Corporal.

Choma, Tomasz, Sergeant

Chomiczewski, Bronisław, Corporal.

Chomko, Kazimierz, Sergeant (Unclear
how many times awarded)

Chrostowski, Bronisław, Chaplain.
(Awarded Twice)

Chruściak, Jan, Corporal.

Chruściel, Kazimierz, Sergeant.

Chruslicki, Stanisław, Gunner.

Chruszcz, Mikołaj, Second Lieutenant.

Chruszczewski, Zdzisław, Cadet Officer.

Chrzanowski, Stanisław, Lance Corporal.

Chrzanowski, Roman, Corporal.

Chrzanowski, Władysław, Corporal.

Chudowski, Jan, Lance Corporal.

Chudzik, Czesław, Lance Corporal.

Chwalik, Feliks, Corporal.

Chwisowski, Borys, Sergeant.

Chwistecki, Stanisław, Lance Corporal.

Chyliński, Stanisław, Corporal.

Chyliński, Stefan, Sergeant.
(Awarded Twice)

Chyrek, Franciszek, Private.
(Awarded Twice)

Ciachoń, Michał, Lance Corporal.
(Awarded Twice)

Cichowski, Józef, Lance Corporal.

Cichoń, Antoni, Private. (P)

Cichoń, Ryszard, Sergeant.
(Awarded Twice)

Cichowski, Michał, Corporal.

Cichy, Henryk, Sergeant. (Awarded Twice)

Ciechanowicz, Bolesław, Lance Corporal.

Ciemechowicz, Czesław, Cadet Officer.

Ciepliński, Józef, Lance Corporal.

Cieplik, Alojzy, Cadet Officer.

Ciepły, Władysław, Corporal.

Cierpucha, Piotr, Lance Corporal.

Cieśla, Jozef, Lance Corporal.

Ciesielski, Wojciech, Bombardier.

Cieślak, Czesław, Corporal.

Cieślak, Henryk, Corporal.

Cieślik, Bonifacy, Private.

Cieślik, Witold, Sergeant.

Cieśliński, Herman, Captain.
(Awarded Four Times)

Cieśliński, Kazimierz, Cadet Officer.
(Awarded Twice)

Cieśliński, Tadeusz, Second Lieutenant.
(Awarded Twice)

Ciężak, Franciszek, Lance Corporal.
(Awarded Three Times)

Ciężkowski, Kazimierz, Corporal.

Cincio, Franciszek, Lieutenant.

Ciochan, Mikołaj, Lance Corporal.

Ciok, Jan, Sergeant.

Cipko, Edward, Private.

Ciszewski, Tadeusz, Gunner.
(Awarded Twice)

Ciuba, Edward, Lance Corporal.

Ciuraszkiewicz, Mieczysław, Corporal.

Ciżyk, Teodor, Private.

Complak, Karol, Lieutenant Colonel.
(Awarded Three Times)

Cukiernik, Henryk, Lance Corporal.
(Awarded Twice)

Cwiok, Jan, Corporal.

Cybulski, Florian, Private.

Cyma, Jan, Lance Corporal.

Cymborowski, Jan, Lance Corporal.

Cymerman, Edward, Corporal.

Cytryn, Michał, Private. (P)

Czaban, Jan, Corporal.

Czajka, Bolesław, Lance Corporal.

Czajka, Jan, Private. (P)

Czajkowski, Benon, Lance Corporal.

Czajkowski, Franciszek, Private.

Czajkowski, Henryk, Corporal.

Czajkowski, Henryk, Lance Corporal.
(Awarded Twice)

Czajkowski, Kazimierz, Sergeant.
(Awarded Twice0

Czapiewski, Augustyn, Bombardier.

Czapiewski, Józef, Private.

Czapski, Kazimierz, Sergeant.

Czarczyński, Gerard, Sergeant.

Czarkowski, Stanisław, Corporal.

Czarkowski-Golejewski, Cyryl, Lieutenant.

Czarnecki, Edmund, Lance Corporal.

Czarnecki, Józef, Lance Corporal.

Czarnecki, Jerzy, Second Lieutenant.
(Awarded Twice)

Czarnecki, Marian. N, Major.
(Awarded Three Times)

Czarnecki, Kamil. B, Captain.
(Awarded Twice)

Czarnecki, Kazimierz, Lance Corporal.

Czarnecki, Stanisław, Lance Corporal.

Czarniecki, Eugeniusz, Sergeant.

Czarnik, Stanisław, Lance Corporal.
(Awarded Twice)

Czarnodolski, Tadeusz, Lance Corporal.

Czarnota, Bolesław, Lance Corporal.

Czarnota, Stefan, Lieutenant.

Czartoryski, Aleksander, Lance Corporal.

Czawa, Mikołaj, Lance Corporal.

Czech, Emil, Lance Corporal.
(Awarded Twice)

Czeczot, Franciszek, Lance Corporal.

Czerkas, Władysław, Sergeant.

Czerkies, Józef, Lance Corporal.

Czerski, Bronisław, Private.
(Awarded Twice [P])

Czerniawski, Adolf, Corporal.

Czerny, Adam, Sergeant.

Czerny, Stanisław, Second Lieutenant.
(Awarded Three Times)

Czerwiński, Stefan, Gunner.

Czortek, Bronisław, Private.

Czuj, Jan, Corporal.

Czulak, Józef, Captain.

Czupałła, Karol, Cadet Officer.
(Awarded Twice)

Czyruk, Stefan, Corporal.

Czyszek, Feliks, Sergeant.

Czyż, Ignacy, Lance Corporal.

Czyżewski, Jan, Bombardier.

Dąb, Franciszek, Private.

Dąbek, Karol, Lance Corporal.

Dąbrowski, Edward, Corporal.

Dąbrowski, Florian, Corporal.

Dąbrowski, Kazimierz, Lance Corporal.

Dąbrowski, Kazimierz, Lance Corporal.

Dąbrowski, Stanislaw, Bombardier.

Dadlez, Jerzy, Private.

Dajka, Augustyn, Corporal.

Dalcyński, Władysław, Lieutenant.
(Awarded Twice)

Dambski, Jerzy, Second Lieutenant.

Damn, Jerzy, Cadet Officer.

Dancewicz, Stanisław, Lance Corporal.

Danielak, Henryk, Corporal.

Danielewicz, Józef, Lieutenant.

Danielewski, Władysław, Gunner.

Danko, Kazimierz, Lance Corporal.

Dębicki, Paweł, Lance Corporal.

Dębiński, Edward, Lance Corporal.

Dębiński, Józef, Bombardier.

Dębski, Zygmunt, Sergeant.

Dębowski, Jan, Sergeant.

Dec, Władysław, Lieutenant Colonel.

Dedski, Jan, Second Lieutenant.

Delikat, Tadeusz, Corporal.

Dembek, Władysław, Corporal.

Dembek, Edmund, Private. (P)

Demianczuk, Jozef, Sergeant

Demka, Artur, Lance Corporal.

Demkowski, Bronisław, Corporal.

Denek, Władysław, Corporal. (P)

Deneszczuk, Józef, Lance Corporal.

Depta, Józef, Lance Corporal.

Derela, Stefan, Corporal.

Desmond, Wilhelm, Lance Corporal.

Diaczuk, Władysław, Private.

Diamand, Władysław, Private.

Dick, Wincenty, Bombardier.

Długi, Józef, Lance Corporal.

Długosz, Roman, Corporal.
(Awarded Twice)

Długosz, Stanisław, Sergeant.

Długoszewski, Jerzy, Gunner.

Dmitruk, Konstanty, Lance Corporal.

Dmochowski, Czesław, Captain.

Dobek, Franciszek, Sergeant.

Dobiecki, Stanisław, Second Lieutenant.

Dobras, Jan, Corporal. (P)

Dobrecki, Franciszek, Sergeant.

Dobrowolski, Józef, Sergeant.

Dobry, Jan, Sergeant.

Dobrzański, Edmund, Sergeant.
(Awarded Twice)

Doktor, Franciszek, Lance Corporal.

Dolaciński, Jan, Private.

Dolecki, Jan, Lance Corporal.

Domański, Paweł, Gunner.

Domaradzki, Marian, Corporal.
(Awarded Twice)

Domaszuk, Zygmunt, Lance Corporal.

Domicewicz, Adam, Corporal.

Donimirski, Marian, Cadet Officer.

Doruch, Józef, Second Lieutenant.

Dowbór, Roman, Colonel,
(Awarded Three Times)

Drobiuk, Stanisław, Sergeant.

Drahun, Władysław, Sergeant.

Dreher, Andrzej, Sergeant.

Drewczyński, Jan, Private.

Drewiczak, Antoni, Private.

Drewniak, Michał, Corporal.

Drewny, Jerzy, Private.

Drobot, Jan, Cadet Officer.

Drop, Piotr, Lance Corporal.

Drozdowicz, Leopold, no rank given.
(Awarded Four Times)

Drozdowski, Tadeusz, Second Lieutenant
(Doctor).

Drozdzik, Józef, Corporal.
(Awarded Twice)

Drożak, Stefan, Captain,
(Awarded Four Times)

Droźdź, Józef, Sergeant.

Drwęcki, Józef, Corporal.

Dżugała, Jan, Sergeant Major.
(Awarded Twice)

Drygas, Marian, Sergeant.

Drygas, Wojciech, Lance Corporal.

Drymler, Mordochaj, Trooper.

Drzewicki, Franciszek, Corporal.

Drzewiecki, Bolesław, Bombardier.

Drzewiecki, Jerzy, Cadet Officer.

Drzewiński, Stanisław, Major.

Drzymałkowski, Moniek, Lance Corporal.

Drzyk, Maksymilian, Lance Corporal.

Dubicki, Paweł, Lance Corporal.

Dubicki, Zygmunt, Private.

Dubla, Wiesław, Corporal.

Dubrański, Zbigniew, Second Lieutenant.

Duda, Damian, Corporal. (Awarded Twice)

Duda, Kazimierz, Captain.

Duda, Wilhelm, Lance Corporal.

Duda, Stefan, Cadet Officer.

Dudek, Franciszek, Lance Corporal.

Dudek, Stanisław, Corporal.

Dudek, Wacław, Lieutenant.

Dudziak, Władysław, Lance Corporal.

Dudzic, Edmund, Corporal.

Dudziński, Teodor, Sergeant Major.

Duk, Adam, Lance Corporal.

Dul, Tadeusz, Cadet Officer.
(Awarded Twice)

Dulka, Bronisław, Corporal.

Dulski, August, Bombardier.

Dulski, Władysław, Second Lieutenant.

Dumała, Stanisław, Sergeant Major.

Dunajski, Bruno, Lance Corporal.

Duracz, Tadeusz, Lieutenant.

Durhalec, Karol, Gunner.

Duś, Józef, Lance Corporal.

Duś, Władysław, Bombardier.

Dworaczyński, Wilhelm, Corporal.

Dworak, Izydor, Corporal.

Dworok, Karol, Sergeant. (P)

Dworzak, Jan, Lance Corporal.

Dybała, Antoni, Sergeant. (P)

Dybek, Andrzej, Corporal.

Dybowski, Zygmunt, Lance Corporal.

Dydzyński, Władysław, Corporal.

Dygos, Józef, Lance Corporal.

Dylewski, Zygmunt, Lance Corporal.

Dymny, Józef, Lance Corporal.

Duszyński, Stanisław, Sergeant.

Dziadkowski, Henryk, Cadet Officer.

Dzianot, Juliusz, Lieutenant.

Dziaszyk, Jan, Lance Corporal.

Dzięcioł, Piotr, Corporal.

Dzięcioł, Zdzisław, Second Lieutenant.

Dzięcioła, Mikołaj, Corporal.

Dziedzic, Józef, Corporal.

Dziedziuch, Franciszek, Corporal.

Dzierzbiński, Wincenty, Sergeant.
(Awarded Twice)

Dzierżek, Adam, Lieutenant.

Dzierżek, Stanisław, Corporal.

Dziewit, Stefan, Lance Corporal.

Dziki, Władysław, Sergeant. (P)

Dziki, Zygmunt, Private.

Dzila, Józef, Lance Corporal.

Dziubany, Alojzy, Lance Corporal.

Dziubanowski, Władysław,
Sergeant Major.

Dziubański, Michał, Sapper.

Dziubek, Jan, Cadet Officer.

Dziubkowski, Edward, Lance Corporal.

Dziurzyński, Alfred, Corporal.

Dziurzyński, Tadeusz, Cadet Officer.

Dziwiński, Antoni, Lance Corporal.

Dżugaj, Janusz, Second Lieutenant.

Dżugaj, Włodzimierz, Cadet Officer.

Edelstein, Samuel, Trooper.

Eibin, Franciszek, Lance Corporal.

Elertowicz, Władysław, Gunner.

Eliasiewicz, Witold, Lieutenant. (P).

Eliński, Antoni, Lance Corporal.

Eljan, Wiktor, Corporal.

Eminowicz, Stefan, Second Lieutenant.

Englot, Jan, Private. (P)

Faber, Józef, Sergeant.

Fabiański, Władysław, Sergeant.

Faron, Władysław, Bombardier.

Fawłowski, Jerzy, Second Lieutenant.

Fec, Wojciech, Corporal.

Fedor, Stefan, Second Lieutenant.

Fedorowicz, Bolesław, Second Lieutenant.

Fedyczek, Kazimierz, Bombardier.

Fedyszyn, Jarosław, Corporal

Fesiak, Dymitr, Gunner.

Fiałka, Kazimierz, Corporal.

Fica, Alojzy, Private.

Figas, Jan. F, Lance Corporal.

Figiel, Mieczysław, Cadet Officer.

Fikus, Marian, Cadet Officer.

Filary, Czesław, Sergeant.

Filip, Stanisław, Corporal.
(Awarded Twice)

Filip, Tadeusz, Sergeant.

Filipiszyn, Paweł, Lance Corporal.

Finger, Witold, Corporal.

Flak, Czesław, Trooper.

Flasza, Władysław, Staff Sergeant.

Fligiel, Edward, Sergeant.
(Awarded Twice [P])

Flisak, Franciszek, Private. (P)

Florczyk, Bronisław, Gunner.

Fojcik, Bronisław, Lance Corporal.

Fojcik, Gustaw, Corporal.

Fojtowski, Jan, Corporal.

Foltyński, Janusz, Second Lieutenant.

Forster, Paweł, Lieutenant.
(Awarded Twice)

Fortuna, Wacław, Lance Corporal.
(Awarded Twice).

Fraczek, Jan, Lance Corporal.

Fraczek, Wilhelm. J, Second Lieutenant,
(Awarded Three Times)

Franaszczyk, Stefan, Corporal.

Franieczek, Jan, Lance Corporal.

Franczak, Antoni, Sergeant.
(Awarded Twice)

Frankowski, Władysław, Dragoon.

Frankowski, Wiktor, Private.

Frant, Bertold, Lance Corporal.

Frelek, Bolesław, Dragoon.

Friebe, Wenanciusz, Lieutenant.
(Awarded Twice)

Freidrich, Jerzy, Lieutenant.
(Awarded Three Times)

Front, Bronisław, Major.

Frydmański, Bolesław, Lance Corporal.

Frymarz, Paweł, Corporal.

Fuchs, Stanisław, Sapper.

Furmankski, Tadeusz, Sergeant.

Gabryjel, Jan, Corporal.

Gabryjelewski, Gabriel, Second Lieutenant.

Gackowski, Jerzy, Lance Corporal.

Gaczyński, Marian, Corporal.

Gadzikiewicz, Witold, Second Lieutenant.
(Awarded Twice [P])

Gadziński, Edward, Corporal.

Gaede, Jan, Lance Corporal.

Gaik, Zygmunt, Corporal.
(Awarded Twice)

Gajczak, Eryk, Lance Corporal.

Gajda, Antoni, Chaplain.

Gajewski, Włodzimierz, Second
Lieutenant.

Gajowy, Kazimierz, Corporal.
(Awarded Twice)

Galas, Czesław, Private.

Gała, Lucjan, Corporal.

Gałecki, Stanisław, Lance Corporal.

Gałęziewski, Władysław, Lance Corporal.

Gałuński, Edmund, Lance Corporal.

Galusek, Jan, Corporal.

Gałuszka, Erwin, Corporal.

Gamoń, Franciszek, Dragoon.

Gancarczyk, Karol, Sergeant.

Garbaj, Edward, Lance Corporal.

Garbiński, Zbigniew, Corporal.
(Awarded Twice)

Garczewski, Wacław, Sergeant.

Garczyński, Feliks, Sergeant.

Gardowski, Konrad, Lance Corporal.

Gardzielewski, Feliks, Cadet Officer.

Garwicki, Alfred, Lance Corporal.

Garwin, Brunon, Lance Corporal.

Gasiecki, Józef, Corporal.

Gąsienica, Jan, Lance Corporal.

Gąsior, Edward, Corporal.

Gasis, Feliks, Second Lieutenant.

Gaskiewicz, Grzegorz, Second Lieutenant.

Gasper, Feliks, Lance Corporal.

Gaszka, Rudolf, Private.

Gaszyński, Andrzej, Lance Corporal.
(Awarded Twice)

Gatarek, Stefan, Sergeant.

Gawelczyk, Maksymilian, Lance Corporal.

Gaweł, Józef, Lance Corporal.
(Awarded Three Times)

Gawlik, Jan, Lance Corporal.

Gawlikowski, Stanisław, Sergeant.

Gawliński, Andrzej, Lieutenant.

Gawski, Jan, Corporal. (Awarded Twice)

Gawryś, Edmund, Sergeant.

Gazdecki, Romuald,
Regimental Sergeant Major.

Gazdziewicz, Marian, Sergeant.

Gburek, Edmund, Staff Sergeant.

Gdaniec, Jan, Corporal.

Gebel, Franciszek, Corporal.

Giebus, Mikołaj, Corporal.

Gełesz, Ludwik, Sergeant Major.
(Awarded Twice)

Gerdon, Paweł, Sergeant. (Awarded Twice)

Gersteberger, Jan. H, Sergeant.
(Awarded Twice)

Gibes, Władysław, Corporal.

Gielniewski, Marian, Lance Corporal.

Giergiel, Alfred, Lieutenant.
(Awarded Twice)

Giera, Zbigniew, Captain. (Awarded Twice)

Gierula, Michał, Sapper.

Gierula, Władysław, Corporal.
(Awarded Twice)

Gietka, Julian, Corporal.

Gilewicz, Jerzy, Lieutenant.

Ginda, Lesław, Cadet Officer.

Gisicz, Józef, Corporal. (P)

Gize, Eugeniusz, Cadet Officer.
(Awarded Three Times)

Gizycki, Zbigniew, Captain.

Glabs, Mieczysław, Corporal.

Glaser, Wilhelm, Lance Corporal.

Głażewski, Andrzej, Chaplain.
(Awarded Twice)

Głębocki, Feliks, Corporal.

Głogowski, Józef, Sergeant.
(Awarded Twice)

Głowacki, Bruno, Lance Corporal.

Głowacki, Piotr, Lance Corporal.

Głowczewski, Władysław, Sapper.

Głowiński, Józef, Lance Corporal.

Głużewski, Józef, Bombardier.

Gmiterek, Jan, Private.

Gocławski, Zygmunt, Corporal.

Goczoł, Jan. A, Cadet Officer.

Godlewski, Jan, Lance Corporal. (Awarded Twice)

Godlewski, Julian, Second Lieutenant.

Godlewski, Zygmunt, Second Lieutenant.

Godowski, Adam, Second Lieutenant. (P)

Gogołka, Jan, Lance Corporal.

Gogos, Jakub, Lance Corporal.

Gola, Stefan, Sergeant. (Awarded Twice)

Goldberg, Chaim, Lance Corporal.

Golej, Aleksander, Sergeant. (Awarded Twice)

Golis, Leon, Sergeant Major.

Goll, Franciszek, Lance Corporal. (Awarded Twice)

Golonka, Piotr, Sergeant Major.

Golowski, Zygmunt, Corporal.

Gołąb, Jan, Private.

Gołąb, Stanisław, Gunner.

Gołąbek, Stanisław, Corporal.

Gołebiowski, Henryk, Corporal.

Gołyński, Stanisław, Lance Corporal. (Awarded Twice)

Gomuła, Antoni, Bombardier.

Gomułka, Jan, Gunner.

Gonciarz, Tadeusz, Bombardier.

Gonet, Franciszek, Second Lieutenant. (Awarded Three Times)

Gorayski, Adam, Second Lieutenant. (Awarded Twice)

Gordoński, Stanisław, Lance Corporal. (Awarded Twice)

Gościewski, Czesław, Lance Corporal.

Gostowski, Franciszek, Sergeant.

Goszkowski, Jan, Corporal.

Gorzad, Bronisław, Corporal.

Gorzeński, Marian, Captain. (Doctor)

Góra, Antoni, Lance Corporal.

Góra, Jan, Corporal.

Góral, Piotr, Lance Corporal. (P)

Góralik, Jan, Second Lieutenant. (Awarded Four Times)

Górecki, Sylwester, Lieutenant.

Górka, Jan, Corporal. (P)

Górniak, Tadeusz, Gunner.

Górniak, Lance Corporal.

Górnik, Jan, Lance Corporal. (Awarded Twice)

Górny, Walerian, Lance Corporal.

Górny, Władysław, Private.

Górowski, Jan, Private.

Górowski, Wacław, Private.

Górski, Bernard, Corporal.

Górski, Jan, Corporal.

Górski, Kazimierz, Lance Corporal.

Górski, Stanisław, Sergeant.

Górski, Tadeusz, Cadet Officer. (Awarded Twice)

Grabania, Tadeusz, Lieutenant. (P)

Grabarczyk, Franciszek, Corporal.

Grabiec, Bolesław, Lance Corporal.

Grabiec, Ignacy, Corporal.

Grabowski, Józef, Lance Corporal. (P)

Grabowski, Stanisław, Lieutenant.

Grabowski, Władysław, Corporal. (Awarded Twice)

Grabowski, Zygmunt, Lance Corporal.

Grabowski, Józef, Major. (Awarded Twice)

Graczyk, Władysław, Bombardier.

Graczykowski, Stanisław, Sergeant.

Grad, Konstanty, Second Lieutenant.

Grainer, Kazimierz, Second Lieutenant.

Grajkowski, Jan, Colonel. (Awarded Twice)

Gral, Leon, Private.

Grambor, Stanisław, Sergeant. (Awarded Twice)

Granowski, Franciszek, Private.

Gratkowski, Kazimierz, Sergeant.

Gregorasz, Włodzimierz, Cadet Officer. (Awarded Twice)

Greiner, Henryk, Lieutenant. (Awarded Three Times)

Grendowicz, Stefan, Sergeant.

Grochowski, Marian, Cadet Officer.

Grodecki, Jerzy, Cadet Officer.

Grom, Józef, Lance Corporal. (Awarded Twice)

Gromadkiewicz, Zygmunt, Lance Corporal.

Gros, Jan, Corporal.

Grot, Franciszek, Lance Corporal.

Grotger, Paweł, Lance Corporal. (P)

Gruca, Józef, Bombardier.

Gruca, Kazimierz, Second Lieutenant.

Gruchałła, Albin, Lieutenant. (Awarded Twice)

Gruczek, Czesław, Corporal.

Grudniewicz, Stanisław, Second Lieutenant. (Awarded Twice)

Grudzień, Józef, Lance Corporal.

Grudziński, Antoni, Colonel. (Awarded Twice)

Grudziński, Edward, Corporal.

Gruntkowski, Edward, Corporal.

Gruszczyński, Stanisław, Dragoon.

Gruszeczka, Stanisław, Sergeant.

Gruszak, Antoni, Sergeant.

Gruza, Bolesław, Sergeant.

Grygierczyk, Józef, Corporal.

Grynbaum, Sucher, Corporal.

Gryszan, Bronisław, Corporal.

Grzebalski, Mieczysław, Lieutenant. (Awarded Three Times)

Grzeczkowski, Jan, Sapper.

Grzedziński, Jan, Lance Corporal.

Grzegolec, Antoni, Sergeant.

Grzegorzewski, Mieczysław, Corporal. (P)

Grzelachowski, Bohdan, Lieutenant. (Awarded Twice)

Grzesiak, Stanisław, Trooper. (Awarded Twice)

Grzesik, Witold, Sergeant.

Grześkiewicz, Kazimierz, Lance Corporal.

Grzeszczak, Apolinary, Captain.

Grzeszczyński, Stanisław, Second Lieutenant. (Awarded Three Times)

Grzyb, Tadeusz, Sergeant.

Grzybek, Walenty, Corporal.

Grzybowski, Zygmunt, Lance Corporal.

Grzywa, Stanisław, Sergeant.

Grzywacz, Stanisław, Corporal.

Grzywacz, Franciszek, Sergeant.

Guć, Stanisław, Corporal.

Gudowski, Stanisław, Sergeant.

Gulin, Mieczysław, Captain.

Gumiński, Wacław, Sergeant. (Awarded Twice)

Gunerski, Józef, Lance Corporal.

Gunsberg, Abraham, Second Lieutenant (Doctor).

Gurecki, Władysław, Sapper.

Gurowski, Ludwik, Corporal.

Gusztaw, Jan, Corporal. (P)

Gut, Adam, Sergeant.

Gutowski, Michał, Major. (Awarded Three Times)

Gutowski, Mieczysław, Corporal.

Guzik, Jan, Sergeant.

Guzina, Tomasz, Corporal.

Guzowski, Jan, Private.

Guzowski, Włodzimierz, Corporal.

Gwozdowicz, Stanisław, Bombardier.

Gwoździewicz, Władysław, Lieutenant.

Gwoździewicz, Władysław, Second Lieutenant.

Gwoźdź-Bargiełło, Tadeusz, Second Lieutenant. (Awarded Twice)

Gzawa, Mikołaj, Corporal.

Haas, Zygmunt, Private.

Habant, Bronisław, Lance Corporal.

Habura, Jan, Lance Corporal. (P)

Hadała, Jan, Corporal.

Hajduk, Bohdan, Private.

Hajduk, Klemens, Corporal.

Halapup, Tadeusz, Cadet Officer.

Hałabura, Władysław, Corporal. (Awarded Twice)

Hałusa, Stanisław, Corporal.

Haman, Edward, Sergeant. (Awarded Twice)

Hamela, Eugeniusz, Lance Corporal.

Han, Władysław, Corporal. (Awarded Twice)

Handelsman, Józef, Lieutenant.

Hapka, Piotr, Cadet Officer.

Harnasz, Ryszard, Dragoon.

Hartman, Władysław, Lance Corporal.

Hauska, Rudolf, Captain.

Heber, Tadeusz, Cadet Officer.

Hendlik, Stanisław, Lance Corporal.

Herman, Jacek, Cadet Officer.

Herman, Mieczysław, Sergeant.

Herok, Jan, Second Lieutenant.

Hertoń, Henryk, Sergeant.

Hilert, Czesław, Lance Corporal.

Hilkner, Zygmunt, Lieutenant.

Hincz, Paweł, Sergeant.

128

Hoffman, Jan, Cadet Officer.

Hojnecki, Stanisław, Lance Corporal.

Hołub, Wacław, Staff Sergeant.

Hombek, Tadeusz. J, Sergeant.

Horbaczewski, Jerzy, Corporal.

Hornberger, Roman, Sergeant.

Horodecki, Jukub, Lance Corporal.
(Awarded Twice)

Horosko, Jerzy, Bombardier.

Horowski, Edward, Corporal. (P)

Hosowicz, Henryk, Sergeant.

Hrynowiecki, Stanisław, Lance Corporal.
(Awarded Twice)

Hryorkiewicz, Leonard, Sergeant.

Hubczak, Jan, Sapper.

Hubner, Zygmunt, Corporal.

Hulewicz, Mikołaj, Lance Corporal.

Hurykowicz, Walenty, Private.

Hasarewicz, Maksymilian, Private.

Hytrek, Paweł, Private.

Ignasiak, Walenty, Lance Corporal.

Indyk, Zygmunt, Corporal.

Iwańczyszak, Stanisław, Corporal.
(Awarded Twice)

Iwanicki, Józef, Cadet Officer.

Iwaniec, Roman, Second Lieutenant.

Iwaniszyn, Józef, Dragoon.

Iwaniuk, Wacław, Second Lieutenant.

Iwanowski, Jerzy, Captain.

Izbicki, Jan, Lance Corporal.

Izydorczuk, Zenon, Private.

Iżycki, Stanisław, Corporal.

Jabłonka, Andrzej, Bombardier.
(Awarded Twice)

Jabłoński, Bohdan, Second Lieutenant.
(Awarded Twice)

Jabłoński, Franciszek, Sapper.

Jabłoński, Olgierd, Cadet Officer.

Jabłoński, Stanisław, Bombardier.

Jabłoński, Stefan, Private. (P)

Jagielski, Bernard, Private.

Jagondziński, Leon, Corporal.

Jagondziński, Sylwester, Corporal.

Jagusiak, Franciszek, Corporal.

Jagusiak, Michał, Sergeant.

Jakimowicz, Stanisław, Lance Corporal.

Jaksik, Roman, Corporal.

Jakubiec, Antoni, Lance Corporal. (P)

Jakubiec, Jan, Sergeant.

Jakubiec, Władysław, Lieutenant.

Jamros, Józef, Sergeant.

Jamrozik, Józef, Gunner.

Janczewski, Alfons, Private.

Janeczko, Michał, Lance Corporal.

Jandula, Józef, Corporal. (Awarded Twice)

Jandziak, Karol, Corporal.
(Awarded Twice)

Janicki, Augustyn, Corporal.

Janiec, Adam, Corporal. (Awarded Twice)

Janik, Stefan, Private.

Janiszewski, Stanisław, Sergeant Major.

Jankowski, Franciszek, Second Lieutenant.

Jankowski, Franciszek, Sergeant. (P)

Jankowski, Jan, Corporal.

Jankowski, Józef, Captain.

Jankowski, Józef, Sergeant. (P)

Jankowski, Robert, Private.

Jankowski, Bernard, Sapper.

Jankowski, Eugeniusz, Corporal.

Janusz, Edward, Cadet Officer.

Janusz, Ludwik, Lance Corporal.

Januszajtis, Jerzy, Second Lieutenant.

Januszewski, Kazimierz, Corporal.

Januszewski, Wincenty, Corporal.

Jaracz, Ferdynand, Lance Corporal.

Jaracz, Zygmunt, Private. (P)

Jaraszkiewicz, Leon, Lance Corporal.

Jarecki, Maksymilian, Sergeant Major.

Jarecki, Otto, Corporal.

Jarecki, Stanisław, Cadet Officer.

Jarmoluk, Mikołaj, Corporal.

Jarmoszuk, Mikołaj, Sergeant.

Jarmulski, Jan, Second Lieutenant.
(Awarded Three Times)

Jarmułowicz, Witold, Lance Corporal.
(Awarded Twice)

Jarmuszczak, Leon, Corporal.
(Awarded Twice)

Jarmuzek, Florian, Sergeant.

Jarocki, Jakub, Lance Corporal.

Jaroński, Józef, Captain.

Jarosz, Brunon, Lance Corporal.

Jarosz, Józef, Second Lieutenant.
(Awarded Twice)

Jarosz, Roman, Private.

Jaroszyński, Bronisław, Sergeant.

Jarzembiński, Jan, Sergeant.

Jasieński, Włodzimierz, Lieutenant.

Jasiniewski, Klemens, Staff Sergeant.

Jasiński, Antoni, Lance Corporal.

Jasiński, Stefan, Lance Corporal.

Jaskulski, Edward, Dragoon.

Jaśniak, Stanisław, Corporal.

Jasiulewicz, Jan, Staff Sergeant.

Jaszczurek, Dominik, Sergeant.

Jaworski, Feliks, Lance Corporal.

Jaworski, Jan, Sergeant.

Jaworski, Wacław, Corporal.

Jaworski, Zbigniew, Captain.

Jazdowski, Oskar, Captain.

Jazwiński, Jarosław, Lieutenant.

Jazwiński, Kazimierz, Sergeant.

Jedrzejczak, Władysław, Sergeant.

Jedrzejowicz, Adam, Lieutenant.
(Awarded Twice)

Jedrzejowski, Teofil, Lance Corporal.

Jeleń, Gerard, Lance Corporal.

Jeleński, Konstanty, Cadet Officer.

Jełowicki, Marian, Second Lieutenant.

Jena, Władysław, Lance Corporal.

Jerczak, Antoni, Sergeant.
(Awarded Twice [P])

Jerecki, Otto, Lance Corporal.

Jergas, Gustaw, Lance Corporal.

Jermakow, Paweł, Sergeant. (P)

Jezierski, Jan, Sapper.

Jeziorny, Stanisław, Lance Corporal.

Jeziorski, Jan, Lance Corporal.

Jeż, Eugeniusz, Lieutenant.
(Awarded Twice)

Jochymczyk, Rufin, Sergeant.

Jodłowski, Karol, Corporal.

Jopek, Wincenty, Staff Sergeant.

Józefowicz, Henryk, Captain.
(Awarded Three Times)

Jóźwiak, Stanisław, Sergeant. (P)

Juchnicki, Bolesław, Cadet Officer.

Juchta, Albin, Second Lieutenant.

Judkowiak, Edward, Captain.
(Awarded Twice [P])

Juraszyk, Gerard, Private.

Jurczyk, Edward, Lance Corporal.

Jurczyk, Józef, Corporal.

Jurdziński, Bogusław, Corporal.

Jurgielewicz, Stefan. W, Second Lieutenant.

Jurkiewicz, Tadeusz, Private.

Jurkowski, Franciszek, Lance Corporal.

Juśkow, Roman, Second Lieutenant.

Juszkiewicz, Wincenty, Sergeant.

Juszkiewicz, Wacław, Staff Sergeant.

Kacałaj, Władysław, Corporal.

Kachel, Eugeniusz, Private.

Kacperek, Henryk, Lance Corporal.

Kacperek, Szczepan, Second Lieutenant.

Kaczanowski, Tadeusz, Second Lieutenant.

Kaczmarek, Alfons, Lance Corporal.

Kaczmarek, Stefan, Sergeant.

Kaczmarczyk, Tadeusz, Corporal.
(Awarded Twice)

Kaczmarczyk, Kazimierz, Private.

Kaczyński, Stanisław, Corporal.

Kaczyk, Jan, Sergeant.

Kadukowski, Zygmunt, Private.

Kadziołko, Henryk, Second Lieutenant.

Kaja, Adolf, Lance Corporal.

Kajat, Edward, Lance Corporal.

Kajetanowicz, Józef, Dragoon.
(Awarded Twice [P])

Kaleciński, Stanisław, Corporal.

Kaleta, Adam, Dragoon.

Kaleta, Mieczysław, Lance Corporal.
(Awarded Twice)

Kaletka, Zygmunt, Sergeant.

Kalinkiewicz, Kazimierz, Lieutenant.

Kalinowski, Jan, Corporal.

Kalinowski, Józef, Sergeant.

Kalinowski, Paweł, Corporal.
(Awarded Twice)

Kalinowski, Władysław, Corporal.

Kalinowski, Władysław, Lance Corporal.

Kaliski, Bruno, Lance Corporal.

Kałamarz, Piotr, Private.

Kałuski, Janusz, Sapper.

Kałuśniak, Stefan, Sergeant.

Kałużny, Kazimierz, Corporal.

Kamala, Edward, Lance Corporal.

Kamela, Eugeniusz, Private.

Kamieniecki, Karol, Private.

Kamiński, Henryk, Sergeant.

Kamiński, Lucjan, Second Lieutenant.

Kamiński, Marian, Cadet Officer.

Kamiński, Zygmunt, Corporal.

Kania, Zygmunt, Corporal.

Kanciak, Kazimierz, Sapper.

Kantoch, Mieczysław, Corporal.

Kański, Jan. W, Major.
(Awarded Three Times)

Kapcia, Jan, Private.

Kapecki, Zdzisław, Lance Corporal.

Kaper, Ludwik, Sergeant.

Kapis, Aleksander, Lieutenant.

Kapłon, Mieczysław, Bombardier.

Kapsa, Jan Lieutenant.

Kapuściński, Tadeusz, Bombardier.

Kapusta, Stanisław, Second Lieutenant.
(Awarded Three Times)

Karaś, Jan, Corporal.

Karcz, Jan. W, Lieutenant.
(Awarded Twice)

Karcz, Jan, Corporal.

Karczewski, Eugeniusz, Dragoon.

Karczewski, Jan, Lance Corporal.

Karczewski, Wacław, Cadet Officer.

Karczmarz, Zygmunt, Lance Corporal.

Kardasz, Adam, Lance Corporal.
(Awarded Twice)

Karłowski, Alfred, Corporal.
(Awarded Twice)

Karmelita, Piotr, Lance Corporal.

Karolczak, Artur, Corporal.

Karolczak, Stefan, Sergeant.

Karp, Juliusz, Second Lieutenant.

Karpiel, Gerard, Bombardier.

Karpiński, Retigiusz, Corporal.

Karpowicz, Stanisław, Corporal.

Karwiński, Jan, Sergeant.

Kasiński, Jan, Sergeant.

Kasprzak, Stanisław, Corporal.

Kasprzycki, Kazimierz, Captain.

Kasprzyk, Władysław, Corporal.

Kaszki, Julian, Captain. (Awarded Twice)

Kaszuba, Józef, Dragoon.

Kaszubowski, Jan, Major.
(Awarded Three Times)

Kaszymierz, Henryk, Sergeant.

Kaszyński, Wojciech, Corporal.

Kat, Jan, Corporal.

Kata, Franciszek, Corporal.

Katny, Henryk, Lieutenant.

Kawaler, Szymon, Lance Corporal.
(Awarded Twice)

Kazek, Stanisław, Corporal.

Kazimierzczak, Stefan, Major.

Kazimierski, Józef, Lance Corporal.

Kędzia, Wawrzyniec, Private.

Kelhoffer, Rudolf, Cadet Officer.

Keller, Władysław, Private.

Kępny, Ryszard, Private.

Kępiński, Józef, Second Lieutenant.
(Awarded Twice)

Kern, Jerzy, Major.

Kiciak, Jerzy, Cadet Officer.

Kiczek, Jan, Sergeant. (Awarded Twice)

Kida, Jan, Sergeant. (Three Times)

Kidron, Jan, Corporal.

Kiedos, Stefan, Sergeant. (P)

Kielam, Józef, Corporal.

Kietliński, Wacław, Lieutenant.

Kijenia, Władysław, Lance Corporal.

Kikłowicz, Michał, Lance Corporal.

Kintzi, Zbigniew, Lieutenant.
(Awarded Twice)

Kintzl, Stanisław, Second Lieutenant.

Kirschke, Jan, Cadet Officer. (P)

Kiersz, Wiesław, Major.
(Awarded Three Times [P])

Kita, Bolesław, Sergeant.

Kita, Jan, Sergeant.

Kiwatycki, Bazyli, Lance Corporal.

Klaczek, Teofil, Trooper.

Klamecki, Kazimierz, Corporal.

Klaski, Grzegorz, Lance Corporal.

Klej, Seweryn, Sergeant. (Awarded Twice)

Klepacz, Michał, Sergeant.

Klimczak, Józef, Second Lieutenant.

Klimek, Antoni, Lance Corporal.

Klimonda, Jerzy, Lieutenant.

Klukowski, Leon, Corporal.

Kluz, Nikodem, Lieutenant. (P)

Klużniak, Jan, Captain. (Awarded Twice)

Kłaptocz, Władysław,
Second Lieutenant. (P)

Kłobukowski, Antoni, Second Lieutenant.

Kłodziński, Zygmunt, Captain.
(Awarded Four Times)

Kłos, Franciszek, Private.

Kłos, Michał, Corporal.

Kłos, Władysław, Corporal.

Kłosowski, Zygmunt, Corporal.

Knafel, Roman, Corporal.

Knot, Julian, Bombardier.

Knowczyński, Stanisław, Corporal.

Kobielarz, Marcin, Corporal. (P)

Kobierny, Stanisław, Corporal.

Koblański, Józef, Corporal.

Kobryner, Jerzy, Lieutenant.

Kobrzyński, Franciszek, Corporal.

Kobylański, Czesław, Cadet Officer.

Kobyłański, Edmund, Gunner.

Kobyłecki, Antoni, Sergeant.
(Awarded Twice)

Kochan, Mieczysław, Second Lieutenant.

Kochańczyk, Eugeniusz, Lieutenant.

Kochanowicz, Czesław, Corporal.

Kochanowski, Marian, Captain.
(Awarded Twice)

Kochański, Franciszek, Private. (P)

Kochański, Tadeusz, Corporal.

Kochel, Eugeniusz, Private.

Kochutnicki, Władysław, Second
Lieutenant. (Awarded Twice)

Kociołkowski, Zygmunt, Corporal.

Kock, Jerzy, Cadet Officer.

Kocmierski, Ludwik, Corporal.

Koczula, Paweł, Second Lieutenant.

Kogut, Marian, Sapper.

Kojat, Leopold, Trooper.

Kokat, Stanisław, Sergeant Major.

Kołotek, Gerhard, Private.

Kokowski, Jan, Corporal.

Kolański, Mieczysław, Corporal.

Koloński, Józef, Corporal.

Kołat, Jan, Private.

Kołaziński, Władysław, Lance Corporal.
(Awarded Twice)

Kołecki, Stanisław, Corporal.
(Awarded Twice)

Kołodziejski, Jan, Corporal. (P)

Komar, Herman, Corporal.

Kominek, Antoni, Captain (Doctor)
(Awarded Three Times)

Komisarz, Marian, Sergeant.

Komornicki, Stefan, Lieutenant.

Komorowski, Władysław, Lance Corporal.

Konarzewski, Gustaw, Bombardier.

Konarzewski, Witold, Second Lieutenant.

Końcowoj, Józef, Lance Corporal.

Konczanin, Jan, Lance Corporal.

Kondoł, Józef, Lance Corporal.

Kondracki, Edward, Sergeant.

Kondratowicz, Florian, Sergeant.

Konieczny, Ignacy, Corporal.

Konieczny, Władysław, Sergeant Major.

Konik, Antoni, Private.

Koniuszek, Roman, Corporal.

Konkiel, Stanisław, Dragoon.

Konkol, Kazimierz, Sergeant.

Konopiełko, Stanisław, Lance Corporal.

Konrad, Kazimierz, Corporal.

Koński, Jan, Second Lieutenant.
(Awarded Twice)

Konożczak, Jan, Private.

Kopacki, Ryszard, Corporal.

Kopala, Józef, Corporal.

Kopeć, Teofil, Regimental Sergeant Major.

Koperski, Czesław, Private.

Kopka, Franciszek, Private.

Kopytko, Jan, Lance Corporal.

Korab, Roman, Lance Corporal.

Kordas, Henryk, Lance Corporal.

Kordus, Antoni, Lieutenant.

Kordyl, Jan, Second Lieutenant.

Kordylewski, Józef, Captain.

Kordziński, Ludwik, Lance Corporal.

Korhel, Paweł, Lance Corporal. (P)

Kornacki, Alfons, Sergeant.

Korniłoff, Aleksander, Private.

Korona, Konstanty, Corporal.

Korościk, Stanisław, Dragoon.

Korsak, Jan, Bombardier. (Awarded Twice)

Korzeniowski, Henryk, Second Lieutenant.

Korzeniowski, Stanisław, Sergeant.
(Awarded Twice)

Kos, Józef, Lance Corporal.

Kos, Michał, Private.

Kos, Roman, Sergeant.

Kos, Wacław, Corporal.

Kos, Zygmunt, Private. (P)

Kościukiewicz, Michał, Sergeant.

Kościuszek, Franciszek, Sergeant.

Kosecki, Mieczysław, Lance Corporal.

Kosibor, Franciszek, Corporal.

Kosicki, Adam, Sergeant.

Kosik, Norbert, Lance Corporal. (P)

Kosiński, Józef, Lance Corporal.
(Awarded Twice)

Kosiński, Stanisław, Lance Corporal.

Kosiński, Wiktor, Corporal.

Koślacz, Aleksander, Captain.

Kosmała, Ryszard, Lance Corporal.
(Awarded Twice)

Kosmeda, Stanisław, Lance Corporal.

Kosmina, Grzegorz, Lance Corporal.

Kossakowski, Jan, Lieutenant.
(Awarded Twice)

Kossowski, Władysław, Sergeant.

Kostecki, Adam, Cadet Officer.

Kostelicki, Eugeniusz, Lieutenant.

Kostrzewski, Stefan, Lieutenant.
(Awarded Twice)

Kostyniuk, Włodzimierz, Corporal.

Kostura, Brunon, Lance Corporal.

Kosyluk, Józef, Lance Corporal.

Kosztubajda, Jan, Private. (P)

Koszutski, Stanisław, Lieutenant Colonel.
(Awarded Three Times)

Kot, Leon, Private. (P)

Kot, Władysław, Lance Corporal.

Kotlarz, Jan, Second Lieutenant.

Kotowski, Edward, Corporal.
(Awarded Twice)

Kotuchna, Leopold, Corporal.

Kotulański, Bolesław, Lieutenant.

Kotyło, Mieczysław, Bombardier.

Kowal, Borys, Private.

Kowal, Jan, Captain.

Kowal, Rafał, Lance Corporal.

Kowalczewski, Wiktor, Lance Corporal.

Kowalczyk, Andrzej, Lance Corporal.

Kowalczyk, Franciszek, Lance Corporal.
(Awarded Twice)

Kowalczyk, Jan, Corporal. (P)

Kowalczyk, Józef, Lieutenant.

Kowalczyk, Leon, Captain.
(Awarded Three Times)

Kowalczyk, Stanisław, Lance Corporal. (P)

Kowalczyk, Zygmunt, Lance Corporal.

Kowalewski, Kazimierz, Corporal.

Kowalewski, Konstanty, Lance Corporal.

Kowalik, Kazimierz, Corporal.

Kowalik, Władysław, Private.

Kowalski, Eugeniusz, Sergeant Major.

Kowalski, Franciszek, Corporal. (P)

Kowalski, Henryk, Bombardier.
(Awarded Twice)

Kowalski, Jan, Lance Corporal. (P)

Kowalski, Jan, Corporal.

Kowalski, Jan, Sergeant.

Kowalski, Mieczysław, Gunner.
(Awarded Twice)

Kowalski, Stanisław, Lance Corporal.

Kowalski, Stefan, Corporal. (P)

Kowerko, Jan, Sergeant. (P)

Kownas, Wacław, Captain. (P)

Kozak, Michał, Lance Corporal.

Kozak, Stanisław, Corporal.

Kozak, Zbigniew, Second Lieutenant.
(Awarded Twice)

Kozakiewicz, Leon, Bombardier
(Artillery Corporal)

Kozakiewicz, Tadeusz, Private.

Kozdoń, Jan, Sapper.

Koziaczy, Antoni, Sergeant.

Koziełł-Poklewski, Witold. Z, Lieutenant.

Kozierowski, Stanisław, Second Lieutenant.

Kozikowski, Jan, Sergeant.
(Awarded Twice)

Kozikowski, Leonard, Corporal. (P)

Kozioł, Emil, Lance Corporal.

Kozioł, Franciszek, Private.

Koziołkowski, Michał, Private. (P)

Kozłowski, Eugeniusz, Private.

Kozłowski, Henryk, Lance Corporal.

Kozłowski, Marek, Lieutenant.

Kozłowski, Paweł, Sapper.

Kozłowski, Władysław, Sergeant.

Kozub, Bolesław, Corporal.

Kraczkiewicz, Tadeusz, Captain.

Krajewski, Jan, Dragoon. (P)

Krajewski, Teofil, Sergeant.

Kral, Jan, Corporal.

Kram, Franciszek, Corporal.

Kramner, Kazimierz, Sergeant.

Krasiński, Emil, Lance Corporal.

Kraska, Józef, Private.

Krasny, Stefan, Corporal.

Krasucki, Władysław, Trooper.

Kraszewski, Jan, Corporal.

Krautwald, Józef, Colonel.

Krawczyk, Anastazy, Lance Corporal.

Krawczyk, Józef, Lance Corporal.

Krayer, Erwin, Corporal.

Kredlewski, Zenon, Second Lieutenant.

Krelmal, Juliusz, Lance Corporal.

Krenz, Henryk, Corporal.

Kreppel. Karol, Second Lieutenant.

Kretkowski, Ryszard, Private.

Kroglec, Stefan, Sergeant.

Krogulec, Stefan, Sergeant.

Krok, Władysław, Lance Corporal.

Krokoszyński, Zbigniew,
Second Lieutenant.

Król, Karol, Lance Corporal.

Król, Wacław, Bombardier.

Królewski, Kazimierz, Trooper.

Kropidło, Czesław, Staff Sergeant.

Krowicki, Stanisław, Lance Corporal.

Kruczan, Mateusz, Gunner.

Kruczek, Jan, Corporal. (P)

Krupa, Gustaw, Sergeant. (Awarded Twice)

Krupowicz, Władysław, Captain.

Krzak, Adam, Dragoon.

Krzeczkowski, Stanisław, Corporal.

Krzemień, Stanisław, Sergeant.

Krzemionka, Stanisław, Corporal.

Krzempek, Antoni, Lance Corporal.

Krzempek, Piotr, Bombardier.

Krzesaj, Antoni, Bombardier.

Krzysztofik, Józef, Bombardier.

Krzywoń, Karol, Private.

Krzyżaniak, Stanisław, Sergeant.

Krzyżaniak, Tadeusz, Second Lieutenant.

Krzyżanowski, Tadeusz, Corporal.
(Awarded Twice)

Krzyżanowski, Władysław, Lance
Corporal. (Awarded Twice)

Krzyżowski, Rafał, Lance Corporal.

Krynicki, Józef, Corporal.

Krynicki, Marceli, Private.

Kryskiewicz, Wiktor, Private. (P)

Krysta, Jan, Second Lieutenant.

Krywiecki, Eustachy, Lance Corporal.

Książek, Józef, Corporal.

Księżycki, Wojciech, Cadet Officer.

Kubacki, Adam, Adam, Corporal.

Kubacki, Feliks, Gunner. (Awarded Twice)

Kubala, Józef, Sergeant. (Awarded Twice)

Kubatek, Jan, Lance Corporal. (P)

Kubiak, Florian, Corporal.

Kubiak, Jan, Captain. (Awarded Twice)

Kubiak, Jan, Private.

Kubień, Józef, Private.

Kubit, Augustyn, Second Lieutenant.

Kuc, Michał, Trooper.

Kuc, Stanisław, Second Lieutenant.

Kuca, Kazimierz, Lance Corporal.

Kucbajski, Tadeusz, Private. (P)

Kucharczyk, Stefan, Corporal.

Kucharski, Józef, Lance Corporal. (P)

Kucia, Damian, Cadet Officer.
(Awarded Twice)

Kucma, Henryk, Corporal.

Kucowicz, Józef, Private.

Kuczerawy, Józef, Gunner.

Kuczerenko, Anatal, Private.

Kuczyński, Henryk, Private.

Kuczyński, Zygmunt, Second Lieutenant.

Kudelski, Józef, Lance Corporal.

Kuder, Stanisław, Corporal.

Kukuła, Kazimierz, Corporal.
(Awarded Twice)

Kula, Eugeniusz, Sergeant.
(Awarded Twice [P])

Kula, Kazimierz, Lieutenant. (P)

Kulczycki, Kazimierz, Corporal.

Kulsza, Tadeusz, Corporal. (Awarded Twice [P])

Kulsza, Władysław, Second Lieutenant.

Kulig, Henryk, Lance Corporal.

Kulig, Władysław, Second Lieutenant.

Kuliński, Wiktor, Corporal.

Kulka, Franciszek, Lance Corporal.

Kulka, Stanisław, Lance Corporal.

Kułaczkowski, Mieczysław, Corporal.

Kułakowski, Eugeniusz, Lance Corporal.

Kunachowicz, Jerzy, Captain. (Awarded Twice)

Kuprys, Romuald, Corporal.

Kurc, Edward, Lance Corporal.

Kurcab, Czesław, Cadet Officer.

Kurczyk, Jan, Sergeant.

Kurczyk, Rudolf, Corporal.

Kurczyński, Paweł, Lance Corporal.

Kurdziel, Władysław, Sergeant.

Kurek, Antoni, Bombardier.

Kurek, Hieronim, Major. (Awarded Twice)

Kurek, Jerzy, Corporal.

Kurjanowicz, Stefan, Dragoon. (P)

Kurka, Józef, Lance Corporal.

Kurłowicz, Antoni, Sergeant.

Kurowski, Jan, Captain.

Kurpet, Franciszek, Lance Corporal.

Kurpiel, Stanisław, Lieutenant.

Kurtz, Julian, Second Lieutenant.

Kurzeja, Leonard, Corporal.

Kurzydło, Franciszek, Sergeant. (Awarded Twice)

Kuś, Karol, Bombardier.

Kusiński, Ignacy, Corporal.

Kusmirek, Henryk, Lieutenant. (Awarded Twice)

Kuszewski, Zygmunt, Lance Corporal.

Kutno, Zygfryd, Private. (P)

Kuziemski, Marian, Lance Corporal.

Kuznik, Roman, Sergeant.

Kwaczyński, Michał, Corporal. (P)

Kwas, Franciszek, Lance Corporal.

Kwaśniewski, Edmund, Lance Corporal.

Kwaśnik, Michał, Lance Corporal.

Kwaśnik, Zygmunt, Lance Corporal.

Kwiatek, Antoni, Corporal.

Kwiatek, Stanisław, Sergeant.

Kwiatowski, Alfons, Corporal. (P)

Kwiatowski, Andrzej, Corporal.

Kwiatowski, Benedykt, Bombardier.

Kwiatowski, Józef, Captain.

Kwiecień, Józef, Sergeant.

Kwiecień, Władysław, Sergeant. (P)

Kwiecień, Zbigniew, Lance Corporal.

Kwiecień, Zygmunt, Cadet Officer.

Kwieciński, Antoni, Lance Corporal.

Kwieciński, Mikołaj, Corporal. (Awarded Three Times)

Kwieciński, Zygmunt, Lance Corporal.

Kwik, Eryk, Private.

Kwoczek, Marcin, Sergeant.

Lach, Jan, Bombardier.

Lalewicz, Romuald, Corporal.

Lalko, Jan, Lance Corporal.

Landa, Józef, Corporal.

Landau, Marceli, Second Lieutenant.

Landsberg, Jan, Corporal.

Langauer, Karol, Lance Corporal.

Lange, Wiktor,

Lampara, Jan, Corporal.

Lapa, Józef, Lance Corporal.

Larkowski, Józef, Sergeant.

Larwa, Jan, Corporal.

Las, Jan, Lance Corporal.

Las, Witold, Lance Corporal. (P)

Lasia, Stefan, Lance Corporal.

Laskowski, Alfons, Lance Corporal. (P)

Laskowski, Bolesław, Sergeant Major. (Awarded Twice [P])

Lasoń, Jan, Corporal.

Lasota, Józef, Private.

Laszczyk, Władysław, Captain.

Laszczyk, Władysław, Corporal. (Awarded Twice)

Latkowski, Marian, Sergeant.

Latusek, Paweł, Chaplain.

Lebioda, Jerzy, Lance Corporal.

Lech, Jerzy, Lieutenant. (Awarded Twice)

Ledwoń, Józef, Second Lieutenant.

Legeżyński, Tadeusz, Major.

Lejewski, Jan, Lieutenant. (Awarded Four Times)

Leloch, Jan, Corporal. (Awarded Twice)

Lenarcik, Franciszek, Lance Corporal.

Lenczowski, Franciszek, Cadet Officer. (Awarded Four Times)

Leporowski, Alfred, Cadet Officer. (Awarded Twice)

Leskow, Efreim, Dragoon.

Leskow, Jan, Second Lieutenant.

Leśniak, Józef, Sergeant.

Leśniewski, Wacław, Corporal.

Leszczyński, Aleksander, Corporal.

Leszczyński, Czesław, Corporal.

Lewak, Zbigniew, Lieutenant.

Lewandowski, Bronisław, Gunner.

Lewandowski, Stanisław, Sergeant.

Lewandowski, Stanisław, Lance Corporal.

Lewandowski, Zygmunt, Sergeant.

Lewandowski, Zygmunt, Lance Corporal.

Lewicki-Szczęsny, Bolesław, Lieutenant.

Lewiński, Stanisław, Corporal.

Lewkiewicz, Wilhelm, Second Lieutenant.

Lewkowicz, Karol, Trooper.

Lewkowski, Edward, Lance Corporal.

Lewoniewski, Kazimierz, Private.

Liberda, Stanisław, Lance Corporal.

Liboszka, Adam, Lance Corporal.

Lichoś, Leon, Lance Corporal.

Liehr, Jerzy, Captain.

Likos, Władysław, Corporal.

Limberger, Władysław, Lieutenant.

Lin, Jan, Lance Corporal.

Lindan, Olgierd, Second Lieutenant.

Linke, Ryszard, Second Lieutenant. (Awarded Three Times)

Lipiec, Stanisław, Sergeant. (Awarded Twice)

Lipiński, Florian, Sergeant.

Lipiński, Kazimierz, Sergeant.

Lipiński, Stanisław, Second Lieutenant.

Lipiński, Paweł, Corporal. (Awarded Twice)

Lipincki, Stanisław, Sergeant.

Lipski, Wacław, Lance Corporal.

Lipszyc, Maurycy, Lance Corporal.

Lis, Antoni, Corporal.

Lisowski, Antoni, Dragoon. (Awarded Twice)

Lisowski, Bolesław, Private.

Listewnik, Maksymilian, Private.

Litewiak, Stanisław, Lance Corporal. (Awarded Twice)

Litwin, Andrzej, Corporal.

Litwińczuk, Zbigniew, Private. (Awarded Twice)

Loba, Ludwik, Lance Corporal. (P)

Lorbiecki, Brunon, Sergeant.

Lorek, Józef, Second Lieutenant.

Lorenz, Bolesław, Sergeant.

Lorenz, Edward, Corporal.

Lorenz, Leopold, Second Lieutenant.

Lubas, Stefan, Corporal.

Labaszewski, Stefan, Sergeant.

Lubiarz, Marian, Corporal.

Lubieniecki, Walenty, Lieutenant. (Awarded Twice)

Lubomirski, Wincenty, Sergeant.

Ludwiczak, Jan, Trooper.

Łaba, Jan, Corporal.

Łaba, Roman, Lance Corporal.

Łabno, Edward, Captain. (Awarded Four Times)

Łach, Józef, Lance Corporal.

Łaciuk, Alojzy, Private.

Łaczkowski, Józef, Staff Sergeant.

Łaniewski, Aleksander, Lance Corporal.

Łapiński, Wacław, Cadet Officer.

Łasłowski, Marian, Lieutenant. (Awarded Twice)

Łaszczewski, Zbigniew, Private.

Łazorowicz, Albert, Lance Corporal.

Łazorowicz, Jan, Lance Corporal.

Łochocki, Konstanty, Sergeant.

Łokieć, Leib, Bombardier.

Łopaciński, Wacław, Cadet Officer.

Łuczkiewicz, Jerzy, Lance Corporal.

Łukasiewicz, Edward, Corporal.

Łukasiewicz, Jan, Corporal.

Łukasik, Józef, Gunner.

Łukasik, Mieczysław, Lance Corporal.

Łukawski, Józef, Sergeant Major.

Łukiewicz, Bohdan, Lieutenant.

Łukowski, Tomasz, Lance Corporal.

Łukowski, Zygmunt, Lieutenant.

Łuszczyński, Józef, Staff Sergeant.

Łutczyk, Mieczysław, Corporal.

Łysakowski, Tomasz, Sergeant.

Łysiak, Paweł, Corporal.

Łysik, Mikołaj, Corporal.

Łyska, Ryszard, Corporal.

Macek, Henryk, Lance Corporal.

Macfalda, Franciszek, Corporal.

Machlarz, Stanisław, Corporal. (P)

Machnik, Wilhelm, Sergeant.
(Awarded Twice)

Machura, Stefan, Lieutenant.

Maciejczyk, Wojciech, Sergeant.
(Awarded Twice)

Maciejewski, Leon, Private.

Maciejewski, Zbigniew, Second Lieutenant.

Maciejewski, Zygfryd, Lance Corporal.

Maciejowski, Bronisław, Lance Corporal.

Maczuba, Jan, Major.

Madaliński, Antoni, Lance Corporal.

Madej, Jan, Corporal.

Madeński, Edmund, Second Lieutenant.
(Awarded Twice)

Madrawski, Józef, Lance Corporal.

Magoński, Władysław, Lieutenant.

Majchrzak, Czesław, Lance Corproal.

Majerski, Edward, Sergeant.
(Awarded Twice)

Majewski, Henryk, Cadet Officer.

Majewski, Herbert, Second Lieutenant.

Majewski, Jan, Sergeant Major.

Majewski, Leon, Sergeant.
(Awarded Twice)

Majewski, Tadeusz, Colonel.
(Awarded Three Times)

Majkowski, Bronisław, Lance Corporal.

Majkowski, Stefan, Corporal.

Majkowski, Władysław, Cadet Officer.

Majkut, Kazimierz, Lance Corporal.

Majsnerowicz, Leon, Lance Corporal.

Mąka, Tadeusz, Lance Corporal. (P)

Makarczyk, Michał, Corporal.

Makarus, Paweł, Lance Corporal.

Makowski, Alojzy, Sergeant.

Makowski, Edward, Lance Corporal.

Makowski, Jan, Lance Corporal.

Makowski, Zygmunt, Bombardier.

Makówka, Wacław, Corporal.

Maksymiuk, Leon, Sergeant.

Makuch, Józef, Gunner.

Makuch, Kazimierz, Captain.

Malcherczyk, Jan, Corporal.

Malec, Jan, Corporal. (P)

Maleszewski, Tadeusz, Captain.
(Awarded Twice)

Malicki, Henryk, Private.

Malicki, Stefan, Bombardier.

Malinowski, Józef, Sergeant.

Malinowski, Leon, Private.

Malinowski, Mieczysław, Major. (P)

Malinowski, Paweł, Corporal.

Malkiewicz, Mieczysław, Lance Corporal.

Malkiewicz, Mieczysław, Lance Corporal.

Malkiewicz, Paweł, Lieutenant.
(Awarded Twice)

Małecki, Edwin, Private.

Małko, Franciszek, Lance Corporal.

Małodobry, Leopold, Sergeant.

Mały, Władysław, Sergeant.

Małyszko, Czesław, Sergeant.

Mamczarczyk, Józef, Lieutenant.
(Awarded Three Times)

Mańczak, Czesław, Corporal.

Mandrela, Józef, Lance Corporal.

Mania, Czesław, Private.

Mania, Józef, Private.

Mankiewicz, Andrzej, Lance Corporal.

Mańkowski, Jerzy, Private.

Mantykowski, Antoni, Sapper.

Marc, Edward, Sergeant.

Marchocki, Mikołaj, Lance Corporal.

Marcińczak, Stanisław, Sergeant. (P)

Marcińczyk, Franciszek, Lance Corporal.

Marciniak, Czesław, Sergeant.

Marciniak, Józef, Lance Corporal.

Marcinkiewicz, Adam, Second Lieutenant.
(Awarded Twice)

Marcinkiewicz, Franciszek, Corporal.

Marcinkiewicz, Karol, Corporal.

Marcinkowski, Bolesław, Major.

Marcinkowski, Bronisław, Second
Lieutenant. (Awarded Three Times)

Marcinowicz, Henryk, Gunner.

Marczak, Władysław, Lance Corporal.

Marczuk, Bazyli, Lance Corporal.

Maresch, Karol, Lieutenant Colonel.
(Awarded Three Times)

Margiel, Władysław, Corporal.

Markiewicz, Cezary, Sergeant.

Markiewicz, Tadeusz,
Second Lieutenant (Doctor).

Markowski, Karol, Corporal.

Markus, Jan, Dragoon.

Marowski, Jan, Major.

Mars, Władysław, Sergeant.

Marski, Alfred, Private.

Martini, Florian, Captain.

Martul, Julian, Gunner.

Martynoga, Stanisław, Lieutenant.
(Awarded Four Times)

Marzantowicz, Jerzy, Corporal.

Masalski, Paweł, Lance Corporal.

Masłowski, Tadeusz, Second Lieutenant.
(Awarded Twice)

Masłowski, Zygmunt, Bombardier.

Mass, Antoni, Sergeant.

Maszczyk, Władysław, Lance Corporal.

Maszkiewicz, Józef, Sergeant Major.

Maszkowski, Andrzej, Lieutenant.

Masztalerz, Marian, Corporal.

Matejak, Henryk, Sapper.

Matosz, Tadeusz, Corporal.

Matulanis, Jerzy, Lieutenant.
(Awarded Three Times)

Matulewicz, Alfons, Gunner.

Matusiak, Stanisław, Sergeant.

Matuszak, Józef, Corporal.

Matuszewski, Jan, Lance Corporal.

Matych, Feliks, Private.

Matysiak, Franciszek, Corporal.
(Awarded Twice)

Maziarski, Henryk, Lieutenant.

Maziarz, Leszek, Cadet Officer.

Mazur, Jan, Corporal.

Mazur, Mikołaj,
Regimental Sergeant Major.

Mazur, Tadeusz, Lance Corporal.

Mazur, Tadeusz, Sergeant.

Mazurek, Mieczysław, Corporal.

Mazurek, Roman, Second Lieutenant. (P)

Mazurkiewicz, Erwin, Cadet Officer.
(Awarded Twice)

Mazurkiewicz, Zenon, Bombardier.

Mazurowski, Ignacy, Lance Corporal.

Max, Stanisław, Lieutenant.

Medwicki, Adam, Lieutenant.
(Awarded Three Times)

Meisnerowicz, Jan, Lieutenant,
(Awarded Twice)

Mędrala, Antoni, Sergeant.

Mendroch, Franciszek, Private.

Meniw, Bazyli, Lance Corporal.

Menkis, Zygfryd, Lance Corporal.

Mereczko, Paweł, Lance Corporal.
(Awarded Twice)

Merker, Wilhelm, Lieutenant.

Meus, Jan, Corporal.

Miazga, Marcin, Lance Corporal.

Michalak, Stefan, Lance Corporal.
(Awarded Twice)

Michalczyk, Czesław, Major.

Michalik, Czesław, Cadet Officer.

Michalski, Józef, Corporal.
(Awarded Twice)

Michalski, Józef, Cadet Officer.

Michalski, Marian. T, Lieutenant.
(Awarded Twice)

Michalski, Miron, Second Lieutenant.

Michalski, Wacław, Lance Corporal.

Michałek, Albert, Dragoon.

Michałowski, Tadeusz, Second Lieutenant.

Michna, Stefan, Lance Corporal.

Michniewicz, Ignacy, Bombardier.

Mickiewicz, Stefan, Corporal.

Miczyk, Bolesław, Cadet Officer.

Mielczarek, Antoni, Sergeant.

Mielczarek, Stanisław, Corporal.

Mielec, Andrzej, Sergeant.
(Awarded Twice)

Milewski, Józef, Lance Corporal.

Milewski, Stefan, Lance Corporal. (P)

133

Mielniczuk, Mieczysław, Trooper.
Mierzwiak, Artur, Corporal.
Mikołajczak, Józef, Corporal.
Mikołajczyk, Antoni, Corporal.
Mikołajewski, Stanisław, Lance Corporal.
Mikowski, Franciszek, Dragoon.
Mikuszewski, Robert, Corporal.
Miller, Ignacy, Private.
Miłkowski, Józef, Corporal.
Mincer, Andrzej, Second Lieutenant.
(Awarded Three Times)
Mincer, Bohdan, Major,
(Awarded Three Times)
Mindel, Feliks, Lance Corporal.
Miński, Jan, Private.
Mioskowski, Franciszek, Dragoon.
Mirecki, Jerzy, Lieutenant.
Miś, Sebastian, Second Lieutenant.
Miscierewicz, Jan, Gunner.
Misiak, Andrzej, Corporal.
Misiuk, Włodzimierz, Lance Corporal.
Miśniakiewicz, Tadeusz, Private.
Misczyk, Alojzy, Corporal.
(Awarded Three Times)
Mizerka, Henryk, Sergeant.
Mleczko, Karol, Corporal.
Młynarski, Michał, Lance Corporal.
Młynarz, Karol, Second Lieutenant.
(Awarded Twice)
Mogilski, Tadeusz, Cadet Officer.
Mohilenko, Bronisław, Trooper.
Mojzesowicz, Krzysztof, Second
Lieutenant. (Awarded Three Times)
Mokrzycki, Zygmunt, Sergeant.
Molik, Andrzej, Corporal. (P)
Molin, Jan, Gunner.
Mollin, Leon, Sergeant.
Moncik, Kazimierz, Private.
Morawski, Czesław, Second Lieutenant. (P)
Morowski, Leon, Sergeant.
Morowski, Zbigniew, Lieutenant.
Moro, Józef, Lance Corporal.
Morski, Kazimierz, Lance Corporal.
(Awarded Twice)
Mosiewicz, Jan, Second Lieutenant.
Moskal, Władysław, Second Lieutenant.
Moszczyński, Eugeniusz, Sergeant.
Możdżeń, Jerzy, Second Lieutenant. (P)
Mozdżonek, Stanisław, Lance Corporal.
Mroczko, Marian, Sapper.
Mróz, Józef, Lieutenant.
Mróz, Zdzisław, Lance Corporal.
Mrozek, Alojzy, Private.
Mucha, Michał, Corporal.
Mucha, Władysław, Sergeant Major.
(Awarded Twice)
Mudrewicz, Julian, Lieutenant.
Mudryk, Bronisław, Sapper.
Multarzyński, Tadeusz, Private.
(Awarded Twice)
Mura, Nikodem, Lance Corporal.

Muraszko, Aleksander, Captain.
Murawiecki, Konstanty, Corporal.
(Awarded Twice)
Murkowski, Czesław, Corporal.
Musiał, Henryk, Sergeant.
Musiał, Mieczysław, Corporal.
Musiał, Stanisław, Lance Corporal.
Musiał, Wacław, Corporal.
Musiał, Walenty, Sergeant.
Musiałowski, Andrzej, Private.
Musiński, Kazimierz, Private.
Musioł, Edmund, Second Lieutenant.
Muszalski, Józef, Corporal.
Muszarski, Antoni, Corporal.
Muszyński, Jan, Corporal.
Muszyński, Ksawery, Corporal.
Muszyński, Mieczysław, Lance Corporal.
Muszyński, Stanisław, Lance Corporal.
Muszyński, Stefan, Lance Corporal.
Muter, Wacław, Sergeant.
Myrda, Józef, Chaplain.
Myszor, Wilhelm, Corporal.
Mytkowski, Kazimierz, Lance Corporal. (P)
Nadolny, Roman, Corporal.
Nadolski, Zbigniew, Second Lieutenant.
Nadzieja, Józef, Private.
Nadziński, Paweł, Lance Corporal.
Nadgoński, Stanisław, Sergeant.
Nagórny, Leon, Lance Corporal.
Namysłowski, Ludwik, Private.
Napierała, Feliks, Bombardier.
Naprawa, Feliks, Sergeant.
Narloch, Józef, Chaplain.
Narolski, Zygmunt, Sergeant Major.
(Awarded Twice)
Narożny, Władysław, Cadet Officer.
Natanek, Jan, Second Lieutenant.
Naturalny, Józef, Corporal.
Nawrocki, Alfred, Private.
Nawrocki, Paweł, Cadet Officer.
Nawrot, Edmund, Dragoon.
Nawrotny, Tadeusz, Sergeant.
Nebelski, Szymon, Cadet Officer.
Nędza, Henryk, Lieutenant.
(Awarded Twice)
Nelson, Eryk, Dragoon.
Niedziela, Józef, Lance Corporal.
Niedzielski, Adam, Major.
Niedzielski, Eugeniusz, Lance Corporal.
Niemczycki, Zbigniew, Lance Corporal.
Niemiec, Antoni, Lance Corporal.
Niemiec, Jan, Sergeant.
Niermira, Lucjan, Sergeant Major.
(Awarded Twice)
Nieroda, Władysław, Private.
Niesyto, Ludwik, Lance Corporal.
Niewiadomski, Walerian, Sergeant.
Niewiem, Ernest, Second Lieutenant. (P)
Niewinowski, Jerzy, Second Lieutenant.
(Awarded Three Times)
Niezgocki, Bronisław, Private.

Nikiel, Henryk, Lance Corporal.
Nikolin, Konstanty, Lance Corporal.
Nita, Władysław, Lance Corporal.
(Awarded Twice)
Nitka, Bronisław, Captain
Nitosławski, Mieczyslaw, Cadet Officer.
Nizioł, Aleksander, Sergeant.
(Awarded Twice)
Noakowski, Wilhelm, Corporal.
Nocoń, Antoni, Lance Corporal.
Nodelski, Mieczysław, Cadet Officer.
Noel, Bronisław, Colonel. (Awarded Twice)
Nojman, Leon, Corporal. (Awarded Twice)
Noras, Franciszek, Corporal.
Nord, Salomon, Corporal.
Nosalik, Kazimierz, Captain.
Nowacki, Brunon, Private.
Nowaczyński, Aleksander, Lieutenant
Colonel. (Awarded Three Times)
Nowak, Antoni, Gunner.
Nowak, Antoni, Private.
Nowak, Franciszek, I, Lance Corporal.
Nowak, Franciszek, II, Lance Corporal.
Nowak, Ignacy, Sergeant.
Nowak, Jan, Corporal. (Awarded Twice)
Nowak, Józef, Lance Corporal.
(Awarded Twice)
Nowak, Józef, Sergeant.
Nowak, Mieczysław, Private.
Nowak, Michał, Sergeant Major.
Nowak, Paweł, Staff Sergeant.
Nowak, Stefan, Dragoon.
Nowak, Tomasz, Corporal.
Nowak, Władysław, Sapper.
Nowak, Władysław, Sergeant.
Nowakowski, Janusz, Captain.
(Awarded Twice)
Nowakowski, Piotr, Sergeant.
Nowakowski, Tadeusz, Corporal.
Nowakowski, Zygmunt, Lance Corporal.
Nowicki, Julian, Lance Bombardier.
Nowosiad, August, Dragoon.
Nydza, Franciszek, Corporal.
Nytkowski, Edward, Private. (P)
Obara, Stanisław, Gunner.
Obraniak, Jan, Corporal.
Ochab, Jan, Private.
Ochab, Kazimierz, Captain.
Ochałek, Franciszek, Private.
Ochyra, Stanisław, Cadet Officer.
Ogiński, Paweł, Corporal.
Ogon, Stanisław, Private.
Ogorzaly, Stanisław, Cadet Officer.
Ojrzanowski, Marian, Second Lieutenant.
Ojrzyński, Tomasz, Corporal.
Okoniewski, Jan, Cadet Officer.
Oktawiec, Jerzy, Private.
Olczak, Władysław, Corporal.
Olech, Tadeusz, Lance Corporal.
Olejniczak, Teodor, Lance Corporal.
Olencki, Edward, Private.

Olesiński, Józef, Lieutenant. (Awarded Three Times)
Oleksiak, Władysław, Bombardier.
Oleksy, Jan, Lance Corporal.
Oleśnicki, Zbigniew, Lance Corporal.
Olsowski, Teodor, Lance Corporal.
Olszak, Feliks, Corporal.
Olszański, Zygmunt, Lance Corporal.
Olszewski, Jan, Lance Corporal.
Olszewski, Stanisław, Bombardier.
Olszewski, Stanisław, Corporal.
Olszowy, Wiktor, Corporal.
Opaliński, Stanisław, Corporal.
Opaszewski, Paweł, Lance Corporal.
Opiłka, Jan, Private.
Oprychał, Antoni, Corporal.
Opryszko, Aleksander, Corporal.
Orbiński, Szczepan, Lance Corporal.
Orendosz, Karol, Sergeant.
Orkan, Alojzy, Gunner.
Orlak, Stanisław, Private.
Orlik, Jerzy, Lance Corporal.
Orlikowski, Józef, Corporal.
Orłowski, Jerzy, Bombardier.
Orłowski, Paweł, Private.
Orpiszewski, Józef, Captain. (Awarded Three Times)
Orszulik, Ernest, Private.
Orwat, Franciszek, Corporal.
Orzechowski, Bronisław, Private.
Orzeł, Edward, Corporal.
Orzeł, Walter, Sapper.
Orzełek, Czesław, Dragoon.
Osipowicz, Stanisław, Sergeant Major.
Oslizłok, Wiktor, Lance Corporal.
Osmelak, Jan, Lance Corporal.
Osnowski, Alfons, Corporal.
Osowski, Bronisław, Lance Corporal.
Osowicz, Włodzimierz, Sergeant Major. (Awarded Twice)
Ostiadel, Jan. W, Second Lieutenant.
Ostroga, Stanisław, Lance Corporal. (Awarded Twice)
Ostromęcki, Adam, Second Lieutenant. (Awarded Twice)
Ostrowski, Hipolit, Private. (P)
Ostrowski, Piotr, Sergeant.
Owczarkowski, Franciszek, Sergeant Major.
Ozdowski, Roch, Lieutenant.
Ożarski, Andrzej, Lieutenant.
Ożog, Antoni, Sergeant.
Paczos, Jan, Lance Corporal.
Pająk, Franciszek, Lance Corporal.
Pajewski, Józef, Cadet Officer.
Pakulski, Janusz, Lieutenant.
Palarczyk, Karol, Second Lieutenant.
Palczuk, Chaskiel, Lance Corporal.
Palenczak, Józef, Corporal.
Palichleb, Franciszek, Lance Corporal.
Paliwoda, Stanisław, Sergeant.

Palmowski, Antoni, Private.
Palmowski, Wacław, Corporal.
Palowski, Karol, Lance Corporal. (Awarded Twice)
Palubski, Maksymilian, Bombardier.
Paluchniak, Stanisław, Corporal.
Pałucha, Kazimierz, Corporal.
Pałyga, Piotr, Corporal.
Pałys, Alfons, Gunner.
Pałys, Jan, Lance Corporal.
Panek, Tadeusz, Lieutenant.
Panowicz, Józef, Private.
Papée, Henryk, Cadet Officer. (Awarded Twice)
Paprzycki, Aleksander, Second Lieutenant. (Awarded Three Times)
Parol, Jan, Sergeant.
Parszyk, Bolesław, Lance Corporal. (Awarded Twice)
Parzybut, Edward, Lance Corporal.
Parzycki, Aleksander, Second Lieutenant. (Awarded Twice)
Paschek, Alfons, Corporal.
Paszek, Władysław, Second Lieutenant. (Awarded Twice)
Paszki, Julian, Captain.
Paszkiewicz, Edward, Private.
Paszkowski, Roman, Private.
Patalas, Antoni, Sergeant. (Awarded Twice)
Patejczuk, Maksymilian, Lance Corporal.
Pateluch, Jan, Corporal.
Pater, Wawrzyniec, Sergeant.
Paternak, Wawrzyniec, Regimental Sergeant Major. (Awarded Twice)
Paternoga, Zygmunt, Corporal.
Patko, Stanisław, Corporal.
Patorski, Józef. W, Second Lieutenant.
Patryn, Zygmunt, Lieutenant.
Pawelski, Jan, Private.
Pawelski, Mieczysław, Second Lieutenant.
Pawelski, Władysław, Corporal.
Pawelaczyk, Józef, Sergeant.
Pawlak, Tadeusz, Sergeant.
Pawlewski, Zbigniew, Second Lieutenant.
Pawliczek, Gerard, Bombardier.
Pawlikowski, Paweł, Corporal.
Pawłowicz, Czesław, Second Lieutenant.
Pawłowicz, Tadeusz, Sergeant.
Pawłowski, Antoni, Cadet Officer.
Pawłowski, Edward, Lance Corporal.
Pawłowski, Eugeniusz, Second Lieutenant. (Awarded Twice)
Pawłowski, Waldermar, Cadet Officer.
Pazowski, Lesław, Second Lieutenant. (Awarded Twice)
Pęcak, Jakub, Lance Corporal.
Pędziwiatr, Józef, Corporal.
Pelczarski, Stanisław, Corporal. (Awarded Twice)
Pepliński, Jan, Lance Corporal. (P)
Penar, Kazimierz, Regimental Sergeant Major.

Perlo, Czesław, Lance Corporal.
Peszkowski, Wiesław, Corporal.
Petela, Bronisław, Lance Corporal.
Petelczyc, Tadeusz, Lance Corporal.
Peterman, Ray, Corporal.
Petreyko, Mieczysław, Second Lieutenant.
Petryk, Bazyli, Private.
Petryla, Stanisław, Lance Corporal.
Pfeiffer, Stanisław, Cadet Officer.
Piasecki, Stanisław, Sergeant.
Piątek, Józef, Private.
Piątek, Józef, Corporal. (Awarded Twice)
Piątkowski, Grzegorz, Private.
Piątkowski, Jerzy, Lieutenant. (Awarded Twice)
Piechota, Antoni, Second Lieutenant, Second Lieutenant.
Piechota, Józef, Sergeant. (Awarded Twice)
Piecyk, Stanisław, Corporal. (P)
Pieczyński, Kazimierz, Corporal. (Awarded Twice)
Piekarski, Władysław, Sergeant.
Pieniążek, Julian, Lance Corporal.
Piętka, Antoni, Corporal.
Piętka, Stanisław, Lance Corporal.
Pietras, Jan, Trooper.
Pietraszek, Ludwik, Corporal.
Pietraszek, Stanisław, Bombardier.
Pietrusiński, Aleksander, Sergeant.
Pietruszek, Antoni, Sergeant.
Pietruszek, Roman, Lance Corporal. (P)
Pietrzak, Stefan, Lance Corporal.
Pikiel, Czesław, Sergeant Major.
Pikus, Franciszek, Corporal.
Pilarz, Tadeusz, Lance Corporal.
Pilch, Jan, Sergeant.
Pilecki, Kazimierz, Sergeant.
Pilecki, Kurt, Corporal.
Piliszewski, Zbigniew, Bombardier.
Pilny, Ignacy, Lance Corporal. (Awarded Twice)
Piotrowicz, Teodor, Lance Corporal.
Piotrowski, Antoni, Lance Corporal. (Awarded Twice)
Piotrowski, Feliks, Lance Corporal.
Piotrowski, Feliks, Sergeant.
Piotrowski, Franciszek, Lance Corporal. (Awarded Twice)
Piotrowski, Jan, Dragoon.
Piotrowski, Stanisław, Corporal. (Awarded Twice)
Piotrowski, Wacław, Captain. (Awarded Twice)
Piórkowski, Antoni, Corporal.
Piperek, Ferdynand, Dragoon. (Awarded Twice)
Piputa, Wacław, Staff Sergeant.
Pirog, Jan, Lance Corporal. (Awarded Twice)
Piskozub, Tadeusz, Trooper.
Pisulewski, Stefan, Corporal.
Pitakowski, Alojzy, Captain.

135

Pitorak, Florian, Corporal.

Piwowarczyk, Antoni, Lance Corporal.

Pjanka, Jan, Corporal.

Placek, Karol, Lance Corporal.

Plaster, Augustyn, Lance Corporal.

Pleskarzyński, Zbigniew, Cadet Officer.

Plewa, Stanisław, Corporal.

Plichciński, Henryk, Private.

Pluciński, Wacław, Lance Corporal. (P)

Pluta, Józef, Corporal.

Płaszczyk, Józef, Lance Corporal.

Płonka, Stanisław, Dragoon.

Płoszyński, Bronisław, Lance Corporal.

Poczekaj, Józef, Lance Corporal.

Poborca, Stanisław, Private.

Pobudkowski, Janusz, Cadet Officer.

Pogojski, Franciszek, Dragoon.

Podgórski, Henryk, Corporal.

Podkówka, Jan, Private.

Podlewski, Czesław, Second Lieutenant.

Pododworny, Bolesław, Dragoon.

Podolczuk, Włodzimierz, Private.

Podoski, Jan, Captain.

Pogorzelski, Bronisław, Bombardier.

Pogorzelski, Henryk, Lieutenant.

Pogorzelski, Władysław, Corporal.
(Awarded Twice)

Pojdak, Witold, Lance Corporal.

Pojmicz, Stanisław, Lance Corporal.

Pokora, Roman, Lance Corporal.

Pokorski, Józef, Lance Corporal.

Pokrywka, Antoni, Corporal.

Polak, Eugeniusz, Lieutenant. (P)

Polak, Jan, Lieutenant. (Awarded Twice)

Polak, Jordan, Corporal.

Polak, Stefan, Second Lieutenant,
(Awarded Twice)

Polan, Władysław, Lance Corporal.

Poliński, Jan, Corporal.

Politańczuk, Józef, Lance Corporal.

Politowicz, Feliks, Corporal.

Politowski, Józef, Second Lieutenant.

Politowski, Stanisław, Corporal.

Położyński, Antoni, Lieutenant.

Pomianowski, Leszek, Lance Corporal.

Ponc, Karol, Second Lieutenant.

Poncet de Sandon, Leon, Bombardier.

Poniatowski, Bogusław, Lance Corporal.

Ponikowski, Cezary, Second Lieutenant.

Popiak, Aleksander, Second Lieutenant.
(Awarded Twice)

Popiel, Janusz, Lieutenant.
(Awarded Four Times)

Popieluch, Edward, Second Lieutenant.

Popiołkiewicz, Mieczysław, Private.

Popiuk, Mikołaj, Private. (P)

Popławski, Arkadiusz, Second Lieutenant.

Porczyński, Józef, Lieutenant.

Porębski, Adolf, Regimental Sergeant
Major. (Awarded Twice)

Potapczyk, Wacław, Sergeant.
(Awarded Twice [P])

Potiszyl, Karol, Cadet Officer.

Potoczny, Jan, Sergeant.

Potworowski, Jan, Second Lieutenant.
(Awarded Twice)

Pozdrowski, Jan, Lance Corporal.

Praiss, Jan, Corporal.

Prażmowski, Wincenty, Lance Corporal.

Pres, Wiesław, Second Lieutenant.

Priga, Józef, Second Lieutenant.

Prostak, Marcin, Lance Corporal.

Proszek, Roman. Captain.
(Awarded Four Times)

Próg, Jan, Lance Corporal.

Pruchnik, Paweł, Dragoon.

Prudel, Stanisław, Lance Corporal.

Prus, Bolesław, Corporal.

Prystupa. Edward, Lance Corporal.

Przanowski, Jan, Captain.
(Awarded Four Times)

Prądka, Józef, Lance Bombardier.

Przedborski, Mirosław, Lieutenant (Doctor)

Przeor, Bolesław, Staff Sergeant.
(Awarded Twice)

Przepióra, Kazimierz, Lance Corporal.

Przewoży, Ignacy, Sergeant.

Przyborowski, Czesław, Private.

Przybycień, Eugeniusz, Lance Corporal.

Przybliński, Wincenty, Private.

Przybylski, Tadeusz, Cadet Officer

Przyblowski, Wacław, Private.

Przybysz, Józef, Sergeant. (Awarded Twice)

Przybysz, Marian, Corporal.

Przybyszewski, Wincenty, Private. (P)

Przydryga, Adolf, Corporal.

Przykuta, Ernest, Corporal.

Przywieczerski, Leonard, Lance Corporal.

Przywitowski, Franciszek, Sergeant Major.

Pszczoła, Tadeusz, Sergeant.

Pszczołkowski, Wacław, Sergeant.

Ptaszyński, Bronisław, Lance Corporal.
(Awarded Twice)

Pucek, Alfred, Second Lieutenant.
(Awarded Twice)

Pucek, Wojciech, Cadet Officer.

Puchalski, Stanisław, Lance Corporal.

Pupka, Wawrzyniec, Lance Corporal.

Purchla, Jerzy, Bombardier.

Purzycki, Stanisław, Cadet Officer.
(Awarded Twice)

Pustuł, Kazimierz, Bombardier.

Putaj, Franciszek, Lance Corporal.

Puza, Ryszard, Private.

Puzio, Jan, Corporal.

Pyka, Emil, Lance Corporal.

Pyrtek, Jan, Staff Sergeant.

Pytlak, Edmund, Second Lieutenant.

Racławski, Jan, Lance Corporal.

Raczkiewicz, Józef, Sergeant.

Raczkowski, Wiesław, Dragoon. (P)

Raczyński, Konrad, Second Lieutenant.

Raczyński, Tadeusz, Sergeant.

Radecki, Czesław, Lance Corporal.
(Awarded Twice)

Radkiewicz, Stefan, Lieutenant.

Radomski, Tadeusz, Corproal.

Radomski, Władysław, Corporal.

Raduła, Teodor, Second Lieutenant.

Radwański, Michał, Corporal.

Radzikowski, Stefan, Lieutenant.
(Awarded Twice)

Radziwiłł, Konrad, Lance Corporal.

Radki, Franciszek, Corporal.
(Awarded Twice)

Rady, Wiktor, Lance Corporal.
(Awarded Twice)

Ranbuć, Michał, Lance Corporal.

Raganowicz, Michał,
Regimental Sergeant Major.

Rago, Edward. B, Cadet Officer.
(Awarded Twice)

Rajski, Czesław, Private.

Rajski, Eugeniusz, Lance Corporal.

Rakowski, Władysław, Major.
(Awarded Four Times)

Rapecki, Tadeusz, Lance Corporal.

Rarog, Jan, Private.

Rataj, Jan, Corporal. (P)

Raube, Ryszard, Sergeant.
(Awarded Twice)

Raubic, Emil, Lance Corporal.

Rausch, Zdzisław, Corporal.

Rąbalski, Henryk, Second Lieutenant.

Reczek, Antoni, Sergeant.

Rejman, Józef, Major.

Reissman, Joel, Second Lieutenant.

Remski, Eugeniusz, Lance Corporal.

Repak, Bolesław, Sergeant.

Rewer, Wojciech, Captain.

Riezler, Marian, Corporal.

Roczmierowski, Franciszek,
Lance Corporal.

Rode, Feliks, Private. (P)

Rodziewicz, Antoni, Cadet Officer.

Rogalka, Jan, Lance Corporal.

Rogers, Karol, Corporal

Rogiński, Tadeusz, Corporal.

Rogowski, Emil, Lance Corporal.

Rogoziński, Antoni, Second Lieutenant.

Rogulski, Bolesław,
Regimental Sergeant Major.

Rogus, Jan, Sergeant.

Rohatyn, Ferdynand, Cadet Officer.

Rojca, Jerzy, Lance Corporal.

Rokicki, Władysław, Lance Corporal.

Rokoszyński, Zbigniew, Cadet Officer.

Roman, Adam, Lance Corporal.

Roman, Eugeniusz, Lance Corporal.
(Awarded Twice)

Romanek, Stanisław, Lieutenant.

Romer, Adam, Second Lieutenant.

Romer, Stefan, Second Lieutenant.

Romostowski, Julian, Captain.
(Awarded Twice)
Rosa, Stanisław, Sergeant.
Rosiński, Edmund, Lance Corporal.
Rosiński, Jerzy, Lieutenant.
Rosiński, Zbigniew, Second Lieutenant.
Rostek, Tadeusz, Cadet Officer.
Rostkowski, Józef, Trooper.
Roszkowski, Wiktor, Corporal.
Roszkiewicz, Wacław, Lieutenant.
Rouppert, Bolesław, Lieutenant. (P)
Rowiński, Tadeusz, Lieutenant.
Rozdżynski, Franciszek, Sergeant.
Rozwadowski, Jan, Captain.
(Awarded Twice)
Rozwadowski, Franciszek,
Second Lieutenant.
Rozwadowski, Franciszek, Sergeant Major.
Rożek, Edward, Lieutenant.
(Awarded Three Times)
Rożnowski, Stefan, Second Lieutenant.
Rożycki, Zbigniew, Lance Corproal.
Ruczkowski, Stefan, Second Lieutenant.
Ruda, Ryszard, Cadet Officer.
Rudawski, Aleksander, Sergeant.
Rudnicki, Janusz, Major.
Rudnicki, Zygmunt, Corporal.
Rudickowski, Bronisław, Corporal.
Rumak, Krzysztof, Corporal.
Rumian, Stanisław,
Lieutenant Colonel (Doctor)
Runge, Brunon, Gunner.
(Awarded Three Times)
Rupiński, Antoni, Bombardier.
Rupiak, Marcin, Lieutenant.
(Awarded Twice)
Rusek, Zygmunt, Lance Corporal.
(Awarded Twice)
Rusiecki, Ryszard, Captain.
Rutkiewicz, Józef, Lance Corporal.
Rutkowski, Feliks, Corporal.
Rutkowski, Mikołaj, Sergeant.
Rutkowski, Władysław, Private.
Rybak, Adam, Second Lieutenant.
Rybak, Józef, Sergeant.
Rybczyński, Ignacy, Corporal.
Rybiński, Jan, Sergeant.
Rybka, Franciszek, Corporal.
Rybka, Robert, Lance Corporal.
Rycharski, Marian, Sergeant.
Rychlik, Jan, Sergeant.
Rychlik, Józef, Corporal. (Awarded Twice)
Ryczkowski, Władysław, Captain.
Rydel, Stanisław, Sergeant.
Rydzewski, Józef, WO2.
Ryś, Eugeniusz, Lance Corporal.
Ryś, Jan, Corporal. (Awarded Twice)
Ryszkowski, Czesław, Corporal.
(Awarded Twice)
Ryznar, Julian, Lieutenant.
Rzadecki, Stefan, Corporal.
Rzeczycki, Napoleon, Corporal. (P)

Rzeznikowski, Stanisław, Lance Corporal.
Rzegociński, Mieczysław, Corporal.
Sabat, Władysław, Corporal. (P)
Sachse, Bronisław, Lieutenant.
(Awarded Twice)
Sadecki, Teodor, Sergeant.
Sadowski, Józef, Second Lieutenant.
Sadło, Stefan, Corporal.
Sadłowski, Mieczysław, Cadet Officer.
Sagan, Piotr, Corporal.
Sagan, Zdzisław, Cadet Officer.
Sajdak, Klemens, Dragoon.
Sala, Paweł, Private.
Sala, Tadeusz, Lieutenant.
Salamon, Alfred, Lance Corporal.
Salamon, Józef, Lance Corporal.
Salmacki, Aleksander, Corporal.
Salwa, Jan, Captain. (Awarded Twice)
Sało, Mikołaj, Sergeant.
Samborski, Jerzy, Lieutenant.
Samulski, Bohdan, Lieutenant.
Sandomierski, Roman, Lance Corporal.
Sapa, Józef, Lance Corporal.
Sarna, Andrzej, Corporal.
Saron, Edmund, Lance Corporal.
Sasanek, Stanisław, Bombardier.
Sasin, Czesław, Lance Corporal.
Sawicki, Wincenty, Lance Corporal.
Sawko, Władysław, Sergeant.
Schiele, Jan, Second Lieutenant.
Schile, Jan, Sergeant.
Schwalb, Elkune, Cadet Officer.
Schweiter, Karol, Cadet Officer.
(Awarded Twice)
Sciepuro, Witold, Lance Corporal.
Seid, Henryk, Second Lieutenant (Doctor).
(Awarded Twice)
Sek, Franciszek, Bombardier.
Sekul, Wacław, Sergeant Major.
Sekulski, Władysław, Corporal.
Sekuła, Antoni, Lieutenant.
Sendys, Zachariusz, Corporal.
Serafin, Jan, Captain.
Serafin, Ludwik, Corporal.
(Awarded Three Times)
Serafinowicz, Antoni, Sergeant.
Seroczyński, Wacław, Lance Corporal.
Seroka, Henryk, Lance Corporal.
(Awarded Twice)
Sezol, Wincenty, Lance Corporal.
Siamro, Mikołaj, Lance Corporal.
Siarczyński, Kazimierz, Sergeant.
Siedlański, Hubert, Dragoon.
Siedlecki, Eugeniusz, Corporal.
Siedlecki, Eugeniusz, Lieutenant.
(Awarded Twice)
Siekerka, Andrzej, Lance Corporal.
Sielski, Wiktor, Bombardier.
Siemienas, Franciszek, Sergeant.
Sieniewicz, Włodzimierz, Gunner.
(Awarded Twice)

Sieńko, Czesław, Sergeant.
(Awarded Four Times)
Sieńko, Jan, Cadet Officer.
Sieńko, Zygmunt, Second Lieutenant.
Siepiela, Kazimierz, Sergeant.
Sieradzki, Ryszard, Lance Corporal.
Sidor, Józef, Lance Corporal.
(Awarded Twice)
Sidorowski, Wiktor, Gunner.
Sidoruk, Teodor, Lance Corporal.
Sikora, Oskar, Corporal.
Sikorski, Stanisław, Corporal.
Sikorski, Stanisław, WO2.
Siłko, Józef, Sergeant Major.
Sino-Misiewicz, Władysław, Lieutenant.
(Awarded Twice [P])
Sioło, Zbigniew, Cadet Officer.
(Awarded Twice)
Siómak, Władysław, Corporal.
(Awarded Twice)
Siudut, Franciszek, Lieutenant.
Siuszczyński, Stanisław, Corporal.
Siwczyński, Edward, Lance Corporal.
Siwicki, Ryszard, Lance Corporal.
Skalicki, Eugeniusz, Lance Corporal.
Skalski, Bolesław, Corporal.
Skąpski, Jan, Corporal.
Skiba, Michał, Corporal.
Skibiński, Franciszek, Colonel.
(Awarded Twice)
Skibiński, Marian, Cadet Officer.
Skibiński, Zygmunt, Private.
(Awarded Twice)
Skierkowski, Apolinary, Bombardier.
Skobelski, Walenty, Lance Corporal.
Skoczek, Jan, Lance Corporal.
Skok, Stefan, Lance Corporal.
Skonieczny, Franciszek, Corporal.
Skorecki, Alfred, Second Lieutenant.
Skorecki, Piotr, Dragoon.
Skorzyński, Piotr, Sergeant Major.
Skotarek, Józef, Captain. (Doctor)
Skowronek, Jan, Corporal.
Skowronek, Witold, Lance Corporal.
Skrobol, Paweł, Corporal.
Skulicz, Bronisław, Major.
Skupiński, Zdzisław, Lance Corporal.
(Awarded Twice)
Skutecki, Józef, Corporal.
Skwarek, Władysław, Corporal.
Skwaron, Kazimierz, Private.
Skrzetuski, Leon, Lance Corporal.
Skrzydło, Jan, Corporal. (P)
Skrzpczyk, Adam, Corporal. (P)
Skrzypek, Władysław, Corporal. (P)
Slaga, Józef, Lance Corporal.
Slesarczuk, Sergiusz,
Regimental Sergeant Major.
Slesiński, Wacław, Lance Corporal.
Slesiński, Władysław, Lance Bombardier.
Slesorajtis, Mieczysław, Cadet Officer.
Slezak, Stanisław, Lance Corporal.

Slezak, Szymon, Lance Corporal.

Slizowski, Lesław, Second Lieutenant.

Słabczyński, Henryk, Second Lieutenant.

Sławnik, Piotr, Sergeant Major.

Słobodzian, Tadeusz, Lance Corporal.

Słomczewski, Stanisław, Gunner.

Słomka, Bronisław, Sapper.

Słoniecki, Alfons, Bombardier.

Słowik, Franciszek, Sergeant.

Słowik, Piotr, Corporal.

Słowik, Władysław, Corporal.

Słowikowski, Jerzy, Lieutenant.

Sługocki, Władysław, Dragoon.

Smalec, Zbigniew, Lieutenant.
(Awarded Twice)

Smalecki, Edward, Corporal.

Smarzyński, Sylwester, Sergeant.

Smender, Józef, Corporal. (Awarded Twice)

Smoczek, Jan, Lance Corporal.

Smoczkiewicz, Bolesław, Private.

Smok, Bolesław, Sergeant. (Sergeant)

Smolarek, Leon, Lance Corporal.

Smoleń, Stanisław, Private.

Smoleń, Władysław, Sergeant.

Smoliński, Jan, Private.

Smrokowski, Stanisław, Captain.

Smusz, Alojzy, Corporal.

Smutek, Andrzej, Lance Corporal.
(Awarded Twice)

Smyczek, Reinhold, Cadet Officer.

Smyja, Alfons, Lance Corporal.

Sobański, Jan, Private. (P)

Sobczak, Stefan, Private.

Sobczak, Zygmunt, Lance Corporal.

Sobielga, Władysław, Corporal.

Sobik, Jan, Corporal.

Sobik, Michał, Corporal.

Sobik, Teofil, Lance Corporal.

Sobolewski, Bolesław, Trooper.

Sobelewski, Stanisław, Sergeant.

Sobelewki, Piotr, Corporal.

Sobota, Józef, Bombardier.

Socha, Stanisław, Corporal.

Socha, Stefan, Sergeant.

Socha, Witold, Lance Corporal.

Sochacki, Jan, Captain.

Sochacki, Jan, Corporal.

Sokolnicki, Feliks, Corporal.

Sokoł, Mieczysław, Trooper.

Sokołow, Leon, Corporal.

Sokołower, Chonek, Second Lieutenant.

Sokołowski, Jan, Lance Corporal.

Sokołowski, Jan, Second Lieutenant.

Sokołowski, Michał, Lance Corporal.

Solarz, Roman, Dragoon.

Sołtowski, Kazimierz, Lance Corporal.

Sołtys, Henryk, Second Lieutenant.
(Awarded Three Times)

Sołtysiak, Jan, Second Lieutenant.

Sołtysiak, Jan, Trooper.

Sołtyski, Jan, Major.

Sordyl, Kazimierz, Second Lieutenant.
(Awarded Twice)

Soroczyński, Jan, Corporal.
(Awarded Twice)

Sorokowski, Edmund, Corporal.

Sosna, Klemens, Corporal.

Sosnkowski, Edmund, Corporal.

Sowa, Jan, Captain.

Sowiak, Stanisław, Lance Corporal.

Sowiński, Czesław, Private.

Sowiński, Zdzisław, Lance Corporal.

Sowula, Mieczysław, Lance Corporal. (P)

Spaliński, Mieczysław, Cadet Officer.

Spałek, Tadeusz, Sergeant.

Spiewak, Piotr, Lance Corporal.

Spyczak, Paweł, Corporal.

Srama, Karol, Corporal.

Srogi, Jan, Lance Corporal.
(Awarded Twice)

Sroka, Józef, Lance Corporal.

Srzednicki, Janusz,
Second Lieutenant. (Doctor)

Stachiewicz, Juliusz, Private.

Stachiewicz, Bohdan, Private.

Stachowiak, Franciszek, Corporal.

Stachowicz, Jan, Major. (Awarded Twice)

Stadnicki, Edward, Lance Corporal.

Stanco, Franciszek, Corporal.

Stanczewski, Zenon, Sergeant.

Stańczyc, Władysław, Corporal.

Stanek, Jan, Lance Corporal.

Staniaszek, Stanisław, Lance Corporal.

Staniczek, Konrad, Corporal.

Stankiewicz, Józef, Lance Corporal.

Stankiewicz, Juliusz, Cadet Officer.

Stankiewicz, Ludwik, Major.
(Awarded Twice)

Stankiewicz, Stanisław, Cadet Officer.

Stankiewicz, Wacław, Sergeant.

Stankowiak, Wiktor, Gunner.

Stański, Hieronim, Lance Corporal.

Stapor, Ludwik, Private.

Starczyk, Stanisław, Second Lieutenant.

Staroń, Jan, Corporal.

Starzyński, Zygmunt, Captain.
(Awarded Three Times)

Staszak, Jan, Sergeant.

Stawarz, Stanisław, Bombardier.

Stawiński, Mieczysław, Cadet Officer.

Stawiński, Franciszek, Corporal.
(Awarded Twice)

Stec, Józef, Sergeant Major.

Stefański, Henryk, Lance Corporal.

Stefanowicz, Aleksander, Major.
(Awarded Three Times)

Stefanowicz, Zenon, Dragoon.

Steinhart, Konstanty, Lance Corporal.
(Awarded Twice)

Stelmach, Andrzej, Private.

Stembalski, Lesław, Private.

Stemplewski, Kazimierz, Corporal.

Stępek, Mieczysław, Second Lieutenant.

Stępień, Konrad, Major.
(Awarded Twice [P])

Stępień, Tadeusz, Captain.
(Awarded Three Times)

Stępniewski, Tadeusz, Sergeant.

Stern, Lajzor, Cadet Officer.
(Awarded Twice)

Stifter, Karol, Sergeant.

Stocki, Marian, Lance Corporal.

Stojowski, Leon, Second Lieutenant.

Stolarz, Roman, Second Lieutenant.
(Awarded Twice)

Stopa, Alfons, Chaplain.

Strekowski, Paweł, Corporal.

Streszkowski, Bolesław, Private.

Strusiak, Władysław, Lance Corporal.

Struś, Witold, Bombardier.

Strycharski, Józef, Cadet Officer.

Stryczyński, Tadeusz, Lance Corporal.

Strtjecki, Zygfryd, Cadet Officer.

Strzelecki, Józef, Sergeant.

Strzyzewski, Stefan, Sergeant.

Styczyński, Władysław, Lieutenant.

Stypkowski, Jerzy, Sergeant.

Suchcitz, Jerzy, Sergeant.

Suchecki, Jan, Lance Corporal.

Suchodolski, Ludwik, Lance Corporal.

Suchoń, Stefan, Corporal.

Suchorski, Antoni, Lieutenant.

Sudowicz, Uszel, Corporal.

Sugiero, Jerzy, Second Lieutenant.

Sulej, Kazimierz, Lance Corporal.

Sulek, Tadeusz, Lance Corporal.

Sulewski, Aleksander, Major.

Sulkowski, Tadeusz, Sergeant.

Sumiński, Albert, Lieutenant.

Surawski, Stanisław, Second Lieutenant.
(Awarded Twice)

Surma, Jan, Corporal.

Surowiec, Antoni, Corporal.

Suska, Kazimierz, Sergeant Major.
(Awarded Twice)

Suwiński, Włodzimierz, Lieutenant.

Swetnik, Leon, Cadet Officer.

Swinarski, Włodzimierz, Sergeant.

Swiszczewski, Bohdan, Cadet Officer. (P)

Swoboda, Józef, Private.

Swoboda, Kazimierz, Sergeant Major.

Swołek, Józef, Corporal. (P)

Sycewicz, Jan, Bombardier.

Synowiec, Bronisław, Sergeant.

Sypniewicz, Kazimierz, Private.

Szabat, Jan, Sergeant.
(Awarded Three Times)

Szabla, Józef, Trooper.

Szablewski, Teofil, Lance Corporal.
(Awarded Twice)

Szadura, Stanisław, Lance Corporal.

Szafir, Jerzy, Cadet Officer.
(Awarded Twice)

Szajsinger, Chaim, Lance Corporal.

Szajda, Kazimierz, Sergeant.

Szajowski, Andrzej, Major.

Szałkowski, Władysław, Corporal.

Szaniawski, Jerzy, Lieutenant.

Szarek, Emil, Sergeant.

Szast, Michał, Cadet Officer.

Szatkowski, Jan, Sergeant.
(Awarded Twice)

Szatkowski, Władysław, Corporal.

Szawiński, Jan, Lance Corporal.
(Awarded Three Times)

Szawłowski, Zbigniew, Gunner.

Szczawiński, Stanisław, Second Lieutenant.

Szczechła, Aleksander, Regimental
Sergeant Major.

Szczekała, Piotr, Gunner.

Szczeniowski, Wacław, Lieutenant.
(Awarded Twice [P])

Szczepaniak, Stanisław, Lance Corporal.

Szczepanowski, Jerzy, Lance Corporal.
(Awarded Twice)

Szczepanowski, Stanisław, Lance Corporal.

Szczepański, Eugeniusz, Corporal.

Szczepański, Henryk, Private.

Szczepański, Karol, Sergeant.

Szczepański, Michał,
Lance Bombardier. (P)

Szczodrok, Franciszek, Private.

Szczodrowski, Józef, Private.

Szczuka, Karol, Bombardier.

Szczurek, Józef, Corporal.
(Awarded Three Times)

Szczurek, Władysław, Lance Corporal.

Szczygieł, Leon, Dragoon.

Szczygieł, Stanisław, Lieutenant.

Szczygłowski, Stanisław, Lance Corporal.
(Awarded Twice [P])

Szczyrba, Edmund, Lance Corporal.

Szegidowicz, Alej, Corporal.

Szejner, Michał, Sergeant.

Szelagowski, Ryszard, Sergeant.
(Awarded Twice)

Szeliga, Władysław, Corporal.

Szeliga, Wojciech, Captain.
(Awarded Four Times)

Szembida, Franciszek, Bombardier.

Szemro, Karol, Corporal. (Awarded Twice)

Szepetiuk, Jan, Gunner.

Szepioła, Aleksander, Corporal.

Szercman, Natan, Gunner.

Szewc, Andrzej, Trooper.

Szewczuk, Antoni, Corporal.

Szewczuk, Antoni, Lance Corporal.

Szewczyk, Kazimierz, Sergeant.

Szkaradek, Józef, Lance Corporal.

Szklar, Zygmunt, Trooper.

Szklarek, Bronisław, Second Lieutenant.

Szklinik, Tadeusz, Second Lieutenant.

Szkólka, Franciszek, Corporal.

Szkuta, Kazimierz, Lieutenant.
(Awarded Twice)

Szlachta, Józef, Corporal.

Szlachta, Józef, Corporal.

Szlachta, Stanisław, Sergeant.

Szlotawa, Paweł, Lance Corporal.

Szłamas, Leonard, Second Lieutenant.

Szmeller, Roland, Corporal.

Szmidt, Stanisław, Private.

Szmyd, Stanisław, Private.

Sznaj, Stanisław, Dragoon.

Sznejder, Wilhelm, Lance Corporal.

Szojkowicz, Tadeusz, Second Lieutenant.

Szołomiak, Aleksander, Corporal.

Szołtysek, Karol, Lance Corporal.

Szomko, Stanisław, Corporal.

Szopa, Jan, Private. (P)

Szostak, Wojciech, Lance Corporal.

Szot, Stanisław, Corporal.

Szott, Józef, Trooper. (Awarded Twice)

Szrama, Feliks, Corporal.

Szpałek, Jan, Sapper.

Szpejnowski, Aleksander, Regimental
Sergeant Major. (Awarded Twice)

Szperber, Adam, Second Lieutenant.

Szpunar, Józef, Sergeant. (Awarded Twice)

Szpytma, Jan, Corporal.

Sztumpf, Zbigniew, Lieutenant.
(Awarded Three Times)

Szubarga, Andrzej, Lieutenant.
(Awarded Twice)

Szubert, Emil, Lance Corporal.

Szukała, Marian, Private.

Szulc, Julian, Lance Corporal.

Szulc, Wacław, Lance Corporal.
(Awarded Three Times)

Szuler, Michał, Sergeant.

Szulżycki, Leon, Corporal.

Szumański, Zbigniew, Captain.

Szumiłowski, Józef, Corporal.

Szumlański, Tadeusz, Gunner.

Szwarcman, Józef,
Second Lieutenant. (Doctor)

Szwed, Marian, Lance Corporal.

Szwedowski, Józef, Private.

Szwedzicki, Witold, Lieutenant.

Szybalski, Karol, Cadet Officer.

Szychliński, Alojzy, Bombardier. (P)

Szychowski, Zdzisław, Corporal.

Szydłowski, Ludomir, Captain.

Szydłowski, Zdzisław, Lieutenant Colonel.
(Awarded Four Times)

Szygowski, Ludwik, Second Lieutenant.

Szyldkrecht, Edward, Sergeant.

Szymański, Jan, Lieutenant.
(Awarded Three Times)

Szymański, Jan, Lance Corporal.
(Awarded Twice)

Szymański, Franciszek, Dragoon.

Szymański, Karol, Corporal.

Szymański, Paweł, Corporal.

Szymański, Tadeusz, Lance Corporal.

Szymański, Teofil, Bombardier.

Szymberski, Bolesław, Second Lieutenant.

Szymczyński, Józef, Sergeant.

Szymecki, Adolf, Corporal.

Szymik, Jan, Corporal. (Awarded Twice)

Szymkowski, Leon, Second Lieutenant.
(Awarded Three Times)

Szymura, Zygmunt, Private.

Szyndler, Roman, Gunner.

Szyniec, Edmund, Corporal.

Szyszko, Tadeusz, Sergeant. (P)

Ślązak, Stanisław, Staff Sergeant.

Śledź, Józef, Lance Corporal.

Ślimak, Zbigniew, Lance Corporal.

Śliwa, Teodor, Trooper.

Śliwarski, Rudolf, Lance Corporal.

Śliwiński, Bronisław, Corporal. (P)

Śliwiński, Bolesław, Cadet Officer.

Śliwiński, Jan, Lance Corporal.
(Awarded Twice)

Śliwiński, Józef, Sergeant.

Śliwiński, Zenon, Lance Corporal.

Śliwowski, Tomasz, Private.

Śmiechowski, Rudolf, Lance Corporal.

Śmigiel, Wacław, Private.

Śmigielski, Józef, Dragoon.

Śniadecki, Edward, Corporal.

Świątkowski, Władysław,
Second Lieutenant.

Święcicki, Kazimierz, Sapper.

Święcicki, Zbigniew, Second Lieutenant.

Świerczyński, Jan, Corporal.

Świergot, Adolf, Lance Corporal.
(Awarded Twice)

Świerszcz, Czesław, Lieutenant.
(Awarded Twice)

Świerszcz, Paweł, Sapper.

Świerszcz, Stefan, Private.

Świdziński, Paweł, Lance Corporal.

Świtalski, Władysław, Corporal.

Taszewski, Adolf, Corporal.

Tabęcki, Antoni, Second Lieutenant.
(Awarded Three Times)

Tabus, Julian, Sergeant.

Tanasiewicz, Stanisław, Second Lieutenant.

Taranek, Wacław, Private. (P)

Taras, Stanisław, Lieutenant.
(Awarded Three Times)

Targosz, Józef, Corporal.

Tarnowski, Stanisław,
Second Lieutenant. (Awarded Twice)

Tarwid, Antoni, Corporal.

Tas, Tadeusz, Corporal.

Teder, Piotr, Trooper.

Telesz, Ludwik, Second Lieutenant.

Telka, Antoni, Sergeant.

Terczyński, Stefan, Sergeant Major.

Terelak, Jan, Lance Corporal.

Terlicki, Józef, Sergeant.

Terlikowski, Zygmunt,
Lance Corporal. (Awarded Twice)

Terpiłowski, Dominik, Sergeant.

Tkacz, Stanisław, Lieutenant.

Tkaczuk, Jan, Sapper.

Tkaczyk, Jan, Sergeant.
Tłusty, Paweł, Lance Corporal.
Tobiasz, Tadeusz, Lieutenant.
Toczek, Kazimierz, Gunner.
Toczyski, Roman, Corporal.
Todorski, Mieczysław, Corporal.
Tokarski, Stanisław, Corporal.
Tolkowiec, Adam, Gunner.
Tolwiński, Jan, Captain (Doctor)
Tomala, Justyn, Corporal.
Tomaszek, Stefan, Sergeant.
Tomaszewski, Aleksander, Cadet Officer.
Tomaszewski, Bolesław, Bombardier.
Tomaszewski, Marian, Cadet Officer.
Tomaszewski, Stanisław, Sergeant.
(Awarded Twice)
Tomczak, Kazimierz, Lance Corporal.
Tomczyński, Tadeusz, Corporal.
Tomczyk, Józef, Lance Corporal.
Tomczyk, Stanisław, Corporal.
(Awarded Twice)
Tomczyk, Stefan, Lance Corporal.
Tomkowski, Edward, Sergeant.
Toper, Jerzy, Cadet Officer. (P)
Toperek, Jan, Corporal.
Toporowski, Jan, Corporal.
Torczelewski, Ignacy, Lance Corporal.
Torżewski, Władysław, Second Lieutenant.
Torżyk, Piotr, Lance Corporal.
Trębacz, Stanisław, Second Lieutenant.
(Awarded Twice)
Tredlewski, Zenon, Lieutenant.
Trembecki, Marian, Corporal.
(Awarded Twice)
Trenzinger, Henryk, Sergeant.
Trochimczuk, Lucjan, Corporal.
Trofimowicz, Jarosław, Private.
Trojak, Alojzy, Lance Corporal. (P)
Trojca, Stanisław, Lance Corporal.
Trusz, Władysław, Lance Corporal.
Truszkiewicz, Mieczysław, Lieutenant.
Trybus, Bronisław, Second Lieutenant.
Trynka, Tadeusz, Lieutenant.
Trzebiński, Stanisław,
 Second Lieutenant. (Awarded Twice)
Trzelecki, Stanisław, Corporal.
Trzesiecki, Stanisław, Corporal.
Trzęsiok, Henryk, Sergeant.
(Awarded Twice)
Tucewicz, Zygmunt, Captain.
(Awarded Twice)
Tucholski, Mieczysław, Gunner.
Turek, Michał, Sergeant. (P)
Turko, Jan, Corporal.
Turowski, Henryk, Lance Corporal.
Turowski, Franciszek, Gunner.
Turowski, Marian, Sergeant.
Turzański, Marian, Sergeant.
Turzański, Tadeusz, Lance Corporal.
Tutkaj, Jan, Corporal.
Twarożek, Arkadiusz, Second Lieutenant.

Tworkowski, Tadeusz, Cadet Officer.
Tylek, Bartłomiej, Private.
Tymosiak, Bronisław, Bombardier.
Typer, Roman, Lieutenant.
(Awarded Twice)
Tyrcz, Zbigniew, Second Lieutenant. (P)
Tyrol, Konrad.
Ubermanowicz, Rafał, Second Lieutenant.
Ujma, Stefan, Sergeant.
Uljasz, Jan, Lance Corporal.
Urban, Tadeusz, Dragoon.
Urbaniak, Józef, Lieutenant.
Urbaniak, Stefan, Corporal.
Urbaniak, Franciszek, Corporal.
Urbanowicz, Andrzej, Lance Corporal.
Urbanowicz, Antoni, Private. (P)
Urbanowicz, Karol, Corporal.
Uściński, Edward, Captain.
(Awarded Twice)
Wabner, Ryszard, Second Lieutenant.
Wacnik, Jan, Cadet Officer.
(Awarded Twice)
Wachała, Władysław, Lance Corporal.
Wachlarz, Eugeniusz, Sapper.
Wachoń, Henryk, Sergeant.
Wacławski, Tadeusz, Corporal.
Wadlewski, Wiktor, Corporal.
Wageżewski, Paweł, Corporal.
Wagner, Wacław, Lance Corporal.
Wainryb, Józef, Lance Corporal.
Walas, Ignacy, Sergeant.
(Awarded Twice [P])
Walczak, Franciszek, Sergeant.
Walczyński, Jan, Cadet Officer.
Walek, Zbigniew, Lieutenant.
Walenciak, Stanisław, Corporal.
Walewicz, Tadeusz,
Second Lieutenant. (Awarded Twice)
Walewski, Grzegorz, Trooper.
Waliński, Władysław, Private.
Waliłko, Antoni, Sergeant Major.
Walkiewicz, Antoni, Sergeant.
(Awarded Twice)
Walkowiak, Maksymilian, Private.
Walkowski, Jan, Lieutenant.
Walkowski, Jan, Captain (Doctor).
(Awarded Twice)
Walkowski, Karol, Corporal.
Walla, Antoni, Dragoon.
Walter, Paweł, Sergeant Major.
Wałaszewski, Brunon,
Second Lieutenant. (Awarded Twice)
Wandel, Józef, Lance Corporal.
Wanderski, Tadeusz, Lance Corporal.
Wanic, Wiesław, Cadet Officer.
(Awarded Twice)
Warchoł, Edward, Private.
Wareczko, Rudolf, Private.
Warm, Abram, Private.
Warmiński, Stanisław, Second Lieutenant.
Wartak, Stanisław, Captain.
Warzewski, Bolesław, Sergeant.

Wąsik, Wiktor, Lance Corporal.
Wasko, Władysław, Lance Corporal.
Waśkowicz, Wilhelm, Lance Corporal.
Waśniowski, Józef, Lance Corporal.
Wasicki, Franciszek, Sapper.
Wasiewicz, Jan, Second Lieutenant.
Wasiewski, Mieczysław, Corporal.
Wasilewski, Antoni, Corporal.
Wasilewski, Jerzy, Major. (Awarded Twice)
Wasilewski, Jerzy, Lance Corporal.
Wasilewski, Roman, Second Lieutenant.
Wasilewski, Zbigniew, Lance Corporal.
(Awarded Three Times)
Wasilkiewicz, Józef, Sergeant.
Wąsowicz, Michał, Major.
Wąsowicz, Władysław, Sergeant.
Waszak, Józef, Corporal.
Wawreczko, Rudolf, Lance Corporal.
Wawro, Franciszek, Second Lieutenant.
Wawrowski, Walenty, Corporal.
Wawrzyniak, Stanisław,
Sergeant Major. (Awarded Twice)
Wdowiak, Józef, Lance Corporal.
Weber, Aleksander, Private.
Węcławs, Sylwester, Lance Corporal.
Węgiel, Piotr, Sergeant.
Węgliński, Janusz, Dragoon.
Węgrzyn, Jan, Staff Sergeant.
Węgrzyn, Jan, Lance Corporal.
Wejssager, Wilhelm, Second Lieutenant.
Wejna, Józef, Sergeant.
Wendorff, Bohdan, Lieutenant.
Wentk, Jan, Sergeant.
Werachowski, Bazyli, Corporal.
(Awarded Twice)
Wereszczyński, Mirosław, Sergeant.
Wergau, Karol, Private.
Werys, Władysław, Sergeant.
Wesołowski, Józef, Private.
Wesołowski, Kazimierz, Lance Corporal.
Wesoły, Andrzej, Sergeant.
(Awarded Twice)
Whitehead, Franciszek, Second Lieutenant.
Wiatrowski, Tadeusz, Second Lieutenant.
Wicher, Henryk, Corporal.
Wichlaj, Józef, Corporal. (P)
Wichowski, Czesław, Corporal.
(Awarded Twice)
Wiciński, Tadeusz, Lance Corporal.
Widło, Roman, Corporal. (Awarded Twice)
Wiechno, Jan, Corporal.
Więcław, Florian, Sergeant.
(Awarded Twice)
Wieczorek, Adolf, Lance Corporal.
Wieczorek, Franciszek, Private.
Wieczorek, Henryk, Private.
Wierczorkiewicz, Bronisław, Sergeant.
Wieglus, Józef, Lance Corporal.
(Awarded Four Times)
Wielogórski, Tadeusz, Lieutenant.
Wientort, Mieczysław, Lance Corporal.

Wieremejczuk, Kazimierz, Dragoon.

Wieroński, Marian, Colonel.

Wierzbicki, Antoni, Lance Corporal.

Wierzchowski, Jan, Corporal.

Wiercigroch, Józef, Private.
(Awarded Three Times)

Wierdak, Leopold, Second Lieutenant.

Wiese, Leonard, Corporal.

Wiezik, Jan, Lance Corporal.

Wijas, Albin, Corporal. (Awarded Twice)

Wiktorowicz, Stanisław, Corporal.

Wilczyński, Antoni, Private.

Wilczyński, Jerzy, Lieutenant.

Wilewicz, Karol, Lance Corporal.

Wilgan, Szymon, Lance Corporal.

Wilhelm, Franciszek, Private.

Wilk, Bolesław, Private.

Wilk, Jan, Sergeant.

Winawer, Edward, Lance Corporal.

Wincza, Leon, Cadet Officer.

Winczakiewicz, Jan, Cadet Officer.

Winiarski, Mieczysław, Corporal.

Winnicki, Leon, Sergeant.

Wińsko, Antoni, Trooper.

Wiosna, Edward, Bombardier.

Wiśniewski, Daniel, Lance Corporal.

Wiśniewski, Jan, Bombardier.

Wiśniewski, Julian, Second Lieutenant.

Wiśniowski, Stanisław, Sergeant Major.

Wiśniowski, Zbigniew, Second Lieutenant.

Wisz, Kazimierz, Cadet Officer.

Wiszniewski, Edward, Lieutenant.

Wiszniewski, Wojciech, Corporal.

Wiszniewski, Rudolf, Corporal.

Wiszniowski, Jan, Lieutenant Colonel.
(Awarded Three Times)

Witek, Czesław, Lance Corporal.

Witkowski, Leopold, Lance Corporal.

Wito, Tadeusz, Corporal.

Wlizło, Józef, Corporal.

Wład, Franciszek, Second Lieutenant.

Włodarczyk, Józef, Private.

Włodarski, Franciszek, Corporal.

Włodarski, Wojciech, Corporal.

Wnuczek, Szczepan, Corporal.
(Awarded Twice)

Wodakowski, Józef, Lance Corporal.

Wojciechowski, Edmund, Trooper.

Wojciechowski, Jan, Second Lieutenant.

Wojciechowski, Józef, Corporal.

Wojciechowski, Marian,
Second Lieutenant.

Wojciechowski, Olgierd, Lieutenant.

Wojciechowski, Zbigniew, Gunner.

Wojciechowski, Zygmunt, Lieutenant.

Wojcieszek, Stefan, Lance Corporal.

Wojcieszewski, Aleksander, Private.

Wójcik, Jan, Corporal. (Awarded Twice)

Wójcik, Franciszek, Second Lieutenant.

Wójcik, Stanisław, Sergeant.

Wójcik, Stanisław, Lance Corporal.

(Awarded Twice)

Wójcik, Stanisław, Private.

Wójcik, Władysław, Corporal.

Wojdylak, Jan, Lance Corporal.

Wojec, Leon, Sergeant. (Awarded Twice)

Wojnar, Zdzisław, Bombardier.

Wojnarski, Witold, Corporal.

Wojno, Piotr, Dragoon. (Awarded Twice)

Wojtanek, Jan, Corporal.

Wojtaszek, Jan, Cadet Officer.

Wojtaszek, Kazimierz, Lance Corporal.

Wojtkiewicz, Władysław, Regimental
Sergeant Major.

Wojtkowski, Konrad, Private.

Wojtowicz, Mieczysław, Corporal.
(Awarded Twice)

Wojtowicz, Stanisław, Sergeant.

Wolański, Marian, Second Lieutenant.

Wolański, Kazimierz, Lance Corporal.

Wolicki, Maciej, Cadet Officer.

Wolnik, Michał, Captain.

Wolny, Antoni, Private.

Wolny, Rudolf, Second Lieutenant.

Wolny, Sylwester, Corporal.

Wolski, Bolesław, Corporal.

Wolszakiewicz, Franciszek, Lieutenant.

Wołodko, Franciszek, Corporal.
(Awarded Twice)

Wołowiec, Jan, Sergeant.

Wołyncewicz, Wacław, Captain (Doctor).

Worobiec, Mieczysław,
Lieutenant. (Awarded Twice)

Worobiej, Witold, Lance Corporal.

Worsa, Piotr, Private.

Woszczyna, Antoni, Private.

Woźniak, Jan, Bombardier.

Woźniak, Sebastian, Cadet Officer.
(Awarded Twice)

Woźniak, Stanisław, Second Lieutenant.

Woźniak, Stanisław, Lance Corporal.

Woźniak, Tadeusz, Second Lieutenant.

Woźnica, Herbert, Corporal.

Wróbel, Andrzej, Sergeant.

Wróbel, Franciszek, Lance Corporal.

Wróbel, Lucjan, Lance Corporal.

Wróbel, Ryszard, Second Lieutenant.

Wróblewski, Alfons, Private.
(Awarded Twice)

Wróblewski, Czesław, Corporal.

Wróblewski, Jerzy, Lieutenant.

Wróblewski, Józef, Corporal.

Wroblewski, Ryszard, Sergeant.

Wrona, Julian, Second Lieutenant.
(Awarded Twice)

Wronecki, Konrad, Corporal.

Wroński, Jerzy, Second Lieutenant.

Wrzoł, Franciszek, Private. (P)

Wrzos, Leon, Corporal.

Wyka, Zygmunt, Second Lieutenant.

Wyrwalski, Karol, Captain.

Wysocki, Stanisław, Lance Corporal.

Wywrocki, Jan, Lance Corporal.

Zabłocki, Wacław, Lieutenant.
(Awarded Twice)

Zabojski, Witold, Lieutenant.

Zacharewicz, Mieczysław, Second
Lieutenant.

Zachariasiewicz, Tadeusz, Sapper.

Zachariasz, Julian, Corporal.

Zachowski, Kazimierz, Sergeant.

Zadorożny, Michał, Trooper. (P)

Zadworny, Stanisław, Lance Corporal.

Zagadzki, Alfons, Lance Corporal.

Zagórski, Jacek, Second Lieutenant.

Zagórski, Jerzy, Lieutenant.

Zagorzecki, Leopold, Corporal.

Zając, Antoni, Sergeant.

Zając, Bolesław, Bombardier.

Zając, Franciszek, Corporal.

Zajączek, Brunon, Private.

Zajer, Edward, Lance Corporal.

Zakrocki, Tadeusz, Second Lieutenant.
(Awarded Twice)

Zakrzewski, Brunon, Private.
(Awarded Twice)

Zaleski, Andrzej, Second Lieutenant.

Zalewski, Leszek, Cadet Officer.

Zalewski, Piotr, Sergeant.

Zalewski, Stefan, Lieutenant.

Załuczkowski, Franciszek, Corporal.

Zamecznik, Władysław,
Second Lieutenant.

Zamoyski, Krzysztof, Second Lieutenant.

Zandek, Franciszek, Corporal.

Zantuan, Eugeniusz, Lance Corporal.

Zaporowicz, Władysław, Lance Corporal.

Zaremba, Stanisław, Lieutenant. (P)

Zaremba, Teofil, Lance Corporal.

Zaremba, Zygmunt, Sergeant.

Zarychta, Wincenty, Sergeant.

Zatorski, Ryszard, Second Lieutenant.

Zawadziński, Jan, Private.

Zawadzki, Adam, Second Lieutenant.

Zawadzki, Józef,
Regimental Sergeant Major.

Zawadzki, Michał, Dragoon.

Zawisza, Andrzej, Major.

Zawisza, Józef, Private.

Zawoda, Jan, Private.

Zawodniak, Edward, Corporal.

Zbichowki, Józef, Lance Corporal.

Zbieranowski, Jan, Private.

Zborowski, Bolesław, Private.

Zborowski, Stanisław, Private.

Zborowski, Stefan, Second Lieutenant.

Zbroski, Jan, Major. (Awarded Twice)

Zdanowicz, Albin, Corporal.
(Awarded Twice)

Zdanowicz, Kazimierz, Corporal.

Zdanowicz, Mieczysław, Corporal.

Zdrojewski, Stanisław, Sergeant. (P)

Zdun, Józef, Sergeant. (Awarded Twice)

141

Zdybel, Józef, Sergeant. (Awarded Twice)
Zdziechowski, Stanisław, Second Lieutenant.
Zegartowski, Marian, Second Lieutenant.
Zeltzer, Włodzimierz, Captain.
Zemlik, Jakób, Corporal.
Zgorzelski, Władysław, Major. (Awarded Four Times)
Zięba, Józef, Corporal.
Zieliński, Antoni, Lance Corporal. (Awarded Twice)
Zieliński, Bohdan, Sergeant. (P)
Zieliński, Czesław, Sergeant. (Awarded Twice)
Zieliński, Ryszard, Sergeant. (Awarded Twice)
Zieliński, Stefan, Lieutenant.
Zieliński, Stefan, Second Lieutenant.
Zieliński, Teodor. Sergeant.
Zienkiewicz, Józef, Corporal.
Zimand, Wilhelm, Private.
Ziemnicki, Konstanty, Corporal. (Awarded Twice)
Zimny, Józef, Corporal.
Ziobrowski, Antoni, Private.
Zioło, Władysław, Corporal. (Awarded Twice)

Zip, Sylwester, Lance Corporal.
Zipser, Gustaw, Second Lieutenant.
Złotnik, Edward, Captain.
Złotorowicz, Tadeusz, Lance Corporal.
Zmierzchoł, Konrad, Corporal.
Zmyślany, Andrzej, Lance Corporal.
Zodziewski, Antoni, Corporal.
Zorza, Bernard, Lance Corporal.
Zozański, Bernard, Corporal.
Zazuliński, Eugeniusz, Lance Corporal.
Zwierzyński, Józef, Lance Corporal.
Zwirko, Bronisław, Lance Corporal.
Zubert, Karol, Captain.
Zubowicz, Jan, Lieutenant.
Zubrzycki, Tadeusz, Lance Corporal.
Zurański, Adam, Lance Corporal.
Zuwala, Bolesław, Corporal.
Zych, Jan, Private. (P)
Zych, Witold, Corporal.
Zychiewicz, Franciszek, Corporal.
Zygiert, Henryk, Trooper.
Zysman, Szloma, Lance Corporal.
Żarkow, Benjamin, Corporal.
Żarski, Jan, Second Lieutenant.
Żarski, Jerzy, Lieutenant.

Żebrowski, Marian, Major.
Żelechowski, Stanisław, Second Lieutenant.
Żelewski, Emil, Lance Corporal.
Żelezny, Franciszek, Trooper.
Żmijewski, Zygmunt, Lance Corporal.
Żmudzki, Dyonizy, Lance Corporal.
Żochowski, Bolesław, Sergeant.
Żudziewski, Antoni, Corporal.
Żołkiewicz, Wiktor, Second Lieutenant.
Żorski, Wiktor, Lance Corporal.
Żuchowski, Stanisław, Regimental Sergeant Major. (Awarded Twice)
Żukowski, Adolf, Lieutenant.
Żukowski, Paweł, Lance Corporal.
Żur, Stefan, Lance Corporal.
Żurawski, Czesław, Private. (Awarded Twice)
Żyliński, Jerzy, Dragoon.
Żyłka, Alojzy, Lance Corporal.
Żyrmont, Edward, Sergeant. (P)
Żytyński, Antoni, Private.
Żywczyk, Bronisław, Bombardier.
Żywicki, Jan, Private.

Krzyż Zasługi z Mieczami (Service Cross with Swords)

Awarded:
Gold Cross   64 Soldiers.
Silver Cross   296 Soldiers.
Bronze Cross   2031 Soldiers.

Medal Wojska – Army Medal (Service Medal)

Awarded to 12,336 soldiers.
Foreign Decorations Awarded to Members of the First Polish Armoured Division
(FOR SERVICE IN NORTH-WEST EUROPE 1944–45).

Belgium

Grand Officier de l'Ordre de la Couronne avec Palme

Maczek, Stanisław, Lieutenant General.

Commandeur de l'Ordre de la Couronne avec Palme

Dworek, Kazimierz, Major General.   Rudnicki, Klemens, Major General.

Commandeur de l'Ordre de Leopold II avec Palme

Majewski, Tadeusz, Colonel.

Officier de l'Ordre de Leopold avec Palme

Dec, Władysław, Colonel.   Noel, Bronisław, Colonel.   Szydłowski, Zdzisław, Colonel.

Officier de l'Ordre la Couronne avec Palme

Stankiewicz, Ludwik, Lieutenant Colonel.

Stefanowicz, Aleksander, Lieutenant Colonel.

Zgorzelski, Władysław, Lieutenant Colonel.

Officier de l'Ordre de Leopold II avec Palme

Marowski, Jan, Major.

Wasilewski, Jerzy, Major.

Chevalier de l'Ordre de Leopold avec Palme

Bergander, Stefan, Captain.
Bojanowski, Zbigniew, Captain.
Borowski, Bohdan, Captain.
Drożak, Stefan, Captain.
Grabowski, Stanisław, Captain.

Horbaczewski, Jerzy, Captain.
Iwaszkiewicz, Jan, Captain. (Doctor)
Jazdowski, Oskar, Captain.
Kłodziński, Zygmunt, Captain.
Popiel, Janusz, Captain.

Rozwadowski, Jan, Captain.
Starzyński, Zygmunt, Captain.
Zuber, Karol, Captain.

Chevalier de l'Ordre de la Couronne avec Palme

Biernacki, Władysław, Lieutenant.
Kozłowski, Marek, Lieutenant.
Marcinkiewicz, Adam, Lieutenant.

Sadowski, Józef, Lieutenant.
Walewicz, Tadeusz, Second Lieutenant.
Wasiewicz, Jan, Second Lieutenant.

Wrona, Julian, Second Lieutenant.

Chevalier de l'Ordre de Leopold II avec Palme

Andrejczuk, Józef, Staff Sergeant.
Błasiak, Władysław, Sergeant.
Brzyski, Stanisław, Sergeant.
Buller, Tadeusz, Corporal.
Czajkowski, Kazimierz, Sergeant.
Czarczyński, Gerard, Sergeant.
Furmankowski, Tadeusz, Sergeant.
Gerstenburger, Jan, Sergeant.
Giebus, Mikołaj, Corporal.
Gołowski, Zygmunt, Corporal.
Hlebowicz, Kazimierz, Sergeant.
Jarmużek, Florian, Sergeant.

Jorer, Wincenty, Staff Sergeant.
Kochanowski, Mikołaj, Sergeant.
Kociołek, Edmund, Sergeant.
Krupiński, Bronisław, Corporal.
Lasocki, Zygmunt, Corporal.
Łaba, Franciszek, Staff Sergeant.
Marcinkiewicz, Karol, Corporal.
Maskiewicz, Józef, Sergeant.
Maślanka, Stanisław, Sergeant.
Naprawa, Feliks, sergeant.
Nocoń, Wacław, Sergeant.
Pełda, Władysław, Sergeant.

Piszczyński, Antoni, Corporal.
Rudnikowski, Bronisław, Corporal.
Rybak, Józef, Sergeant.
Sanecki, Rudolf, Sergeant.
Sawczak, Stefan, Sergeant.
Stypułkowski, Józef, Sergeant.
Tomczyński, Tadeusz, Sergeant.
Wawrzyniak, Stanisław, Sergeant.
Wesoły, Andrzej, Sergeant.
Wittholz, Tadeusz, Sergeant.
Wojtasz, Czesław, Sergeant.
Żochowski, Bolesław, Sergeant.

Croix de Guerre 1940 avec Palme

9th Flanders Rifle Battalion (9BS).

Adamczyk, Jan, Corporal.
Andrejczuk, Józef, Staff Sergeant.
Antosiewicz, Stanisław, Lance Corporal.
Baraczewski, Eugeniusz, Second Lieutenant.
Basser, Henryk, Lieutenant.
Bejster, Augustyn, Second Lieutenant.
Bergander, Stefan, Captain.
Bielecki, Julian, Lance Corproal.
Biernacki, Władysław, Lieutenant.
Bilicki, Tadeusz, Corporal.
Błasiak, Władysław, Sergeant.
Bogdanowicz, Henryk, Lieutenant.

Bojanowski, Zbigniew, Captain.
Bojarski, Zbigniew, Captain.
Borkowski, Arkadiusz, Sergeant.
Borowski, Bohdan, Captain.
Brzozowski, Bohdan, Lieutenant.
Brzyski, Stanisław, Sergeant.
Budziszewski, Tadeusz, Sergeant.
Buller, Tadeusz, Corporal.
Buryło, Piotr, Captain.
Charżewski, Czesław, Major.
Czajkowski, Henryk, Corporal.
Czajkowski, Kazimierz, Sergeant.

Czarczyński, Gerard, Sergeant.
Czarnecki, Kamil, Major.
Czarnecki, Marian, Major.
Cyganowski, Józef, Lieutenant.
Dalecki, Jan, Corporal.
Dec, Władysław, Colonel.
Drożak, Stefan, Captain.
Drozdowicz, Leopold, Captain.
Duda, Ludwik, Corporal.
Dworak, Kazimierz, Major General.
Fawryszewski, Marian, Corporal.
Fribe, Wenancjusz, Lieutenant.

Furmankowski, Tadeusz, Sergeant.
Gawryś, Edmund, Sergeant.
Gazdecki, Romuald, Staff Sergeant.
Gburek, Edmund, Staff Sergeant.
Gerstenburger, Jan, Sergeant.
Giebus, Mikołaj, Corporal.
Giera, Zbigniew, Captain.
Gil, Leon, Corporal.
Golej, Aleksander, Sergeant.
Gołowski, Zygmunt, Corporal.
Gorzeński, Marian, Major (Doctor).
Grabowski, Stanisław, Captain.
Grinberg, Henryk, Lieutenant.
Grudziński, Antoni, Colonel.
Grygosiński, Jerzy, Second Lieutenant.
Gunsberg, Abraham, Second Lieutenant.
Guzik, Jan, Sergeant.
Hlebowicz, Kazimierz, sergeant.
Horbaczewski, Jerzy, Captain.
Iwaszkiewicz, Jan, Captain.
Jarmużek, Florian, Sergeant.
Jaworski, Marian, Corporal.
Jazdowski, Oskar, Captain.
Jesionkowicz, Alojzy, Corporal.
Jorer, Wincenty, Staff Sergeant.
Kapecke, Zdzisław, Corporal.
Kaszubowski, Jan, Major.
Kiszewski, Edmund, Corporal.
Kłodzinski, Zygmunt, Captain.
Kociołek, Edward, Sergeant.
Kochanowski, Mikołaj, Sergeant.
Kolny, Alojzy, Corporal.
Kominek, Antoni, Captain (Doctor).
Komornicki, Stefan, Lieutenant.
Konieczny, Franciszek, Corporal.
Kordyl, Jan, Second Lieutenant.
Kozłowski, Józef, Corporal.
Kozłowski, Marek, Lieutenant.
Kraczkiewicz, Tadeusz, Captain.
Krappel, Maksymilian, Captain.
Krupiński, Bronisław, Corporal.
Kujawa, Edmund, Lance Corporal.
Kunachowicz, Jerzy, Captain.
Kurzydym, Franciszek, Corporal.
Lasocki, Zygmunt, Corporal.
Lasoń, Jan, Sergeant.
Lasto, Stefan, Corporal.
Lesser, Teodor, Major.
Lipiński, Benedykt, Corporal.
Łaba, Franciszek, Staff Sergeant.
Łabno, Edward, Captain.
Łapicki, Ireneusz, Second Lieutenant.
Łapiński, Józef, Corporal.
Łopaciński, Second Lieutenant.
Maczek, Stanisław, Lieutenant General.
Majewski, Tadeusz, Colonel.
Makowski, Wincenty, Corporal.

Makuch, Kazimierz, Captain.
Marcinkiewicz, Adam, Lieutenant.
Marcinkiewicz, Karol, Corporal.
Marowski, Jan, Major.
Maskiewicz, Józef, Sergeant.
Maslanies, Wojciech, Corporal.
Maślanka, Stanisław, Sergeant.
Matulanis, Jerzy, Lieutenant.
Michalczyk, Czesław, Major.
Naprawa, Feliks, Sergeant.
Nocoń, Wacław, Sergeant.
Noel, Bronisław, Colonel.
Nosalik, Kazimierz, Captain.
Nowak, Józef, Corporal.
Nowak, Stefan, Corporal.
Nowicki, Marian, Second Lieutenant.
Olszewski, Eugeniusz, Captain.
Ordyński, Ryszard, Corporal.
Ostromęcki, Adam, Lieutenant.
Ostrycharz, Marian, Corporal.
Pełda, Władysław, Sergeant.
Pinar, Kazimierz, Staff Sergeant.
Peszkowski, Wiesław, Corporal.
Piątkowski, Jerzy, Captain.
Piekarski, Władysław, Sergeant.
Piotrkowski, Antoni, Staff Sergeant.
Piszczyński, Antoni, Corporal.
Popiel, Janusz, Captain.
Popieluch, Edward, Lieutenant.
Potworowski, Jan, Lieutenant.
Proszek, Roman, Major.
Przybylski, Jan, Corporal.
Przysiecki, Tadeusz, Sergeant.
Pury, Aleksander, Corporal.
Rączka, Stanisław, Corporal.
Rau, Wacław, Corporal.
Repak, Bolesław, Sergeant.
Rozwadowski, Jan, Captain.
Rudnicki, Klemens, Major General.
Rudnikowski, Bronisław, Corporal.
Rumian, Stanisław,
Lieutenant Colonel (Doctor)
Rusiecki, Ryszard, Captain.
Rybak, Józef, Sergeant.
Sadowski, Józef, Lieutenant.
Sanecki, Rudolf, Sergeant.
Sarna, Andrzej, Corporal.
Sas, Przbysław, Corporal.
Sawczak, Stefan, Sergeant.
Sawko, Władysław, Sergeant.
Seroka, Henryk, Corporal.
Skalski, Bolesław, Corporal.
Skolimowski, Zbigniew,
Second Lieutenant.
Słoniecki, Alfons, Corporal.
Słowiński, Antoni, Captain (Doctor).
Sługocki, Władysław, Corporal.
Sroka, Józef, Corproal.

Stankiewicz, Ludwik, Lieutenant Colonel.
Starczyk, Stanisław, Second Lieutenant.
Starzyński, Zygmunt, Captain.
Stefanowicz, Aleksander,
Lieutenant Colonel.
Sternik, Wiktor, Corporal.
Stypułkowicz, Józef, Sergeant.
Stryna, Franciszek, Corporal.
Suchecki, Jerzy, Corporal.
Suchomski, Jan, Corporal.
Sulek, Tadeusz, Corporal.
Suwiński, Włodzimierz, Lieutenant.
Swięcicki, Zbigniew, Second Lieutenant.
Skotniak, Ludwik, Corporal.
Szuberski, Franciszek, Corporal.
Szydłowski, Zdzisław, Corporal.
Szymczak, Józef, Corporal.
Tasak, Stanisław, Corporal.
Tomczyński, Tadeusz, Sergeant.
Trzaska, Tadeusz, Corporal.
Turowski, Henryk, Corporal.
Twardowski, Józef, Corporal.
Tyrol, Edward, Corporal.
Walewicz, Tadeusz, Second Lieutenant.
Wasiewicz, Jan, Second Lieutenant.
Wasilewski, Jerzy, Major.
Wasilewski, Zbigniew, Corporal.
Wawrzyniak, Stanisław, Sergeant.
Wendorff, Bohdan, Lieutenant.
Wesołowski, Józef, Corporal.
Wesoły, Andrzej, Sergeant.
Wielaszewicz, Paweł, Sergeant.
Wielechowski, Ryszard, Sergeant.
Wiercigroch, Józef, Lance Corporal.
Wiśniewski, Daniel, Corporal.
Wiszniewski, Edward, Captain.
Witholtz, Tadeusz, Sergeant.
Włodarski, Wojciech, Corporal.
Wojnicki, Aleksander, Corporal.
Wojtasz, Czesław, Sergeant.
Wołyncewicz, Wacław, Captain (Doctor).
Wrona, Julian, Second Lieutenant.
Wysocki, Tadeusz, Major.
Zajdel, Jan, Sergeant.
Zalechowski, Stanisław,
Second Lieutenant.
Zawada, Bronisław, Corporal.
Zawałowski, Józef, Corporal.
Zdybel, Józef, Sergeant.
Zgorzelski, Władysław,
Lieutenant Colonel.
Zięba, Paweł, Sergeant.
Zmroczek, Franciszek, Lieutenant.
Zuber, Karol, Captain.
Żaboklicki, Zbigniew, Corporal.
Żarski, Jan, Lieutenant.
Żochowski, Bolesław, Sergeant.
Żurowski, Stanisław, Staff Sergeant.

Decoration Militaire de 2e Classe avec Palme

Adamczyk, Jan, Corporal.
Bilicki, Tadeusz, Corporal.
Czajkowski, Henryk, Corporal.
Dalecki, Jan, Corporal.
Duda, Ludwik, Corporal.
Fawryszewicz, Marian, Corporal.
Gil, Leon, Corporal.
Jaworski, Marian, Corporal.
Jesionkowicz, Alojzy, Corporal.
Kapecke, Zdzisław, Corporal.
Kiszewski, Edmund, Corporal.
Kolny, Alojzy, Corporal.
Konieczny, Franciszek, Corporal.
Kozłowski, Józef, Corporal.
Kujawa, Edmund, Lance Corporal.
Kurzydym, Franciszek, Corporal.
Lasota, Stefan, Corporal.

Lipiński, Benedykt, Corporal.
Łapiński, Józef, Corporal.
Makowski, Stefan, Corporal.
Maslanies, Wojciech, Corporal.
Nowak, Stefan, Corporal.
Ordyński, Ryszard, Corporal.
Peszkowski, Wiesław, Corporal.
Przybylski, Jan, Corporal.
Raczka, Stanisław, Corporal.
Rau, Wacław, Corporal.
Sas, Przybysław, Corporal.
Seroka, Henryk, Corporal.
Skalski, Bolesław, Corporal.
Słoniecki, Alfons, Corporal.
Sługocki, Władysław, Corporal.
Sroka, Józef, Corporal.
Sternik, Wiktor, Corporal.

Suchecki, Jerzy, Corporal.
Suchomski, Jan, Corporal.
Skotniak, Ludwik, Corporal.
Szuszek, Józef, Corporal.
Szymczak, Józef, Corporal.
Tasak, Stanisław, Corporal.
Trzaska, Tadeusz, Corporal.
Twardowski, Józef, Corporal.
Tyrol, Konrad, Corporal.
Wasilewski, Zbigniew, Corporal.
Wesołowski, Józef, Corporal.
Wiercigroch, Józef, Lance Corporal.
Wiśniewski, Daniel, Corporal.
Włodarski, Wojciech, Corporal.
Wojnicki, Aleksander, Corporal.
Zawada, Bronisław, Corporal.

France

Legion d'Honneur Commander

Maczek, Stanisław, Lieutenant General.

Legion d'Honneur Officier

Dworak, Kazimierz, Colonel.

Legion d'Honneur Chevalier

Czarnecki, Marian, Major.
Dec, Władysław, Colonel.
Grudziński, Antoni, Colonel.

Majewski, Tadeusz, Colonel.
Marowski, Jan, Major.
Noel, Bronisław, Major.

Popiel, Janusz, Captain.
Skibiński, Franciszek, Colonel.
Stankiewicz, Ludwik, Colonel.

Croix de Guerre avec Palme

Czarnecki, Marian, Major.
Dec, Władysław, Colonel.
Dorantt, Jan, Lieutenant Colonel.
Dworak, Kazimierz, Colonel.
Grajkowski, Jan, Colonel.
Grudziński, Antoni, Colonel.
Gutowski, Michał, Major.

Maczek, Stanisław, Lieutenant General.
Majewski, Tadeusz, Colonel.
Maresch, Karol, Colonel.
Marowki, Jan, Major.
Noel, Bronisław, Colonel.
Nowakowski, Janusz, Major.
Popiel, Janusz, Captain.

Skibiński, Franciszek, Colonel.
Stankiewicz, Ludwik, Lieutenant Colonel.
Tarnowski, Jan, Second Lieutenant.

Croix de Guerre with Gold Star

Berendt, Witold, Major.
Borchulski, Władysław, Lieutenant.
Complak, Karol, Lieutenant Colonel.
Friedrich, Jerzy, Lieutenant.
Juskow, Roman, Lieutenant.
Kaszubowski, Jan, Major.
Kochanowski, Marian, Captain.
Kominek, Antoni, Captain (Doctor).

Kurek, Hieronim, Major.
Młynek, Stefan, Private.
Nowaczyński, Aleksander, Lieutenant Colonel.
Piątkowski, Jerzy, Captain.
Piotrkowski, Wacław, Captain.
Sikorski, Stanisław, Cadet Officer.
Stefanowicz, Aleksander, Lieutenant Colonel.

Szablewski, Teofil, Lance Corporal.
Szpunar, Józef, Sergeant.
Tobolski, Antoni, Sergeant.
Wasilewski, Jerzy, Major.
Wołyncewicz, Wacław, Captain (Doctor)
Wysocki, Tadeusz, Major.
Żebrowski, Marian, Major.

Croix de Guerre with Silver Star

Borzemski, Paweł, Lieutenant.
Buraczewski, Józef, Gunner.

Chabrzyński, Edward, Regimental Sergeant Major.

Choma, Tomasz, Sergeant.
Cieślik, Bonifacy, Lance Corporal.

Dick, Wincenty, Bombardier.
Gałęzki, Sylwester, Sergeant.
Gumiński, Wacław, Sergeant.
Konieczny, Władysław, Sergeant.
Kontrym, Bolesław, Captain.
Koziar, Stanisław, Sergeant.

Makowiec, Tadeusz, Lieutenant.
Moszczyński, Eugeniusz, Sergeant.
Opolski, Stanisław, Lance Corporal.
Pelc, Antoni, Sergeant.
Rewer, Wojciech, Captain.
Rowiński, Kazimierz, Corporal.

Sokołow, Leon, Corporal.
Spoliński, Antoni, Corporal.
Szczurek, Józef, Corporal.
Waliłko, Antoni, Sergeant Major.
Wierzbicki, Józef, Staff Sergeant.
Wolański, Marian, Lieutenant.

Holland

Orde van Oranje Nassau Class III

Maczek, Stanisław, Lieutenant General.

Rudnicki, Klemens, Major General.

Orde van Oranje Nassau Class IV

Marowski, Jan, Major.

Stankiewicz, Ludwik, Lieutenant Colonel.

Orde van Oranje Nassau Class V

Podoski, Jan, Captain.
De Bronzen Leeuw
Adamik, Gerard, Lance Corporal.
Complak, Karol, Lieutenant Colonel.
Ejsymont, Otton, Major.
Grudziński, Antoni, Colonel.
Koński, Jan, Lieutenant.
Majewski, Tadeusz, Colonel.

Neklaws, Wiktor, Major.
Noel, Bronisław, Colonel.
Nowaczyński, Aleksander, Lieutenant Colonel.
Rakowski, Władysław, Major.
Skibiński, Franciszek, Colonel.
Wereszczyński, Mirosław, Sergeant.
Het Bronzen Kruis

Kowalski, Kazimierz, Corporal.
Puszyński, Włodzimierz, Corporal.
Śrama, Karol, Sergeant.
Wesołowski, Józef, Lance Corporal.
Kruis van Verdiensten Wegens Dapperheid
Maszkowski, Bernard, Corporal.

United Kingdom

Order of the Bath: Commander

Maczek, Stanisław, Lieutenant General.

Order of the British Empire: Companion

Dworak, Kazimierz, Colonel.

Majewski, Tadeusz, Colonel.

Order of the British Empire: Officer

Deskur, Jerzy, Colonel.
Grajkowski, Jan, Colonel.

Grudziński, Antoni, Colonel.
Fryzendorff, Edward, Lieutenant Colonel.

Marowski, Jan, Major.
Pawłowicz, Władysław, Lieutenant Colonel (Doctor)

Order of the British Empire: Member

Bachurzewski, Zbigniew, Lieutenant.
Czarnecki, Marian, Major.
Fryzendorff, Edward, Major.

Jedraszak, Stefan, Cadet Officer.
Pieńkowski, Wacław, Cadet Officer.
Podoski, Jan, Captain.

Wąsowicz, Michał, Major.
Wołyncewicz, Wacław, Captain (Doctor).

Distinguished Service Order

Berendt, Witold, Major.
Complak, Karol, Lieutenant Colonel.
Dec, Władysław, Colonel.

Dorantt, Jan, Lieutenant Colonel.
Dowbor, Romuald, Lieutenant Colonel.
Koszutski, Stanisław, Lieutenant Colonel.

Maczek, Stanisław, Lieutenant General.
Majewski, Tadeusz, Colonel.
Maresch, Karol, Colonel.

Noel, Bronisław, Colonel.

Nowaczyński, Aleksander, Lieutenant Colonel.

Skibiński, Franciszek, Colonel.

Stankiewicz, Ludwik, Lieutenant Colonel.

Stefanowicz, Aleksander, Lieutenant Colonel.

Szydłowski, Zbigniew, Lieutenant Colonel.

Zgorzelski, Władysław, Lieutenant Colonel.

Military Cross

Antonowicz, Mikołaj, Lieutenant.

Barbacki, Roman, Captain.

Bartosiński, Marian, Major. (P)

Bletek, Tadeusz, Lieutenant.

Błędowski, Władysław, Second Lieutenant.

Bobula, Adam, Lieutenant.

Bojanowski, Zbigniew, Captain.

Dzierżek, Adam, Lieutenant.

Jakubiec, Władysław, Captain.

Józefowicz, Henryk, Captain.

Kłodziński, Zygmunt, Captain.

Marcinkiewicz, Adam, Second Lieutenant.

Rudniak, Marcin, Lieutenant.

Salwa, Jan, Captain.

Sołtys, Henryk, Second Lieutenant.

Stojowski, Leon, Second Lieutenant.

Sumiński, Albert, Captain.

Szczygieł, Stanisław, Lieutenant.

Szubarga, Andrzej, Captain.

Wasilewski, Jerzy, Major.

Wyrwalski, Karol, Captain.

British Empire Medal

Grambor, Stanisław, Sergeant.

Sobiech, Hieronim, Sergeant.

Zajdel, Andrzej, Sergeant.

Distinguished Conduct Medal

Dzierzbiński, Wincenty, Sergeant.

Gros, Konrad, Sapper.

Roczmierowski, Władysław, Lance Corporal.

Siodmak, Władysław, Lance Corporal.

Szalkowski, Władysław, Corporal.

Military Medal

Bec, Nikodem, Corporal.

Bogdan, Antoni, Private.

Budzyński, Władysław, Corporal.

Ciężak, Franciszek, Lance Corporal.

Doruch, Józef, Cadet Officer.

Drygała, Jan, Sergeant.

Fec, Wojciech, Sergeant.

Fligiel, Edward, Sergeant. (P)

Gacyk, Leon, Sergeant.

Górski, Stanisław, Sergeant.

Han, Władysław, Corporal.

Hasiuk, Stanisław, Corporal.

Kamienicki, Karol, Private.

Koźmina, Władysław, Lance Corporal.

Lenczowski, Franciszek, Staff Sergeant.

Łysakowski, Stefan, Sergeant.

Mitek, Stanisław, Dragoon.

Mogilski, Władysław, Cadet Officer.

Olden, Franciszek, Sergeant.

Olszyk, Leon, Sergeant.

Rozum, Jan, Sergeant.

Sagin, Zygmunt, Lance Corporal.

Strzyżewski, Stefan, Sergeant.

Terlecki, Józef, Sergeant.

Urgacz, Marian, Corporal.

Waliłko, Antoni, Sergeant.

Campaign Medals

14,301 soldiers awarded the 1939 Star.
18,724 soldiers awarded France and Germany Star.

The United States of America

The Legion of Merit: Degree of Legionnaire

Gutowski, Michał, Major.

The Legion of Merit: Bronze Star

Lewicki, Bolesław, Lieutenant.

Rogalski, Antoni, Sergeant.

Rum, Wacław, Sergeant.

Starczewski, Franciszek, Corporal.

Złotnik, Edward, Captain. [149]

Notes

1. N. Davies, *Heart of Europe: A Short History of Poland*, Oxford, Oxford University Press, 1986, p. 161.

2. Ibid. p. 162.

3. N. Davies, *God's Playground: A History of Poland Volume II, 1795 to the Present*, Oxford, Oxford University Press, 1981, p. 368.

4. Davies, *Heart of Europe*, pp. 116–118.

5. N. Davies, *White Eagle, Red Star: The Polish-Soviet War, 1919–20*, London, Orbis Books, 1983, pp. 222–223.

6. Ibid. p. 197.

7. Jozef Pilsudski, *Rok 1920*, London, Polska Fundacja Kulturna, 1987, 6th edition, p. 165.

8. Andrew A. Michta, *The Soldier-Citizen: The Politics of the Polish Army After Communism*, London, Macmillan, 1997, p. 26.

9. Jerzy W. Wiatr, *The Soldier and the Nation: The Role of the Military in Polish Politics, 1918–1985*, Boulder, Colorado, Westview Press, 1988, p. 63.

10. Peter D. Stachura (ed), *Themes of Modern Polish History: Proceedings of a Symposium on 28 March 1992. In Honour of the Century* of *General Stanislaw Maczek*, Glasgow, The Polish Social and Educational Society, 1992, p. 2.

11. Witold A Deimel, 'The Life and Career of General Stanislaw Maczek: An Appreciation' in Stachura op.cit., p. 12.

12. Ibid. p. 12.

13. John Keegan, *Six Armies in Normandy: From D-Day to the Liberation of Paris, June 6th – August 25th 1944*, London, Jonathan Cape, 1982, p. 264. Also Dr Andrew Maczek, in conversation by telephone with the author, June 2000.

14. Dr Andrew Maczek, June 2000.

15. Deimel, p. 12.

16. Keegan, op.cit. p. 264.

17. Deimel, p. 12.

18. Keegan, op.cit. p. 264.

19. Tadeusz Walewicz, Letter to the author, 4 January, 2001.

20. Deimel, p. 12.

21. Walewicz, letter to author, 4 January, 2001.

22. Deimel, p. 13.

23. Ibid. p. 13.

24. Walewicz, letter, 4 January, 2001.

25. Deimel, p. 13.

26. P. A. Szudek, 'The 1st Polish Armoured Division in the Second World War' in Peter D. Stachura (ed) *Themes of Modern Polish History: Proceedings of a Symposium on 28 March 1992 In Honour of the Century of General Stanislaw Maczek*, Glasgow, The Polish Social and Educational Society, 1992. p. 35.

27. Szudek, op.cit. p. 36.

28. Ibid. p. 36.

29. A basis of Polish-Soviet co-operation, later to have serious political consequences for Poland. See Keith Sword, *Deportation and Exile: Poles in the Soviet Union 1939–48*, London, Macmillan, 1996

30. Szudek, op.cit. p. 36.

31. Ibid. p. 36.

32. Ibid. p. 36.

33. Ibid. p. 37.

34. Szudek, op.cit. p. 37.

35. Ibid. pp. 37–38.

36. Szudek, op.cit. p. 38.

37. Both men have recorded their experiences: Chaim Goldberg, *I Remember Like Now: The Odyssey of Polish Jew*, edited by Jo Atkinson & Colin Atkinson, Windsor, Ontario, Canada, Black Moss Press, 1994; Antoni Polozynski, *Z Drogi i Przydroza*, Warsaw, Vipart, 1997.

38. I am grateful to Mr. Polozynski, resident in West Yorkshire, died June 2003, for the many conversations which we had about the 1st Polish Armoured Division and how he came to join it. For a more detailed account of his escape from Poland see: Polozynski, op.cit. pp. 7–53.

39. Goldberg, op.cit. p. 38.

40. Chaim Goldberg, Letter to author, 3 December 2000. For detailed accounts of Goldberg's journey see: Goldberg, op.cit. pp. 9–41.

41. Szudek, op.cit. p. 38.

42. Ibid. pp. 38–39.

43. Ibid. p. 39.

44. Ibid. p. 39.

45. Ibid. p. 40.

46. Szudek, op.cit. p. 40.

47. Ibid. pp. 40–42.

48. Ibid. pp. 41–42.

49. *The Economist*, (London) 30 September 1944, 7 October 1944. Jozef Beck was Polish Foreign Minister during the 1930s and was responsible for much of the co-operation between Germany and Poland between 1933 and 1939.

50. Jozef Garlinski, *Poland in the Second World War*, London, Macmillan, 1985, p. 233.

51. Szudek, op.cit. p. 40.

52. Antoni Polozynski, *Z Drogi i Przydroza*, Warsaw, Vipart, 1997, p. 65. P. A. Szudel, 'The 1st Polish Armoured Division in the Second World War' in *Themes of Polish History: Proceedings of a Symposium on 28 March 1992 In Honour of the Century of General Stanislaw Maczek*, Glasgow, The Polish Social and Educational Society, 1992, p. 42.

53. Tadeusz, A. Wysocki, *I Polska Dywizja Pancerna 1939 – 1947: Geneza i Dzieje*, Warsaw, Wydawnictwo Bellona, 1994, pp. 105–106.

54. *I Dywizja Pancerna W Walce Praca Zbrorowa*, Brussels, La Colonne, 1946, p. 46.

55. Henry Maule, *Normandy Breakout*, New York, Quadrangle, 1977.

56. Wysocki, op.cit. pp. 107–108.

57. Szudek, op.cit. p. 45.

58. Terry Copp, 'Our Polish Comrades' *Legion Magazine* (Canada) January/February 2000, pp. 42–44.

59. Ibid. p. 42. See also Roman Johann Jarymowycz, *Tank Tactics: From Normandy to Lorraine Boulder*, Lynne Rienner, 2001. p. 169.

60. Ibid. p. 42. Perrun also comments upon Simonds's tactics. See Jody Perrun, 'Best Laid Plans: Guy Simonds and Operation Totalize, 7 – 10 August 1944' *The Journal of Military History*, 2003, Vol. 67, pp. 137 – 171.

61. Szudek, op.cit. p. 44.

62. Ibid. p. 44.

63. Franciszek Skibinski, *O Sztuce Wojennej: Na Polnocno-Zachodnim Teatrze Dzialan Wojennych 1944–1945*, Warsaw, Wydawnictwo Ministerwa Obrony Naradowej, undated, p. 159.

64. Stanislaw Maczek, *Avec Mes Blindes: Pologne, France, Belgique, Allemagne*. Paris, Presses de la Cite, 1967. p. 183.

65. Maule. Op.cit. p. 115.

66. Maczek. Op.cit. p. 183.

67. *10 Pulk Strzelcow Konnych w Kampanii 1944–45: Praca Zbiorowa*, Nuremberg, 1947. p. 9.

68. Alexander McKee, *Caen: Anvil of Victory*, London, 2000. pp. 332–333.

69. Maule. Op.cit. p. 117.

70. Ibid. pp. 117–118. Perrun disputes this. Perrun. Op.cit.

71. Hubert Meyer, *The History of the 12. SS-Panzerdivision Hitlerjugend*, English Translation by H. Harri Henschler, Winnipeg, J. J. Fedorowicz Publishing Inc, 1994. p. 173.

72. Antoni Polozynski in conversation with the author.

73. *10 Pulk Strzelcow Konnych*. p. 9–11.

74. Tadeusz Walewicz, Letter to the author, 26 February 2001.

75. Wysocki, op.cit. p. 112.

76. Meyer, op.cit. p. 174.

77. *10 Pulk Strzelcow Konnych*. p. 11.

78. Copp. Op.cit. p. 43. Polozynski in conversation with the author.

79. George H. Stein, *The Waffen SS: Hitler's Elite Guard, 1939–1945*, Ithaca, New York, Cornell University Press, 1977. pp. 225–226.

80. *10 Pulk Strzelcow Konnych*. p. 16.

81. See Timothy Harrison Place's discussion of the vulnerability of tank crews in close range infantry attacks in : Timothy Harrison Place, *Military Training in the British Army, 1940 – 1944: From Dunkirk to D-Day*, London, Frank Cass, 2000. pp. 129–133.

82. For an overall view of the early battles of 10 PSK see: *10 Pulk Strzelcow Konnych*, pp. 9–18.

83. Wysocki, op.cit. p. 116.

84. Meyer. Op.cit. 180.

85. Max Hastings, *Overlord: D-Day and the Battle for Normandy, 1944*, London, Guild Publishing, 1984, pp. 300–301.

86. Terry Copp, 'Our Polish Comrades' in *Legion Magazine* (Canada) January/February 2000. p. 43. Antoni Polozynski, commander of a Cromwell tank (10 PSK) recalled that he and others, learnt this method of protection from German tank crews. Conversation with the author.

87. Copp. Op.cit. p. 43.

88. *10 Pulk Strzelcow Konnych w Kampanii 1944–1945*, Nuremburg, 1947. p. 19.

89. Tadeusz Wysocki, *I Polska Dywizja Pancerna 1939–1947: Geneza i Dzieje*, Warsaw, Wydawnictwo Bellona, 1994. p. 121.

90. Hubert Meyer, *The History of the 12-Panzerdivision Hitlerjugend*, Translated by H. Harri Henschler, Winnipeg, J. J. Fedorowicz Publishing Inc, 1994. p. 185.

91. *I Dywizja Pancerna w Walce: Prace Zbrorowa*, Brussels, La Colonne, 1947. p. 85.

92. *I Dywizja Pancerna w Walce*, pp. 85–87.

93. For more detailed account of 10 PSK's activities at Jort on 15 August 1944, see: *10 Pulk Strzelcow* Konnych, pp. 19 –25. See also Meyer, op.cit. pp. 186–187.

94. Wysocki, op.cit. p. 129.

95. Wysocki, op.cit. p. 129.

96. *10 Pulk Strzelcow*, pp. 25–26.

97. Meyer, op.cit. p. 192.

98. Wysocki, op.cit. pp. 129–130.

99. *10 Pulk Strzelcow Konnych*, pp. 29–30.

100. Wysocki, op.cit. p. 130.

101. Meyer. Op.cit. p. 188.

102. Wysocki, op.cit. pp. 130–131.

103. *10 Pulk Strzelcow Konnych*, p. 31.

104. *The Daily Telegraph* (London) reported that the French guide was killed by German rifle fire. See: 'Poles Lucky Mistake in Falaise Gap' in *The Daily Telegraph*, 2 September 1944.

105. Tadeusz Walewicz' Letter to the author. 26 February 2001.

106. *The Daily Telegraph*, 2 September 1944.

107. Stanisław Koszutski, *Wspomnienia z Roznych Pobojowisk*, London, Wydawnictwo Przegladu Kawalerii i Broni Pancernej Nr. 3, 1972, pp. 195–201.

108. John Keegan, *Six Armies in Normandy: From D-Day to the Liberation of Paris, June 6th – August 25th 1944*, London, Jonathan Cape, 1982, pp. 272–273.

109. See Henry Maule, *Normandy Breakout*, New York, Quadrangle, 1977, p. 166.

110. See Hubert Meyer, *The History of the 12 SS-Panzerdivision Hitlerjugend*, Winnipeg, Canada, J. J. Fedrowicz, 1994, p. 199.

111. Franciszek Skibinski, *O Sztuce Wojennej: Na Polnocno-Zachodnim Teatrze Działan Wojennych 1944–1945*, Warsaw, Wydawnictwo Ministerwa Obrony Narodowej, 1977, p. 174.

112. There were reports that the Poles held a grudge against the Germans owing to the treatment of Poland by the Nazis. Many Poles interviewed in Normandy had a sense of revenge for Poland. *The Daily Telegraph*, 12 August 1944. After bitter hand to hand fighting in the Quesay Wood and at the village of Potigny, German wounded, fearful that Polish troops had poisoned the drinking water being offered to them, made the Poles drink the water first. *The Daily Telegraph*, 16 August 1944.

113. *10 Pulk Strzelcow Konnych w Kampanii 1944–45: Praca Zbiorowa*. Nuremberg, 1947. p. 30–39.

114. P. A. Szudek, 'The 1st Polish Armoured Division in the Second World War' in Peter D. Stachura (ed) *Themes of Modern Polish History: Proceedings of a Symposium on 28 March 1992. In Honour of the Century of General Stanisław Maczek*, Glasgow, The Polish Social and Educational Society, 1992. pp. 48–49.

115. Keegan. Op.cit. pp. 277–278.

116. Keegan, op.cit. p. 279.

117. A. S. 'Trzydniowa Bitwa O 'Macuge' in *I Dywizja Pancerna w Walce, Prace Zbrorowa*, Brussels, La Colonne, 1947. pp. 110–117.

118. 'Poles Great Fight: Defeated Two SS Corps and Closed the Gap' in *The Tank*, 26, 1944 p. 78.

119. Keegan. op.cit. p. 282.

120. Max Hastings, *Overlord: D-Day and the Battle for Normandy, 1944*. London, Guild Publishing, 1983. p. 313.

121. Tadeusz A. Wysocki, *1 Polska Dywizja Pancerna 1939–1947: Geneza i Dzieje*, Warsaw, Wydawnictwo Bellona, 1994. p. 151.

122. Wysocki, op.cit. pp. 151–155.

123. Wysocki, op.cit. pp. 154–155. Meyer would seem to contradict allied figures concerning 12 SS Division. See Hubert Meyer, *The History of the 12 SS-Panzerdivision Hitlerjugend* Translated by H. Harri Henschler, Winnipeg, J. J. Fedrowicz Publishing, 1994. p. 204.

124. *10 Pulk Strzecow Konnych w Kampanii 1944–45: Praca Zboirowa*, Nuremberg, 1947. pp. 38–39.

125. *10 Pulk Strzelcow Konnych*, pp. 38–39.

126. *10 Pulk Strzelcow Konnych*, pp. 39–41.

127. P. A. Szudek, 'The 1st Polish Armoured Division in the Second World War' in Peter D. Stachura (ed) *Themes of Modern Polish History: Proceedings of a Symposium on 28 March 1992 In Honour of the Century of General Stanisław Maczek*, Glasgow, The Polish Social and Educational Society. p. 51.

128. Tadeusz A. Wysocki, *1 Dywizja Pancerna 1939–1947: Geneza i Dzieje*, Warsaw, Wydawnicto Bellona, 1994. pp. 157–160.

129. Translated from the Polish, *10 Pulk Strzelcow Konnych w Kampanii 1944–1945: Praca Zbiorowa*, Nuremberg, 1947, pp. 50–72.

130. Tadeusz A. Wysocki, *I Polska Dywizya Pancerna 1939–1947: Geneza i Dzieje*, Warsaw, 1994, p.162.

131. Stefan Drozak, 'Wspomnienia Z Ypres' in *I Dywizja w Walce: Prace Zbiorowa*, Brussels, La Colonne, 1947, pp. 150–152.

132. Second Lieutenant (2nd Tank Regiment) 'Ruysselede – "Małe Chambois"' in *I Dywizja w Walce* pp. 156–157.

133. *10 Pulk Strzelcow Konnych w Kampanii 1944–45: Praca Zbiorowa*, Nuremberg, 1946, pp. 74–76.

134. Wysocki, op.cit. pp. 163–164.

135. *10 Pulk Strzelcow Konnych w Kampanii 1944–45*, pp. 74–78.

136. Tadeusz Wysocki, *1 Polska Dywizja Pancerna 1939–1947: Geneza i Dzieje* Warsaw, 1994, pp. 169-170.

137. Tadeusz Krzytzaniak, 'Z Wałk O Bredê' in *I Pancerna W Walce: Praca Zbiorowa*, Brussels, La Colonne, 1947, pp. 232–233.

138. *10 Pulk Strzelcow Konnych W Kampanii 1944–45: Praca Zbiorowa* Nuremberg, 1947, pp. 78–136.

139. Tadeusz Walewicz. Letter to the author, 4 April 2001.

140. Wysocki, pp. 182–183.

141. Tadeusz A. Wysocki, *1 Polska Dywizja Pancerna 1939–1947: Geneza i Dzieje*, Warsaw, Wydawnictwo Bellona, 1994, p. 187

142. Antoni Położyñski, *Z Drogi i Przydroza*, Warsaw, Vipart, 1997, p. 85.

143. '*Uwolnienie (Koncowy Fragment P. T. 'R D Z A' 'Mieczysława'* in *I Dywizja Pancerna w Walce: Praca Zborowa*, Brussels, La Colonne, 1947 pp. 338–340. Jamar records that 1726 women from the Polish Underground were discovered in the camp. K. Jamar, *Śladami Gąsienic Pierwszej Dywizji Pancernej*, Hengelo, Netherlands, HL. Smith & ZN, 1946, p. 305.

144. KOL 298/40, Archives at the Polish Institute and General Sikorski Museum, London.

145. Hubert Meyer, *The History of the 12. SS-Panzerdivision Hitlerjugend.* Translated by H. Harri Henschler, Winnipeg, Canada, J. J. Fedorowicz, 1994, p. 188.

146. Wysocki, op.cit. p. 209.

147. See Evan McGilvray 'General Stanisław Maczek and Post-War Britain' in *The Poles in Britain 1940-2000. From Betrayal to Assimilation*, Peter D. Stachura (ed) London, Frank Cass, 2004, pp. 59–68.

148. Antoni Położyñski, conversation with the author.

149. Based on Stanisław Maczek, *Od Podwody Do Czołga. Wspomnienia Wojenne 1918–1945*, Edinburgh, Tomar Publishers, 1961. pp. 251–293.

Bibliography

Correspondence and Interviews

Chaim Goldberg
Dr Andrew Maczek
Antoni Położyński
Tadeusz Walewicz

Archives

Polish Institute and General Sikorski Museum, London. Kol 298/40.

Published Primary Sources

Anon *I Dywizja Pancerna w Walce Praca Zborowa*. Brussels, La Colonne, 1946.
Anon *10 Pułk Strzelców Konnych w Kampanii 1944–45. Praca Zbiorowa*. Nuremberg, 1947.

Secondary Sources

Davies, Norman, *Heart of Europe. A Short History of Poland*. Oxford, Oxford University Press, 1986.

Davies, Norman, *White Eagle, Red Star. The Polish-Soviet War, 1919–20*. London, Orbis Books, 1983.

Davies, Norman, *God's Playground: A History of Poland. Vol. 2, 1795 to the Present*. Oxford, Oxford University Press, 1981.

Garlinski, Józef, *Poland in the Second World War*. London, Macmillan, 1985.

Goldberg, Chaim, *I Remember Like Now: The Odyssey of a Polish Jew*. Edited by Jo Atkinson & Colin Atkinson, Windsor, Ontario, Black Moss Press, 1994.

Harrison Place, Timothy, *Military Training in the British Army, 1940–1944: From Dunkirk to D-Day*. London, Frank Cass, 2000.

Hastings, Max, *Overlord: D-Day and the Battle for Normandy, 1944*. London, Guild Publishing, 1984.

Jamar, K, *Śladami Gąsienic Pierwszej Pancernej*. Hengelo, Netherlands, HL. Smith & ZN, 1946.

Jarymowycz, Roman Johann, *Tank Tactics: From Normandy to Lorraine*. Boulder, Lynne Rienner, 2001.

Keegan, John, *Six Armies in Normandy: From D-Day to the Liberation of Paris, June 6th – August 25th 1944*. London, Jonathan Cape, 1982.

Koszutski, Stanisław, *Wspomnienia z Roznych Pobojowski*. London, Wydawnictwo Przegladu Kawalerri i Broni Pancernej nr.3, 1972.

Maczek, Stanisław, *Od Podwody do Czołga. Wspomnienia Wojenne, 1918–1945*. Edinburgh, Tomar Publishers, 1961.

Maczek, Stanisław, *Avec Mes Blindes: Pologne, France, Belgique, Allemande*. Paris, Presses de la Cité, 1967.

Maule, Henry, *Normandy Breakout*. New York, Quadrangle, 1977.

McKee, Alexander, *Caen: Anvil of Victory*. London, 2000.

Meyer, Hubert, *The History of the 12. SS Panzerdivision Hitlerjugend*. English translated by H. Harri Henschler. Winnipeg, J. J. Fedorowicz Publishing Inc, 1994.

Michta, Andrew A, *The Soldier-Citizen: The Politics of the Polish Army after Communism*. London, Macmillan, 1997.

Piłsudski, Józef, *Rok 1920*, London, Polska Fundacji Kulturna, 1987. 6th Edition.

Plołożyński, Antoni, *Z Drogi i Przydroża*. Warsaw, Vipart, 1997.

Skibinski, Franciszek, *O Sztuce Wojennej: Na Polnocno-Zachodnim Teatrze Dzialan Wojennych 1944–1945*. Warsaw, Wydawnictwo Ministerwa Obrony Naradowej, undated.

Stachura, Peter D., (ed) *The Poles in Britain 1940–2000. From Betrayal to Assimilation*. London, Frank Cass, 2004.

Stachura, Peter D., (ed) *Themes of Modern Polish History: Proceedings of a Symposium on 28 March 1992. In Honour of the Century of General Stanisław Maczek*. Glasgow, The Polish Social and Educational Society, 1992.

Stein, George H, *The Waffen SS: Hitler's Elite Guard, 1939–1945*. Ithaca, New York: Cornell University Press, 1977.

Sword, Keith, *Deportation and Exile: Poles in the Soviet Union 1939–48*. London, Macmillan, 1996.

Wiatr, Jerzy W, *The Soldier and the Nation: The Role of the Military in Polish Politics, 1918–1985*. Boulder, Colorado, Westview Press, 1988.

Wysocki, Tadeusz A, *I Polska Dywizja Pancerna 1939–1947: Geneza i Dzieje*. Warsaw, Wydawnictwo Bellona, 1994.

Journals and Newspapers

The Daily Telegraph (London) 1939–1945.

The Economist (London) 1939–1945.

The Tank, 1944.

Copp, Terry, 'Our Polish Comrades' *Legion Magazine* (Canada) January-February 2000.

Perron, Jody, 'Best Laid Plans: Guy Simonds and Operation Totalize, 7–10 August 1944' *The Journal of Military History* vol. 67 (2003) pp. 131–171.